TRAVELS INTO THE
INTERIOR OF AFRICA

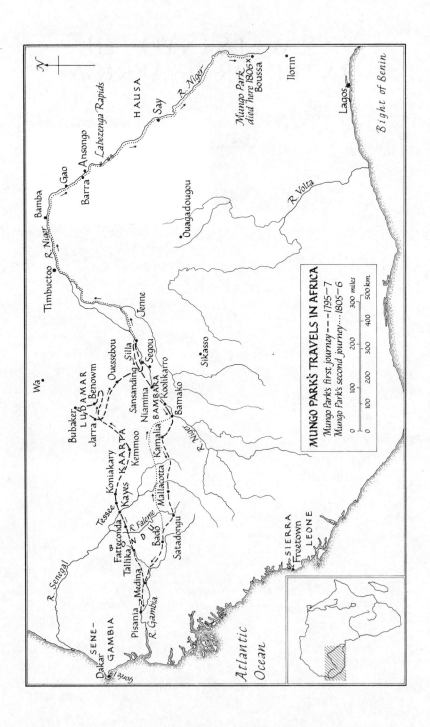

MUNGO PARK'S TRAVELS IN AFRICA

Mungo Park's first journey ---- 1795-7
Mungo Park's second journey ···· 1805-6

0   100   200   300 miles
0   100   200   300   400   500 km

N

HAUSA

R. Niger

Mungo Park died here 1805 ×   Boussa

Ilorin

Lagos

Bight of Benin

Say

Labezenga Rapids

Ansongo

Barra

Gao

Bamba

R. Niger

R. Volta

Ouagadougou

Timbuctoo

Jenne

Sikasso

Wa

Ouessebou

Silla

Sansanding

Segou

LUDAMAR   Benowm

Bubaker   Niamina   Koolikarro

Jarra   BAMBARA   Bamako

Kamalia   R. Niger

KAARTA   Kemmoo

Koniakary

Tesee   Maillaootta

Kayes   Bado

Fattaconda   Satadongu

Tallika   R. Falome

Pisania   Medina

Dakar   R. Gambia

SENE-   R. Senegal

GAMBIA

SIERRA   Freetown

LEONE

Atlantic
Ocean

Goree

TRAVELS INTO THE INTERIOR OF AFRICA

MUNGO PARK

Illustrated with plates based on Mungo Park's own drawings

WITH A NEW PREFACE BY
JEREMY SWIFT

ELAND, LONDON
&
HIPPOCRENE BOOKS, INC., NEW YORK

Published by
ELAND BOOKS
53 Eland Road London SW11 5JX

This edition first published by
J.M. Dent in 1954

ISBN 0 907871 55 0
First issued in this paperback edition 1983
Reprinted 1986

Printed and bound in Great Britain
by Redwood Burn Ltd, Trowbridge, Wiltshire

NEW PREFACE

Mungo Park could hardly have picked a worse time to make the two journeys he describes in this book. What then appeared to him to be a savage and dangerous place had earlier had several centuries of relative peace and prosperity. The warring kingdoms he crossed had once had strong central government.

In 1300 the Mali empire covered the whole area travelled by Park, from the Atlantic coast between the Senegal and Gambia rivers as far east as Gao and the present day borders of Nigeria. In 1324-5 the Mali ruler, Mansa Musa, went on an extravagant overland pilgrimage to Mecca, taking with him at least 8,000 people and enough gold to push its value on the Cairo market down by over 10 percent. At home he had a huge army and an efficient civil service.

The great traveller Ibn Battuta visited the Mali empire in 1352-3 and reported in some detail on its geography and customs. In a section of his account entitled "What I approved of and what I disapproved of" he noted of the inhabitants of Mali that "one of their good features is their lack of oppression. They are the farthest removed of people from it and their Sultan does not permit anyone to practise it. Another is the security embracing the whole country, so that neither traveller there nor dweller has anything to fear from thief or usurper." (Among the things the prudish Ibn Battuta disapproved of was the way women servants and slave girls went around completely naked "with their privy parts uncovered," and also that the people ate dogs and donkeys.)

The Mali empire collapsed early in the 15th century, and was replaced by the Songhay, based at Gao on the Niger, who took over most of the territory of Mali and extended it north and east into the desert. Despite continuing upheavals, prosperity lasted until the Moroccans invaded in 1591. But the Moroccans were unable to administer this distant province. The orderly government gradually built up throughout the western Sudan by Ghana, Mali and Songhay, and the resulting development of domestic production and trade, was replaced by anarchy and destruction. Trans-Saharan trade, which had been developing well under the Songhay administration, declined and then shifted east to more peaceful caravan bases. At home, famine, rare for several hundred years, again became a constant danger. Central government was replaced by small states and warring tribes.

By the time Mungo Park made his first journey through this area in 1795, two hundred years of chaos had left the western Sudan impoverished and fragmented. In the west were several tiny Mande states, already under strong Islamic influence. The Fulani or Fulbe, nomadic cattle herders from the Senegal river valley, were entrenched in northern Senegal, the Gambia (where in 1621 Richard

Jobson had compared them to the gypsies of Europe), the Futa
Jallon mountains in Guinea, and in the Maasina on the middle
Niger. On the upper Senegal river, the theocratic state of Futa Toro
had been formed by Muslim Tucolor to fight off Muslim Moors. On
the upper Niger, the small Mande state which had succeeded Songhay
was being metamorphosed into the powerful Bambara kingdom of
Segu, and was about to go to war with the neighbouring and related
kingdom of Kaarta. Everywhere on the marches were Moor and
Twareg nomads, who as herders, traders and warriors were able to
raid far down into the sedentary farming areas. It is not surprising
that Mungo Park's journey at times reads like an ethnography of
banditry: there can hardly have been an important tribe in the
western Sudan which did not rob him at one time or another. The
surprising thing is that he emerged from his first trip at all.

Two influences were especially important in this confusion. Islam
had long been spreading both by the peaceful influence of Muslim
traders, and by the military conquests of more impatient proselyt-
izers. The Saharan Berber nomads, Twareg and Moors, had been
converted following successive Arab invasions of north Africa,
especially that of the Banu Hilaal in the 11th and 12th centuries.
The invaders did not necessarily want to conquer the Sahara and the
Sudan, but they did want to trade. Muslim traders from north
Africa settled in market towns south of the Sahara and were an
important religious influence on the surrounding people, in whose
minds success in trade became increasingly linked with the Muslim
faith. Islam and trade thus became closely linked in the western
Sudan, and a Muslim cleric like Ibn Battuta could in the 14th century travel peacefully throughout the region relying on the hospitality
of traders and of kings unwilling to alienate such a powerful
community.

Islam also provided the motive for some peaceful and some violent
missionary campaigns. Islamic fervour, quiet for several centuries,
was beginning to heat up again in the 18th century, and from about
1750 it was an important political force in the region. Religious
brotherhoods seeking peaceful converts by argument and example,
and straightforward military campaigns presented as holy wars,
transformed the western Sudan. Fulbe townspeople and nomads
played a crucial role. At the time of Mungo Park's trips, the Fulbe
of the Futa Jallon to the south of his route had already established
an aggressive theocracy, and the Torobe or clerical class of the
Tucolor from the Senegal river valley had also created a theocratic
state; Park did not meet its ruler, the Almamy Abd al-Qaadir, but
he was already an important and threatening figure, and 50 years
later his successor al-hajj Umar sacked the area visited by Park in
the name of a purer Islam. Further east, just beyond the area visited

by Park, Uthman dan Fodio was already engaged in the best known of these holy wars, which founded the Sokoto empire. As a Christian, and more generally a non-Muslim, Park was taking his life in his hands in an area so dangerously on the edge of wars and preparations for war.

A second important influence on the area crossed by Mungo Park was the slave trade. The Atlantic slave trade had started with the Portuguese discovery of the west African coast, and with their trading posts set up there in the mid-15th century. Taken over by the English and French, the trade prospered, and at its peak between 1750 and 1790 about 60,000 slaves were shipped from Africa across the Atlantic each year. The development of a local slave economy was made difficult by the relatively late exploration of west Africa, and considerable local resistance which would have made it hard to organise a plantation labour force; but the local states were ready to trade, at first in gold, ivory and Guinea peppers, later in a slave labour force to replace the Indian populations of America wiped out at conquest. In fact the export of slaves from Senegal and Gambia was never huge: at its high point in the 1710s the region exported about 3,000 slaves a year, only 15 percent of the total number of slaves exported by the English and French from Africa. Many of these slaves probably came from the new Bambara kingdom at Segu, then being set up, whose king Mansong was later so careful about receiving Park.

Although the total number of slaves exported from west Africa increased slowly or stagnated during the 18th century, the most important part of the trade shifted south to the Bight of Biafra and to southern Africa; during this time Senegambia exported fewer and fewer slaves, with the numbers dropping (particularly in the 1790s when Park made his first journey) as a result of Anglo-French rivalry at sea during the Napoleonic wars. But although the trade had recently declined rapidly in the areas visited by Park, it was by no means dead (Senegambia exported about 400 slaves a year across the Atlantic during the 1790s), and the memory of the intense trade of earlier decades was still alive. Fear of being enslaved or reenslaved was a powerful force among Park's African companions, and the trade had contributed greatly to the disruption of the countryside he travelled through.

In the second half of the 18th century in England, little was known of the history and geography of inland west Africa. Ibn Battuta's books were not available and knowledge was limited to classical authors such as Herodotus, and the equally second-hand accounts of Leo Africanus and al-Idrisi, both the latter of whom had said that the Niger flowed from east to west. At a time when much of the rest of the world was being opened up to Europeans for the first time, inland west Africa remained a mystery; this was especially surprising given the legends about the wealth of Timbuktu, perhaps started by Mansa Musa's extravagances in Cairo nearly 500 years before. Merchants, too busy shipping slaves to the Americas, had scarcely thought about where their slaves came from. To remedy this, in 1788 a group of 12 gentlemen founded in London a new society, the African Association, to encourage exploration of what lay beyond the river mouths. Their motives were mixed. Six members, including Sir Joseph Banks, the Treasurer, were Fellows of the Royal Society, and intellectual curiosity, including a feeling of shame that the Age of Enlightenment knew less about Africa than the Greeks, was important, and at least one member was interested in the abolition of the slave trade. On the other hand, longer term commercial motives were not entirely lacking: the constitution of the Association allowed information gathered to be kept secret, presumably for trading purposes, and one committee member announced that since in Timbuktu even the slaves wore gold, "if we could get our manufactures into that country we should soon have gold enough." Members of the Association also had the comfortable sense of a civilizing mission justifying their work.

Major Daniel Houghton was sent by the Association in 1790 to explore the Niger, but died or was killed not far inland. To follow him, the Association chose Mungo Park, a young Scottish doctor who had already demonstrated a keen amateur interest in botany and a desire to travel. Mungo Park had been born near Selkirk in the Borders on 11 September 1771, the seventh of twelve or thirteen children of a modestly successful tenant farmer of the Duke of Buccleuch. Educated at first by a private tutor, then at local schools and Edinburgh Medical School, Mungo Park had been a shy and studious child, always top of his class. His father wanted him to go into the church, but Mungo Park decided to be a doctor. He showed an early interest in plants, and as a medical student he had joined his sister's husband James Dickson on a botanical tour of the Scottish Highlands. When Park completed his medical training he went to stay with Dickson in London to look for a job.

Through Dickson, Park met Sir Joseph Banks, President of the Royal Society and deeply involved in the African Association which had been founded four years before. Banks had travelled with Captain Cook and was the patron of the most important botanical explorations of the age. He was impressed by Park, and in 1793 found him a job as Surgeon's Mate on the *Worcester*, sailing to Sumatra. Park returned with a competent account of new plants and fishes from the area. He had proved he had the qualities needed for tropical exploration, and when he offered his services to the African Association for the Niger, they accepted him with enthusiasm. He was at once commissioned to go to West Africa, following the route pioneered by Houghton from the Gambia river inland. His instructions were to get to the Niger, to ascertain its course and if possible its beginning and end, to visit the main cities, particularly Timbuktu and "Houssa" (mistakenly thought to be a large town), and to return safely to Europe with this information. Park set off on this daunting mission in May 1795.

Park found the river, noted that it flowed east, and followed its banks for some distance to the edge of the Fulbe state of Maasina near Jenne, some way before the modern town of Mopti. Exhausted by illness, completely impoverished by a series of comprehensive robberies and facing the difficult start of the rains, Park turned back, little wiser about where the Niger went or what Timbuktu was like. He struggled back to the coast where he arrived in June 1796, a year after setting off.

Despite his meagre results, Park returned to a triumphal welcome. His account of his travels appeared in 1799, and in the same year he married Allison Anderson, a childhood friend, settled down as a country doctor at Peebles and had three children. But his mind was more on Africa than Scotland, and 1805 he accepted a second commission from the African Association to complete the exploration of the Niger. Setting off, this time with a military caravan of 45 Europeans, including soldiers, carpenters to build boats on the Niger and his brother in law, he cut through more directly to the river. Although he was better protected this time from casual banditry, he was later in the year than on his first trip, and much slowed down by the size of his party. With the start of the rains his companions started to die, and by the time he reached the river two thirds of them were dead. Park pressed on with a mounting sense of despair. Once on the river he threw away his normal caution and diplomacy, and instead of negotiating his passage with the chiefs he was soon firing on anyone who came near him. Obsessed by a tunnel vision of the river's mouth, he had fewer and fewer contacts with the inhabitants, and, I assume, gathered almost no more information about what went on on the river banks either side of him. He sailed past Timbuktu without visiting the town, past Gao and on to what is now northern Nigeria. He and his three remaining European companions died at Bussa.

Mungo Park does not seem to have been a very engaging person. He was mentally and physically tough, very tough indeed. The increasing succession of disasters on his first trip would have persuaded a less dogged person to turn back much earlier, and probably to despair completely. He was helped by an unemphatic sense of Christian duty but it is doubtful that this was a major part of his resolution. He seems to have been a mild-mannered, diffident man who was socially inept when he returned as a hero to London. On his first trip he behaved courteously to everyone, including those who robbed him, and he never resisted a demand for a present. I suspect a little more charm and some jokes would have helped his trip by making easier the difficult contacts with justly suspicious African chiefs. The few times he relaxed, as when he joked with the women who wanted to know whether Christians were circumcised, were a great success. In general he got on much better with women than with men, perhaps because he was able to joke with them.

Mungo Park saw himself as a gatherer of scientific information, but he brought back rather little wholly new material, although all his observations are careful and most are accurate. He would have greatly resented the idea that he was a scout for imperialism, which was certainly the view of many of the chiefs he visited, and also not entirely absent from Banks' mind when he declared in 1799, just after the publication of Park's account of his first trip, that Park had "opened a gate into the interior of Africa, into which it is easy for every nation to enter and to extend its commerce and discovery . . . A detachment of 500 chosen troops would soon make that road easy, and would build embarcations upon the Joliba—if 200 of these were to embark with field pieces they would be able to overcome the whole forces which Africa could bring against them." But it was the French not the English who followed Park's route to a colonial empire in the western Sudan a century later.

Park is curiously ambivalent on the other great subject of his time, the slave trade. He saw its terrible effects at close quarters and wrote movingly about the misery of slaves on caravans to the coast. But he never wrote or spoke clearly condemning the trade and never gave his support to the Abolition campaign then being organised.

Above all he was very brave and determined, as he slogged on from disaster to unexpected kindness to greater disaster. He must have been a curious sight, dressed in heavy European clothes, his diaries hidden in the crown of a large hat as he swam flooded streams, pressing on relentlessly despite the death of almost all his European companions so laconically recorded in his notes. It is a shame it went so terribly wrong at the end, particularly since there is probably some truth in Major Laing's claim that he left behind an appalling and savage image of Europeans, with his boat floating hopelessly down the Niger to certain doom, refusing all contacts and firing indiscriminately at anyone who came near him. It is an image prophetic of the larger disaster of European colonialism waiting off stage, which was to burst upon the middle Niger almost exactly 100 years later.

© Jeremy Swift 1983

CONTENTS

BOOK I: THE FIRST JOURNEY

Contents

PLATES

*Taken from illustrations in the original 1799
edition, based on Mungo Park's own drawings.*

BOOK ONE

THE FIRST JOURNEY

TRAVELS
IN THE
INTERIOR DISTRICTS OF AFRICA
PERFORMED UNDER THE
DIRECTION AND PATRONAGE
OF THE
AFRICAN ASSOCIATION
IN THE
YEARS 1795, 1796, AND 1797

BY MUNGO PARK, SURGEON

(The following is Park's text verbatim, omitting the dedication, list of subscribers, maps and illustrations, and appendix on "Geographical Illustrations," by J. Rennell.)

MUNGO PARK

From an engraving after the portrait by Henry Ederidge
reproduced as the frontispiece to the Travels

AUTHOR'S PREFACE

THE following Journal, drawn up from original minutes and notices made at the proper moment, and preserved with great difficulty, is now offered to the Public by the direction of my noble and honourable employers, the Members of the African Association. I regret that it is so little commensurate to the patronage I have received. As a composition, it has nothing to recommend it but *truth*. It is a plain unvarnished tale, without pretensions of any kind, except that it claims to enlarge, in some degree, the circle of African geography. For this purpose my services were offered, and accepted by the Association; and, I trust, I have not laboured altogether in vain. The work, however, must speak for itself; and I should not have thought any preliminary observations necessary, if I did not consider myself called upon, both by justice and gratitude, to offer those which follow.

Immediately after my return from Africa, the Acting Committee of the Association,[1] taking notice of the time it would require to prepare an account in detail, as it now appears, and being desirous of gratifying, as speedily as possible, the curiosity which many of the Members were pleased to express concerning my discoveries, determined

[1] This Committee consists of the following noblemen and gentlemen: Earl of Moira, Lord Bishop of Landaff, Right Hon. Sir Joseph Banks, President of the Royal Society, Andrew Stewart, Esq., F.R.S., and Bryan Edwards, Esq., F.R.S. Concerning the original institution of the Society itself, and the progress of discovery, previous to my expedition, the fullest information has already been given in the various publications which the Society have caused to be made.

that an epitome, or abridgment of my travels, should be forthwith prepared from such materials and oral communications as I could furnish, and printed for the use of the Association, and also that an engraved map of my route should accompany it. A memoir, thus supplied and improved, was accordingly drawn up in two parts, by members of the Association, and distributed among the Society; the first consisting of a narrative, in abstract, of my travels, by Bryan Edwards, Esq.; the second, of Geographical Illustrations of my progress, by Major James Rennell, F.R.S. Major Rennell was pleased also to add a map of my route, constructed in conformity to my own observations and sketches, freed from those errors which the Major's superior knowledge, and distinguished accuracy in geographical researches, enabled him to discover and correct.

Availing myself, therefore, on the present occasion, of assistance like this, it is impossible that I can present myself before the public, without expressing how deeply and gratefully sensible I am of the honour and advantage which I derive from the labours of those gentlemen; for Mr. Edwards has kindly permitted me to incorporate, as occasion offered, the whole of his narrative into different parts of my work; and Major Rennell, with equal goodwill, allows me to embellish and elucidate my Travels with the map before mentioned.

Thus aided and encouraged, I should deliver this volume to the world with that confidence of a favourable reception, which no merits of my own could authorise me to claim, were I not apprehensive that expectations have been formed by some of my subscribers, of discoveries to be unfolded which I have not made, and of wonders to be related of which I am utterly ignorant. There is danger that those who feel a disappointment of this nature, finding less to astonish and amuse in my book than they had promised to themselves beforehand, will not even allow me the little

merit which I really possess. Painful as this circumstance
may prove to my feelings, I shall console myself under
it, if the distinguished persons, under whose auspices I
entered on my mission, shall allow that I have executed
the duties of it to their satisfaction; and that they consider
the Journal, which I have now the honour to present to
them, to be, what I have endeavoured to make it, an
honest and faithful report of my proceedings and observations in their service, from the outset of my journey to its
termination.

M. P.

The following African words recurring very frequently in the course of the narrative, it is thought necessary to prefix an explanation of them for the Reader's convenience.

Alkaid. The head magistrate of a town or province, whose office is commonly hereditary.

Baloon. A room in which strangers are commonly lodged.

Bar. Nominal money: a single bar is equal in value to two shillings sterling or hereabouts.

Bentang. A sort of stage, erected in every town, answering the purpose of a town-hall.

Bushreen. A Mussulman.

Calabash. A species of gourd, of which the Negroes make bowls and dishes.

Coffle or Cafila. A caravan of slaves, or a company of people travelling with any kind of merchandise.

Cowries. Small shells, which pass for money in the interior.

Dooty. Another name for the chief magistrate of a town or province; this word is used only in the interior countries.

Kafir. A Pagan native; an unbeliever.

Korree. A watering place where shepherds keep their cattle.

Kouskous. A dish prepared from boiled corn.

Mansa. A king or chief governor.

Minkalli. A quantity of gold, nearly equal in value to ten shillings sterling.

Paddle. A sort of hoe used in husbandry.

Palaver. A court of justice; a public meeting of any kind.

Saphie. An amulet or charm.

Shea tou-lou. Vegetable butter.

Slatees. Free black merchants, who trade chiefly in slaves.

Soofroo. A skin for containing water.

Sonakee. Another term for an unconverted native; it signifies one who drinks strong liquors, and is used by way of reproach.

TRAVELS IN
THE INTERIOR OF AFRICA

CHAPTER I

The Author's motives for undertaking the voyage—His instructions
and departure—Arrives at Jillifree, on the Gambia River—Proceeds to Vintain—Some account of the Feloops—Proceeds up the
river for Jonkakonda—Arrives at Dr. Laidley's—Some account of
Pisania, and the British factory established at that place—The
Author's employment during his stay at Pisania—His sickness
and recovery—The country described—Prepares to set out for
the interior.

Soon after my return from the East Indies in 1793, having
learnt that the noblemen and gentlemen, associated for the
purpose of prosecuting discoveries in the interior of Africa,
were desirous of engaging a person to explore that continent by the way of the Gambia River, I took occasion,
through means of the President of the Royal Society, to
whom I had the honour to be known, of offering myself
for that service. I had been informed, that a gentleman
of the name of Houghton, a captain in the army, and
formerly fort-major at Goree, had already sailed to the
Gambia, under the direction of the Association, and that
there was reason to apprehend he had fallen a sacrifice to
the climate, or perished in some contest with the natives;
but this intelligence, instead of deterring me from my
purpose, animated me to persist in the offer of my services
with the greater solicitude. I had a passionate desire to
examine into the productions of a country so little known,
and to become experimentally acquainted with the modes
of life and character of the natives. I knew that I was
able to bear fatigue; and I relied on my youth and the
strength of my constitution to preserve me from the effects

of the climate. The salary which the Committee allowed was sufficiently large, and I made no stipulation for future reward. If I should perish in my journey, I was willing that my hopes and expectations should perish with me; and if I should succeed in rendering the geography of Africa more familiar to my countrymen, and in opening to their ambition and industry new sources of wealth, and new channels of commerce, I knew that I was in the hands of men of honour, who would not fail to bestow that remuneration which my successful services should appear to them to merit. The Committee of the Association, having made such inquiries as they thought necessary, declared themselves satisfied with the qualifications that I possessed, and accepted me for the service; and with that liberality which on all occasions distinguishes their conduct, gave me every encouragement which it was in their power to grant, or which I could with propriety ask.

It was at first proposed that I should accompany Mr. James Willis, who was then recently appointed Consul at Senegambia, and whose countenance in that capacity it was thought might have served and protected me; but Government afterwards rescinded his appointment, and I lost that advantage. The kindness of the Committee, however, supplied all that was necessary. Being favoured by the Secretary of the Association, the late Henry Beaufoy, Esq., with a recommendation to Dr. John Laidley (a gentleman who had resided many years at an English factory on the banks of the Gambia), and furnished with a letter of credit on him for £200, I took my passage in the brig *Endeavour*, a small vessel trading to the Gambia for bees-wax and ivory, commanded by Captain Richard Wyatt, and I became impatient for my departure.

My instructions were very plain and concise. I was directed, on my arrival in Africa, "to pass on to the river Niger, either by the way of Bambouk, or by such other route as should be found most convenient. That I should ascertain the course, and, if possible, the rise and termination of that river. That I should use my utmost exertions to visit the principal towns or cities in its neighbourhood, particularly Timbuctoo and Houssa; and that I should be afterwards at liberty to return to Europe, either by the way of the Gambia, or by such other route, as, under all the then existing circumstances of my situation and prospects, should appear to me to be most advisable."

We sailed from Portsmouth on the 22nd day of May 1795. On the 4th of June we saw the mountains over Mogadore, on the coast of Africa; and on the 21st of the same month, after a pleasant voyage of thirty days, we anchored at Jillifree, a town on the northern bank of the river Gambia, opposite to James's Island, where the English had formerly a small port.

The kingdom of Barra, in which the town of Jillifree is situated, produces great plenty of the necessaries of life; but the chief trade of the inhabitants is in salt; which commodity they carry up the river in canoes as high as Barraconda, and bring down in return Indian corn, cotton cloths, elephants' teeth, small quantities of gold dust, etc. The number of canoes and people constantly employed in this trade, make the King of Barra more formidable to Europeans than any other chieftain on the river; and this circumstance probably encouraged him to establish those exorbitant duties which traders of all nations are obliged to pay at entry, amounting to nearly £20 on every vessel, great and small. These duties or customs are generally collected in person by the Alkaid, or governor of Jillifree, and he is attended on these occasions by a numerous train of dependents, among whom are found many who, by their frequent intercourse with the English, have acquired a smattering of our language; but they are commonly very noisy and very troublesome—begging for every thing they fancy with such earnestness and importunity, that traders, in order to get quit of them, are frequently obliged to grant their requests.

On the 23rd we departed from Jillifree, and proceeded to Vintain, a town situated about two miles up a creek on the southern side of the river. This is much resorted to by Europeans, on account of the great quantities of bees-wax which are brought hither for sale. The wax is collected in the woods by the Feloops, a wild and unsociable race of people; their country, which is of considerable extent, abounds in rice; and the natives supply the traders, both on the Gambia and Cassamansa rivers, with that article, and also with goats and poultry, on very reasonable terms. The honey which they collect is chiefly used by themselves in making a strong intoxicating liquor, much the same as the mead which is produced from honey in Great Britain.

In their traffic with Europeans, the Feloops generally employ a factor or agent, of the Mandingo nation, who speaks a little English, and is acquainted with the trade of the river.   This broker makes the bargain; and, with the connivance of the European, receives a certain part only of the payment, which he gives to his employer as the whole; the remainder (which is very truly called the *cheating money*) he receives when the Feloop is gone, and appropriates to himself, as a reward for his trouble.

The language of the Feloops is appropriate and peculiar; and as their trade is chiefly conducted, as has been observed, by Mandingoes, the Europeans have no inducement to learn it.   The numerals are as follow : One, *Enory;* Two, *Sickaba* or *Cookaba ;* Three, *Sisajee;* Four, *Sibakeer ;* Five, *Footuck ;* Six, *Footuck-Enory;* Seven, *Footuck-Cookaba;* Eight, *Footuck-Sisajee ;* Nine, *Footuck-Sibakeer ;* Ten, *Sibankonyen.*

On the 26th we left Vintain, and continued our course up the river, anchoring whenever the tide failed us, and frequently towing the vessel with the boat.   The river is deep and muddy, the banks are covered with impenetrable thickets of mangrove, and the whole of the adjacent country appears to be flat and swampy.

The Gambia abounds with fish, some species of which are excellent food ; but none of them that I recollect are known in Europe.   At the entrance from the sea, sharks are found in great abundance ; and higher up, alligators and the hippopotamus (or river horse) are very numerous.   The latter might with more propriety be called the river-elephant, being of enormous and unwieldy bulk, and its teeth furnish good ivory.   This animal is amphibious, with short and thick legs, and cloven hoofs : it feeds on grass, and such shrubs as the banks of the river afford, boughs of trees, etc., seldom venturing far from the water, in which it seeks refuge on hearing the approach of man. I have seen many, and always found them of a timid and inoffensive disposition.

In six days after leaving Vintain, we reached Jonkakonda, a place of considerable trade, where our vessel was to take in part of her lading. The next morning, the several European traders came from their different factories to receive their letters, and learn the nature and amount of the cargo ; and the captain despatched a messenger to Dr. Laidley to inform him of my arrival. He came to Jonkakonda the morning following, when I delivered him Mr. Beaufoy's letter, and he gave me a kind invitation to spend my time at his house until an opportunity should offer of prosecuting my journey. This invitation was too acceptable to be refused ; and being furnished by the Doctor with a horse and guide, I set out from Jonkakonda at daybreak on the 5th of July, and at eleven o'clock arrived at Pisania, where I was accommodated with a room and other conveniences in the Doctor's house.

Pisania is a small village in the king of Yany's dominions, established by British subjects as a factory for trade, and inhabited solely by them and their black servants. It is situated on the banks of the Gambia, sixteen miles above Jonkakonda. The white residents, at the time of my arrival there, consisted only of Dr. Laidley, and two gentlemen who were brothers, of the name of Ainslie, but their domestics were numerous. They enjoyed perfect security under the king's protection ; and being highly esteemed and respected by the natives at large, wanted no accommodation or comfort which the country could supply ; and the greatest part of the trade in slaves, ivory, and gold, was in their hands.

Being now settled for some time at my ease, my first object was to learn the Mandingo tongue, being the language in almost general use throughout this part of Africa ; and without which I was fully convinced that I never could acquire an extensive knowledge of the country or its inhabitants. In this pursuit I was greatly assisted by

Dr. Laidley, who, by a long residence in the country, and constant intercourse with the natives, had made himself completely master of it.   Next to the language, my great object was to collect information concerning the countries I intended to visit.   On this occasion I was referred to certain traders called Slatees.   These are free black merchants, of great consideration in this part of Africa, who come down from the interior countries chiefly with enslaved Negroes for sale; but I soon discovered that very little dependence could be placed on the accounts they gave; for they contradicted each other in the most important particulars, and all of them seemed extremely unwilling that I should prosecute my journey.   These circumstances increased my anxiety to ascertain the truth from my own personal observations.

In researches of this kind, and in observing the manners and customs of the natives, in a country so little known to the nations of Europe, and furnished with so many striking and uncommon objects of nature, my time passed not unpleasantly; and I began to flatter myself that I had escaped the fever, or seasoning, to which Europeans, on their first arrival in hot climates, are generally subject.   But, on the 31st of July, I imprudently exposed myself to the night dew, in observing an eclipse of the moon, with a view to determine the longitude of the place; the next day I found myself attacked with a smart fever and delirium; and such an illness followed, as confined me to the house during the greatest part of August.   My recovery was very slow; but I embraced every short interval of convalescence to walk out, and make myself acquainted with the productions of the country.   In one of those excursions, having rambled farther than usual in a hot day, I brought on a return of my fever, and on the 10th of September I was again confined to my bed.   The fever, however, was not so violent as before; and in the course of three weeks I was able, when the weather would permit, to renew my botanical excursions; and when it rained, I amused myself with drawing plants, etc., in my chamber.   The care and attention of Dr. Laidley contributed greatly to alleviate my sufferings; his company and conversation beguiled the tedious hours during that gloomy season, when the rain falls in torrents ; when suffocating heats oppress by day, and when the night is spent by the terrified traveller in listening to the croaking of frogs (of which the numbers are beyond imagination), the shrill cry of the jackal, and the deep howling of the hyæna ; a dismal concert, interrupted only by the roar of such tremendous thunder as no person can form a conception of but those who have heard it.

The country itself, being an immense level, and very generally covered with woods, presents a tiresome and gloomy uniformity to the eye ; but although nature has denied to the inhabitants the beauties of romantic land-scapes, she has bestowed on them, with a liberal hand, the more important blessings of fertility and abundance. A little attention to cultivation procures a sufficiency of corn; the fields afford a rich pasturage for cattle ; and the natives are plentifully supplied with excellent fish, both from the Gambia river and the Walli creek.

The grains which are chiefly cultivated are Indian corn (*zea mays*); two kinds of *holcus spicatus*, called by the natives *soono* and *sanio ; holcus niger*, and *holcus bicolor ;* the former of which they have named *bassi woolima*, and the latter *bassiqui*. These, together with rice, are raised in consider-able quantities ; besides which the inhabitants in the vicinity of the towns and villages have gardens which produce onions, calavances, yams, cassavi, ground-nuts, pompions, gourds, water-melons, and some other esculent plants.

I observed, likewise, near the towns, small patches of cotton and indigo. The former of these articles supplies them with clothing, and with the latter they dye their cloth of an excellent blue colour, in a manner that will hereafter be described.

In preparing their corn for food, the natives use a large wooden mortar called a *paloon,* in which they bruise the seed until it parts with the outer covering, or husk, which is then separated from the clean corn by exposing it to the wind ; nearly in the same manner as wheat is cleared from the chaff in England. The corn thus freed from the husk is returned to the mortar, and beaten into meal, which is dressed variously in different countries ; but the most common preparation of it among the nations of the Gambia, is a sort of pudding, which they call *kouskous*. It is made by first moistening the flour with water, and then stirring and shaking it about in a large calabash or gourd, till it adheres together in small granules, resembling sago. It is then put into an earthen pot, whose bottom is perforated with a number of small holes ; and this pot being placed upon another, the two vessels are luted together, either with a paste of meal and water, or with cows' dung, and placed upon the fire. In the lower vessel is commonly some animal food and water, the steam or vapour of which ascends through the perforations in the bottom of the upper ve-sel, and softens and prepares the *kouskous*, which is very much esteemed throughout all the countries that I visited. I am informed that the same manner of preparing flour is very generally used on the Barbary coast, and that the dish so prepared is there called by the same name. It is therefore probable that the Negroes borrowed the practice from the Moors.

For gratifying a taste for variety, another sort of pudding called *nealing* is sometimes prepared from the meal of corn ; and they have also adopted two or three different modes of dressing their rice. Of vegetable food, therefore, the natives have no want ; and although the common class of people are but sparingly supplied with animal food, yet this article is not wholly withheld from them.

Their domestic animals are nearly the same as in Europe. Swine are found in the woods, but their flesh is not esteemed ; probably the marked abhorrence in which this animal is held by the votaries of Mahomet has spread itself among the pagans. Poultry of all kinds (the turkey excepted) is everywhere to be had. The Guinea fowl and red partridge abound in the fields ; and the woods furnish a small species of antelope, of which the venison is highly and deservedly prized.

Of the other wild animals in the Mandingo countries, the most common are the hyæna, the panther, and the elephant. Considering the use that is made of the latter in the East

Indies, it may be thought extraordinary that the natives of Africa have not, in any part of this immense continent, acquired the skill of taming this powerful and docile creature, and applying his strength and faculties to the service of man. When I told some of the natives that this was actually done in the countries of the East, my auditors laughed me to scorn, and exclaimed, *Tobaubo fonnio* (a white man's lie)! The Negroes frequently find means to destroy the elephant by fire-arms; they hunt it principally for the sake of the teeth, which they transfer in barter to those who sell them again to the Europeans. The flesh they eat, and consider it as a great delicacy.

The usual beast of burthen in all the Negro territories is the ass. The application of animal labour to the purposes of agriculture is nowhere adopted; the plough, therefore, is wholly unknown. The chief implement used in husbandry is the hoe, which varies in form in different districts; and the labour is universally performed by slaves.

On the 6th of October the waters of the Gambia were at the greatest height, being fifteen feet above the high-water mark of the tide; after which they began to subside —at first slowly, but afterwards very rapidly, sometimes sinking more than a foot in twenty-four hours; by the beginning of November the river had sunk to its former level, and the tide ebbed and flowed as usual. When the river had subsided, and the atmosphere grew dry, I recovered apace, and began to think of my departure— for this is reckoned the most proper season for travelling: the natives had completed their harvest, and provisions were everywhere cheap and plentiful.

Dr. Laidley was at this time employed in a trading voyage at Jonkakonda. I wrote to him to desire that he would use his interest with the Slatees, or slave-merchants, to procure me the company and protection of the first *coffle* (or caravan) that might leave Gambia for the interior country; and in the meantime I requested him to purchase for me a horse and two asses. A few days afterwards the Doctor returned to Pisania, and informed me that a coffle would certainly go for the interior in the course of the dry season; but that as many of the merchants belonging to it had not yet completed their assortment of goods, he could not say at what time they would set out.

As the characters and dispositions of the Slatees, and people that composed the caravan, were entirely unknown to me, and as they seemed rather averse to my purpose, and unwilling to enter into any positive engagements on my account; and the time of their departure being withal very uncertain, I resolved, on further deliberation, to avail myself of the dry season, and proceed without them.

Dr. Laidley approved my determination, and promised me every assistance in his power to enable me to prosecute my journey with comfort and safety.

This resolution having been formed, I made preparations accordingly. And now, being about to take leave of my hospitable friend (whose kindness and solicitude continued to the moment of my departure),[1] and to quit, for many months, the countries bordering on the Gambia, it seems proper, before I proceed with my narrative, that I should, in this place, give some account of the several Negro nations which inhabit the banks of this celebrated river, and the commercial intercourse that subsists between them and such of the nations of Europe as find their advantage in trading to this part of Africa. The observations which have occurred to me on both these subjects will be found in the following chapter.

[1] Dr. Laidley, to my infinite regret, has since paid the debt of nature. He left Africa in the latter end of 1797, intending to return to Great Britain by way of the West Indies; and died soon after his arrival at Barbadoes.

CHAPTER II

Description of the Feloops, the Jaloffs, the Foulahs, and Mandingoes
—Some account of the trade between the nations of Europe and
the natives of Africa, by the way of the Gambia, and between
the native inhabitants of the coast, and the nations of the interior
countries—Their mode of selling and buying, etc.

THE natives of the countries bordering on the Gambia,
though distributed into a great many distinct governments,
may, I think, be divided into four great classes; the
Feloops, the Jaloffs, the Foulahs, and the Mandingoes.
Among all these nations, the religion of Mahomet has
made, and continues to make, considerable progress; but
in most of them, the body of the people, both free and
enslaved, persevere in maintaining the blind but harmless
superstitions of their ancestors, and are called by the
Mahomedans *kafirs*, or infidels.

Of the Feloops, I have little to add to what has been
observed concerning them in the former chapter. They
are of a gloomy disposition, and are supposed never to
forgive an injury. They are even said to transmit their
quarrels as deadly feuds to their posterity; insomuch that
a son considers it as incumbent on him, from a just sense
of filial obligation, to become the avenger of his deceased
father's wrongs. If a man loses his life in one of those
sudden quarrels, which perpetually occur at their feasts,
when the whole party is intoxicated with mead, his son,
or the eldest of his sons (if he has more than one), endeavours to procure his father's sandals, which he wears *once
a year*, on the anniversary of his father's death, until a fit
opportunity offers of avenging his fate, when the object of
his resentment seldom escapes his pursuit. This fierce
and unrelenting disposition is, however, counterbalanced
by many good qualities; they display the utmost gratitude

and affection towards their benefactors; and the fidelity
with which they preserve whatever is intrusted to them is
remarkable.   During the present war they have more than
once taken up arms to defend our merchant vessels from
French privateers; and English property, of considerable
value, has frequently been left at Vintain, for a long time,
entirely under the care of the Feloops, who have uniformly
manifested on such occasions the strictest honesty and
punctuality.   How greatly is it to be wished that the
minds of a people, so determined and faithful, could be
softened and civilised by the mild and benevolent spirit
of Christianity!

The Jaloffs (or Yaloffs) are an active, powerful, and
warlike race, inhabiting great part of that tract which lies
between the river Senegal and the Mandingo states on the
Gambia; yet they differ from the Mandingoes, not only in
language, but likewise in complexion and features.   The
noses of the Jaloffs are not so much depressed, nor the
lips so protuberant, as among the generality of Africans;
and although their skin is of the deepest black, they are
considered by the white traders as the most sightly Negroes
in this part of the continent.

They are divided into several independent states or
kingdoms, which are frequently at war either with their
neighbours, or with each other.   In their manners, superstitions, and government, however, they have a greater
resemblance to the Mandingoes than to any other nation;
but excel them in the manufacture of cotton cloth—spinning the wool to a finer thread, weaving it in a broader
loom. and dyeing it of a better colour.

Their language is said to be copious and significant, and
is often learnt by Europeans trading to Senegal.

The Foulahs (or Pholeys), such of them at least as reside
near the Gambia, are chiefly of a tawny complexion, with
soft silky hair and pleasing features.   They are much
attached to a pastoral life, and have introduced themselves
into all the kingdoms on the windward coast as herdsmen
and husbandmen, paying a tribute to the sovereign of the
country for the lands which they hold.

The Mandingoes constitute in truth the bulk of the inhabitants in all those districts of Africa which I visited; and their language, with a few exceptions, is universally understood, and very generally spoken, in that part of the continent.

They are called Mandingoes, I conceive, as having originally migrated from the interior state of Manding, of which some account will hereafter be given; but, contrary to the present constitution of their parent country, which is republican, it appeared to me that the government in all the Mandingo states, near the Gambia, is monarchical. The power of the sovereign is, however, by no means unlimited. In all affairs of importance, the king calls an assembly of the principal men, or elders, by whose councils he is directed, and without whose advice he can neither declare war, nor conclude peace.

In every considerable town there is a chief magistrate, called the *Alkaid*, whose office is hereditary, and whose business it is to preserve order, to levy duties on travellers, and to preside at all conferences in the exercise of local jurisdiction and the administration of justice. These courts are composed of the elders of the town (of free condition), and are termed *palavers;* and their proceedings are conducted in the open air with sufficient solemnity. Both sides of a question are freely canvassed, witnesses are publicly examined, and the decisions which follow generally meet with the approbation of the surrounding audience.

As the Negroes have no written language of their own, the general rule of decision is an appeal to *ancient custom;* but since the system of Mahomet has made so great progress among them, the converts to that faith have gradually introduced, with the religious tenets, many of the civil institutions of the Prophet; and where the Koran is not found sufficiently explicit, recourse is had to a commentary called *Al Sharra*, containing, as I was told, a complete exposition or digest of the Mahomedan laws, both civil and criminal, properly arranged and illustrated.

This frequency of appeal to written laws, with which the pagan natives are necessarily unacquainted, has given rise in their palavers to (what I little expected to find in Africa) professional advocates, or expounders of the law, who are allowed to appear and to plead for plaintiff or defendant, much in the same manner as counsel in the law courts of Great Britain. They are Mahomedan Negroes who have made, or affect to have made, the laws of the Prophet their peculiar study; and if I may judge from their harangues, which I frequently attended, I believe that in the forensic qualifications of procrastination and cavil, and the arts of confounding and perplexing a cause, they are not always surpassed by the ablest pleaders in Europe. While I was at Pisania a cause was heard which furnished the Mahomedan lawyers with an admirable opportunity of displaying their professional dexterity. The case was this: An ass belonging to a Serawoolli Negro (a native of an interior country near the river Senegal) had broke into a field of corn belonging to one of the Mandingo inhabitants, and destroyed great part of it. The Mandingo having caught the animal in his field, immediately drew his knife and cut its throat. The Serawoolli thereupon called a *palaver* (or in European terms, *brought an action*) to recover damages for the loss of his beast, on which he set a high value. The defendant confessed he had killed the ass, but pleaded a *set off*, insisting that the loss he had sustained, by the ravage in his corn, was equal to the sum demanded for the animal. To ascertain this fact was the point at issue, and the learned advocates contrived to puzzle the cause in such a manner, that after a hearing of three days, the court broke up without coming to any determination upon it; and a second palaver was, I suppose, thought necessary.

The Mandingoes, generally speaking, are of a mild, sociable, and obliging disposition. The men are commonly above the middle size, well shaped, strong, and capable of enduring great labour; the women are good-natured, sprightly and agreeable. The dress of both sexes is composed of cotton cloth, of their own manufacture; that of the men is a loose frock. not unlike a surplice, with drawers which reach half-way down the leg; and they wear sandals on their feet, and white cotton caps on their heads. The women's dress consists of two pieces of cloth, each of which they wrap round the waist, which, hanging down to the ankles, answers the purpose of a petticoat; the other is thrown negligently over the bosom and shoulders.

This account of their clothing is indeed nearly applicable to the natives of all the different countries in this part of Africa; a peculiar national mode is observable only in the head-dresses of the women.

Thus, in the countries of the Gambia, the females wear a sort of bandage, which they call *Jalla*. It is a narrow stripe of cotton cloth, wrapped many times round, immediately over the forehead. In Bondou the head is encircled with strings of white beads, and a small plate of gold is worn in the middle of the forehead. In Kasson, the ladies decorate their heads, in a very tasteful and elegant manner, with white sea-shells. In Kaarta and Ludamar, the women raise their hair to a great height by the addition of a pad (as the ladies did formerly in Great Britain), which they decorate with a species of coral, brought from the Red Sea by pilgrims returning from Mecca, and sold at a great price.

In the construction of their dwelling-houses, the Man-dingoes also conform to the general practice of the African nations on this part of the continent, contenting themselves with small and incommodious hovels. A circular mud wall about four feet high, upon which is placed a conical roof, composed of the bamboo cane, and thatched with grass, forms alike the palace of the king, and the hovel of the slave. Their household furniture is equally simple. A hurdle of canes placed upon upright stakes about two feet from the ground, upon which is spread a mat or bullock's hide, answers the purpose of a bed; a water jar, some earthen pots for dressing their food, a few wooden bowls and calabashes, and one or two low stools, compose the rest.

As every man of free condition has a plurality of wives, it is found necessary (to prevent, I suppose, matrimonial dispute) that each of the ladies should be accommodated with a hut to herself; and all the huts belonging to the same family are surrounded by a fence, constructed of

*B 205

bamboo canes split and formed into a sort of wicker-work.
The whole enclosure is called a *sirk*, or *surk*. A number
of these enclosures, with narrow passages between them,
form what is called a town; but the huts are generally
placed without any regularity, according to the caprice of
the owner. The only rule that seems to be attended to, is
placing the door towards the south-west, in order to admit
the sea-breeze.

In each town is a large stage called the *Bentang*, which
answers the purpose of a public hall or town-house; it is
composed of interwoven canes, and is generally sheltered
from the sun by being erected in the shade of some large
tree. It is here that all public affairs are transacted, and
trials conducted; and here the lazy and indolent meet to
smoke their pipes and hear the news of the day. In most
of the towns the Mahomedans have also a *missura*, or
mosque, in which they assemble and offer up their daily
prayers, according to the rules of the Koran.

In the account which I have thus given of the natives,
the reader must bear in mind that my observations apply
chiefly to persons of *free condition*, who constitute, I suppose,
not more than one-fourth part of the inhabitants at large;
the other three-fourths are in a state of hopeless and
hereditary slavery, and are employed in cultivating the land,
in the care of cattle, and in servile offices of all kinds, much
in the same manner as the slaves in the West Indies. I
was told, however, that the Mandingo master can neither
deprive his slave of life, nor sell him to a stranger, without
first calling a palaver on his conduct, or, in other words,
bringing him to a public trial; but this degree of protection
is extended only to the native or domestic slave. Captives
taken in war, and those unfortunate victims who are condemned to slavery for crimes or insolvency, and, in short,
all those unhappy people who are brought down from the
interior countries for sale, have no security whatever, but
may be treated and disposed of in all respects as the owner
thinks proper. It sometimes happens, indeed, when no
ships are on the coast, that a humane and considerate
master incorporates his purchased slaves among his

domestics; and their offspring at least, if not the parents, become entitled to all the privileges of the native class.

The preceding remarks concerning the several nations that inhabit the banks of the Gambia, are all that I recollect as necessary to be made in this place, at the outset of my journey. With regard to the Mandingoes, however, many particulars are yet to be related, some of which are necessarily interwoven into the narrative of my progress, and others will be given in a summary at the end of my work, together with all such observations as I have collected on the country and climate, which I could not with propriety insert in the regular detail of occurrences. What remains of the present chapter will therefore relate solely to the trade which the nations of Christendom have found means to establish with the natives of Africa by the channel of the Gambia, and the inland traffic which has arisen in consequence of it between the inhabitants of the coast and the nations of the interior countries.

The earliest European establishment on this celebrated river was a factory of the Portuguese, and to this must be ascribed the introduction of the numerous words of that language which are still in use among the Negroes. The Dutch, French, and English afterwards successively possessed themselves of settlements on the coast; but the trade of the Gambia became, and continued for many years, a sort of monopoly in the hands of the English. In the travels of Francis Moore is preserved an account of the Royal African Company's establishments in this river in the year 1730, at which time James's factory alone consisted of a governor, deputy-governor, and two other principal officers; eight factors, thirteen writers, twenty inferior attendants and tradesmen; a company of soldiers, and thirty-two Negro servants, besides sloops, shallops, and boats, with their crews; and there were no less than eight subordinate factories in other parts of the river.

The trade with Europe, by being afterwards laid open, was almost annihilated; the share which the subjects of England at this time hold in it, supports not more than two or three annual ships, and I am informed that the gross value of British exports is under £20,000. The French and Danes still maintain a small share, and the Americans have lately sent a few vessels to the Gambia by way of experiment.

The commodities exported to the Gambia from Europe consist chiefly of fire-arms and ammunition, ironware, spirituous liquors, tobacco, cotton caps, a small quantity of broad cloth, and a few articles of the manufacture of Manchester; a small assortment of India goods, with some glass beads, amber, and other trifles, for which are taken in exchange, slaves, gold dust, ivory, bees-wax, and hides. Slaves are the chief article, but the whole number which at this time are annually exported from the Gambia by all nations, is supposed to be under one thousand.

Most of these unfortunate victims are brought to the coast in periodical caravans, many of them from very remote inland countries, for the language which they speak is not understood by the inhabitants of the maritime districts. In a subsequent part of my work I shall give the best information I have been able to collect concerning the manner in which they are obtained. On their arrival at the coast, if no immediate opportunity offers of selling them to advantage, they are distributed among the neighbouring villages until a slave ship arrives, or until they can be sold to black traders, who sometimes purchase on speculation. In the meanwhile, the poor wretches are kept constantly fettered, two and two of them being chained together, and employed in the labours of the field; and I am sorry to add, are very scantily fed, as well as harshly treated. The price of a slave varies according to the number of purchasers from Europe and the arrival of caravans from the interior; but in general I reckon that a young and healthy male, from sixteen to twenty-five years of age, may be estimated on the spot from £18 to £20 sterling.

The Negro slave merchants, as I have observed in the former chapter, are called *Slatees;* who, besides slaves and the merchandise which they bring for sale to the whites, supply the inhabitants of the maritime districts with native iron, sweet-smelling gums and frankincense, and a commodity called *shea-toulou*, which, literally translated, signifies *tree-butter*. This commodity is extracted, by means of boiling water, from the kernel of a nut, as will be more particularly described hereafter; it has the consistence and appearance of butter; and is in truth an admirable substitute for it. It forms an important article in the food of the natives, and serves also for every domestic purpose in which oil would otherwise be used. The demand for it is therefore very great.

In payment of these articles, the maritime states supply the interior countries with salt, a scarce and valuable commodity, as I frequently and painfully experienced in the course of my journey. Considerable quantities of this article, however, are also supplied to the inland natives by the Moors, who obtain it from the salt pits in the Great Desert, and receive in return corn, cotton cloth, and slaves.

In thus bartering one commodity for another, many inconveniences must necessarily have arisen at first from the want of coined money, or some other visible and determinate medium to settle the balance, or difference of value between different articles, to remedy which the natives of the interior make use of small shells called *cowries*, as will be shown hereafter. On the coast, the inhabitants have adopted a practice which I believe is peculiar to themselves.

In their early intercourse with Europeans, the article that attracted most notice was iron. Its utility, in forming the instruments of war and husbandry, made it preferable to all others; and iron soon became the measure by which the value of all other commodities was ascertained. Thus, a certain quantity of goods, of whatever denomination, appearing to be equal in value to a bar of iron, constituted, in the trader's phraseology, a bar of that particular merchandise. Twenty leaves of tobacco, for instance, were considered as a *bar* of tobacco; and a gallon of spirits (or rather half spirits and half water), as a *bar* of rum; a bar of one commodity being reckoned equal in value to a bar of another commodity.

As, however, it must unavoidably happen, that according

to the plenty or scarcity of goods at market in proportion to the demand, the relative value would be subject to continual fluctuation, greater precision has been found necessary; and at this time the current value of a single bar of any kind is fixed by the whites at two shillings sterling. Thus a slave, whose price is £15, is said to be worth 150 bars.

In transactions of this nature, it is obvious that the white trader has infinitely the advantage over the African, whom, therefore, it is difficult to satisfy; for, conscious of his own ignorance, he naturally becomes exceedingly suspicious and wavering; and indeed, so very unsettled and jealous are the Negroes in their dealings with the whites, that a bargain is never considered by the European as concluded, until the purchase money is paid, and the party has taken leave.

Having now brought together such general observations on the country and its inhabitants, as occurred to me during my residence in the vicinage of the Gambia, I shall detain the reader no longer with introductory matter, but proceed, in the next chapter, to a regular detail of the incidents which happened, and the reflections which arose in my mind, in the course of my painful and perilous journey, from its commencement, until my return to the Gambia.

CHAPTER III

The Author sets out from Pisania—His attendants—Reaches Jindey—
Story related by a Mandingo Negro—Proceeds to Medina, the
capital of Woolli—Interview with the king—Saphies or charms—
Proceeds to Koler—Description of Mumbo Jumbo—Arrives at
Koojar—Wrestling match—Crosses the wilderness, and arrives at
Tallika, in the kingdom of Bondou.

ON the 2nd of December 1795, I took my departure from
the hospitable mansion of Dr. Laidley. I was fortunately
provided with a Negro servant, who spoke both the English
and Mandingo tongues. His name was *Johnson*. He was
a native of this part of Africa; and having in his youth
been conveyed to Jamaica as a slave, he had been made
free, and taken to England by his master, where he had
resided many years; and at length found his way back
to his native country. As he was known to Dr. Laidley,
the Doctor recommended him to me, and I hired him as
my interpreter, at the rate of ten bars monthly, to be paid
to himself, and five bars a month to be paid to his wife
during his absence. Dr. Laidley furthermore provided me
with a Negro boy of his own, named *Demba ;* a sprightly
youth, who besides Mandingo, spoke the language of the
Serawoollies, an inland people (of whom mention will
hereafter be made), residing on the banks of the Senegal ;
and to induce him to behave well, the Doctor promised
him his freedom on his return, in case I should report
favourably of his fidelity and services. I was furnished
with a horse for myself (a small, but very hardy and
spirited beast, which cost me to the value of £7, 10s.),
and two asses for my interpreter and servant. My baggage
was light, consisting chiefly of provisions for two days ; a
small assortment of beads, amber and tobacco, for the
purchase of a fresh supply, as I proceeded ; a few changes
of linen, and other necessary apparel, an umbrella, a pocket

sextant, a magnetic compass, and a thermometer; together with two fowling-pieces, two pairs of pistols, and some other small articles.

A freeman (a Bushreen or Mahomedan), named Madiboo, who was travelling to the kingdom of Bambarra, and two Slatees, or slave merchants of the Serawoolli nation, and of the same sect, who were going to Bondou, offered their services as far as they intended respectively to proceed; as did likewise a Negro named Tami (also a Mahomedan), a native of Kasson, who had been employed some years by Dr. Laidley as a blacksmith, and was returning to his native country with the savings of his labours. All these men travelled on foot, driving their asses before them.

Thus I had no less than six attendants, all of whom had been taught to regard me with great respect, and to consider that their safe return hereafter, to the countries on the Gambia, would depend on my preservation.

Dr. Laidley himself, and Messrs. Ainsley, with a number of their domestics, kindly determined to accompany me the two first days; and, I believe, they secretly thought they should never see me afterwards.

We reached Jindey the same day, having crossed the Walli creek, a branch of the Gambia, and rested at the house of a black woman, who had formerly been the *chère amie* of a white trader named Hewett; and who, in consequence thereof, was called, by way of distinction, *Seniora*. In the evening we walked out to see an adjoining village, belonging to a Slatee named Jemaffoo Mamadoo, the richest of all the Gambia traders. We found him at home; and he thought so highly of the honour done him by this visit, that he presented us with a fine bullock, which was immediately killed, and part of it dressed for our evening's repast.

The Negroes do not go to supper till late, and in order to amuse ourselves while our beef was preparing, a Mandingo was desired to relate some diverting stories; in listening to which, and smoking tobacco, we spent three hours. These stories bear some resemblance to those in the Arabian Nights' Entertainments; but, in general, are of a more ludicrous cast. I shall here abridge one of them for the reader's amusement.

"Many years ago (said the relater), the people of Doomasansa (a town on the Gambia), were much annoyed by a lion, that came every night, and took away some of their cattle. By continuing his depredations, the people were at length so much enraged, that a party of them resolved to go and hunt the monster. They accordingly proceeded in search of the common enemy, which they found concealed in a thicket; and immediately firing at him, were lucky enough to wound him in such a manner, that, in springing from the thicket towards the people, he fell down among the grass, and was unable to rise. The animal, however, manifested such appearance of vigour, that nobody cared to approach him singly; and a consultation was held concerning the properest means of taking him alive; a circumstance, it was said, which, while it furnished undeniable proof of their prowess, would turn out to great advantage, it being resolved to convey him to the coast, and sell him to the Europeans. While some persons proposed one plan, and some another, an old man offered a scheme. This was, to strip the roof of a house of its thatch, and to carry the bamboo frame (the pieces of which are well secured together by thongs), and throw it over the lion. If, in approaching him, he should attempt to spring upon them, they had nothing to do but to let down the roof upon themselves, and fire at the lion through the rafters.

"This proposition was approved and adopted. The thatch was taken from the roof of a hut, and the lion-hunters, supporting the fabric, marched courageously to the field of battle; each person carrying a gun in one hand, and bearing his share of the roof on the opposite shoulder. In this manner they approached the enemy; but the beast had by this time recovered his strength; and such was the fierceness of his countenance, that the hunters, instead of proceeding any further, thought it prudent to provide for their own safety, by covering themselves with the roof. Unfortunately, the lion was too nimble for them; for, making a spring while the roof was setting down, both the beast and his pursuers were caught in the same cage, and the lion devoured them at his leisure, to the great astonishment and mortification of the people of Dooma-sansa; at which place it is dangerous even at this day to tell the story, for it is become the subject of laughter and derision in the neighbouring countries. and nothing will enrage an inhabitant of that town so much as desiring him to catch a lion alive."

About one o'clock in the afternoon of the 3rd of December, I took my leave of Dr. Laidley and Messrs. Ainsley, and rode slowly into the woods. I had now before me a boundless forest, and a country, the inhabitants of which were strangers to civilised life, and to most of whom a white man was the object of curiosity or plunder. I reflected that I had parted from the last European I might probably behold, and perhaps quitted for ever the comforts of Christian society. Thoughts like these would necessarily cast a gloom over the mind, and I rode musing along for about three miles, when I was awakened from my reverie by a body of people, who came running up and stopped the asses, giving me to understand that I must go with them to Peckaba, to present myself to the king of Walli, or pay customs to them. I endeavoured to make them comprehend that the object of my journey not being traffic, I ought not to be subjected to a tax like the Slatees and other merchants who travel for gain; but I reasoned to no purpose. They said it was usual for travellers of all descriptions to make a present to the king of Walli, and without doing so I could not be permitted to proceed. As they were more numerous than my attendants, and withal very noisy, I thought it prudent to comply with their demand, and having presented them with four bars of tobacco, for the king's use, I was permitted to continue my journey, and at sunset reached a village near Kootacunda, where we rested for the night.

In the morning of December 4th, I passed Kootacunda, the last town of Walli, and stopped about an hour at a small adjoining village to pay customs to an officer of the king of Woolli. We rested the ensuing night at a village called Tabajang, and at noon the next day (December 5th) we reached Medina, the capital of the king of Woolli's dominions.

The kingdom of Woolli is bounded by Walli on the west, by the Gambia on the south, by the small river Walli on the north-west, by Bondou on the north-east, and on the east by the Simbani wilderness.

The country everywhere rises into gentle acclivities, which are generally covered with extensive woods, and the towns are situated in the intermediate valleys. Each town is surrounded by a tract of cultivated land, the produce of which, I presume, is found sufficient to supply the wants of the inhabitants; for the soil appeared to me to be everywhere fertile, except near the tops of the ridges, where the red iron-stone and stunted shrubs sufficiently marked the boundaries between fertility and barrenness. The chief pro uctions are cotton, tobacco, and esculent vegetables; all which are raised in the valleys, the rising grounds being appropriated to different sorts of corn.

The inhabitants are Mandingoes; and, like most of the Mandingo nations, are divided into two great sects, the Mahomedans, who are called *Bushreens*, and the Pagans, who are called indiscriminately, *Kafirs* (unbelievers) and *Sonakies* (*i.e.* men who drink strong liquors). The Pagan natives are by far the most numerous, and the government of the country is in their hands, for though the most respectable among the Bushreens are frequently consulted in affairs of importance, yet they are never permitted to take any share in the executive government, which rests solely in the hands of the *Mansa*, or sovereign, and great officers of the state. Of these, the first in point of rank is the presumptive heir of the crown, who is called the *Farbanna*; next to him are the *Alkaids*, or provincial governors, who are more frequently called *Keamos*. Then follow the two grand divisions of freemen and slaves;[1] of the former, the Slatees, so frequently mentioned in the preceding pages,

[1] The term which signifies a man of free condition, is *Horia*; that of a slave, *Jong*.

are considered as the principal; but in all classes great respect is paid to the authority of aged men.

On the death of the reigning monarch, his eldest son (if he has attained the age of manhood) succeeds to the regal authority. If there is no son, or if the son is under the age of discretion, a meeting of the great men is held, and the late monarch's nearest relation (commonly his brother) is called to the government, not as regent, or guardian to the infant son, but in full right, and to the exclusion of the minor. The charges of the government are defrayed by occasional tributes from the people, and by duties on goods transported across the country. Travellers, on going from the Gambia towards the interior, pay customs in European merchandise. On returning they pay in iron and *shea-toulou;* these taxes are paid at every town.

Medina,[1] the capital of the kingdom, at which I was now arrived, is a place of considerable extent; and may contain from eight hundred to one thousand houses. It is fortified in the common African manner, by a surrounding high wall built of clay, and an outward fence of pointed stakes and prickly bushes; but the walls are neglected, and the outward fence has suffered considerably from the active hands of busy housewives, who pluck up the stakes for firewood. I obtained a lodging at one of the king's near relations, who apprised me, that at my introduction to the king, I must not presume *to shake hands with him.* It was not usual, he said, to allow this liberty to strangers. Thus instructed, I went in the afternoon to pay my respects to the sovereign; and ask permission to pass through his territories to Bondou. The king's name was *Jatta.* He was the same venerable old man of whom so favourable an account was transmitted by Major Houghton. I found him seated upon a mat before the door of his hut; a number of men and women were arranged on each side, who were singing and clapping their hands. I saluted him respectfully, and informed him of the purport of my visit.

[1] Medina, in the Arabic, signifies a city. The name is not uncommon among the Negroes, and has probably been borrowed from the Mahomedans.

The king graciously replied, that he not only gave me leave to pass through his country, but would offer up his prayers for my safety. On this, one of my attendants, seemingly in return for the king's condescension, began to sing, or rather to roar, an Arabic song; at every pause of which, the king himself, and all the people present, struck their hands against their foreheads, and exclaimed, with devout and affecting solemnity, *Amen, Amen!*[1] The king told me, furthermore, that I should have a guide the day following, who would conduct me safely to the frontier of his kingdom. I then took my leave, and in the evening sent the king an order upon Dr. Laidley for three gallons of rum, and received in return great store of provisions.

Dec. 6th.—Early in the morning, I went to the king a second time, to learn if the guide was ready. I found his majesty sitting upon a bullock's hide, warming himself before a large fire; for the Africans are sensible of the smallest variation in the temperature of the air, and frequently complain of cold when a European is oppressed with heat. He received me with a benevolent countenance, and tenderly entreated me to desist from my purpose of travelling into the interior, telling me that Major Houghton had been killed in his route, and that, if I followed his footsteps, I should probably meet with his fate. He said that I must not judge of the people of the eastern country by those of Woolli; that the latter were acquainted with white men, and respected them; whereas the people of the east had never seen a white man, and would certainly destroy me. I thanked the king for his affectionate solicitude, but told him that I had considered the matter, and was determined, notwithstanding all dangers, to proceed. The king shook his head, but desisted from further persuasion, and told me the guide should be ready in the afternoon.

About two o'clock, the guide appearing, I went and took

---

[1] It may seem from hence that the king was a Mahomedan; but I was assured to the contrary. He joined in prayer on this occasion probably from the mere dictates of his benevolent mind; considering perhaps that prayers to the Almighty, offered up with true devotion and sincerity, were equally acceptable whether from Bushreen or Pagan.

my last farewell of the good old king, and in three hours
reached Konjour, a small village, where we determined to
rest for the night. Here I purchased a fine sheep for some
beads, and my Serawoolli attendants killed it with all the
ceremonies prescribed by their religion; part of it was
dressed for supper, after which a dispute arose between
one of the Serawoolli Negroes and Johnson, my interpreter,
about the sheep's horns. The former claimed the horns
as his perquisite, for having acted the part of our butcher,
and Johnson contested the claim. I settled the matter by
giving a horn to each of them. This trifling incident is
mentioned as introductory to what follows; for it appeared
on inquiry that these horns were highly valued, as being
easily convertible into portable sheaths, or cases, for containing and keeping secure certain charms or amulets called
saphies, which the Negroes constantly wear about them.
These saphies are prayers, or rather sentences from the
Koran, which the Mahomedan priests write on scraps of
paper, and sell to the simple natives, who consider them to
possess very extraordinary virtues. Some of the Negroes
wear them to guard themselves against the bite of snakes
or alligators, and on this occasion the saphie is commonly
enclosed in a snake's or alligator's skin, and tied round the
ankle. Others have recourse to them in time of war, to
protect their persons against hostile weapons; but the
common use to which these amulets are applied is to prevent or cure bodily diseases, to preserve from hunger and
thirst, and generally to conciliate the favour of superior
powers under all the circumstances and occurrences of
life.[1]

In this case it is impossible not to admire the wonderful
contagion of superstition ; for, notwithstanding that the
majority of the Negroes are pagans, and absolutely reject
the doctrines of Mahomet, I did not meet with a man,
whether a Bushreen or Kafir, who was not fully persuaded
of the powerful efficacy of these amulets. The truth is,
that all the natives of this part of Africa consider the art of

[1] I believe that similar charms or amulets, under the names of *domini*,
grigri, *fetich*, etc., etc., are common in all parts of Africa.

writing as bordering on magic; and it is not in the doctrines of the Prophet, but in the arts of the magician that their confidence is placed. It will hereafter be seen that I was myself lucky enough, in circumstances of distress, to turn the popular credulity in this respect to good account.

On the 7th I departed from Konjour, and slept at a village called Malla (or Mallaing); and on the 8th, about noon, I arrived at Kolor, a considerable town, near the entrance into which I observed, hanging upon a tree, a sort of masquerade habit, made of the bark of trees, which I was told on inquiry belonged to MUMBO JUMBO. This is a strange bugbear, common to all the Mandingo towns, and much employed by the Pagan natives in keeping their women in subjection; for as the Kafirs are not restricted in the number of their wives, every one marries as many as he can conveniently maintain; and as it frequently happens that the ladies disagree among themselves, family quarrels sometimes rise to such a height that the authority of the husband can no longer preserve peace in his household. In such cases, the interposition of Mumbo Jumbo is called in, and is always decisive.

This strange minister of justice (who is supposed to be either the husband himself, or some person instructed by him), disguised in the dress that has been mentioned, and armed with the rod of public authority, announces his coming (whenever his services are required) by loud and dismal screams in the woods near the town. He begins the pantomime at the approach of night; and as soon as it is dark he enters the town, and proceeds to the Bentang, at which all the inhabitants immediately assemble.

It may easily be supposed that this exhibition is not much relished by the women; for as the person in disguise is entirely unknown to them, every married female suspects that the visit may possibly be intended for herself; but they dare not refuse to appear when they are summoned; and the ceremony commences with songs and dances, which continue till midnight, about which time Mumbo fixes on the offender. This unfortunate victim being thereupon immediately seized, is stripped naked, tied to a post,

and severely scourged with Mumbo's rod, amidst the
shouts and derision of the whole assembly; and it is
remarkable, that the rest of the women are the loudest in
their exclamations on this occasion against their unhappy
sister.   Daylight puts an end to this indecent and unmanly
revel.

Dec. 9th,—As there was no water to be procured on the
road, we travelled with great expedition until we reached
Tambacunda; and departing from thence early the next
morning, the 10th, we reached, in the evening, Kooniakary,
a town of nearly the same magnitude as Kolor.   About
noon on the 11th we arrived at Koojar, the frontier town of
Woolli, towards Bondou, from which it is separated by an
intervening wilderness of two days' journey.

The guide appointed by the king of Woolli being now to
return, I presented him with some amber for his trouble;
and having been informed that it was not possible at all
times to procure water in the wilderness, I made inquiry
for men who would serve both as guides and water-bearers
during my journey across it.   Three Negroes, elephant-
hunters, offered their services for these purposes, which I
accepted, and paid them three bars each in advance, and
the day being far spent, I determined to pass the night in
my present quarters.

The inhabitants of Koojar, though not wholly unaccustomed to the sight of Europeans (most of them having
occasionally visited the countries on the Gambia) beheld
me with a mixture of curiosity and reverence, and in the
evening invited me to see a *neobering*, or wrestling match,
at the Bentang.   This is an exhibition very common in all
the Mandingo countries.   The spectators arranged themselves in a circle, leaving the intermediate space for the
wrestlers, who were strong active young men, full of emulation, and accustomed, I suppose, from their infancy to this
sort of exertion.   Being stripped of their clothing, except a
short pair of drawers, and having their skin anointed with
oil, or *shea* butter, the combatants approached each other
on all fours, parrying with and occasionally extending a
hand for some time, till at length one of them sprang

forward, and caught his rival by the knee. Great dexterity
and judgment were now displayed; but the contest was
decided by superior strength; and I think that few Europeans would have been able to cope with the conqueror.
It must not be unobserved that the combatants were
animated by the music of a drum, by which their actions
were in some measure regulated.

The wrestling was succeeded by a dance, in which many
performers assisted, all of whom were provided with little
bells, which were fastened to their legs and arms; and here,
too, the drum regulated their motions. It was beaten with
a crooked stick, which the drummer held in his right hand,
occasionally using his left to deaden the sound, and thus
vary the music. The drum is likewise applied on these
occasions to keep order among the spectators, by imitating
the sound of certain Mandingo sentences: for example,
when the wrestling match is about to begin, the drummer
strikes what is understood to signify *ali bœ see*,—sit all
down; upon which the spectators immediately seat themselves; and when the combatants are to begin, he strikes
amuta amuta,—take hold, take hold.

In the course of the evening I was presented, by way of
refreshment, with a liquor which tasted so much like the
strong beer of my native country (and very good beer, too),
as to induce me to inquire into its composition; and I
learnt, with some degree of surprise, that it was actually
made from corn which had been previously malted, much
in the same manner as barley is malted in Great Britain.
A root yielding a grateful bitter was used in lieu of hops,
the name of which I have forgot; but the corn which yields
the wort is the *holcus spicatus* of botanists.

Early in the morning (the 12th), I found that one of the
elephant-hunters had absconded with the money he had
received from me in part of wages; and in order to prevent
the other two from following his example, I made them
instantly fill their calabashes (or gourds) with water, and as
the sun rose I entered the wilderness that separates the
kingdoms of Woolli and Bondou.

We had not travelled more than a mile before my attendants insisted on stopping, that they might prepare a saphie or charm, to insure us a safe journey.   This was done by muttering a few sentences, and spitting upon a stone, which was thrown before us on the road.   The same ceremony was repeated three times, after which the Negroes proceeded with the greatest confidence; every one being firmly persuaded that the stone (like the scape-goat) had carried with it everything that could induce superior powers to visit us with misfortune.

We continued our journey without stopping any more till noon, when we came to a large tree, called by the natives *Neema Taba*.   It had a very singular appearance, being decorated with innumerable rags or scraps of cloth, which persons travelling across the wilderness had at different times tied to the branches; probably, at first, to inform the traveller that water was to be found near it; but the custom has been so greatly sanctioned by time, that nobody now presumes to pass without hanging up something.   I followed the example, and suspended a handsome piece of cloth on one of the boughs; and being told that either a well, or pool of water, was at no great distance, I ordered the Negroes to unload the asses that we might give them corn, and regale ourselves with the provisions we had brought. In the meantime I sent one of the elephant-hunters to look for the well, intending, if water was to be obtained, to rest here for the night.   A pool was found, but the water was thick and muddy, and the Negro discovered near it the remains of a fire recently extinguished, and the fragments of provisions; which afforded a proof that it had been lately visited either by travellers or banditti.   The fears of my attendants supposed the latter; and believing that robbers lurked near us, I was persuaded to change my resolution of resting here all night, and proceed to another watering-place, which, I was assured, we might reach early in the evening.

We departed accordingly, but it was eight o'clock at night before we came to the watering-place; and being now sufficiently fatigued with so long a day's journey, we kindled a large fire, and lay down, surrounded by our cattle

on the bare ground, more than a gun-shot from any bush
—the Negroes agreeing to keep watch by turns to prevent
surprise.

I know not indeed that any danger was justly to be
dreaded, but the Negroes were unaccountably apprehensive
of banditti during the whole of the journey. As soon
therefore as daylight appeared, we filled our *soofroos* (skins)
and calabashes at the pool, and set out for Tallika, the first
town in Bondou, which we reached about eleven o'clock in
the forenoon (the 13th of December). I cannot, however,
take leave of Woolli, without observing that I was everywhere well received by the natives; and that the fatigues
of the day were generally alleviated by a hearty welcome
at night; and although the African mode of living was at
first unpleasant to me, yet I found at length that custom
surmounted trifling inconveniences, and made everything
palatable and easy.

CHAPTER IV

Some account of the inhabitants of Tallika—The Author proceeds for
Fatteconda—Incidents on the road—Crosses the Neriko—Arrives
at Koorkarany—Reaches the river Falemé—Fishery on that river
—Proceeds along its bank to Naye or Nayemow—Crosses the
Falemé, and arrives at Fatteconda—Has an interview with
Almami, the sovereign of Bondou—Description of the king's
dwelling—Has a second interview with the king, who begs the
Author's coat—Author visits the king's wives—Is permitted to
depart on friendly terms—Journey by night—Arrives at Joag—
Some account of Bondou and its inhabitants, the Foulahs.

TALLIKA, the frontier town of Bondou towards Woolli, is
inhabited chiefly by Foulahs of the Mahomedan religion,
who live in considerable affluence, partly by furnishing
provisions to the *coffles*, or caravans, that pass through the
town, and partly by the sale of ivory, obtained by hunting
elephants ; in which employment the young men are generally very successful.   Here, an officer belonging to the king
of Bondou constantly resides, whose business it is to give
timely information of the arrival of the caravans, which are
taxed according to the number of loaded asses that arrive
at Tallika.

I took up my residence at this officer's house, and agreed
with him to accompany me to Fatteconda, the residence of
the king, for which he was to receive five bars ; and before
my departure I wrote a few lines to Dr. Laidley, and gave
my letter to the master of a caravan bound for the Gambia.
This caravan consisted of nine or ten people with five asses
loaded with ivory.   The large teeth are conveyed in nets,
two on each side of the ass ; the small ones are wrapped
up in skins, and secured with ropes.

Dec. 14*th.*—We left Tallika, and rode on very peaceably
for about two miles, when a violent quarrel arose between
two of my fellow-travellers, one of whom was the blacksmith, in the course of which they bestowed some oppro-

brious terms upon each other; and it is worthy of remark, that an African will sooner forgive a blow than a term of reproach applied to his ancestors.—"Strike me, but do not curse my mother," is a common expression even among the slaves.   This sort of abuse, therefore, so enraged one of the disputants, that he drew his cutlass upon the blacksmith, and would certainly have ended the dispute in a very serious manner, if the others had not laid hold of him, and wrested the cutlass from him.   I was obliged to interfere, and put an end to this disagreeable business, by desiring the blacksmith to be silent, and telling the other, who I thought was in the wrong, that if he attempted in future to draw his cutlass, or molest any of my attendants, I should look upon him as a robber, and shoot him without further ceremony.   This threat had the desired effect, and we marched sullenly along till the afternoon, when we arrived at a number of small villages scattered over an open and fertile plain.   At one of these, called Ganado, we took up our residence for the night.   Here an exchange of presents and a good supper terminated all animosities among my attendants; and the night was far advanced before any of us thought of going to sleep.   We were amused by an itinerant *singing man*,[1] who told a number of diverting stories, and played some sweet airs, by blowing his breath upon a bowstring, and striking it at the same time with a stick.

Dec. 15*th.*—At daybreak, my fellow-travellers, the Serawoollies, took leave of me, with many prayers for my safety. About a mile from Ganado, we crossed a considerable branch of the Gambia, called Neriko.   The banks were steep, and covered with *mimosas;* and I observed in the mud a number of large mussels, but the natives do not eat them.   About noon, the sun being exceedingly hot, we rested two hours in the shade of a tree, and purchased some milk and pounded corn from some Foulah herdsmen, and at sunset reached a town called Koorkarany,

[1] These are a sort of travelling bards and musicians, who sing extempore songs in praise of those who employ them.   A fuller account of them will be given hereafter.

where the blacksmith had some relations; and here we rested two days.

Koorkarany is a Mahomedan town, surrounded by a high wall, and is provided with a mosque. Here I was shown a number of Arabic manuscripts, particularly a copy of the book before mentioned, called *Al Shara*. The *Maraboo* or priest, in whose possession it was, read and explained to me in Mandingo, many of the most remarkable passages; and in return, I showed him Richardson's Arabic grammar, which he very much admired.

On the evening of the second day (Dec. 17th) we departed from Koorkarany. We were joined by a young man who was travelling to Fatteconda for salt; and as night set in we reached Dooggii, a small village about three miles from Koorkarany.

Provisions were here so cheap that I purchased a bullock for six small stones of amber; for I found my company increase or diminish according to the good fare they met with.

Dec. 18th.—Early in the morning we departed from Dooggii, and being joined by a number of Foulahs and other people, made a formidable appearance, and were under no apprehension of being plundered in the woods. About eleven o'clock, one of the asses proving very refractory, the Negroes took a curious method to make him tractable. They cut a forked stick, and putting the forked part into the ass's mouth, like the bit of a bridle, tied the two smaller parts together above his head, leaving the lower part of the stick of sufficient length to strike against the ground if the ass should attempt to put his head down. After this, the ass walked along quietly and gravely enough, taking care, after some practice, to hold his head sufficiently high to prevent the stones or roots of trees from striking against the end of the stick, which experience had taught him would give a severe shock to his teeth. This contrivance produced a ludicrous appearance, but my fellow-travellers told me it was constantly adopted by the Slatees, and always proved effectual.

In the evening we arrived at a few scattered villages, surrounded with extensive cultivation; at one of which, called Buggil, we passed the night in a miserable hut, having no other bed than a bundle of corn stalks, and no provisions but what we brought with us. The wells here are dug with great ingenuity, and are very deep. I measured one of the bucket-ropes, and found the depth of the well to be twenty-eight fathoms.

Dec. 19*th.*—We departed from Buggil, and travelled along a dry, stony height, covered with *mimosas*, till mid-day, when the land sloped towards the east, and we descended into a deep valley, in which I observed abundance of whin-stone and white quartz. Pursuing our course to the eastward, along this valley, in the bed of an exhausted river course, we came to a large village, where we intended to lodge. We found many of the natives dressed in a thin French gauze, which they called *byqui;* this being a light airy dress, and well calculated to display the shape of their persons, is much esteemed by the ladies. The manners of these females, however, did not correspond with their dress, for they were rude and troublesome in the highest degree; they surrounded me in numbers, begging for amber, beads, etc., and were so vehement in their solicitations, that I found it impossible to resist them. They tore my cloak, cut the buttons from my boy's clothes, and were proceeding to other outrages, when I mounted my horse and rode off, followed for half a mile by a body of these harpies.

In the evening we reached Soobrudooka, and as my company was numerous (being fourteen), I purchased a sheep, and abundance of corn for supper; after which we lay down by the bundles, and passed an uncomfortable night in a heavy dew.

Dec. 20*th.*—We departed from Soobrudooka, and at two o'clock reached a large village situated on the banks of the Falémé river, which is here rapid and rocky. The natives were employed in fishing in various ways. The large fish were taken in long baskets made of split cane, and placed in a strong current, which was created by walls of stone built across the stream, certain open places being left, through which the water rushed with great force. Some of these baskets were more than twenty feet long, and when once the fish had entered one of them, the force of the stream prevented it from returning.   The small fish were taken in great numbers in hand-nets, which the natives weave of cotton, and use with great dexterity.   The fish last mentioned are about the size of sprats, and are prepared for sale in different ways; the most common is by pounding them entire as they come from the stream in a wooden mortar, and exposing them to dry in the sun, in large lumps like sugar loaves.   It may be supposed that the smell is not very agreeable; but in the Moorish countries to the north of the Senegal, where fish is scarcely known, this preparation is esteemed as a luxury, and sold to considerable advantage.   The manner of using it by the natives is, by dissolving a piece of this black loaf in boiling water, and mixing it with their *kouskous*.

I thought it very singular, at this season of the year, to find the banks of the Falemé everywhere covered with large and beautiful fields of corn, but on examination I found it was not the same species of grain as is commonly cultivated on the Gambia; it is called by the natives *Manio*, and grows in the dry season; is very prolific, and is reaped in the month of January.   It is the same which, from the depending position of the ear, is called by botanical writers *holcus cernuus*.

On returning to the village, after an excursion to the river side to inspect the fishery, an old Moorish shereef came to bestow his blessing upon me, and beg some paper to write saphies upon.   This man had seen Major Houghton in the kingdom of Kaarta, and told me that he died in the country of the Moors.   I gave him a few sheets of paper, and he levied a similar tribute from the blacksmith; for it is customary for young Mussulmans to make presents to the old ones in order to obtain their blessing, which is pronounced in Arabic, and received with great humility.

About three in the afternoon we continued our course along the bank of the river, to the northward, till eight o'clock, when we reached Nayemow; here the hospitable master of the town received us kindly, and presented us with a bullock. In return, I gave him some amber and beads.

Dec. 21st.—In the morning, having agreed for a canoe to carry over my bundles, I crossed the river, which came up to my knees as I sat on my horse; but the water is so clear that from the high bank the bottom is visible all the way over.

About noon we entered Fatteconda, the capital of Bondou; and in a little time received an invitation to the house of a respectable Slatee; for, as there are no public-houses in Africa, it is customary for strangers to stand at the Bentang, or some other place of public resort, till they are invited to a lodging by some of the inhabitants. We accepted the offer, and in an hour afterwards a person came and told me that he was sent on purpose to conduct me to the king, who was very desirous of seeing me immediately, if I was not too much fatigued.

I took my interpreter with me, and followed the messenger till we got quite out of the town, and crossed some cornfields: when, suspecting some trick, I stopped, and asked the guide whither he was going. Upon which he pointed to a man sitting under a tree at some little distance, and told me that the king frequently gave audience in that retired manner, in order to avoid a crowd of people; and that nobody but myself and my interpreter must approach him. When I advanced, the king desired me to come and sit by him upon the mat; and after hearing my story, on which he made no observation, he asked if I wished to purchase any slaves, or gold: being answered in the negative, he seemed rather surprised, but desired me to come to him in the evening, and he would give me some provisions.

This monarch was called Almami, a Moorish name, though I was told that he was not a Mahomedan, but a Kafir, or Pagan. I had heard that he had acted towards Major Houghton with great unkindness, and caused him to be plundered. His behaviour, therefore, towards myself at this interview, though much more civil than I expected, was far from freeing me from uneasiness. I still appre-

hended some double dealing; and as I was now entirely
in his power, I thought it best to smooth the way by a
present; accordingly I took with me in the evening one
canister of gunpowder, some amber, tobacco, and my
umbrella; and, as I considered that my bundles would
inevitably be searched, I concealed some few articles in
the roof of the hut where I lodged, and I put on my new
blue coat, in order to preserve it.

All the houses belonging to the king and his family are
surrounded by a lofty mud wall, which converts the whole
into a kind of citadel. The interior is subdivided into different courts. At the first place of entrance I observed a
man standing with a musket on his shoulder; and I found
the way to the presence very intricate, leading through many
passages, with sentinels placed at the different doors. When
we came to the entrance of the court in which the king resides, both my guide and interpreter, according to custom,
took off their sandals; and the former pronounced the
king's name aloud, repeating it till he was answered from
within. We found the monarch sitting upon a mat, and
two attendants with him. I repeated what I had before
told him concerning the object of my journey, and my
reasons for passing through his country. He seemed,
however, but half satisfied. The notion of travelling for
curiosity was quite new to him. He thought it impossible,
he said, that any man in his senses would undertake so
dangerous a journey, merely to look at the country and its
inhabitants; however, when I offered to show him the contents of my portmanteau, and everything belonging to me,
he was convinced; and it was evident that his suspicion
had arisen from a belief that every white man must of
necessity be a trader. When I had delivered my presents,
he seemed well pleased, and was particularly delighted with
the umbrella, which he repeatedly furled and unfurled, to
the great admiration of himself and his two attendants,
who could not for some time comprehend the use of this
wonderful machine. After this I was about to take my
leave, when the king, desiring me to stop awhile, began
a long preamble in favour of the whites, extolling their

immense wealth and good dispositions. He next proceeded to an eulogium on my blue coat, of which the
yellow buttons seemed particularly to catch his fancy ; and
he concluded by entreating me to present him with it;
assuring me, for my consolation under the loss of it, that
he would wear it on all public occasions, and inform every
one who saw it of my great liberality towards him. The
request of an African prince, in his own dominions, particularly when made to a stranger, comes little short of a
command. It is only a way of obtaining by gentle means
what he can, if he pleases, take by force ; and, as it was
against my interest to offend him by a refusal, I very quietly
took off my coat, the only good one in my possession, and
laid it at his feet.

In return for my compliance, he presented me with great
plenty of provisions, and desired to see me again in the
morning. I accordingly attended, and found him sitting
upon his bed. He told me he was sick, and wished to
have a little blood taken from him ; but I had no sooner
tied up his arm, and displayed the lancet, than his courage
failed, and he begged me to postpone the operation till the
afternoon, as he felt himself, he said, much better than he
had been, and thanked me kindly for my readiness to serve
him. He then observed that his women were very desirous
to see me, and requested that I would favour them with a
visit. An attendant was ordered to conduct me, and I had
no sooner entered the court appropriated to the ladies,
than the whole seraglio surrounded me, some begging for
physic, some for amber, and all of them desirous of trying
that great African specific, *blood-letting*. They were ten or
twelve in number, most of them young and handsome, and
wearing on their heads ornaments of gold, and beads of
amber.

They rallied me with a good deal of gaiety on different
subjects, particularly upon the whiteness of my skin, and
the prominency of my nose. They insisted that both were
artificial. The first, they said, was produced when I was an
infant, by dipping me in milk ; and they insisted that my
nose had been pinched every day till it had acquired its

present unsightly and unnatural conformation. On my part, without disputing my own deformity, I paid them many compliments on African beauty. I praised the glossy jet of their skins, and the lovely depression of their noses; but they said that flattery, or (as they emphatically termed it) *honey mouth*, was not esteemed in Bondou. In return, however, for my company or my compliments (to which, by the way, they seemed not so insensible as they affected to be), they presented me with a jar of honey and some fish, which were sent to my lodging, and I was desired to come again to the king a little before sunset.

I carried with me some beads and writing paper, it being usual to present some small offering on taking leave, in return for which the king gave me five drachms of gold, observing that it was but a trifle, and given out of pure friendship, but would be of use to me in travelling for the purchase of provision. He seconded this act of kindness by one still greater, politely telling me, that though it was customary to examine the baggage of every traveller passing through his country, yet, in the present instance, he would dispense with that ceremony; adding, I was at liberty to depart when I pleased.

Accordingly, on the morning of the 23rd, we left Fatteconda, and about eleven o'clock came to a small village, where we determined to stop for the rest of the day.

In the afternoon my fellow-travellers informed me, that as this was the boundary between Bondou and Kajaaga, and dangerous for travellers, it would be necessary to continue our journey by night, until we should reach a more hospitable part of the country. I agreed to the proposal, and hired two people for guides through the woods; and as soon as the people of the village were gone to sleep (the moon shining bright), we set out. The stillness of the air, the howling of the wild beasts, and the deep solitude of the forest, made the scene solemn and impressive. Not a word was uttered by any of us but in a whisper; all were attentive and every one anxious to show his sagacity, by pointing out to me the wolves and hyænas as they glided like shadows from one thicket to another. Towards morning we arrived at a village called Kimmoo, where our guides awakened one of their acquaintances, and we stopped to give the asses some corn, and roast a few ground-nuts for ourselves. At daylight we resumed our journey, and in the afternoon arrived at Joag in the kingdom of Kajaaga.

Being now in a country and among a people differing in many respects from those that have as yet fallen under our observation, I shall, before I proceed further, give some account of Bondou (the territory we have left), and its inhabitants, the Foulahs, the description of whom I purposely reserved for this part of my work.

Bondou is bounded on the east by Bambouk; on the south-east and south by Tenda, and the Simbani Wilderness; on the south-west by Woolli; on the west by Foota Torra; and on the north by Kajaaga.

The country, like that of Woolli, is very generally covered with woods, but the land is more elevated, and towards the Falemé river, rises into considerable hills. In native fertility the soil is not surpassed, I believe, by any part of Africa.

From the central situation of Bondou, between the Gambia and Senegal rivers, it is become a place of great resort; both for the Slatees, who generally pass through it, in going from the coast to the interior countries; and for occasional traders who frequently come hither from the inland countries, to purchase salt.

These different branches of commerce are conducted principally by Mandingoes and Serawoollies, who have settled in the country. These merchants likewise carry on a considerable trade with Gedumah, and other Moorish countries, bartering corn and blue cotton cloths for salt, which they again barter in Dentilla and other districts, for iron, shea butter, and small quantities of gold-dust. They likewise sell a variety of sweet-smelling gums packed up in small bags, containing each about a pound. These gums, being thrown on hot embers, produce a very pleasant odour, and are used by the Mandingoes for perfuming their huts and clothes.

The customs, or duties on travellers, are very heavy : in almost every town an ass-load pays a bar of European m rchandise ; and at Fatteconda, the residence of the king, one Indian baft, or a musket, and six bottles of gun-powder, are exacted as a common tribute. By means of these duties, the king of Bondou is well supplied with arms and ammunition ; a circumstance which makes him formidable to the neighbouring states.

The inhabitants differ in their complexions and national manners from the Mandingoes and Serawoollies, with whom they are frequently at war. Some years ago the king of Bondou crossed the Falemé river with a numerous army, and after a short and bloody campaign totally defeated the forces of Samboo, king of Bambouk, who was obliged to sue for peace, and surrender to him all the towns along the eastern bank of the Falemé.

The Foulahs in general (as has been observed in a former chapter) are of a tawny complexion, with small features, and soft silky hair ; next to the Mandingoes they are undoubtedly the most considerable of all the nations in this part of Africa. Their original country is said to be Fooladoo, which signifies the country of the Foulahs ; but they possess at present many other kingdoms at a great distance from each other ; their complexion, however, is not exactly the same in the different districts ; in Bondou and the other kingdoms which are situated in the vicinity of the Moorish territories, they are of a more yellow complexion than in the southern states.

The Foulahs of Bondou are naturally of a mild and gentle disposition, but the uncharitable maxims of the Koran have made them less hospitable to strangers, and more reserved in their behaviour than the Mandingoes. They evidently consider all the Negro natives as their inferiors ; and when talking of different nations, always rank themselves among the white people.

Their government differs from that of the Mandingoes chiefly in this, that they are more immediately under the influence of the Mahomedan laws : for all the chief men (the king excepted) and a large majority of the inhabitants

of Bondou, are Mussulmans, and the authority and laws of
the Prophet are everywhere looked upon as sacred and
decisive. In the exercise of their faith, however, they
are not very intolerant towards such of their countrymen as still retain their ancient superstitions. Religious persecution is not known among them, nor is it
necessary; for the system of Mahomet is made to extend
itself by means abundantly more efficacious. By establish-
ing small schools in the different towns, where many of the
Pagan as well as Mahomedan children are taught to read
the Koran, and instructed in the tenets of the Prophet, the
Mahomedan priests fix a bias on the minds, and form the
character of their young disciples, which no accidents of
life can ever afterwards remove or alter. Many of these
little schools I visited in my progress through the country,
and observed with pleasure the great docility and submis-
sive deportment of the children, and heartily wished they
had had better instructors and a purer religion.

With the Mahomedan faith is also introduced the Arabic
language, with which most of the Foulahs have a slight
acquaintance. The native tongue abounds very much in
liquids, but there is something unpleasant in the manner of
pronouncing it. A stranger on hearing the common conversation of two Foulahs, would imagine that they were
scolding each other.

The industry of the Foulahs, in the occupations of pasturage and agriculture, is everywhere remarkable. Even
on the banks of the Gambia, the greater part of the corn
is raised by them; and their herds and flocks are more
numerous and in better condition than those of the Mandingoes; but in Bondou they are opulent in a high degree,
and enjoy all the necessaries of life in the greatest profusion. They display great skill in the management of
their cattle, making them extremely gentle by kindness and
familiarity. On the approach of night, they are collected
from the woods, and secured in folds, called korrees, which
are constructed in the neighbourhood of the different
villages. In the middle of each korree is erected a small
hut, wherein one or two of the herdsmen keep watch during

the night, to prevent the cattle from being stolen, and to keep up the fires which are kindled round the korree to frighten away the wild beasts.

The cattle are milked in the mornings and evenings: the milk is excellent; but the quantity obtained from any one cow is by no means so great as in Europe. The Foulahs use the milk chiefly as an article of diet, and that not until it is quite sour. The cream which it affords is very thick, and is converted into butter by stirring it violently in a large calabash. This butter, when melted over a gentle fire, and freed from impurities, is preserved in small earthen pots, and forms a part in most of their dishes; it serves likewise to anoint their heads, and is bestowed very liberally on their faces and arms.

But although milk is plentiful, it is somewhat remarkable that the Foulahs, and indeed all the inhabitants of this part of Africa, are totally unacquainted with the art of making cheese. A firm attachment to the customs of their ancestors, makes them view with an eye of prejudice everything that looks like innovation. The heat of the climate and the great scarcity of salt, are held forth as unanswerable objections; and the whole process appears to them too long and troublesome, to be attended with any solid advantage.

Besides the cattle, which constitute the chief wealth of the Foulahs, they possess some excellent horses, the breed of which seems to be a mixture of the Arabian with the original African.

CHAPTER V

Account of Kajaaga—Serawoollies—Their manners and language—
Account of Joag—The Author is ill-treated, and robbed of half
of his effects, by order of Batcheri, the king—Charity of a female
slave—The Author is visited by Demba Sego, nephew of the king
of Kasson, who offers to conduct him in safety to that kingdom—
Offer accepted—The Author and his protector, with a numerous
retinue, set out and reach Samee, on the banks of the Senegal—
Proceed to Kayee, and, crossing the Senegal, arrive in the kingdom
of Kasson.

THE kingdom of Kajaaga, in which I was now arrived, is
called by the French Gallam ; but the name that I have
adopted is universally used by the natives. This country
is bounded on the south-east and south by Bambouk ; on
the west by Bondou and Foota Torra ; and on the north
by the river Senegal.

The air and climate are, I believe, more pure and
salubrious than at any of the settlements towards the
coast ; the face of the country is everywhere interspersed
with a pleasing variety of hills and valleys ; and the
windings of the Senegal river, which descends from the
rocky hills of the interior, make the scenery on its banks
very picturesque and beautiful.

The inhabitants are called Serawoollies, or (as the French
write it) *Seracolets*. Their complexion is a jet black ; they
are not to be distinguished in this respect from the
Jaloffs.

The government is monarchical ; and the regal authority,
from what I experienced of it, seems to be sufficiently
formidable. The people themselves, however, complain
of no oppression, and seemed all very anxious to support
the king, in a contest he was going to enter into with the
sovereign of Kasson. The Serawoollies are habitually a
trading people ; they formerly carried on a great commerce
with the French in gold and slaves, and still maintain some

*c 205

traffic in slaves with the British factories on the Gambia.
They are reckoned tolerably fair and just in their dealings,
but are indefatigable in their exertions to acquire wealth,
and they derive considerable profits by the sale of salt
and cotton cloth in distant countries.   When a Serawoolli
merchant returns home from a trading expedition, the
neighbours immediately assemble to congratulate him
upon his arrival.   On these occasions the traveller displays his wealth and liberality, by making a few presents
to his friends ; but if he has been unsuccessful, his levee
is soon over, and every one looks upon him as a man of
no understanding, who could perform a long journey, and
(as they express it) *bring back nothing but the hair upon
his head.*

Their language abounds much in gutturals, and is not
so harmonious as that spoken by the Foulahs ; it is,
however, well worth acquiring by those who travel through
this part of the African continent ; it being very generally
understood in the kingdoms of Kasson, Kaarta, Ludamar,
and the northern parts of Bambarra.   In all these countries
the Serawoollies are the chief traders.

We arrived at Joag, the frontier town of this kingdom,
on the 24th of December, and took up our residence at
the house of the chief man, who is here no longer known
by the title of *Alkaid.* but is called the *Dooty.*   He was a
rigid Mahomedan, but distinguished for his hospitality.
This town may be supposed, on a gross computation, to
contain two thousand inhabitants.   It is surrounded by
a high wall, in which are a number of port holes, for
musketry to fire through, in case of an attack.   Every
man's possession is likewise surrounded by a wall—the
whole forming so many distinct citadels ; and amongst a
people unacquainted with the use of artillery, these walls
answer all the purposes of stronger fortifications.   To the
westward of the town is a small river on the banks of
which the natives raise great plenty of tobacco and
onions.

The same evening Madiboo the Bushreen, who had
accompanied me from Pisania, went to pay a visit to his

father and mother, who dwelt at a neighbouring town called Dramanet. He was joined by my other attendant the blacksmith ; and as soon as it was dark, I was invited to see the sports of the inhabitants, it being their custom, on the arrival of strangers, to welcome them by diversions of different kinds. I found a great crowd surrounding a party who were dancing by the light of some large fires, to the music of four drums, which were beat with great exactness and uniformity. The dances, however, consisted more in wanton gestures than in muscular exertion or graceful attitudes. The ladies vied with each other in displaying the most voluptuous movements imaginable.

Dec. 25th.—About two o'clock in the morning a number of horsemen came into the town, and having awakened my landlord, talked to him for some time in the Serawoolli tongue, after which they dismounted and came to the Bentang, on which I had made my bed. One of them, thinking that I was asleep, attempted to steal the musket that lay by me on the mat ; but finding that he could not effect his purpose undiscovered, he desisted, and the strangers sat down by me till daylight.

I could now easily perceive, by the countenance of my interpreter Johnson, that something very unpleasant was in agitation. I was likewise surprised to see Madiboo and the blacksmith so soon returned. On inquiring the reason, Madiboo informed me, that as they were dancing at Dramanet, ten horsemen belonging to Batcheri, king of the country, with his second son at their head, had arrived there, inquiring if the white man had passed, and on being told that I was at Joag, they rode off without stopping. Madiboo added, that on hearing this, he and the blacksmith hastened back to give me notice of their coming. Whilst I was listening to this narrative, the ten horsemen mentioned by Madiboo arrived ; and coming to the Bentang, dismounted and seated themselves with those who had come before, the whole being about twenty in number, forming a circle round me, and each man holding his musket in his hand. I took this opportunity to observe to my landlord, that as I did not understand the Serawoolli tongue, I hoped, whatever the men had to say, they would speak in Mandingo. To this they agreed ; and a short man, loaded with a remarkable number of saphies, opened the business in a very long harangue, informing me that I had entered the king's town without having first paid the duties, or given any present to the king, and that, according to the laws of the country, my people, cattle, and baggage were forfeited. He added, that they had received orders from the king to conduct me to Maana,[1] the place of his residence, and if I refused to come with them, their orders were to bring me by force ; upon his saying which, all of them rose up and asked me if I was ready. It would have been equally vain and imprudent in me to have resisted or irritated such a body of men. I therefore affected to comply with their commands, and begged them only to stop a little until I had given my horse a feed of corn, and settled matters with my landlord. The poor blacksmith, who was a native of Kasson, mistook this feigned compliance for a real intention, and taking me away from the company, told me that he had always behaved towards me as if I had been his father and master, and he hoped I would not entirely ruin him by going to Maana ; adding, that as there was every reason to believe a war would soon take place between Kasson and Kajaaga, he should not only lose his little property, the savings of four years' industry, but should certainly be detained and sold as a slave, unless his friends had an opportunity of paying two slaves for his redemption. I saw this reasoning in its full force, and determined to do my utmost to preserve the blacksmith from so dreadful a fate. I therefore told the king's son that I was ready to go with him, upon condition that the blacksmith, who was an inhabitant of a distant kingdom, and entirely unconnected with me, should be allowed to stay at Joag till my return. To this they all objected, and insisted that, as we had all acted contrary to the laws, we were all equally answerable for our conduct.

I now took my landlord aside, and giving him a small

[1] Maana is within a short distance of the ruins of Fort St. Joseph, on the Senegal river, formerly a French factory.

present of gunpowder, asked his advice in so critical a situation. He was decidedly of opinion that I ought not to go to the king. He was fully convinced, he said, that if the king should discover anything valuable in my possession, he would not be over scrupulous about the means of obtaining it. This made me the more solicitous to conciliate matters with the king's people ; and I began by observing, that what I had done did not proceed from any want of respect towards the king, nor from any wish to violate his laws, but wholly from my own inexperience and ignorance, being a stranger, totally unacquainted with the laws and customs of their country. I had indeed entered the king's frontier without knowing that I was to pay the duties beforehand, but I was ready to pay them now, which I thought was all they could reasonably demand. I then tendered them, as a present to the king, the five drachms of gold which the king of Bondou had given me; this they accepted, but insisted on examining my baggage, which I opposed in vain. The bundles were opened, but the men were much disappointed in not finding in them so much gold and amber as they expected. They made up the deficiency, however, by taking whatever things they fancied ; and after wrangling and debating with me till sunset, they departed, having first robbed me of half my goods. These proceedings dispirited my people, and our fortitude was not strengthened by a very indifferent supper after a long fast. Madiboo begged me to turn back ; Johnson laughed at the thoughts of proceeding without money, and the blacksmith was afraid to be seen, or even to speak, lest any one should discover him to be a native of Kasson. In this disposition we passed the night by the side of a dim fire, and our situation the next day was very perplexing. It was impossible to procure provisions without money, and I knew that if I produced any beads or amber, the king would immediately hear of it, and I should probably lose the few effects I had concealed. We therefore resolved to combat hunger for the day, and wait some favourable opportunity of purchasing or begging provisions.

Towards evening, as I was sitting upon the Bentang, chewing straws, an old female slave passing by with a basket upon her head, asked me *if I had got my dinner.* As I thought she only laughed at me, I gave her no answer ; but my boy, who was sitting close by, answered for me, and told her that the king's people had robbed me of all my money. On hearing this, the good old woman, with a look of unaffected benevolence, immediately took the basket from her head, and showing me that it contained ground-nuts, asked me if I could eat them ; being answered in the affirmative, she presented me with a few handfuls, and walked away before I had time to thank her for this seasonable supply. This trifling circumstance gave me peculiar satisfaction. I reflected with pleasure on the conduct of this poor untutored slave, who, without examining into my character or circumstances. listened implicitly to the dictates of her own heart. Experience had taught her that hunger was painful, and her own distresses made her commiserate those of others.

The old woman had scarcely left me, when I received information that a nephew of Demba Sego Jalla, the Mandingo king of Kasson, was coming to pay me a visit. He had been sent on an embassy to Batcheri, king of Kajaaga, to endeavour to settle the disputes which had arisen between his uncle and the latter ; but after debating the matter four days without success, he was now on his return ; and hearing that a white man was at Joag, on his way to Kasson, curiosity brought him to see me. I represented to him my situation and distresses, when he frankly offered me his protection, and said he would be my guide to Kasson (provided I would set out the next morning), and be answerable for my safety. I readily and gratefully accepted his offer, and was ready, with my attendants, by daylight on the morning of the 27th of December.

My protector, whose name was Demba Sego, probably after his uncle, had a numerous retinue. Our company at leaving Joag consisted of thirty persons and six loaded asses ; and we rode on cheerfully enough for some hours, without any remarkable occurrence, until we came to a species of tree, for which my interpreter Johnson had made frequent inquiry. On finding it, he desired us to stop; and producing a white chicken, which he had purchased at Joag for the purpose, he tied it by the leg to one of the branches, and then told us we might now safely proceed, for that our journey would be prosperous. This circumstance is mentioned merely to illustrate the disposition of the Negroes, and to show the power of superstition over their minds; for although this man had resided seven years in England, it was evident that he still retained the prejudices and notions he had imbibed in his youth. He meant this ceremony, he told me, as an offering or sacrifice to the spirits of the wood, who were, he said, a powerful race of beings of a white colour, with long flowing hair. I laughed at his folly, but could not condemn the piety of his motives.

At noon we had reached Gungadi, a large town, where we stopped about an hour, until some of the asses that had fallen behind came up. Here I observed a number of date trees, and a mosque built of clay, with six turrets, on the pinnacles of which were placed six ostrich eggs. A little before sunset we arrived at the town of Samee, on the banks of the Senegal, which is here a beautiful, but shallow river, moving slowly over a bed of sand and gravel. The banks are high and covered with verdure; the country is open and cultivated, and the rocky hills of Felow and Bambouk add much to the beauty of the landscape.

Dec. 28*th.*—We departed from Samee, and arrived in the afternoon at Kayee, a large village, part of which is situated on the north, and part on the south side of the river. A little above this place is a considerable cataract, where the river flows over a ledge of whinstone rock, with great force; below this, the river is remarkably black and deep; and here it was proposed to make our cattle swim over. After hallowing and firing some muskets, the people on the Kasson side observed us, and brought over a canoe to carry our baggage. I did not, however, think it possible to get the cattle down the bank, which is here more than forty feet above the water; but the Negroes seized the horses, and launched them, one at a time, down a sort of trench or gully that was almost perpendicular, and seemed to have been worn smooth by this sort of use. After the terrified cattle had been plunged in this manner to the water's edge, every man got down as well as he could. The ferryman then taking hold of the most steady of the horses by a rope, led him into the water, and paddled the canoe a little from the brink; upon which a general attack commenced upon the other horses, who finding themselves pelted and kicked on all sides, unanimously plunged into the river, and followed their companion. A few boys swam in after them, and by laving water upon them when they attempted to return, urged them onwards, and we had the satisfaction, in about fifteen minutes, to see them all safe on the other side. It was a matter of greater difficulty to manage the asses; their natural stubbornness of disposition made them endure a great deal of pelting and shoving before they would venture into the water; and when they had reached the middle of the stream four of them turned back, in spite of every exertion to get them forwards. Two hours were spent in getting the whole of them over; an hour more was employed in transporting the baggage; and it was near sunset before the canoe returned, when Demba Sego and myself embarked in this dangerous passage-boat, which the least motion was like to overset. The king's nephew thought this a proper time to have a peep into a tin box of mine that stood in the forepart of the canoe; and in stretching out his hand for it, he unfortunately destroyed the equilibrium, and overset the canoe. Luckily we were not far advanced, and got back to the shore without much difficulty; from whence, after wringing the water from our clothes, we took a fresh departure, and were soon afterwards safely landed in Kasson.

CHAPTER VI

Arrival at Teesee—Interview with Tiggity Sego, the king's brother
—The Author's detention at Teesee—Some account of that place
and its inhabitants—Incidents which occurred there—Rapacious
conduct of Tiggity Sego toward the Author on his departure—
Sets out for Kooniakary, the capital of the kingdom—Incidents on
the road, and arrival at Kooniakary.

WE no sooner found ourselves safe in Kasson, than Demba
Sego told me that we were now in his uncle's dominions,
and he hoped I would consider, being now out of danger,
the obligation I owed to him, and make him a suitable
return for the trouble he had taken on my account, by
a handsome present. This, as he knew how much had
been pilfered from me at Joag, was rather an unexpected
proposition; and I began to fear that I had not much
improved my condition by crossing the water; but as it
would have been folly to complain, I made no observation upon his conduct, and gave him seven bars of amber,
and some tobacco, with which he seemed to be content.

After a long day's journey, in the course of which I
observed a number of large loose nodules of white granite,
we arrived at Teesee on the evening of December 29, and
were accommodated in Demba Sego's hut. The next
morning he introduced me to his father, Tiggity Sego,
brother to the king of Kasson, chief of Teesee. The
old man viewed me with great earnestness, having never,
he said, beheld but one white man before, whom by his
description I immediately knew to be Major Houghton.
I related to him, in answer to his inquiries, the motives
that induced me to explore the country. But he seemed
to doubt the truth of what I asserted, thinking, I believe,
that I secretly meditated some project which I was afraid
to avow. He told me it would be necessary I should go to
Kooniakary, the residence of the king, to pay my respects

to that prince, but desired me to come to him again before I left Teesee.

In the afternoon one of his slaves eloped; and a general alarm being given, every person that had a horse rode into the woods in the hopes of apprehending him; and Demba Sego begged the use of my horse for the same purpose. I readily consented; and in about an hour they all returned with the slave, who was severely flogged, and afterwards put in irons. On the day following (Dec. 31), Demba Sego was ordered to go, with twenty horsemen, to a town in Gedumah, to adjust some dispute with the Moors, a party of whom were supposed to have stolen three horses from Teesee. Demba begged, a second time, the use of my horse; adding, that the sight of my bridle and saddle would give him consequence among the Moors. This request also I readily granted, and he promised to return at the end of three days. During his absence I amused myself with walking about the town, and conversing with the natives, who attended me everywhere with great kindness and curiosity, and supplied me with milk, eggs, and what other provisions I wanted, on very easy terms.

Teesee is a large unwalled town, having no security against the attack of an enemy, except a sort of citadel, in which Tiggity and his family constantly reside. This town, according to the report of the natives, was formerly inhabited only by a few Foulah shepherds, who lived in considerable affluence by means of the excellent meadows in the neighbourhood, in which they reared great herds of cattle. But their prosperity attracting the envy of some Mandingoes, the latter drove out the shepherds, and took possession of their lands.

The present inhabitants, though they possess both cattle and corn in abundance, are not over nice in articles of diet; rats, moles squirrels, snakes, locusts, etc., are eaten without scruple by the highest and lowest. My people were one evening invited to a feast given by some of the townsmen, where, after making a hearty meal of what they thought fish and kouskous, one of them found a piece of hard skin in the dish, and brought it along with him, to show me what sort of fish they had been eating. On examining the skin, I found they had been feasting on a large snake. Another custom still more extraordinary is, that no woman is allowed to *eat an egg*. This prohibition, whether arising from ancient superstition, or from the craftiness of some old Bushreen who loved eggs himself, is rigidly adhered to, and nothing will more affront a woman of Teesee than to offer her an egg. The custom is the more singular, as the men eat eggs without scruple in the presence of their wives, and I never observed the same prohibition in any other of the Mandingo countries.

The third day after his son's departure, Tiggity Sego held a palaver on a very extraordinary occasion, which I attended; and the debates on both sides of the question displayed much ingenuity. The case was this: A young man, a Kafir, of considerable affluence, who had recently married a young and handsome wife, applied to a very devout Bushreen, or Mussulman priest of his acquaintance, to procure him saphies for his protection during the approaching war. The Bushreen complied with the request; and in order, as he pretended, to render the saphies more efficacious, enjoined the young man to avoid any nuptial intercourse with his bride for the space of six weeks. Severe as the injunction was, the Kafir strictly obeyed; and without telling his wife the real cause, absented himself from her company. In the meantime it began to be whispered at Teesee, that the Bushreen, who always performed his evening devotions at the door of the Kafir's hut, was more intimate with the young wife than he ought to be. At first, the good husband was unwilling to suspect the honour of his sanctified friend, and one whole month elapsed before any jealousy rose in his mind; but hearing the charge repeated, he at last interrogated his wife on the subject, who frankly confessed that the Bushreen had seduced her. Hereupon the Kafir put her into confinement, and called a palaver upon the Bushreen's conduct. The fact was clearly proved against him; and he was sentenced to be sold into slavery, or to find two slaves for his redemption, according to the pleasure of the complainant. The injured husband, however, was unwilling to proceed against his friend to such extremity, and desired rather to have him publicly flogged before Tiggity Sego's gate. This was agreed to, and the sentence was immediately executed. The culprit was tied by the hands to a strong stake; and a long black rod being brought forth, the executioner, after flourishing it round his head for some time, applied it with such force and dexterity to the Bushreen's back, as to make him roar until the woods resounded with his screams. The surrounding multitude, by their hooting and laughing, manifested how much they enjoyed the punishment of this old gallant; and it is worthy of remark, that the number of stripes was precisely the same as are enjoined by the Mosaic law, *forty, save one.*

As there appeared great probability that Teesee, from its being a frontier town, would be much exposed, during the war, to the predatory excursions of the Moors of Gadumah, Tiggity Sego had, before my arrival, sent round to the neighbouring villages, to beg or to purchase as much provisions as would afford subsistence to the inhabitants for one whole year, independently of the crop on the ground, which the Moors might destroy. This project was well received by the country people, and they fixed a day on which to bring all the provisions they could spare to Teesee; and as my horse was not yet returned, I went in the afternoon of January 4th, 1796, to meet the escort with the provisions.

It was composed of about four hundred men, marching in good order, with corn and ground-nuts in large calabashes upon their heads. They were preceded by a strong guard of bowmen, and followed by eight musicians or singing men. As soon as they approached the town, the latter began a song, every verse of which was answered by the company, and succeeded by a few strokes on the large drums. In this manner they proceeded, amidst the acclamations of the populace, till they reached the house of Tiggity Sego, where the loads were deposited; and in the evening they all assembled under the Bentang tree, and spent the night in dancing and merriment. Many of these strangers remained at Teesee for three days, during which time I was constantly attended by as many of them as could conveniently see me; one party giving way to another, as soon as curiosity was gratified.

On the 5th of January an embassy of ten people belonging to Almami Abdulkader, king of Foota Torra, a country to the west of Bondou, arrived at Teesee; and desiring Tiggity Sego to call an assembly of the inhabitants, announced publicly their king's determination to this effect: —"That unless all the people of Kasson would embrace the Mahomedan religion, and evince their conversion by saying eleven public prayers, he (the king of Foota Torra) could not possibly stand neuter in the present contest, but would certainly join his arms to those of Kajaaga." A message of this nature, from so powerful a prince, could not fail to create great alarm; and the inhabitants of Teesee, after a long consultation, agreed to conform to his good pleasure, humiliating as it was to them. Accordingly, one and all publicly offered up eleven prayers, which were considered a sufficient testimony of their having renounced paganism, and embraced the doctrines of the Prophet.

It was the 8th of January before Demba Sego returned with my horse; and being quite wearied out with the delay, I went immediately to inform his father that I should set out for Kooniakary early the next day. The old man made many frivolous objections; and at length gave me to understand, that I must not think of departing without first paying him the same duties he was entitled to receive from all travellers; besides which he expected, he said, some acknowledgment for his kindness towards me. Accordingly, on the morning of the 9th, my friend Demba, with a number of people, came to me, and said that they were sent by Tiggity Sego for my present, and wished to see what goods I had appropriated for that purpose. I knew that resistance was hopeless, and complaint unavailing; and being in some measure prepared by the intimation I had received the night before, I quietly offered him seven bars of amber and five of tobacco. After surveying these articles for some time very coolly, Demba laid them down,

and told me this was not a present for a man of Tiggity
Sego's consequence, who had it in his own power to take
whatever he pleased from me.   He added, that if I did not
consent to make him a larger offering, he would carry all
my baggage to his father, and let him choose for himself.
I had not time for reply, for Demba and his attendants
immediately began to open my bundles, and spread the
different articles upon the floor, where they underwent
a more strict examination than they had done at Joag.
Everything that pleased them, they took without scruple;
and amongst other things, Demba seized the tin box which
had so much attracted his attention in crossing the river.
Upon collecting the scattered remains of my little fortune
after these people had left me, I found that, as at Joag, I
had been plundered of half; so here, without even the
shadow of accusation, I was deprived of half the remainder.
The blacksmith himself, though a native of Kasson, had
also been compelled to open his bundles, and take an
oath that the different articles they contained were his own
exclusive property.   There was, however, no remedy; and
having been under some obligation to Demba Sego for his
attention towards me in the journey from Joag, I did not
reproach him for his rapacity, but determined to quit
Teesee at all events the next morning.   In the meanwhile,
in order to raise the drooping spirits of my attendants, I
purchased a fat sheep, and had it dressed for our dinner.

Early in the morning of January 10th, therefore, I left
Teesee, and about mid-day ascended a ridge, from whence
we had a distant view of the hills round Kooniakary.   In
the evening we reached a small village, where we slept,
and departing from thence the next morning, crossed in
a few hours a narrow but deep stream called Krieko, a
branch of the Senegal.   About two miles farther to the
eastward, we passed a large town called Madina; and at
two o'clock came in sight of Jumbo, the blacksmith's
native town, from whence he had been absent more than
four years.   Soon after this his brother, who had by some
means been apprised of his coming, came out to meet
him, accompanied by a singing man; he brought a horse

for the blacksmith, that he might enter his native town in a dignified manner; and he desired each of us to put a good charge of powder into our guns. The singing man now led the way, followed by the two brothers; and we were presently joined by a number of people from the town, all of whom demonstrated great joy at seeing their old acquaintance, the blacksmith, by the most extravagant jumping and singing. On entering the town, the singing man began an extempore song in praise of the blacksmith, extolling his courage in having overcome so many difficulties; and concluding with a strict injunction to his friends to dress him plenty of victuals.

When we arrived at the blacksmith's place of residence, we dismounted and fired our muskets. The meeting between him and his relations was very tender; for these rude children of nature, free from restraint, display their emotions in the strongest and most expressive manner. Amidst these transports, the blacksmith's aged mother was led forth, leaning upon a staff. Every one made way for her; and she stretched out her hand to bid her son welcome. Being totally blind, she stroked his hands, arms, and face with great care, and seemed highly delighted that her latter days were blessed by his return, and that her ears once more heard the music of his voice. From this interview I was fully convinced, that whatever difference there is between the Negro and European in the conformation of the nose and the colour of the skin, there is none in the genuine sympathies and characteristic feelings of our common nature.

During the tumult of these congratulations, I had seated myself apart, by the side of one of the huts, being unwilling to interrupt the flow of filial and parental tenderness; and the attention of the company was so entirely taken up with the blacksmith, that I believe none of his friends had observed me. When all the people present had seated themselves, the blacksmith was desired by his father to give them some account of his adventures; and silence being commanded, he began; and after repeatedly thanking God for the success that had attended him, related every material occurrence that had happened to him from his leaving Kasson to his arrival at the Gambia, his employment and success in those parts, and the dangers he had escaped in returning to his native country. In the latter part of his narration, he had frequently occasion to mention me; and after many strong expressions concerning my kindness to him, he pointed to the place where I sat, and exclaimed, *Affiille ibi siring*, "see him sitting there." In a moment all eyes were turned upon me; I appeared like a being dropped from the clouds; every one was surprised that they had not observed me before; and a few women and children expressed great uneasiness at being so near a man of such an uncommon appearance. By degrees, however, their apprehensions subsided; and when the blacksmith assured them that I was perfectly inoffensive, and would hurt nobody, some of them ventured so far as to examine the texture of my clothes, but many of them were still very suspicious; and when by accident I happened to move myself, or look at the young children, their mothers would scamper off with them with the greatest precipitation. In a few hours, however, they all became reconciled to me.

With these worthy people I spent the remainder of that, and the whole of the ensuing day, in feasting and merriment; and the blacksmith declared he would not quit me during my stay at Kooniakary, for which place we set out early on the morning of the 14th of January, and arrived about the middle of the day at Soolo, a small village three miles to the south of it.

As this place was somewhat out of the direct road, it is necessary to observe that I went thither to visit a Slatee, or Gambia trader, of great note and reputation, named Salim Daucari. He was well known to Dr. Laidley, who had trusted him with effects to the value of five slaves, and had given me an order for the whole of the debt. We luckily found him at home, and he received me with great kindness and attention.

It is remarkable, however, that the king of Kasson was by some means immediately apprised of my motions; for

I had been at Soolo but a few hours, before Sambo Sego, his second son, came thither with a party of horse, to inquire what had prevented me from proceeding to Kooniakary, and waiting immediately upon the king, who, he said, was impatient to see me. Salim Daucari made my apology, and promised to accompany me to Kooniakary the same evening; we accordingly departed from Soolo at sunset, and in about an hour entered Kooniakary. But as the king had gone to sleep, we deferred the interview till next morning, and slept at the hut of Sambo Sego.

My interview with the king, and the incidents which occurred to me in the kingdoms of Kasson and Kaarta, will be the subject of the ensuing chapter.

CHAPTER VII

The Author admitted to an audience of the king of Kasson, whom he finds well disposed towards him—Incidents during the Author's stay at Kooniakary—Departs thence for Kemmoo, the capital of Kaarta—Is received with great kindness by the king of Kaarta, who dissuades him from prosecuting his journey, on account of approaching hostilities with the king of Bambarra—The Author determines, notwithstanding, to proceed; and the usual route being obstructed, takes the path to Ludamar, a Moorish kingdom—Is accommodated by the king with a guide to Jarra, the frontier town of the Moorish territories; and sets out for that place, accompanied by three of the king's sons, and two hundred horsemen.

ABOUT eight o'clock in the morning of January 15, 1796, we went to an audience of the king (Demba Sego Jalla); but the crowd of people to see me was so great, that I could scarcely get admittance. A passage being at length obtained, I made my bow to the monarch, whom we found sitting upon a mat, in a large hut; he appeared to be a man of about sixty years of age; his success in war, and the mildness of his behaviour in time of peace, had much endeared him to all his subjects. He surveyed me with great attention; and when Salim Daucari explained to him the object of my journey, and my reasons for passing through his country, the good old king appeared not only perfectly satisfied, but promised me every assistance in his power. He informed me that he had seen Major Houghton, and presented him with a white horse; but that after crossing the kingdom of Kaarta, he had lost his life among the Moors; in what manner he could not inform me. When this audience was ended, we returned to our lodging, and I made up a small present for the king out of the few effects that were left me; for I had not yet received anything from Salim Daucari. This present, though inconsiderable in itself, was well received by the king, who sent me in return a large white bullock. The sight of this animal quite delighted my attendants; not so much on account of its bulk, as from its being of a white colour, which is considered as a particular mark of favour. But although the king himself was well disposed towards me, and readily granted me permission to pass through his territories, I soon discovered that very great and unexpected obstacles were likely to impede my progress. Besides the war which was on the point of breaking out between Kasson and Kajaaga, I was told that the next kingdom of Kaarta, through which my route lay, was involved in the issue; and was furthermore threatened with hostilities on the part of Bambarra. The king himself informed me of these circumstances, and advised me to stay in the neighbourhood of Kooniakary, till such time as he could procure proper information respecting Bambarra, which he expected to do in the course of four or five days, as he had already, he said, sent four messengers into Kaarta for that purpose. I readily submitted to this proposal, and went to Soolo, to stay there till the return of one of those messengers. This afforded me a favourable opportunity of receiving what money Salim Daucari could spare me on Dr. Laidley's account. I succeeded in receiving the value of three slaves, chiefly in gold dust; and being anxious to proceed as quickly as possible, I begged Daucari to use his interest with the king to allow me a guide by the way of Fooladoo, as I was informed that the war had already commenced between the kings of Bambarra and Kaarta. Daucari accordingly set out for Kooniakary on the morning of the 20th, and the same evening returned with the king's answer, which was to this purpose; that the king had many years ago made an agreement with Daisy, king of Kaarta, to send all merchants and travellers through his dominions; but that if I wished to take the route through Fooladoo, I had his permission so to do; though he could not, consistently with his agreement, lend me a guide. Having felt the want of regal protection in a former part of my journey, I was unwilling to hazard a repetition of the hardships I had then experienced, especially as the money I had received was probably the last supply that I should obtain; I therefore determined to wait for the return of the messengers from Kaarta.

In the interim it began to be whispered abroad that I had received plenty of gold from Salim Daucari; and on the morning of the 23rd Sambo Sego paid me a visit with a party of horsemen. He insisted upon knowing the exact amount of the money I had obtained, declaring, that whatever the sum was, one half of it must go to the king; besides which, he intimated that he expected a handsome present for himself, as being the king's son, and for his attendants, as being the king's relations. The reader will easily perceive, that if all these demands had been satisfied, I should not have been overburdened with money; but though it was very mortifying to me to comply with the demands of injustice, and so arbitrary an exaction, yet, thinking it was highly dangerous to make a foolish resistance, and irritate the lion when within the reach of his paw, I prepared to submit; and if Salim Daucari had not interposed, all my endeavours to mitigate this oppressive claim would have been of no avail. Salim at last prevailed upon Sambo to accept sixteen bars of European merchandise, and some powder and ball, as a complete payment of every demand that could be made upon me in the kingdom of Kasson.

Jan. 26th.—In the forenoon, I went to the top of a high hill to the southward of Soolo, where I had a most enchanting prospect of the country. The number of towns and villages, and the extensive cultivation around them, surpassed everything I had yet seen in Africa. A gross calculation may be formed of the number of inhabitants in this delightful plain by considering that the king of Kasson can raise four thousand fighting men by the sound of his war drum. In traversing the rocky eminences of this hill, which are almost destitute of vegetation, I observed a number of large holes in the crevices and fissures of the rocks, where the wolves and hyænas take refuge during the day. Some of these animals paid us a visit on the evening of the 27th; their approach was discovered by the dogs of the village; and on this occasion, it is remarkable that the dogs did not bark, but howl in the most dismal manner. The inhabitants of the village no sooner heard them, than, knowing the cause, they armed themselves; and providing bunches of dry grass, went in a body to the inclosure in the middle of the village where the cattle were kept. Here they lighted the bunches of grass, and, waving them to and fro, ran hooping and hallooing towards the hills. This manoeuvre had the desired effect of frightening the wolves away from the village, but, on examination, we found that they had killed five of the cattle, and torn and wounded many others.

Feb. 1*st.*—The messengers arrived from Kaarta, and brought intelligence that the war had not yet commenced between Bambarra and Kaarta, and that I might probably pass through Kaarta before the Bambarra army invaded that country.

Feb. 3*rd.*—Early in the morning two guides on horse-back came from Kooniakary to conduct me to the frontiers of Kaarta. I accordingly took leave of Salim Daucari, and parted, for the last time, from my fellow-traveller, the blacksmith, whose kind solicitude for my welfare had been so conspicuous; and about ten o'clock departed from Soolo. We travelled this day through a rocky and hilly country, along the banks of the river Krieko, and at sunset came to the village of Soomo, where we slept.

Feb. 4*th.*—We departed from Soomo, and continued our route along the banks of the Krieko, which are everywhere well cultivated, and swarm with inhabitants. At this time they were increased by the number of people that had flown thither from Kaarta on account of the Bambarra war. In the afternoon we reached Kimo, a large village, the residence of Madi Konko, governor of the hilly country of Kasson, which is called Sorroma. From hence the guides appointed by the king of Kasson returned to join in the expedition against Kajaaga; and I waited until the 6th before I could prevail on Madi Konko to appoint me a guide to Kaarta.

Feb. 7th.—Departing from Kimo, with Madi Konko's son as a guide, we continued our course along the banks of the Krieko until the afternoon, when we arrived at Kangee, a considerable town. The Krieko is here but a small rivulet. This beautiful stream takes its rise a little to the eastward of this town, and descends with a rapid and noisy current until it reaches the bottom of the high hill called Tappa, where it becomes more placid, and winds gently through the lovely plains of Kooniakary; after which, having received an additional branch from the north, it is lost in the Senegal, somewhere near the falls of Felow.

Feb. 8th.—This day we travelled over a rough stony country, and having passed Seimpo and a number of other villages, arrived in the afternoon at Lackerago, a small village which stands upon the ridge of hills that separates the kingdoms of Kasson and Kaarta. In the course of the day we passed many hundreds of people flying from Kaarta, with their families and effects.

Feb. 9th.—Early in the morning we departed from Lackerago, and a little to the eastward came to the brow of a hill, from whence we had an extensive view of the country. Towards the south-east were perceived some very distant hills, which our guide told us were the mountains of Fooladoo. We travelled with great difficulty down a stony and abrupt precipice, and continued our way in the bed of a dry river-course; where the trees, meeting overhead, made the place dark and cool. In a little time we reached the bottom of this romantic glen, and about ten o'clock emerged from between two rocky hills, and found ourselves on the level and sandy plains of Kaarta. At noon we arrived at a Korree, or watering place, where, for a few strings of beads, I purchased as much milk and corn-meal as we could eat; indeed provisions are here so cheap, and the shepherds live in such affluence, that they seldom ask any return for what refreshments a traveller receives from them. From this Korree we reached Feesurah at sunset, where we took up our lodging for the night.

Feb. 10th.—We continued at Feesurah all this day, to

have a few clothes washed, and learn more exactly the situation of affairs before we ventured towards the capital.

Feb. 11*th.*—Our landlord, taking advantage of the unsettled state of the country, demanded so extravagant a sum for our lodging, that suspecting he wished for an opportunity to quarrel with us, I refused to submit to his exorbitant demand; but my attendants were so much frightened at the reports of approaching war, that they refused to proceed any further, unless I could settle matters with him, and induce him to accompany us to Kemmoo, for our protection on the road. This I accomplished with some difficulty, and by a present of a blanket which I had brought with me to sleep in, and for which our landlord had conceived a very great liking. Matters were at length amicably adjusted, and he mounted his horse and led the way. He was one of those Negroes who, together with the ceremonial part of the Mahomedan religion, retain all their ancient superstitions, and even drink strong liquors. They are called Johars, or Jowers, and in this kingdom form a very numerous and powerful tribe. We had no sooner got into a dark and lonely part of the first wood, than he made a sign for us to stop, and taking hold of a hollow piece of bamboo, that hung as an amulet round his neck, whistled very loud, three times. I confess I was somewhat startled, thinking it was a signal for some of his companions to come and attack us; but he assured me that it was done merely with a view to ascertain what success we were likely to meet with on our present journey. He then dismounted, laid his spear across the road, and having said a number of short prayers, concluded with three loud whistles; after which he listened for some time, as if in expectation of an answer, and receiving none, told us we might proceed without fear, for there was no danger. About noon we passed a number of large villages quite deserted, the inhabitants having fled into Kasson to avoid the horrors of war. We reached Karankalla at sunset; this formerly was a large town, but having been plundered by the Bambarrans about four years ago, nearly one half of it is still in ruins.

Feb. 12*th.*—At daylight we departed from Karankalla, and as it was but a short day's journey to Kemmoo, we travelled slower than usual, and amused ourselves by collecting such eatable fruits as grew near the roadside. In this pursuit I had wandered a little from my people, and being uncertain whether they were before or behind me, I hastened to a rising ground to look about me. As I was proceeding towards this eminence, two Negro horsemen, armed with muskets, came galloping from among the bushes; on seeing them I made a full stop; the horsemen did the same; and all three of us seemed equally surprised and confounded at this interview. As I approached them their fears increased, and one of them, after casting upon me a look of horror, rode off at full speed; the other, in a panic of fear, put his hands over his eyes, and continued muttering prayers until his horse, seemingly without the rider's knowledge, conveyed him slowly after his companion. About a mile to the westward, they fell in with my attendants, to whom they related a frightful story. It seems their fears had dressed me in the flowing robes of a tremendous spirit; and one of them affirmed that, when I made my appearance, a cold blast of wind came pouring down upon him from the sky, like so much cold water. About noon we saw at a distance the capital of Kaarta, situated in the middle of an open plain, the country for two miles round being cleared of wood, by the great consumption of that article for building and fuel, and we entered the town about two o'clock in the afternoon.

We proceeded, without stopping, to the court before the king's residence; but I was so completely surrounded by the gazing multitude that I did not attempt to dismount, but sent in the landlord and Madi Konko's son to acquaint the king of my arrival. In a little time they returned, accompanied by a messenger from the king, signifying that he would see me in the evening; and in the meantime, the messenger had orders to procure me a lodging, and see that the crowd did not molest me. He conducted me into a court, at the door of which he stationed a man, with a stick in his hand, to keep off the mob, and then showed me a large hut, in which I was to lodge. I had scarcely seated myself in this spacious apartment, when the mob entered; it was found impossible to keep them out, and I was surrounded by as many as the hut could contain. When the first party, however, had seen me, and asked a few questions, they retired to make room for another company; and in this manner the hut was filled and emptied thirteen different times.

A little before sunset the king sent to inform me that he was at leisure, and wished to see me. I followed the messenger through a number of courts surrounded with high walls, where I observed plenty of dry grass, bundled up like hay, to fodder the horses in case the town should be invested. On entering the court in which the king was sitting I was astonished at the number of his attendants, and at the good order that seemed to prevail among them. They were all seated—the fighting men on the king's right hand, and the women and children on the left, leaving a space between them for my passage. The king, whose name was Daisy Koorabarri, was not to be distinguished from his subjects by any superiority in point of dress; a bank of earth about two feet high, upon which was spread a leopard's skin, constituted the only mark of royal dignity. When I had seated myself upon the ground before him, and related the various circumstances that had induced me to pass through his country, and my reasons for soliciting his protection he appeared perfectly satisfied; but said it was not in his power at present to afford me much assistance, for that all sort of communication between Kaarta and Bambarra had been interrupted for some time past; and as Mansong, the king of Bambarra, with his army, had entered Fooladoo in his way to Kaarta, there was but little hope of my reaching Bambarra by any of the usual routes, inasmuch as, coming from an enemy's country, I should certainly be plundered or taken for a spy. If his country had been at peace, he said, I might have remained with him until a more favourable opportunity offered; but, as matters stood at present, he did not wish me to continue in Kaarta, for fear some accident should befall me, in which case my countrymen might say that he had murdered a white man. He would therefore advise me to return into Kasson, and remain there until the war should terminate, which would probably happen in the course of three or four months ; after which, if he was alive, he said, he would be glad to see me, and if he was dead, his sons would take care of me.

This advice was certainly well meant on the part of the king, and perhaps I was to blame in not following it ; but I reflected that the hot months were approaching, and I dreaded the thoughts of spending the rainy season in the interior of Africa. These considerations, and the aversion I felt at the idea of returning without having made a greater progress in discovery, made me determine to go forwards ; and though the king could not give me a guide to Bambarra, I begged that he would allow a man to accompany me as near the frontiers of his kingdom as was consistent with safety. Finding that I was determined to proceed, the king told me that one route still remained, but that, he said, was by no means free from danger ; which was to go from Kaarta into the Moorish kingdom of Ludamar, from whence I might pass, by a circuitous route, into Bambarra. If I wished to follow this route, he would appoint people to conduct me to Jarra, the frontier town of Ludamar. He then inquired very particularly how I had been treated since I had left the Gambia, and asked in a jocular way how many slaves I expected to carry home with me on my return. He was about to proceed, when a man mounted on a fine Moorish horse, which was covered with sweat and foam, entered the court, and signifying that he had something of importance to communicate, the king immediately took up his sandals, which is the signal to strangers to retire. I accordingly took leave, but desired my boy to stay about the place in order to learn something of the intelligence that this messenger had brought. In about an hour the boy returned, and informed me that the Bambarra army had left Fooladoo, and was on its march towards Kaarta ; that the man I had seen, who had brought this intelligence, was one of the scouts or watchmen employed by the king, each of whom has his particular station (commonly on some rising ground) from whence he has the best view of the country, and watches the motions of the enemy.

In the evening the king sent me a fine sheep; which was very acceptable, as none of us had tasted victuals during the day. Whilst we were employed in dressing supper, evening prayers were announced; not by the call of the priest, as usual, but by beating on drums, and blowing through large elephants' teeth, hollowed out in such a manner as to resemble bugle horns; the sound is melodious, and, in my opinion, comes nearer to the human voice than any other artificial sound. As the main body of Daisy's army was, at this juncture, at Kemmoo, the mosques were very much crowded; and I observed that the disciples of Mahomet composed nearly one half of the army of Kaarta.

Feb. 13*th.*—At daylight I sent my horse-pistols and holsters as a present to the king, and being very desirous to get away from a place which was likely soon to become the seat of war, I begged the messenger to inform the king that I wished to depart from Kemmoo as soon as he should find it convenient to appoint me a guide. In about an hour the king sent his messenger to thank me for the present, and eight horsemen to conduct me to Jarra. They told me that the king wished me to proceed to Jarra with all possible expedition, that they might return before anything decisive should happen between the armies of Bambarra and Kaarta. We accordingly departed forthwith from Kemmoo, accompanied by three of Daisy's sons, and about two hundred horsemen, who kindly undertook to see me a little way on my journey.

CHAPTER VIII

Journey from Kemmoo to Funingkedy—Some account of the lotus—
    A youth murdered by the Moors—Interesting scene at his death—
    Author passes through Simbing—Some particulars concerning
    Major Houghton—Author reaches Jarra—Situation of the sur-
    rounding states at the period of his arrival there, and a brief
    account of the war between Kaarta and Bambarra.

On the evening of the day of our departure from Kemmoo
(the king's eldest son and great part of the horsemen having
returned) we reached a village called Marina, where we
slept.   During the night some thieves broke into the hut
where I had deposited my baggage, and having cut open
one of my bundles, stole a quantity of beads, part of my
clothes, and some amber and gold, which happened to be
in one of the pockets.   I complained to my protectors, but
without effect.   The next day (Feb. 14) was far advanced
before we departed from Marina, and we travelled slowly,
on account of the excessive heat, until four o'clock in the
afternoon, when two Negroes were observed sitting among
some thorny bushes at a little distance from the road.   The
king's people, taking it for granted that they were runaway
slaves, cocked their muskets, and rode at full speed in
different directions through the bushes, in order to surround
them, and prevent their escaping.   The Negroes, however,
waited with great composure until we came within bowshot
of them, when each of them took from his quiver a handful
of arrows, and putting two between his teeth and one in
his bow, waved to us with his hand to keep at a distance ;
upon which one of the king's people called out to the
strangers to give some account of themselves.   They said
that they were natives of Toorda, a neighbouring village,
and had come to that place to gather *tomberongs*.   These
are small farinaceous berries, of a yellow colour and de-

licious taste, which I knew to be the fruit of the *Rhamnus lotus* of Linnæus. The Negroes showed us two large basketfuls, which they had collected in the course of the day. These berries are much esteemed by the natives, who convert them into a sort of bread, by exposing them for some days to the sun, and afterwards pounding them gently in a wooden mortar, until the farinaceous part of the berry is separated from the stone. This meal is then mixed with a little water, and formed into cakes, which, when dried in the sun, resemble in colour and flavour the sweetest ginger-bread. The stones are afterwards put into a vessel of water, and shaken about so as to separate the meal which may still adhere to them This communicates a sweet and agreeable taste to the water, and with the addition of a little pounded millet, forms a pleasant gruel called *fondi*, which is the common breakfast in many parts of Ludamar during the months of February and March. The fruit is collected by spreading a cloth upon the ground, and beating the branches with a stick.

The lotus is very common in all the kingdoms which I visited, but is found in the greatest plenty on the sandy soil of Kaarta, Ludamar, and the northern parts of Bambarra, where it is one of the most common shrubs of the country. I had observed the same species at Gambia. The leaves of the desert shrub are, however, much smaller, and more resembling, in that particular, those represented in the engraving given by Desfontaines in the *Mémoires de l'Académie Royale des Sciences*, 1788, p. 443.

As this shrub is found in Tunis, and also in the Negro kingdoms, and as it furnishes the natives of the latter with a food resembling bread, and also with a sweet liquor which is much relished by them, there can be little doubt of its being the lotus mentioned by Pliny as the food of the Lybian Lotophagi. An army may very well have been fed with the bread I have tasted, made of the meal of the fruit, as is said by Pliny to have been done in Lybia ; and as the taste of the bread is sweet and agreeable, it is not likely that the soldiers would complain of it.

We arrived in the evening at the village of Toorda, when

all the rest of the king's people turned back except two, who remained with me as guides to Jarra.

Feb. 15*th.*—I departed from Toorda, and about two o'clock came to a considerable town called Funingkedy. As we approached the town the inhabitants were much alarmed; for, as one of my guides wore a turban, they mistook us for some Moorish banditti. This misapprehension was soon cleared up, and we were well received by a Gambia Slatee, who resides at this town, and at whose house we lodged.

Feb. 16*th.*—We were informed that a number of people would go from this town to Jarra on the day following; and as the road was much infested by the Moors, we resolved to stay and accompany the travellers. In the meantime, we were told, that a few days before our arrival, most of the Bushreens and people of property in Funingkedy had gone to Jarra, to consult about removing their families and effects to that town, for fear of the approaching war ; and that the Moors, in their absence, had stolen some of their cattle.

About two o'clock, as I was lying asleep, upon a bullock's hide behind the door of the hut, I was awakened by the screams of women, and a general clamour and confusion among the inhabitants. At first I suspected that the Bambarrans had actually entered the town ; but observing my boy upon the top of one of the huts, I called to him to know what was the matter. He informed me that the Moors were come a second time to steal the cattle, and that they were now close to the town. I mounted the roof of the hut, and observed a large herd of bullocks coming towards the town, followed by five Moors on horseback, who drove the cattle forward with their muskets. When they had reached the wells, which are close to the town, the Moors selected from the herd sixteen of the finest beasts, and drove them off at full gallop.

During this transaction, the townspeople, to the number of five hun red, stood collected close to the walls of the town ; and when the Moors drove the cattle away, though they passed within pistol shot of them, the inhabitants scarcely made a show of resistance. I only saw four muskets fired, which, being loaded with gunpowder of the

Rhamnus Lotus

Negroes' own manufacture, did no execution. Shortly after this I observed a number of people supporting a young man upon horseback, and conducting him slowly towards the town. This was one of the herdsmen, who, attempting to throw his spear. had been wounded by a shot from one of the Moors. His mother walked on before, quite frantic with grief, clapping her hands, and enumerating the good qualities of her son. *Ee maffo fonio* (he never told a lie), said the disconsolate mother, as her wounded son was carried in at the gate;—*Ee maffo fonio abada* (he never told a lie ; no, never). When they had conveyed him to his hut, and laid him upon a mat, all the spectators joined in lamenting his fate, by screaming and howling in the most piteous manner.

After their grief had subsided a little, I was desired to examine the wound. I found that the ball had passed quite through his leg, having fractured both bones a little below the knee ; the poor boy was faint from the loss of blood, and his situation withal so very precarious, that I could not console his relations with any great hopes of his recovery. However, to give him a possible chance, I observed to them that it was necessary to cut off his leg above the knee. This proposal made every one start with horror ; they had never heard of such a method of cure, and would by no means give their consent to it ; indeed they evidently considered me as a sort of cannibal for proposing so cruel and unheard of an operation, which in their opinion would be attended with more pain and danger than the wound itself. The patient was therefore committed to the care of some old Bushreens, who endeavoured to secure him a passage into paradise, by whispering in his ear some Arabic sentences, and desiring him to repeat them. After many unsuccessful attempts, the poor heathen at last pronounced, *La illah el allah, Mahomet rasowl allahi,*[1] and the disciples of the Prophet assured his mother that her son had given sufficient evidence of his faith, and would be happy in a future state. He died the same evening.

Feb. 17*th.*—My guides informed me, that in order to

---

[1] There is but one God, and Mahomet is his Prophet.

avoid the Moorish banditti, it was necessary to travel in the night; we accordingly departed from Funingkedy in the afternoon, accompanied by about thirty people, carrying their effects with them into Ludamar, for fear of the war. We travelled with great silence and expedition until midnight, when we stopped in a sort of inclosure, near a small village; but the thermometer being so low as 68°, none of the Negroes could sleep on account of the cold.

At daybreak on the 18th, we resumed our journey, and at eight o'clock passed *Simbing*, the frontier village of Ludamar, situated in a narrow pass between two rocky hills, and surrounded with a high wall. From this village Major Houghton (being deserted by his Negro servants, who refused to follow him into the Moorish country), wrote his last letter with a pencil to Dr. Laidley. This brave but unfortunate man, having surmounted many difficulties, had taken a northerly direction, and endeavoured to pass through the kingdom of Ludamar, where I afterwards learned the following particulars concerning his melancholy fate. On his arrival at Jarra, he got acquainted with certain Moorish merchants who were travelling to Tisheet (a place near the salt pits in the Great Desert, ten days' journey to the northward) to purchase salt; and the major, at the expense of a musket and some tobacco, engaged them to convey him thither. It is impossible to form any other opinion on this determination, than that the Moors intentionally deceived him either with regard to the route that he wished to pursue, or the state of the intermediate country between Jarra and Timbuctoo. Their intention probably was to rob and leave him in the desert. At the end of two days he suspected their treachery, and insisted on returning to Jarra. Finding him persist in this determination, the Moors robbed him of everything he possessed, and went off with their camels; the poor major being thus deserted, returned on foot to a watering place in possession of the Moors, called Tarra. He had been some days without food, and the unfeeling Moors refusing to give him any, he sunk at last under his distresses. Whether he actually perished of hunger, or was murdered outright by the savage

Mahomedans, is not certainly known ; his body was dragged into the woods, and I was shown, at a distance, the spot where his remains were left to perish.

About four miles to the north of Simbing we came to a small stream of water, where we observed a number of wild horses ; they were all of one colour, and galloped away from us at an easy rate, frequently stopping and looking back. The Negroes hunt them for food, and their flesh is much esteemed.

About noon we arrived at Jarra, a large town situated at the bottom of some rocky hills. But before I proceed to describe the place itself, and relate the various occurrences which befell me there, it will not be improper to give my readers a brief recital of the origin of the war which induced me to take this route—an unfortunate determination, the immediate cause of all the misfortunes and calamities which afterward befell me. The recital which I propose to give in this place will prevent interruptions hereafter.

This war, which desolated Kaarta soon after I had left that kingdom, and spread terror into many of the neighbouring states, arose in the following manner. A few bullocks belonging to a frontier village of Bambarra having been stolen by a party of Moors, were sold to the Dooty, or chief man of a town in Kaarta. The villagers claimed their cattle, and being refused satisfaction, complained of the Dooty to their sovereign, Mansong, king of Bambarra, who probably beheld with an eye of jealousy the growing prosperity of Kaarta, and availed himself of this incident to declare hostilities against that kingdom.

With this view he sent a messenger and a party of horsemen to Daisy, king of Kaarta, to inform him that the king of Bambarra, with nine thousand men, would visit Kemmoo in the course of the dry season ; and to desire that he (Daisy) would direct his slaves to sweep the houses, and have everything ready for their accommodation. The messenger concluded this insulting notification by presenting the king with a pair of *iron sandals;* at the same time adding, that "until such time as Daisy had worn out these sandals in his flight, he should never be secure from the arrows of Bambarra."

*D 205

Daisy, having consulted with his chief men about the best means of repelling so formidable an enemy, returned an answer of defiance, and made a Bushreen write in Arabic, upon a piece of thin board, a sort of proclamation, which was suspended to a tree in the public square; and a number of aged men were sent to different places to explain it to the common people. This proclamation called upon all the friends of Daisy to join him immediately; but to such as had no arms, or were afraid to enter into the war, permission was given to retire into any of the neighbouring kingdoms; and it was added, that provided they observed a strict neutrality, they should always be welcome to return to their former habitations. If, however, they took any active part against the Kaarta, they had then "broken the key of their huts, and could never afterwards enter the door." Such was the expression.

This proclamation was very generally applauded; but many of the Kaartans, and amongst others the powerful tribes of Jower and Kakaroo, availing themselves of the indulgent clause, retired from Daisy's dominions, and took refuge in Ludamar and Kasson. By means of these desertions, Daisy's army was not so numerous as might have been expected; and when I was at Kemmoo, the whole number of effective men, according to report, did not exceed four thousand; but they were men of spirit and enterprise, and could be depended on.

On the 22nd of February (four days after my arrival at Jarra), Mansong, with his army, advanced towards Kemmoo; and Daisy, without hazarding a battle, retired to Joko, a town to the north-west of Kemmoo, where he remained three days, and then took refuge in a strong town called Gedingooma, situated in the hilly country, and surrounded with high walls of stone. When Daisy departed from Joko, his sons refused to follow him, alleging that "the singing men would publish their disgrace, as soon as it should be known that Daisy and his family had fled from Joko without firing a gun." They were therefore left behind, with a number of horsemen, to defend Joko; but, after many skirmishes, they were totally defeated; and one of Daisy's sons taken prisoner; the remainder fled to Gedingooma, which Daisy had stored with provisions, and where he determined to make his final stand.

Mansong, finding that Daisy was determined to avoid a pitched battle, placed a strong force at Joko to watch his motions; and, separating the remainder of his army into small detachments, ordered them to overrun the country, and seize upon the inhabitants before they had time to escape. These orders were executed with such promptitude, that in a few days the whole kingdom of Kaarta became a scene of desolation. Most of the poor inhabitants of the different towns and villages being surprised in the night, fell an easy prey; and their corn, and everything which could be useful to Daisy, was burnt and destroyed. During these transactions, Daisy was employed in fortifying Gedingooma. This town is built in a narrow pass between two high hills, having only two gates, one towards Kaarta and the other towards Jaffnoo. The gate towards Kaarta was defended by Daisy in person, and that towards Jaffnoo was committed to the charge of his sons. When the army of Bambarra approached the town they made some attempts to storm it, but were always driven back with great loss; and Mansong, finding Daisy more formidable than he expected, resolved to cut off his supplies, and starve him into submission. He accordingly sent all the prisoners he had taken into Bambarra, and having collected a considerable quantity of provisions, remained with his army two whole months in the vicinity of Gedingooma without doing anything decisive. During this time he was much harassed by sallies from the besieged; and his stock of provisions being nearly exhausted, he sent to Ali, the Moorish king of Ludamar, for two hundred horsemen, to enable him to make an attack upon the north gate of the town, and give the Bambarrans an opportunity of storming the place. Ali, though he had made an agreement with Mansong at the commencement of the war to afford him assistance, now refused to fulfil his engagement, which so enraged Mansong, that he marched part of his army to Funingkedy, with a view to surprise the camp of Benowm; but the Moors having received intelligence of his design, fled to the northward, and Mansong, without attempting anything farther, returned to Sego. This happened while I was myself in captivity in Ali's camp, as will hereafter be seen.

As the king of Kaarta had now got quit of his most formidable antagonist, it might have been hoped that peace would have been restored to his dominions ; but an extra-ordinary incident involved him, immediately afterwards, in hostilities with Kasson, the king of which country dying about that time, the succession was disputed by his two sons. The younger (Sambo Sego, my old acquaintance) prevailed ; and drove his brother from the country. He fled to Gedingooma ; and being pursued thither, Daisy, who had lived in constant friendship with both the brothers, refused to deliver him up—at the same time declaring that he would not support his claim, nor any way interfere in the quarrel. Sambo Sego, elated with success, and proud of the homage that was paid him as sovereign of Kasson, was much displeased with Daisy's conduct, and joined with some disaffected fugitive Kaartans in a plundering expedition against him. Daisy, who little expected such a visit, had sent a number of people to Joko to plant corn, and collect together such cattle as they might find straying in the woods, in order to supply his army. All these people fell into the hands of Sambo Sego, who carried them to Kooniakary, and afterwards sent them in caravans to be sold to the French at Fort Louis, on the river Senegal.

This attack was soon retaliated ; for Daisy, who was now in distress for want of provisions, thought he was justified in supplying himself from the plunder of Kasson. He accordingly took with him eight hundred of his best men, and marching secretly through the woods, surprised in the night three large villages near Kooniakary, in which many of his traitorous subjects who were in Sambo's expedition had taken up their residence. All these, and indeed all the able men that fell into Daisy's hands, were immediately put to death.

After this expedition, Daisy began to indulge the hopes of peace. Many of his discontented subjects had returned to their allegiance, and were repairing the towns which had been desolated by the war. The rainy season was approaching, and everything wore a favourable appearance, when he was suddenly attacked from a different quarter.

The Jowers, Kakaroos, and some other Kaartans, who had deserted from him at the commencement of the war, and had shown a decided preference to Mansong and his army during the whole campaign, were now afraid or ashamed to ask forgiveness of Daisy, and being very powerful in themselves, joined together to make war upon him. They solicited the Moors to assist them in their rebellion (as will appear hereafter), and having collected a considerable army, they plundered a large village belonging to Daisy, and carried off a number of prisoners.

Daisy immediately prepared to revenge this insult; but the Jowers, and indeed almost all the Negro inhabitants of Ludamar, deserted their towns, and fled to the eastward; and the rainy season put an end to the war of Kaarta, which had enriched a few individuals, but destroyed the happiness of thousands.

Such was the state of affairs among the nations in the neighbourhood of Jarra, soon after the period of my arrival there. I shall now proceed, after giving some description of that place, with the detail of events as they occurred.

CHAPTER IX

Some account of Jarra, and the Moorish inhabitants—The Author applies for, and obtains permission from Ali, the Moorish chief or sovereign of Ludamar, to pass through his territories—Departs from Jarra, and arrives at Deena—Ill treated by the Moors—Proceeds to Sampaka—Finds a Negro who makes gunpowder—Continues his journey to Samee, where he is seized by some Moors who are sent for that purpose by Ali—Is conveyed a prisoner to the Moorish camp at Benowm, on the borders of the Great Desert.

THE town of Jarra is of considerable extent; the houses are built of clay and stone intermixed, the clay answering the purpose of mortar. It is situated in the Moorish kingdom of Ludamar; but the major part of the inhabitants are Negroes, from the borders of the southern states, who prefer a precarious protection under the Moors, which they purchase by a tribute, rather than continue exposed to their predatory hostilities. The tribute they pay is considerable; and they manifest towards their Moorish superiors the most unlimited obedience and submission, and are treated by them with the utmost indignity and contempt. The Moors of this and the other states adjoining the country of the Negroes resemble in their persons the Mulattoes of the West Indies to so great a degree as not easily to be distinguished from them; and in truth, the present generation seem to be a mixed race between the Moors (properly so called) of the north, and the Negroes of the south, possessing many of the worst qualities of both nations.

Of the origin of these Moorish tribes, as distinguished from the inhabitants of Barbary, from whom they are divided by the Great Desert, nothing farther seems to be known than what is related by John Leo, the African, whose account may be abridged as follows:—

Before the Arabian Conquest, about the middle of the

seventh century, all the inhabitants of Africa, whether they were descended from Numidians, Phœnicians, Carthaginians, Romans, Vandals, or Goths, were comprehended under the general name of *Mauri*, or Moors. All these nations were converted to the religion of Mahomet during the Arabian empire under the Caliphs. About this time many of the Numidian tribes, who led a wandering life in the Desert, and supported themselves upon the produce of their cattle, retired southward across the Great Desert, to avoid the fury of the Arabians ; and by one of those tribes, says Leo (that of Zanhaga), were discovered and conquered the Negro nations on the Niger. By the Niger is here undoubtedly meant the river of Senegal, which in the Mandingo language is called *Bafing*, or the Black River.

To what extent these people are now spread over the African continent it is difficult to ascertain. There is reason to believe that their dominion stretches from west to east, in a narrow line or belt, from the mouth of the Senegal (on the northern side of that river) to the confines of Abyssinia. They are a subtle and treacherous race of people, and take every opportunity of cheating and plundering the credulous and unsuspecting Negroes. But their manners and general habits of life will be best explained as incidents occur in the course of my narrative.

On my arrival at Jarra, I obtained a lodging at the house of Daman Jumma, a Gambia Slatee. This man had formerly borrowed goods from Dr. Laidley, who had given me an order for the money, to the amount of six slaves ; and though the debt was of five years' standing, he readily acknowledged it, and promised me what money he could raise. He was afraid, he said, in his present situation, he could not pay more than two slaves' value. He gave me his assistance, however, in exchanging my beads and amber for gold, which was a more portable article, and more easily concealed from the Moors.

The difficulties we had already encountered, the unsettled state of the country, and, above all, the savage and overbearing deportment of the Moors, had so completely frightened my attendants, that they declared they would rather relin-

quish every claim to reward, than proceed one step farther
to the eastward.   Indeed the danger they incurred of being
seized by the Moors, and sold into slavery, became every
day more apparent; and I could not condemn their apprehensions.   In this situation, deserted by my attendants,
and reflecting that my retreat was cut off by the war behind
me, and that a Moorish country of ten days' journey lay
before me, I applied to Daman to obtain permission from
Ali, the chief or sovereign of Ludamar, that I might pass
through his country unmolested, into Bambarra; and I
hired one of Daman's slaves to accompany me thither, as
soon as such permission should be obtained.   A messenger
was dispatched to Ali, who at this time was encamped near
Benowm ; and as a present was necessary in order to insure
success, I sent him five garments of cotton cloth, which I
purchased of Daman for one of my fowling-pieces.   Fourteen days elapsed in settling this affair ; but, on the evening
of the 26th of February, one of Ali's slaves arrived with
directions, as he pretended, to conduct me in safety as far
as Goomba ; and told me I was to pay him one garment
of blue cotton cloth for his attendance.   My faithful boy,
observing that I was about to proceed without him, resolved
to accompany me ; and told me that though he wished me
to turn back, he never had entertained any serious thoughts
of deserting me, but had been advised to it by Johnson, with
a view to induce me to return immediately for Gambia.

Feb. 27th.—I delivered most of my papers to Johnson,
to convey them to Gambia as soon as possible, reserving a
duplicate for myself in case of accidents.   I likewise left in
Daman's possession a bundle of clothes and other things
that were not absolutely necessary ; for I wished to diminish
my baggage as much as possible, that the Moors might have
fewer inducements to plunder us.

Things being thus adjusted, we departed from Jarra in
the forenoon, and slept at Troomgoomba, a small walled
village inhabited by a mixture of Negroes and Moors.   On
the day following (Feb. 28th) we reached Quira ; and on
the 29th, after a toilsome journey over a sandy country, we
came to Compe, a watering place belonging to the Moors :

from whence, on the morning following, we proceeded to Deena, a large town, and, like Jarra, built of stone and clay. The Moors are here in greater proportion to the Negroes than at Jarra. They assembled round the hut of the Negro where I lodged, and treated me with the greatest insolence. They hissed, shouted, and abused me; they even spat in my face with a view to irritate me, and afford them a pretext for seizing my baggage. But, finding such insults had not the desired effect, they had recourse to the final and decisive argument, that I was a Christian, and of course that my property was lawful plunder to the followers of Mahomet. They accordingly opened my bundles, and robbed me of everything they fancied. My attendants, finding that everybody could rob me with impunity, insisted on returning to Jarra.

The day following (March 2nd) I endeavoured by all means in my power to prevail upon my people to go on; but they still continued obstinate; and having reason to fear some further insult from the fanatic Moors, I resolved to proceed alone. Accordingly the next morning, about two o'clock, I departed from Deena. It was moonlight; but the roaring of wild beasts made it necessary to proceed with caution.

When I had reached a piece of rising ground about half a mile from the town, I heard somebody halloo, and looking back, saw my faithful boy running after me. He informed me that Ali's man had gone back to Benowm, and that Daman's Negro was about to depart for Jarra; but he said he had no doubt, if I would stop a little, that he could persuade the latter to accompany us. I waited accordingly, and in about an hour the boy returned with the Negro; and we continued travelling over a sandy country, covered chiefly with the *Asclepias giganteo*, until mid-day, when we came to a number of deserted huts; and seeing some appearances of water at a little distance, I sent the boy to fill a soofroo; but as he was examining the place for water, the roaring of a lion, that was probably on the same pursuit, induced the frightened boy to return in haste, and we submitted patiently to the disappointment. In the afternoon we reached a town inhabited chiefly by Foulahs, called Samamingkoos.

Next morning (March 4th) we set out for Sampaka, which place we reached about two o'clock. On the road we observed immense quantities of locusts: the trees were quite black with them. These insects devour every vegetable that comes in their way, and in a short time completely strip a tree of its leaves. The noise of their excrement falling upon the leaves and withered grass, very much resembles a shower of rain. When a tree is shaken or struck, it is astonishing to see what a cloud of them will fly off. In their flight they yield to the current of the wind, which at this season of the year is always from the north-east. Should the wind shift, it is difficult to conceive where they could collect food, as the whole of their course was marked with desolation.

Sampaka is a large town, and when the Moors and Bam-barrans were at war, was thrice attacked by the former; but they were driven off with great loss, though the king of Bambarra was afterwards obliged to give up this, and all the other towns as far as Goomba, in order to obtain a peace. Here I lodged at the house of a Negro who practised the art of making gunpowder. He showed me a bag of nitre, very white, but the crystals were much smaller than common. They procure it in considerable quantities from the ponds which are filled in the rainy season, and to which the cattle resort for coolness during the heat of the day. When the water is evaporated, a white efflorescence is observed on the mud, which the natives collect and purify in such a manner as to answer their purpose. The Moors supply them with sulphur from the Mediterranean; and the process is completed by pounding the different articles together in a wooden mortar. The grains are very unequal, and the sound of its explosion is by no means so sharp as that produced by European gunpowder.

March 5th.—We departed from Sampaka at daylight. About noon we stopped a little at a village called Dangali; and in the evening arrived at Dalli. We saw upon the road two large herds of camels feeding. When the Moors turn their camels to feed, they tie up one of their fore legs, to prevent their straying. This happened to be a feast day at Dalli, and the people were dancing before the Dooty's house. But when they were informed that a white man was come into the town, they left off dancing, and came to the place where I lodged, walking in regular order, two and two, with the music before them. They play upon a sort of flute; but instead of blowing into a hole in the side, they blow obliquely over the end, which is half shut by a thin piece of wood; they govern the holes on the side with their fingers, and play some simple and very plaintive airs. They continued to dance and sing until midnight; during which time I was surrounded by so great a crowd as made it necessary for me to satisfy their curiosity by sitting still.

March 6th—We stopt here this morning because some of the townspeople, who were going to Goomba on the day following, wished to accompany us; but in order to avoid the crowd of people which usually assembled in the evening, we went to a Negro village to the east of Dalli, called Samee, where we were kindly received by the hospitable Dooty, who on this occasion killed two fine sheep, and invited his friends to come and feast with him.

March 7th.—Our landlord was so proud of the honour of entertaining a white man, that he insisted on my staying with him and his friends until the cool of the evening, when he said he would conduct me to the next village. As I was now within two days' journey of Goomba, I had no apprehensions from the Moors, and readily accepted the invitation. I spent the forenoon very pleasantly with these poor Negroes; their company was the more acceptable, as the gentleness of their manners presented a striking contrast to the rudeness and barbarity of the Moors. They enlivened their conversation by drinking a fermented liquor made from corn—the same sort of beer that I have described in a former chapter—and better I never tasted in Great Britain.

In the midst of this harmless festivity I flattered myself that all danger from the Moors was over. Fancy had already placed me on the banks of the Niger, and presented to my imagination a thousand delightful scenes in my future progress, when a party of Moors unexpectedly entered the hut, and dispelled the golden dream. They came, they said, by Ali's orders, to convey me to his camp at Benowm. If I went peaceably, they told me I had nothing to fear; but if I refused, they had orders to bring me by force. I was struck dumb by surprise and terror, which the Moors observing, endeavoured to calm my apprehensions by repeating the assurance that I had nothing to fear. Their visit, they added, was occasioned by the curiosity of Ali's wife, Fatima, who had heard so much about Christians, that she was very anxious to see one. As soon as her curiosity should be satisfied, they had no doubt, they said, that Ali would give me a handsome present, and send a person to conduct me to Bambarra. Finding entreaty and resistance equally fruitless, I prepared to follow the messengers, and took leave of my landlord and his company with great reluctance. Accompanied by my faithful boy (for Daman's slave made his escape on seeing the Moors), we reached Dalli in the evening, where we were strictly watched by the Moors during the night.

March 8th.—We were conducted by a circuitous path through the woods to Dangali, where we slept.

March 9th.—We continued our journey, and in the afternoon arrived at Sampaka. On the road we saw a party of Moors, well armed, who told us that they were hunting for a runaway slave; but the townspeople informed us that a party of Moors had attempted to steal some cattle from the town in the morning, but were repulsed; and on their describing the persons, we were satisfied that they were the same banditti that we had seen in the woods.

Next morning (March 10th) we set out for Samamingkoos. On the road we overtook a woman and two boys, with an ass; she informed us that she was going for Bambarra, but had been stopped on the road by a party of Moors, who had taken most of her clothes, and some gold from her; and that she would be under the necessity of returning to Deena till the fast moon was over. The same evening the new moon was seen, which ushered in the month Rhamadan.

Large fires were made in different parts of the town, and a greater quantity of victuals than usual dressed upon the occasion.

March 11*th.*—By daylight the Moors were in readiness; but as I had suffered much from thirst on the road, I made my boy fill a soofroo of water for my own use; for the Moors assured me that they should not taste either meat or drink until sunset. However, I found that the excessive heat of the sun, and the dust we raised in travelling, overcame their scruples, and made my soofroo a very useful part of our baggage. On our arrival at Deena, I went to pay my respects to one of Ali's sons. I found him sitting in a low hut, with five or six more of his companions, washing their hands and feet, and frequently taking water into their mouths, gargling, and spitting it out again. I was no sooner seated, than he handed me a double-barrelled gun, and told me to dye the stock of a blue colour, and repair one of the locks. I found great difficulty in persuading him that I knew nothing about the matter. However, says he, if you cannot repair the gun, you shall give me some knives and scissors immediately; and when my boy, who acted as interpreter, assured him that I had no such articles, he hastily snatched up a musket that stood by him, cocked it, and putting the muzzle close to the boy's ear, would certainly have shot him dead upon the spot, had not the Moors wrested the musket from him, and made signs for us to retreat. The boy, being terrified at this treatment, attempted to make his escape in the night, but was prevented by the vigilance of the Moors, who guarded us with strict attention; and at night always went to sleep by the door of the hut, in such a situation that it was almost impossible to pass without stepping upon them.

March 12*th.*—We departed from Deena towards Benowm, and about nine o'clock came to a Korree, whence the Moors were preparing to depart to the southward, on account of the scarcity of water; here we filled our soofroo, and continued our journey over a hot sandy country, covered with small stunted shrubs, until about one o'clock, when the heat of the sun obliged us to stop. But our water being expended, we could not prudently remain longer than a few minutes to collect a little gum, which is an excellent succedaneum for water, as it keeps the mouth moist, and allays for a time the pain in the throat.

About five o'clock we came in sight of Benowm, the residence of Ali. It presented to the eye a great number of dirty-looking tents, scattered without order, over a large space of ground; and among the tents appeared large herds of camels, cattle, and goats. We reached the skirts of the camp a little before sunset, and, with much entreaty, procured a little water. My arrival was no sooner observed, than the people who drew water at the wells threw down their buckets, those in the tents mounted their horses, and men, women, and children came running or galloping towards me. I soon found myself surrounded by such a crowd that I could scarcely move; one pulled my clothes, another took off my hat, a third stopped me to examine my waistcoat buttons, and a fourth called out, *La illah el allah Mahomet rasowl allahi*,[1] and signified, in a threatening manner, that I must repeat those words. We reached at length the king's tent, where we found a great number of people, men and women, assembled. Ali was sitting upon a black leather cushion, clipping a few hairs from his upper lip; a female attendant holding up a looking-glass before him. He appeared to be an old man, of the Arab cast, with a long white beard; and he had a sullen and indignant aspect. He surveyed me with attention, and inquired of the Moors if I could speak Arabic; being answered in the negative, he appeared much surprised, and continued silent. The surrounding attendants, and especially the ladies, were abundantly more inquisitive; they asked a thousand questions, inspected every part of my apparel, searched my pockets, and obliged me to unbutton my waistcoat, and display the whiteness of my skin; they even counted my toes and fingers, as if they doubted whether I was in truth a human being. In a little time the priest announced evening prayers; but before the people departed, the Moor, who had acted as interpreter, informed me that Ali

[1] See p. 77.

A View of Ali's Tent at the Camp of Benowm

was about to present me with something to eat; and looking round, I observed some boys bringing a wild hog, which they tied to one of the tent strings, and Ali made signs to me to kill and dress it for supper. Though I was very hungry, I did not think it prudent to eat any part of an animal so much detested by the Moors, and therefore told him that I never ate such food. They then untied the hog, in hopes that it would run immediately at me—for they believe that a great enmity subsists between hogs and Christians—but in this they were disappointed, for the animal no sooner regained his liberty, than he began to attack indiscriminately every person that came in his way, and at last took shelter under the couch upon which the king was sitting. The assembly being thus dissolved, I was conducted to the tent of Ali's chief slave, but was not permitted to enter, nor allowed to touch anything belonging to it. I requested something to eat, and a little boiled corn, with salt and water, was at length sent me in a wooden bowl; and a mat was spread upon the sand before the tent, on which I passed the night, surrounded by the curious multitude.

At sunrise, Ali, with a few attendants, came on horseback to visit me, and signified that he had provided a hut for me, where I would be sheltered from the sun. I was accordingly conducted thither, and found the hut comparatively cool and pleasant. It was constructed of corn stalks set up on end, in the form of a square, with a flat roof of the same materials, supported by forked sticks, to one of which was tied the wild hog before mentioned. This animal had certainly been placed there by Ali's order, out of derision to a Christian; and I found it a very disagreeable inmate, as it drew together a number of boys, who amused themselves by beating it with sticks, until they had so irritated the hog that it ran and bit at every person within its reach.

I was no sooner seated in this my new habitation, than the Moors assembled in crowds to behold me; but I found it rather a troublesome levee, for I was obliged to take off one of my stockings, and show them my foot, and even to take off my jacket and waistcoat to show them how my clothes were put on and off; they were much delighted with the curious contrivance of buttons. All this was to be repeated to every succeeding visitor; for such as had already seen these wonders, insisted on their friends seeing the same; and in this manner I was employed, dressing and undressing, buttoning and unbuttoning, from noon to night. About eight o'clock, Ali sent me for supper some kouskous and salt and water, which was very acceptable, being the only victuals I had tasted since morning.

I observed that, in the night, the Moors kept regular watch, and frequently looked into the hut to see if I was asleep; and if it was quite dark, they would light a wisp of grass. About two o'clock in the morning, a Moor entered the hut, probably with a view to steal something, or perhaps to murder me; and groping about, he laid his hand upon my shoulder. As night visitors were at best but suspicious characters, I sprang up the moment he laid his hand upon me: and the Moor, in his haste to get off, stumbled over my boy, and fell with his face upon the wild hog, which returned the attack by biting the Moor's arm. The screams of this man alarmed the people in the king's tent, who immediately conjectured that I had made my escape, and a number of them mounted their horses, and prepared to pursue me. I observed upon this occasion that Ali did not sleep in his own tent, but came galloping up on a white horse from a small tent at a considerable distance: indeed, the tyrannical and cruel behaviour of this man made him so jealous of every person around him, that even his own slaves and domestics knew not where he slept. When the Moors had explained to him the cause of this outcry, they all went away, and I was permitted to sleep quietly until morning.

March 13*th.*—With the returning day commenced the same round of insult and irritation: the boys assembled to beat the hog, and the men and women to plague the Christian. It is impossible for me to describe the behaviour of a people who study mischief as a science, and exult in the miseries and misfortunes of their fellow-creatures. It is sufficient to observe that the rudeness, ferocity, and fanaticism, which distinguish the Moors from the rest of mankind, found here a proper subject whereon to exercise their propensities. I was a *stranger*, I was *unprotected*, and I was a *Christian;* each of these circumstances is sufficient to drive every spark of humanity from the heart of a Moor; but when all of them, as in my case, were combined in the same person, and a suspicion prevailed withal, that I had come as a *spy* into the country, the reader will easily imagine that, in such a situation, I had everything to fear. Anxious, however, to conciliate favour, and, if possible, to afford the Moors no pretence for ill treating me, I readily complied with every command, and patiently bore every insult; but never did any period of my life pass away so heavily: from sunrise to sunset was I obliged to suffer, with an unruffled countenance, the insults of the rudest savages on earth.

CHAPTER X

Various occurrences during the Author's confinement at Benowm—Is visited by some Moorish ladies—A funeral and wedding—The Author receives an extraordinary present from the bride—Other circumstances illustrative of the Moorish character and manners.

THE Moors, though very indolent themselves are rigid taskmasters, and keep every person under them in full employment. My boy Demba was sent to the woods to collect withered grass for Ali's horses; and, after a variety of projects concerning myself, they at last found out an employment for me; this was no other than the respectable office of *barber*. I was to make my first exhibition in this capacity in the royal presence, and to be honoured with the task of shaving the head of the young prince of Ludamar. I accordingly seated myself upon the sand, and the boy, with some hesitation, sat down beside me. A small razor, about three inches long, was put into my hand, and I was ordered to proceed; but whether from my own want of skill, or the improper shape of the instrument, I unfortunately made a slight incision in the boy's head, at the very commencement of the operation; and the king observing the awkward manner in which I held the razor, concluded that his son's head was in very improper hands, and ordered me to resign the razor, and walk out of the tent. This I considered as a very fortunate circumstance; for I had laid it down as a rule, to make myself as useless and insignificant as possible, as the only means of recovering my liberty.

March 18th.—Four Moors arrived from Jarra with Johnson, my interpreter, having seized him before he had received any intimation of my confinement: and bringing with them a bundle of clothes that I had left at Daman Jumma's house, for my use, in case I should return by the way of Jarra. Johnson was led into Ali's tent and examined; the bundle was opened, and I was sent for to explain the use of the different articles. I was happy, however, to find that Johnson had committed my papers to the charge of one of Daman's wives. When I had satisfied Ali's curiosity respecting the different articles of apparel, the bundle was again tied up, and put into a large cowskin bag, that stood in a corner of the tent. The same evening Ali sent three of his people to inform me, that there were many thieves in the neighbourhood, and that to prevent the rest of my things from being stolen, it was necessary to convey them all into his tent. My clothes, instruments, and everything that belonged to me, were accordingly carried away; and though the heat and dust made clean linen very necessary and refreshing, I could not procure a single shirt out of the small stock I had brought along with me. Ali was, however, disappointed, by not finding among my effects the quantity of gold and amber that he expected; but to make sure of everything, he sent the same people, on the morning following, to examine whether I had anything concealed about my person. They, with their usual rudeness, searched every part of my apparel, and stripped me of all my gold, amber, my watch, and one of my pocket compasses. I had fortunately, in the night, buried the other compass in the sand; and this, with the clothes I had on, was all that the tyranny of Ali had now left me.

The gold and amber were highly gratifying to Moorish avarice, but the pocket compass soon became an object of superstitious curiosity. Ali was very desirous to be informed why that small piece of iron, the needle, always pointed to the Great Desert; and I found myself somewhat puzzled to answer the question. To have pleaded my ignorance, would have created a suspicion that I wished to conceal the real truth from him; I therefore told him, that my mother resided far beyond the sands of Sahara, and that whilst she was alive the piece of iron would always point that way, and serve as a guide to conduct me to her, and that if she was dead, it would point to her grave. Ali now looked at the compass with redoubled amazement;

turned it round and round repeatedly; but observing that
it always pointed the same way, he took it up with great
caution, and returned it to me, manifesting that he thought
there was something of magic in it, and that he was afraid
of keeping so dangerous an instrument in his possession.

March 20th.—This morning a council of chief men was
held in Ali's tent respecting me; their decisions, though
they were all unfavourable to me, were differently related
by different persons. Some said that they intended to
put me to death; others, that I was only to lose my right
hand; but the most probable account was that which I
received from Ali's own son, a boy about nine years of age,
who came to me in the evening, and, with much concern,
informed me that his uncle had persuaded his father to put
out my eyes, which they said resembled those of a cat, and
that all the Bushreens had approved of this measure. His
father, however, he said, would not put the sentence into
execution until Fatima the queen, who was at present in the
north, had seen me.

March 21st.—Anxious to know my destiny, I went to the
king early in the morning; and as a number of Bushreens
were assembled, I thought this a favourable opportunity of
discovering their intentions. I therefore began by begging his permission to return to Jarra; which was flatly
refused; his wife, he said, had not yet seen me, and I must
stay until she came to Benowm, after which I should be at
liberty to depart; and that my horse, which had been
taken away from me the day after I arrived, should be
again restored to me. Unsatisfactory as this answer was,
I was forced to appear pleased; and as there was little
hopes of making my escape, at this season of the year, on
account of the excessive heat, and the total want of water
in the woods, I resolved to wait patiently until the rains
had set in, or until some more favourable opportunity
should present itself—but *hope deferred maketh the heart
sick.* This tedious procrastination from day to day, and
the thoughts of travelling through the Negro kingdoms in
the rainy season, which was now fast approaching, made
me very melancholy; and having passed a restless night,

I found myself attacked, in the morning, by a smart fever. I had wrapped myself close up in my cloak, with a view to induce perspiration, and was asleep when a party of Moors entered the hut, and, with their usual rudeness, pulled the cloak from me. I made signs to them that I was sick, and wished much to sleep; but I solicited in vain ; my distress was matter of sport to them, and they endeavoured to heighten it by every means in their power. This studied and degrading insolence, to which I was constantly exposed, was one of the bitterest ingredients in the cup of captivity, and often made life itself a burden to me. In these distressing moments I have frequently envied the situation of the slave, who, amidst all his calamities, could still possess the enjoyment of his own thoughts; a happiness to which I had for some time been a stranger. Wearied out with such continual insults, and perhaps a little peevish from the fever, I trembled lest my passion might unawares overleap the bounds of prudence, and spur me to some sudden act of resentment, when death must be the inevitable consequence. In this perplexity I left my hut, and walked to some shady trees at a little distance from the camp, where I lay down. But even here persecution followed me, and solitude was thought too great an indulgence for a distressed Christian. Ali's son, with a number of horsemen, came galloping to the place, and ordered me to rise and follow them. I begged they would allow me to remain where I was, if it was only for a few hours; but they paid little attention to what I said; and after a few threatening words, one of them pulled out a pistol from a leather bag, that was fastened to the pummel of his saddle, and presenting it towards me, snapped it twice. He did this with so much indifference, that I really doubted whether the pistol was loaded; he cocked it a third time, and was striking the flint with a piece of steel, when I begged them to desist, and returned with them to the camp. When we entered Ali's tent, we found him much out of humour. He called for the Moor's pistol, and amused himself for some time with opening and shutting the pan; at length, taking up his powder-horn, he fresh primed it ; and turning round to me with a menacing look, said something in Arabic, which I did not understand. I desired my boy, who was sitting before the tent, to inquire what offence I had committed; when I was informed that having gone out of the camp without Ali's permission, they suspected that I had some design of making my escape; and that in future, if I was seen without the skirts of the camp, orders had been given that I should be shot by the first person that observed me.

In the afternoon, the horizon, to the eastward, was thick and hazy, and the Moors prognosticated a sand wind; which accordingly commenced on the morning following, and lasted, with slight intermissions, for two days. The force of the wind was not in itself very great; it was what a seaman would have denominated a *stiff breeze;* but the quantity of sand and dust carried before it, was such as to darken the whole atmosphere. It swept along from east to west, in a thick and constant stream, and the air was at times so dark and full of sand, that it was difficult to discern the neighbouring tents. As the Moors always dress their victuals in the open air, this sand fell in great plenty among the kouskous; it readily adhered to the skin, when moistened by perspiration, and formed a cheap and universal hair-powder. The Moors wrap a cloth round their face to prevent them from inhaling the sand, and always turn their backs to the wind when they look up, to prevent the sand falling into their eyes.

About this time, all the women of the camp had their feet and the ends of their fingers, stained of a dark saffron colour. I could never ascertain whether this was done from motives of religion, or by way of ornament. The curiosity of the Moorish ladies had been very troublesome to me ever since my arrival at Benowm; and on the evening of the 25th (whether from the instigation of others, or impelled by their own ungovernable curiosity, or merely out of frolic, I cannot affirm), a party of them came into my hut, and gave me plainly to understand that the object of their visit was to ascertain, by actual inspection, whether the rite of circumcision extended to the Nazarenes (Christians), as well as to the followers of Mahomet. The reader

will easily judge of my surprise at this unexpected decla-
ration ; and in order to avoid the proposed scrutiny, I
thought it best to treat the business jocularly. I observed
to them, that it was not customary in my country to give
ocular demonstration in such cases, before so many beautiful women ; but that if all of them would retire, except
the young lady to whom I pointed (selecting the youngest
and handsomest), I would satisfy her curiosity. The ladies
enjoyed the jest, and went away laughing heartily and the
young damsel herself to whom I had given the preference
(though she did not avail herself of the privilege of inspection), seemed no way displeased at the compliment, for
she soon afterwards sent me some meal and milk for my
supper.

March 28th.—This morning a large herd of cattle arrived
from the eastward ; and one of the drivers, to whom Ali
had lent my horse, came into my hut with the leg of an
antelope as a present, and told me that my horse was
standing before Ali's tent. In a little time Ali sent one
of his slaves to inform me, that, in the afternoon, I must
be in readiness to ride out with him, as he intended to
show me to some of his women.

About four o'clock, Ali, with six of his courtiers, came
riding to my hut, and told me to follow them. I readily
complied. But here a new difficulty occurred. The Moors,
accustomed to a loose and easy dress, could not reconcile
themselves to the appearance of my *nankeen breeches*, which
they said were not only inelegant, but, on account of their
tightness, very indecent : and as this was a visit to ladies,
Ali ordered my boy to bring out the loose cloak which I
had always worn since my arrival at Benowm, and told
me to wrap it close round me. We visited the tents of
four different ladies, at every one of which I was presented with a bowl of milk and water. All these ladies
were remarkably corpulent, which is considered here as
the highest mark of beauty. They were very inquisitive,
and examined my hair and skin with great attention ; but
affected to consider me as a sort of inferior being to
themselves, and would knit their brows, and seemed to

shudder, when they looked at the whiteness of my skin. In the course of this evening's excursion, my dress and appearance afforded infinite mirth to the company, who galloped round me, as if they were baiting a wild animal; twirling their muskets round their heads, and exhibiting various feats of activity and horsemanship, seemingly to display their superior prowess over a miserable captive.

The Moors are certainly very good horsemen. They ride without fear; their saddles being high before and behind, afford them a very secure seat; and if they chance to fall, the whole country is so soft and sandy, that they are very seldom hurt. Their greatest pride, and one of their principal amusements, is to put the horse to his full speed, and then stop him with a sudden jerk, so as frequently to bring him down upon his haunches. Ali always rode upon a milk-white horse, with its tail dyed red. He never walked, unless when he went to say his prayers; and even in the night, two or three horses were always kept ready saddled, at a little distance from his own tent. The Moors set a very high value upon their horses; for it is by their superior fleetness that they are enabled to make so many predatory excursions into the Negro countries. They feed them three or four times a day, and generally give them a large quantity of sweet milk in the evening, which the horses appear to relish very much.

April 3rd.—This forenoon a child, which had been some time sickly, died in the next tent, and the mother and relations immediately began the death howl. They were joined by a number of female visitors, who came on purpose to assist at this melancholy concert. I had no opportunity of seeing the burial, which is generally performed secretly in the dusk of the evening, and frequently at only a few yards' distance from the tent. Over the grave, they plant one particular shrub; and no stranger is allowed to pluck a leaf, or even to touch it, so great a veneration have they for the dead.

April 7th.—About four o'clock in the afternoon, a whirlwind passed through the camp with such violence that it overturned three tents, and blew down one side of my hut. These whirlwinds come from the Great Desert, and at this season of the year are so common, that I have seen five or six of them at one time. They carry up quantities of sand to an amazing height, which resemble, at a distance, so many moving pillars of smoke.

The scorching heat of the sun upon a dry and sandy country makes the air insufferably hot. Ali having robbed me of my thermometer, I had no means of forming a comparative judgment; but in the middle of the day, when the beams of the vertical sun are seconded by the scorching wind from the Desert, the ground is frequently heated to such a degree, as not to be borne by the naked foot; even the Negro slaves will not run from one tent to another without their sandals. At this time of the day, the Moors lie stretched at length in their tents, either asleep, or unwilling to move; and I have often felt the wind so hot, that I could not hold my hand in the current of air, which came through the crevices of my hut, without feeling sensible pain.

April 8th.—This day the wind blew from the south-west, and in the night there was a heavy shower of rain, accompanied with thunder and lightning.

April 10th.—In the evening the tabala, or large drum, was beat to announce a wedding, which was held at one of the neighbouring tents. A great number of people of both sexes assembled, but without that mirth and hilarity which take place at a Negro wedding : here was neither singing nor dancing, nor any other amusement that I could perceive. A woman was beating the drum, and the other women joining at times like a chorus, by setting up a shrill scream, and at the same time moving their tongues from one side of the mouth to the other with great celerity. I was soon tired, and had returned into my hut, where I was sitting almost asleep, when an old woman entered, with a wooden bowl in her hand, and signified that she had brought me a present from the bride. Before I could recover from the surprise which this message created, the woman discharged the contents of the bowl full in my face. Finding that it was the same sort of holy water with which, among the Hottentots, a priest is said to sprinkle a new married couple, I began to suspect that the old lady was actuated by mischief, or malice; but she gave me seriously to understand that it was a nuptial benediction from the bride's own person, and which, on such occasions, is always received by the young unmarried Moors as a mark of distinguished favour. This being the case, I wiped my face, and sent my acknowledgments to the lady. The wedding drum continued to beat, and the women to sing, or rather whistle, all night. About nine in the morning, the bride was brought in state from her mother's tent, attended by a number of women who carried her tent (a present from the husband), some bearing up the poles, others holding by the strings; and in this manner they marched, whistling as formerly, until they came to the place appointed for her residence, where they pitched the tent. The husband followed, with a number of men leading four bullocks, which they tied to the tent strings; and having killed another, and distributed the beef among the people, the ceremony was concluded.

CHAPTER XI

Occurrences at the camp continued—Information collected by the
Author concerning Houssa and Timbuctoo ; and the situation of
the latter—The route described from Morocco to Benowm—The
Author's distress from hunger—Ali removes his camp to the
northward—The Author is carried prisoner to the new encampment, and is presented to Queen Fatima—Great distress from the
want of water.

ONE whole month had now elapsed since I was led into
captivity, during which time each returning day brought
me fresh distresses.   I watched the lingering course of the
sun with anxiety, and blessed his evening beams as they
shed a yellow lustre along the sandy floor of my hut ; for
it was then that my oppressors left me, and allowed me to
pass the sultry night in solitude and reflection.

About midnight a bowl of kouskous, with some salt and
water, was brought for me and my two attendants ; this
was our common fare, and it was all that was allowed us
to allay the cravings of hunger, and support nature for the
whole of the following day ; for it is to be observed that
this was the Mahomedan Lent ; and as the Moors keep
the fast with a religious strictness, they thought it proper
to compel me, though a Christian, to a similar observance.
Time, however, somewhat reconciled me to my situation.
I found that I could bear hunger and thirst better than
I expected ; and at length I endeavoured to beguile the
tedious hours by learning to write Arabic. The people
who came to see me, soon made me acquainted with the
characters ; and I discovered, that by engaging their attention in this way, they were not so troublesome as otherwise they would have been.   Indeed, when I observed any
person whose countenance I thought bore malice towards
me, I made it a rule to ask him, either to write in the
sand himself, or to decipher what I had already written,

and the pride of showing his superior attainments generally induced him to comply with my request.

April 14*th.*—As Queen Fatima had not yet arrived, Ali proposed to go to the north, and bring her back with him ; but as the place was two days' journey from Benowm, it was necessary to have some refreshment on the road ; and Ali, suspicious of those about him, was so afraid of being poisoned, that he never ate anything but what was dressed under his own immediate inspection. A fine bullock was therefore killed, and the flesh being cut up into thin slices, was dried in the sun : and this with two bags of dry kouskous, formed his travelling provisions.

Previous to his departure the black people of the town of Benowm came, according to their annual custom, to show their arms, and bring their stipulated tribute of corn and cloth. They were but badly armed : twenty-two with muskets, forty or fifty with bows and arrows, and nearly the same number of men and boys, with spears only. They arranged themselves before the tent, where they waited until their arms were examined and some little disputes settled.

About midnight on the 16th, Ali departed quietly from Benowm, accompanied by a few attendants. He was expected to return in the course of nine or ten days.

April 18*th.*—Two days after the departure of Ali, a Shereef arrived with salt and some other articles from Walet, the capital of the kingdom of Biroo. As there was no tent appropriated for him, he took up his abode in the same hut with me. He seemed to be a well-informed man, and his acquaintance both with the Arabic and Bambarra tongues enabled him to travel with ease and safety through a number of kingdoms; for though his place of residence was Walet, he had visited Houssa, and had lived some years at Timbuctoo. Upon my inquiring so particularly about the distance from Walet to Timbuctoo, he asked me if I intended to travel that way; and being answered in the affirmative, he shook his head, and said, *it would not do ;* for that Christians were looked upon there as the devil's children, and enemies to the Prophet. From him I learned the following particulars:—That Houssa was the largest town he had ever seen; that Walet was larger than Timbuctoo; but being remote from the Niger, and its trade consisting chiefly of salt, it was not so much resorted to by strangers; that between Benowm and Walet was ten days' journey; but the road did not lead through any remarkable towns, and travellers supported themselves by purchasing milk from the Arabs who keep their herds by the watering places; two of the day's journeys were over a sandy country, without water. From Walet to Timbuctoo was eleven days more; but water was more plentiful, and the journey was usually performed upon bullocks. He said there were many Jews at Timbuctoo, but they all spoke Arabic, and used the same prayers as the Moors. He frequently pointed his hand to the south-east quarter, or rather the east by south, observing that Timbuctoo was situated in that direction; and though I made him repeat this information again and again, I never found him to vary more than half a point, which was to the southward.

April 24th.—This morning Shereef Sidi Mahomed Moora Abdalla, a native of Morocco, arrived with five bullocks loaded with salt. He had formerly resided some months at Gibraltar, where he had picked up as much English as enabled him to make himself understood. He informed me, that he had been five months in coming from Santa Cruz; but that great part of the time had been spent in trading. When I requested him to enumerate the days employed in travelling from Morocco to Benowm, he gave them as follows:—To Swera, three days; to Agadier, three; to Jiniken, ten; to Wadenoon, four; to Lakeneigh, five; to Zeeriwin-zeriman, five; to Tisheet, ten; to Benowm, ten; in all, fifty days; but travellers usually rest a long while at Jiniken and Tisheet, at the latter of which places they dig the rock salt, which is so great an article of commerce with the Negroes.

In conversing with these Shereefs and the different strangers that resorted to the camp, I passed my time with rather less uneasiness than formerly. On the other hand, as the dressing of my victuals was now left entirely to the care of Ali's slaves, over whom I had not the smallest control, I found myself but ill supplied, worse even than in the fast month ; for two successive nights they neglected to send us our accustomed meal ; and though my boy went to a small Negro town near the camp, and begged with great diligence from hut to hut, he could only procure a few handfuls of ground nuts, which he readily shared with me. Hunger, at first, is certainly a very painful sensation, but when it has continued for some time, this pain is succeeded by languor and debility ; in which case, a draught of water, by keeping the stomach distended, will greatly exhilarate the spirits, and remove for a short time every sort of uneasiness. Johnson and Demba were very much dejected. They lay stretched upon the sand, in a sort of torpid slumber; and even when the kouskous arrived, I found some difficulty in awakening them. I felt no inclination to sleep, but was affected with a deep convulsive respiration, like constant sighing, and, what alarmed me still more, a dimness of sight, and a tendency to faint when I attempted to sit up. These symptoms did not go off until some time after I had received nourishment.

We had been for some days in daily expectation of Ali's return from Saheel (or the north country) with his wife Fatima. In the meanwhile Mansong, king of Bambarra, as I have related in Chapter VIII., had sent to Ali for a party of horse to assist in storming Gedingooma. With this demand Ali had not only refused to comply, but had treated the messengers with great haughtiness and contempt ; upon which Mansong gave up all thoughts of taking the town, and prepared to chastise Ali for his contumacy.

Things were in this situation, when, on the 29th of April, a messenger arrived at Benowm with the disagreeable intelligence that the Bambarra army was approaching the frontiers of Ludamar. This threw the whole country into confusion ; and in the afternoon Ali's son, with about twenty horsemen, arrived at Benowm. He ordered all the cattle to be driven away immediately, all the tents to be struck, and the people to hold themselves in readiness to depart at daylight the next morning.

April 30th.—At daybreak the whole camp was in motion. The baggage was carried upon bullocks, the two tent poles being placed one on each side, and the different wooden articles of the tent distributed in like manner; the tent cloth was thrown over all, and upon this was commonly placed one or two women, for the Moorish women are very bad walkers. The king's favourite concubines rode upon camels, with a saddle of a particular construction, and a canopy to shelter them from the sun. We proceeded to the northward until noon, when the king's son ordered the whole company, except two tents, to enter a thick low wood, which was upon our right. I was sent along with the two tents, and arrived in the evening at a Negro town called Farani; here we pitched the tents in an open place, at no great distance from the town.

The hurry and confusion which attended this decampment prevented the slaves from dressing the usual quantity of victuals; and lest their dry provisions should be exhausted before they reached their place of destination (for as yet none but Ali and the chief men knew whither we were going), they thought proper to make me observe this day as a day of fasting.

May 1st.—As I had some reason to suspect that this day was also to be considered as a fast, I went in the morning to the Negro town of Farani, and begged some provisions from the Dooty, who readily supplied my wants, and desired me to come to his house every day during my stay in the neighbourhood. These hospitable people are looked upon by the Moors as an abject race of slaves, and are treated accordingly. Two of Ali's household slaves, a man and a woman, who had come along with the two tents, went this morning to water the cattle from the town wells, at which there began to be a great scarcity. When the Negro women observed the cattle approaching, they took up their pitchers and ran with all possible haste towards the town; but before they could enter the gate, they were stopped by the slaves, who compelled them to bring back the water they had drawn for their own families, and empty it into the troughs for the cattle. When this was exhausted, they were ordered to draw water until such time as the cattle had all drank; and the woman slave actually broke two wooden bowls over the heads of the black girls, because they were somewhat dilatory in obeying her commands.

May 3rd.—We departed from the vicinity of Farani, and after a circuitous route through the woods, arrived at Ali's camp in the afternoon. This encampment was larger than that of Benowm, and was situated in the middle of a thick wood about two miles distant from a Negro town, called Bubaker. I immediately waited upon Ali, in order to pay my respects to Queen Fatima, who had come with him from Saheel. He seemed much pleased with my coming; shook hands with me, and informed his wife that I was the Christian. She was a woman of the Arab cast, with long black hair, and remarkably corpulent. She appeared at first rather shocked at the thought of having a Christian so near her; but when I had (by means of a Negro boy, who spoke the Mandingo and Arabic tongues) answered a great many questions, which her curiosity suggested, respecting the country of the Christians, she seemed more at ease, and presented me with a bowl of milk, which I considered as a very favourable omen.

The heat was now almost insufferable; all nature seemed sinking under it. The distant country presented to the eye a dreary expanse of sand, with a few stunted trees and prickly bushes, in the shade of which the hungry cattle licked up the withered grass, while the camels and goats picked off the scanty foliage. The scarcity of water was greater here than at Benowm. Day and night the wells were crowded with cattle, lowing and fighting with each other to come at the troughs; excessive thirst made many of them furious; others, being too weak to contend for the water, endeavoured to quench their thirst by devouring the black mud from the gutters near the wells; which they did with great avidity, though it was commonly fatal to them.

This great scarcity of water was felt severely by all the people of the camp, and by none more than myself; for though Ali allowed me a skin for containing water, and

Fatima, once or twice, gave me a small supply when I was in distress, yet such was the barbarous disposition of the Moors at the wells, that when my boy attempted to fill the skin, he commonly received a sound drubbing for his presumption. Every one was astonished that the slave of a Christian should attempt to draw water from wells which had been dug by the followers of the Prophet. This treatment at length so frightened the boy that I believe he would sooner have perished with thirst than attempted again to fill the skin. He therefore contented himself with begging water from the Negro slaves that attended the camp, and I followed his example, but with very indifferent success; for though I let no opportunity slip, and was very urgent in my solicitations, both to the Moors and the Negroes, I was but ill supplied, and frequently passed the night in the situation of Tantalus. No sooner had I shut my eyes than fancy would convey me to the streams and rivers of my native land; there, as I wandered along the verdant brink, I surveyed the clear stream with transport, and hastened to swallow the delightful draught;—but alas! disappointment awakened me, and I found myself a lonely captive, perishing of thirst, amidst the wilds of Africa.

One night, having solicited in vain for water at the camp, and being quite feverish, I resolved to try my fortune at the wells, which were about half a mile distant from the camp. Accordingly, I set out about midnight, and being guided by the lowing of the cattle, soon arrived at the place, where I found the Moors very busy drawing water. I requested permission to drink, but was driven away with outrageous abuse. Passing, however, from one well to another, I came at last to one where there was only an old man and two boys. I made the same request to this man, and he immediately drew me up a bucket of water; but, as I was about to take hold of it, he recollected that I was a Christian, and fearing that his bucket might be polluted by my lips, he dashed the water into the trough, and told me to drink from thence. Though this trough was none of the largest, and three cows were already drinking in it, I resolved to come in for my share; and kneeling down, thrust my head between two of the cows, and drank with great pleasure, until the water was nearly exhausted, and the cows began to contend with each other for the last mouthful.

In adventures of this nature I passed the sultry month of May, during which no material change took place in my situation. Ali still considered me as a lawful prisoner ; and Fatima, though she allowed me a larger quantity of victuals than I had been accustomed to receive at Benowm, had as yet said nothing on the subject of my release. In the meantime the frequent changes of the wind, the gathering clouds, and distant lightning, with other appearances of approaching rain, indicated that the wet season was at hand ; when the Moors annually evacuate the country of the Negroes, and return to the skirts of the Great Desert. This made me consider that my fate was drawing towards a crisis, and I resolved to wait for the event without any seeming uneasiness ; but circumstances occurred which pro-duced a change in my favour more suddenly than I had foreseen, or had reason to expect. The case was this : the fugitive Kaartans, who had taken refuge in Ludamar, as I have related in Chapter VIII., finding that the Moors were about to leave them, and dreading the resentment of their own sovereign, whom they had so basely deserted, offered to treat with Ali for two hundred Moorish horsemen to co-operate with them in an effort to expel Daisy from Gedin-gooma ; for until Daisy should be vanquished or humbled, they considered that they could neither return to their native towns, nor live in security in any of the neighbouring king-doms. With a view to extort money from these people, by means of this treaty, Ali dispatched his son to Jarra, and prepared to follow him in the course of a few days. This was an opportunity of too great consequence to me to be neglected. I immediately applied to Fatima (who, I found, had the chief direction in all affairs of state), and begged her interest with Ali, to give me permission to accompany him to Jarra. This request, after some hesitation, was favourably received. Fatima looked kindly on me, and, I believe, was at length moved with compassion towards me. My bundles were brought from the large cowskin bag that stood in the corner of Ali's tent, and I was ordered to explain the use of the different articles, and show the method of putting on the boots, stockings, etc., with all which I cheerfully complied, and was told that, in the course of a few days, I should be at liberty to depart.

Believing, therefore, that I should certainly find the means of escaping from Jarra, if I should once get thither, I now freely indulged the pleasing hope that my captivity would soon terminate; and happily not having been disappointed in this idea, I shall pause in this place to collect and bring into one point of view such observations on the Moorish character and country, as I had no fair opportunity of introducing into the preceding narrative.

CHAPTER XII

Containing some further miscellaneous reflections on the Moorish character and manners—Observations concerning the Great Desert, its animals, wild and domestic, etc. etc.

THE Moors of this part of Africa are divided into many separate tribes; of which the most formidable, according to what was reported to me, are those of Trasart and Il Braken, which inhabit the northern bank of the Senegal river. The tribes of Gedumah, Jafnoo, and Ludamar, though not so numerous as the former, are nevertheless very powerful and warlike, and are each governed by a chief, or king, who exercises absolute jurisdiction over his own horde, without acknowledging allegiance to a common sovereign. In time of peace the employment of the people is pasturage. The Moors, indeed, subsist chiefly on the flesh of their cattle, and are always in the extreme of either gluttony or abstinence. In consequence of the frequent and severe fasts which their religion enjoins, and the toilsome journeys which they sometimes undertake across the Desert, they are enabled to bear both hunger and thirst with surprising fortitude ; but whenever opportunities occur of satisfying their appetite, they generally devour more at one meal than would serve a European for three. They pay but little attention to agriculture, purchasing their corn, cotton cloth, and other necessaries from the Negroes, in exchange for salt, which they dig from the pits in the Great Desert.

The natural barrenness of the country is such, that it furnishes but few materials for manufacture. The Moors, however, contrive to weave a strong cloth, with which they cover their tents; the thread is spun by their women from the hair of goats, and they prepare the hides of their cattle so as to furnish saddles, bridles, pouches, and other articles

of leather.　They are likewise sufficiently skilful to convert
the native iron, which they procure from the Negroes, into
spears and knives, and also into pots for boiling their food ;
but their sabres and other weapons, as well as their fire-arms
and ammunition, they purchase from the Europeans in exchange for the Negro slaves which they obtain in their
predatory excursions.　Their chief commerce of this kind
is with the French traders on the Senegal river.

The Moors are rigid Mahomedans, and possess, with the
bigotry and superstition, all the intolerance of their sect.
They have no mosques at Benowm, but perform their
devotions in a sort of open shed, or inclosure made of mats.
The priest is at the same time schoolmaster to the juniors.
His pupils assemble every evening before his tent, where,
by the light of a large fire made of brushwood and cow's
dung, they are taught a few sentences from the Koran, and
are initiated into the principles of their creed.　Their
alphabet differs but little from that in Richardson's Arabic
Grammar.　They always write with the vowel points.　Their
priests even affect to know something of foreign literature.
The priest of Benowm assured me that he could read the
writings of the Christians.　He showed me a number of
barbarous characters, which he asserted were the Roman
alphabet; and he produced another specimen, equally unintelligible, which he declared to be the *Kallam il Indi*, or
Persian.　His library consisted of nine volumes in quarto ;
most of them, I believe, were books of religion, for the
name of Mahomet appeared in red letters in almost every
page of each.　His scholars wrote their lessons upon thin
boards, paper being too expensive for general use.　The
boys were diligent enough, and appeared to possess a
considerable share of emulation, carrying their boards
slung over their shoulders when about their common em-
ployments.　When a boy has committed to memory a few
of their prayers, and can read and write certain parts of
the Koran, he is reckoned sufficiently instructed, and with
this slender stock of learning, commences his career of life.
Proud of his acquirements, he surveys with contempt the
unlettered Negro, and embraces every opportunity of dis-

playing his superiority over such of his countrymen as are not distinguished by the same accomplishments.

The education of the girls is neglected altogether; mental accomplishments are but little attended to by the women, nor is the want of them considered by the men as a defect in the female character. They are regarded, I believe, as an inferior species of animals, and seem to be brought up for no other purpose than that of administering to the sensual pleasures of their imperious masters. Voluptuousness is, therefore, considered as their chief accomplishment, and slavish submission as their indispensable duty.

The Moors have singular ideas of feminine perfection. The gracefulness of figure and motion, and a countenance enlivened by expression, are by no means essential points in their standard; with them, corpulence and beauty appear to be terms nearly synonymous. A woman, of even moderate pretensions, must be one who cannot walk without a slave under each arm to support her, and a perfect beauty is a load for a camel. In consequence of this prevalent taste for unwieldiness of bulk, the Moorish ladies take great pains to acquire it early in life; and for this purpose, many of the young girls are compelled by their mothers to devour a great quantity of kouskous, and drink a large bowl of camel's milk every morning. It is of no importance whether the girl has an appetite or not, the kouskous and milk must be swallowed, and obedience is frequently enforced by blows. I have seen a poor girl sit crying, with a bowl at her lips, for more than an hour, and her mother, with a stick in her hand, watching her all the while, and using the stick without mercy, whenever she observed that her daughter was not swallowing. This singular practice, instead of producing indigestion and disease, soon covers the young lady with that degree of plumpness which, in the eye of a Moor, is perfection itself.

As the Moors purchase all their clothing from the Negroes, the women are forced to be very economical in the article of dress. In general they content themselves with a broad piece of cotton cloth, which is wrapped round the middle, and hangs round like a petticoat almost to the ground; to the upper part of this are sewed two square pieces, one before and the other behind, which are fastened together over the shoulders. The head-dress is commonly a bandage of cotton cloth, with some parts of it broader than others, which serve to conceal the face when they walk in the sun; frequently, however, when they go abroad, they veil themselves from head to foot.

The employment of the women varies, according to their degrees of opulence. Queen Fatima, and a few others of high rank, like the great ladies in some parts of Europe, pass their time chiefly in conversing with their visitors, performing their devotions, or admiring their charms in a looking-glass. The women of inferior class employ themselves in different domestic duties. They are very vain and talkative, and when anything puts them out of humour, they commonly vent their anger upon their female slaves, over whom they rule with severe and despotic authority, which leads me to observe, that the condition of these poor captives is deplorably wretched. At daybreak they are compelled to fetch water from the wells in large skins called *girbas*; and as soon as they have brought water enough to serve the family for the day, as well as the horses (for the Moors seldom give their horses the trouble of going to the wells), they are then employed in pounding the corn and dressing the victuals. This being always done in the open air, the slaves are exposed to the combined heat of the sun, the sand, and the fire. In the intervals, it is their business to sweep the tent, churn the milk, and perform other domestic offices. With all this they are badly fed, and oftentimes cruelly punished.

The men's dress among the Moors of Ludamar differs but little from that of the Negroes (which has been already described), except that they have all adopted that characteristic of the Mahomedan sect. the *turban*; which is here universally made of white cotton cloth. Such of the Moors as have long beards, display them with a mixture of pride and satisfaction, as denoting an Arab ancestry. Of this number was Ali himself; but among the generality of the people the hair is short and bushy, and universally black.

And here I may be permitted to observe, that if any one circumstance excited among them favourable thoughts towards my own person, it was my beard, which was now grown to an enormous length, and was always beheld with approbation or envy. I believe in my conscience they thought it too good a beard for a Christian.

The only diseases which I observed to prevail among the Moors, were the intermittent fever and dysentery, for the cure of which nostrums are sometimes administered by their old women; but, in general, nature is left to her own operations. Mention was made to me of the small-pox as being sometimes very destructive; but it had not, to my knowledge, made its appearance in Ludamar while I was in captivity. That it prevails, however, among some tribes of the Moors, and that it is frequently conveyed by them to the Negroes in the southern states, I was assured on the authority of Dr. Laidley, who also informed me that the Negroes on the Gambia practise inoculation.

The administration of criminal justice, as far as I had opportunities of observing, was prompt and decisive. For, although civil rights were but little regarded in Ludamar, it was necessary, when crimes were committed, that examples should sometimes be made. On such occasions the offender was brought before Ali, who pronounced, of his sole authority, what judgment he thought proper. But I understood that capital punishment was seldom or never inflicted, except on the Negroes.

Although the wealth of the Moors consist chiefly in their numerous herds of cattle, yet, as the pastoral life does not afford full employment, the majority of the people are perfectly idle, and spend the day in trifling conversation about their horses, or in laying schemes of depredation on the Negro villages.

The usual place of rendezvous for the indolent is the king's tent, where great liberty of speech seems to be exercised by the company towards each other, while in speaking of their chief they express but one opinion. In praise of their sovereign they are unanimous. Songs are composed in his honour, which the company frequently sing in concert; but they are so loaded with gross adulation that no man but a Moorish despot could hear them without blushing. The king is distinguished by the fineness of his dress, which is composed of blue cotton cloth, brought from Timbuctoo, or white linen or muslin from Morocco. He has likewise a larger tent than any other person, with a white cloth over it; but in his usual intercourse with his subjects, all distinctions of rank are frequently forgotten. He sometimes eats out of the same bowl with his camel driver, and reposes himself during the heat of the day upon the same bed. The expenses of his government and household are defrayed by a tax upon his Negro subjects, which is paid by every householder, either in corn, cloth, or gold dust; a tax upon the different Moorish korrees, or watering places, which is commonly levied in cattle; and a tax upon all merchandise which passes through the kingdom, and is generally collected in kind. But a considerable part of the king's revenue arises from the plunder of individuals. The Negro inhabitants of Ludamar, and the travelling merchants, are afraid of appearing rich; for Ali, who has spies stationed in the different towns to give him information concerning the wealth of his subjects, frequently invents some frivolous plea for seizing their property, and reducing the opulent to a level with their fellow-citizens.

Of the number of Ali's Moorish subjects I had no means of forming a correct estimate. The military strength of Ludamar consists in cavalry. They are well mounted, and appear to be very expert in skirmishing and attacking by surprise. Every soldier furnishes his own horse, and finds his accoutrements, consisting of a large sabre, a double-barrelled gun, a small red leather bag for holding his balls, and a powder horn slung over the shoulder. He has no pay, nor any remuneration but what arises from plunder. This body is not very numerous; for when Ali made war upon Bambarra, I was informed that his whole force did not exceed two thousand cavalry. They constitute, however, by what I could learn, but a very small proportion of his Moorish subjects. The horses are very beautiful, and so highly esteemed that the Negro princes will sometimes give from twelve to fourteen slaves for one horse.

Ludamar has for its northern boundary the Great Desert of Sahara. From the best inquiries I could make, this vast ocean of sand, which occupies so large a space in Northern Africa, may be pronounced almost destitute of inhabitants, except where the scanty vegetation which appears in certain spots affords pasturage for the flocks of a few miserable Arabs, who wander from one well to another. In other places, where the supply of water and pasturage is more abundant, small parties of the Moors have taken up their residence. Here they live in independent poverty, secure from the tyrannical government of Barbary. But the greater part of the Desert, being totally destitute of water, is seldom visited by any human being, unless where the trading caravans trace out their toilsome and dangerous route across it. In some parts of this extensive waste, the ground is covered with low stunted shrubs, which serve as landmarks for the caravans, and furnish the camels with a scanty forage. In other parts the disconsolate wanderer, wherever he turns, sees nothing around him but a vast interminable expanse of sand and sky — a gloomy and barren void, where the eye finds no particular object to rest upon, and the mind is filled with painful apprehensions of perishing with thirst. "Surrounded by this dreary solitude, the traveller sees the dead bodies of birds that the violence of the wind has brought from happier regions; and as he ruminates on the fearful length of his remaining passage, listens with horror to the voice of the driving blast, the only sound that interrupts the awful repose of the Desert." [1]

The few wild animals which inhabit these melancholy regions are the antelope and the ostrich, their swiftness of foot enabling them to reach the distant watering places. On the skirts of the Desert, where water is more plentiful, are found lions, panthers, elephants, and wild boars.

Of domestic animals, the only one that can endure the fatigue of crossing the desert is the camel. By the par-

[1] Proceedings of the African Association, Part I.

ticular conformation of the stomach, he is enabled to carry a supply of water sufficient for ten or twelve days; his broad and yielding foot is well adapted for a sandy country; and by a singular motion of his upper lip, he picks the smallest leaves from the thorny shrubs of the Desert as he passes along.   The camel is, therefore, the only beast of burthen employed by the trading caravans which traverse the Desert in different directions from Barbary to Nigritia.   As this useful and docile creature has been sufficiently described by systematical writers, it is unnecessary for me to enlarge upon its properties.   I shall only add, that his flesh, though to my own taste dry and unsavoury, is preferred by the Moors to any other; and that the milk of the female is in universal esteem, and is indeed sweet, pleasant, and nutritive.

I have observed that the Moors, in their complexion, resemble the Mulattoes of the West Indies; but they have something unpleasant in their aspect, which the Mulattoes have not.   I fancied that I discovered in the features of most of them a disposition towards cruelty and low cunning; and I could never contemplate their physiognomy without feeling sensible uneasiness.   From the staring wildness of their eyes, a stranger would immediately set them down as a nation of lunatics.   The treachery and malevolence of their character are manifested in their plundering excursions against the Negro villages.   Oftentimes, without the smallest provocation, and sometimes, under the fairest professions of friendship, they will suddenly seize upon the Negroes' cattle, and even on the inhabitants themselves.   The Negroes very seldom retaliate. The enterprising boldness of the Moors, their knowledge of the country, and, above all, the superior fleetness of their horses, make them such formidable enemies, that the petty Negro states which border upon the Desert are in continual terror while the Moorish tribes are in the vicinity, and are too much awed to think of resistance.

Like the roving Arabs, the Moors frequently remove from one place to another, according to the season of the year, or the convenience of pasturage.   In the month of

February, when the heat of the sun scorches up every sort of vegetation in the Desert, they strike their tents, and approach the Negro country to the south; where they reside until the rains commence in the month of July. At this time, having purchased corn and other necessaries from the Negroes, in exchange for salt, they again depart to the northward, and continue in the Desert until the rains are over, and that part of the country becomes burnt up and barren.

This wandering and restless way of life, while it inures them to hardships, strengthens, at the same time, the bonds of their little society, and creates in them an aversion towards strangers, which is almost insurmountable. Cut off from all intercourse with civilised nations, and boasting an advantage over the Negroes, by possessing, though in a very limited degree, the knowledge of letters, they are at once the vainest and proudest, and perhaps the most bigoted, ferocious, and intolerant of all the nations on the earth—combining in their character, the blind superstition of the Negro with the savage cruelty and treachery of the Arab.

It is probable that many of them had never beheld a white man before my arrival at Benowm; but they had all been taught to regard the Christian name with inconceivable abhorrence, and to consider it nearly as lawful to murder a European as it would be to kill a dog. The melancholy fate of Major Houghton, and the treatment I experienced during my confinement among them, will, I trust, serve as a warning to future travellers to avoid this inhospitable district.

The reader may probably have expected from me a more detailed and copious account of the manners, customs, superstitions, and prejudices of this secluded and singular people; but it must not be forgotten, that the wretchedness of my situation among them afforded me but few opportunities of collecting information. Some particulars, however, might be added in this place; but being equally applicable to the Negroes of the southward, they will appear in a subsequent page.

CHAPTER XIII

Ali departs for Jarra, and the Author allowed to follow him thither— The Author's faithful servant, Demba, seized by Ali's order, and sent back into slavery—Ali returns to his camp, and permits the Author to remain at Jarra, who, thenceforward, meditates his escape—Daisy, King of Kaarta, approaching with his army towards Jarra, the inhabitants quit the town, and the Author accompanies them in their flight—A party of Moors overtake him at Queira—He gets away from them at daybreak—Is again pursued by another party and robbed; but finally effects his escape.

HAVING, as hath been related, obtained permission to accompany Ali to Jarra, I took leave of Queen Fatima, who, with much grace and civility, returned me part of my apparel; and the evening before my departure, my horse, with the saddle and bridle, were sent me by Ali's orders.

Early on the morning of the 26th of May, I departed from the camp of Bubaker, accompanied by my two attendants, Johnson and Demba, and a number of Moors on horseback; Ali, with about fifty horsemen, having gone privately from the camp during the night. We stopped about noon at Farani, and were there joined by twelve Moors riding upon camels, and with them we proceeded to a watering place in the woods, where we overtook Ali and his fifty horsemen. They were lodged in some low shepherds' tents near the wells. As the company was numerous, the tents could scarcely accommodate us all; and I was ordered to sleep in the open space in the centre of the tents, where every one might observe my motions. During the night there was much lightning from the north-east; and about daybreak a very heavy sand-wind commenced, which continued with great violence until four in the afternoon. The quantity of sand which passed to the westward, in the course of this day, must have been prodigiously great. At times it was impossible to look up; and the cattle were so tormented by the particles lodging in their ears and eyes, that they ran about like mad creatures, and I was in continual danger of being trampled to death by them.

May 28th.—Early in the morning the Moors saddled their horses, and Ali's chief slave ordered me to get in readiness. In a little time the same messenger returned, and taking my boy by the shoulders, told him, in the Mandingo language, that "Ali was to be his master in future"; and then turning to me, "The business is settled at last (said he); the boy, and everything but your horse, goes back to Bubaker; but you may take the old fool (meaning Johnson, the interpreter) with you to Jarra." I made him no answer; but being shocked beyond description at the idea of losing the poor boy, I hastened to Ali, who was at breakfast before his tent, surrounded by many of his courtiers. I told him (perhaps in rather too passionate a strain), that whatever imprudence I had been guilty of in coming into his country, I thought I had already been sufficiently punished for it by being so long detained, and then plundered of all my little property, which, however, gave me no uneasiness, when compared with what he had just now done to me. I observed that the boy which he had now seized upon was not a slave, and had been accused of no offence; he was indeed one of my attendants, and his faithful services in that station had procured him his freedom; his fidelity and attachment had made him follow me into my present situation; and as he looked up to me for protection, I could not see him deprived of his liberty without remonstrating against such an act, as the height of cruelty and injustice. Ali made no reply, but with a haughty air and malignant smile, told his interpreter, that if I did not mount my horse immediately, he would send me back likewise. There is something in the frown of a tyrant which rouses the most secret emotions of the heart; I could not suppress my feelings, and for once entertained an indignant wish to rid the world of such a monster.

Poor Demba was not less affected than myself; he had formed a strong attachment towards me, and had a cheerfulness of disposition which often beguiled the tedious

hours of captivity; he was likewise a proficient in the
Bambarra tongue, and promised on that account to be of
great utility to me in future.   But it was in vain to expect
anything favourable to humanity from people who are
strangers to its dictates. So having shaken hands with
this unfortunate boy, and blended my tears with his,
assuring him, however, that I would do my utmost to
redeem him, I saw him led off by three of Ali's slaves
towards the camp at Bubaker.

When the Moors had mounted their horses, I was
ordered to follow them; and after a toilsome journey
through the woods, in a very sultry day, we arrived in the
afternoon at a walled village, called Doombani; where we
remained two days, waiting for the arrival of some horsemen from the northward.

On the 1st of June we departed from Doombani towards
Jarra.   Our company now amounted to two hundred men,
all on horseback; for the Moors never use infantry in their
wars.   They appeared capable of enduring great fatigue;
but from their total want of discipline, our journey to Jarra
was more like a fox-chase than the march of an army.

At Jarra I took up my lodging at the house of my old
acquaintance Daman Jumma, and informed him of everything that had befallen me. I particularly requested him
to use his interest with Ali to redeem my boy, and promised
him a bill upon Dr. Laidley for the value of two slaves, the
moment he brought him to Jarra. Daman very readily
undertook to negotiate the business; but found that Ali
considered the boy as my principal interpreter, and was
unwilling to part with him, lest he should fall a second
time into my hands, and be instrumental in conducting me
to Bambarra. Ali therefore put off the matter from day to
day; but withal told Daman that if he wished to purchase
the boy for himself, he should have him thereafter at the
common price of a slave; which Daman agreed to pay for
him whenever Ali should send him to Jarra.

The chief object of Ali in this journey to Jarra, as I have
already related, was to procure money from such of the
Kaartans as had taken refuge in his country. Some of

these had solicited his protection, to avoid the horrors of war; but by far the greatest number of them were dissatisfied men, who wished the ruin of their own sovereign. These people no sooner heard that the Bambarran army had returned to Sego without subduing Daisy, as was generally expected, than they resolved to make a sudden attack themselves upon him, before he could recruit his forces, which were now known to be much diminished by a bloody campaign, and in great want of provisions. With this view they solicited the Moors to join them, and offered to hire of Ali two hundred horsemen, which Ali, with the warmest professions of friendship, agreed to furnish, upon condition that they should previously supply him with four hundred head of cattle, two hundred garments of blue cloth, and a considerable quantity of beads and ornaments. The raising this impost somewhat perplexed them; and in order to procure the cattle, they persuaded the king to demand one-half the stipulated number from the people of Jarra, promising to replace them in a short time. Ali agreed to this proposal; and the same evening (June 2nd) the drum was sent through the town, and the crier announced that if any person suffered his cattle to go into the woods, the next morning, before the king had chosen his quota of them, his house should be plundered, and his slaves taken from him. The people dared not disobey the proclamation; and next morning about two hundred of their best cattle were selected, and delivered to the Moors; the full complement was made up afterwards by means equally unjust and arbitrary.

June 8th.—In the afternoon Ali sent his chief slave to inform me that he was about to return to Bubaker; but as he would only stay there a few days, to keep the approaching festival (*Banna Salee*), and then return to Jarra, I had permission to remain with Daman until his return. This was joyful news to me; but I had experienced so many disappointments that I was unwilling to indulge the hope of its being true, until Johnson came and told me that Ali, with part of the horsemen, were actually gone from the town, and that the rest were to follow him in the morning.

June 9th.—Early in the morning the remainder of the Moors departed from the town. They had, during their stay, committed many acts of robbery; and this morning, with the most unparalleled audacity, they seized upon three girls who were bringing water from the wells, and carried them away into slavery.

The anniversary of *Banna Salee*, at Jarra, very well deserved to be called a festival. The slaves were all finely clad on this occasion, and the householders vied with each other in providing large quantities of victuals, which they distributed to all their neighbours with the greatest profusion; hunger was literally banished from the town; man, woman, and child, bond and free, all had as much as they could eat.

June 12th.—Two people, dreadfully wounded, were discovered at a watering place in the woods : one of them had just breathed his last, but the other was brought alive to Jarra. On recovering a little, he informed the people, that he had fled through the woods from Kasson; that Daisy had made war upon Sambo, the king of that country; had surprised three of his towns, and put all the inhabitants to the sword. He enumerated by name many of the friends of the Jarra people, who had been murdered in Kasson. This intelligence made the death howl universal in Jarra for the space of two days.

This piece of bad news was followed by another, not less distressing. A number of runaway slaves arrived from Kaarta on the 14th, and reported that Daisy, having received information concerning the intended attack upon him, was about to visit Jarra. This made the Negroes call upon Ali for the two hundred horsemen which he was to furnish them, according to engagement. But Ali paid very little attention to their remonstrances, and at last plainly told them that his cavalry were otherwise employed. The Negroes, thus deserted by the Moors, and fully apprised that the king of Kaarta would show them as little clemency as he had shown the inhabitants of Kasson, resolved to collect all their forces, and hazard a battle, before the king, who was now in great distress for want of provisions, should become too powerful for them.   They therefore assembled about eight hundred effective men on the whole ; and with these they entered Kaarta, on the evening of the 18th of June.

June 19th.—This morning the wind shifted to the southwest ; and about two o'clock in the afternoon we had a heavy tornado, or thunder-squall, accompanied with rain, which greatly revived the face of nature, and gave a pleasant coolness to the air.   This was the first rain that had fallen for many months.

As every attempt to redeem my boy had hitherto been unsuccessful, and in all probability would continue to prove so, whilst I remained in the country, I found that it was necessary for me to come to some determination concerning my own safety before the rains should be fully set in ; for my landlord, seeing no likelihood of being paid for his trouble, began to wish me away ; and Johnson, my interpreter, refusing to proceed. my situation became very perplexing.   If I continued where I was, I foresaw that I must soon fall a victim to the barbarity of the Moors ; and yet, if I went forward singly, it was evident that I must sustain great difficulties, both from the want of means to purchase the necessaries of life, and of an interpreter to make myself understood.   On the other hand, to return to England, without accomplishing the object of my mission, was worse than either.   I therefore determined to avail myself of the first opportunity of escaping, and to proceed directly for Bambarra, as soon as the rains had set in for a few days, so as to afford me the certainty of finding water in the woods.

Such was my situation when, on the evening of the 24th of June, I was startled by the report of some muskets close to the town, and inquiring the reason, was informed that the Jarra army had returned from fighting Daisy, and that this firing was by way of rejoicing.   However, when the chief men of the town had assembled, and heard a full detail of the expedition, they were by no means relieved from their uneasiness on Daisy's account.   The deceitful Moors having drawn back from the confederacy, after being hired by the Negroes, greatly dispirited the insurgents; who instead of finding Daisy with a few friends concealed in the strong fortress of Gedingooma, had found him at a town near Joka, in the open country, surrounded by so numerous an army, that every attempt to attack him was at once given up : and the confederates only thought of enriching themselves, by the plunder of the small towns in the neighbourhood. They accordingly fell upon one of Daisy's towns, and carried off the whole of the inhabitants; but, lest intelligence of this might reach Daisy, and induce him to cut off their retreat, they returned through the woods by night, bringing with them the slaves and cattle which they had captured.

June 26th.—This afternoon, a spy from Kaarta brought the alarming intelligence that Daisy had taken Simbing in the morning, and would be in Jarra some time in the course of the ensuing day. A number of people were immediately stationed on the tops of the rocks, and in the different passages leading into the town, to give early intelligence of Daisy's motions, and the women set about making the necessary preparations for quitting the town as soon as possible. They continued beating corn, and packing up different articles during the night; and early in the morning nearly one-half of the townspeople took the road for Bambarra, by the way of Deena.

Their departure was very affecting; the women and children crying; the men sullen and dejected . and all of them looking back with regret on their native town, and on the wells and rocks, beyond which their ambition had never tempted them to stray, and where they had laid all their plans of future happiness; all of which they were now forced to abandon, and to seek shelter among strangers.

June 27th.—About eleven o'clock in the forenoon we were alarmed by the sentinels, who brought information that Daisy was on his march towards Jarra, and that the confederate army had fled before him without firing a gun. The terror of the townspeople on this occasion is not easily to be described. Indeed, the screams of the women and children, and the great hurry and confusion that everywhere prevailed, made me suspect that the Kaartans had already entered the town; and although I had every reason to be pleased with Daisy's behaviour to me when I was at Kemmoo, I had no wish to expose myself to the mercy of his army, who might, in the general confusion, mistake me for a Moor. I therefore mounted my horse, and taking a large bag of corn before me, rode slowly along with the townspeople, until we reached the foot of a rocky hill, where I dismounted, and drove my horse up before me. When I had reached the summit I sat down, and having a full view of the town, and the neighbouring country, could not help lamenting the situation of the poor inhabitants, who were thronging after me, driving their sheep, cows, goats, etc., and carrying a scanty portion of provisions, and a few clothes. There was a great noise and crying everywhere upon the road; for many aged people and children were unable to walk, and these, with the sick, were obliged to be carried; otherwise they must have been left to certain destruction.

About five o'clock we arrived at a small farm, belonging to the Jarra people, called Kadeeja; and here I found Daman and Johnson employed in filling large bags of corn to be carried upon bullocks, to serve as provisions for Daman's family on the road.

June 28th.—At daybreak we departed from Kadeeja, and having passed Troongoomba without stopping, arrived in the afternoon at Queira. I remained here two days in order to recruit my horse, which the Moors had reduced to a perfect Rosinante, and to wait for the arrival of some Mandingo Negroes, who were going for Bambarra in the course of a few days.

On the afternoon of the 1st of July, as I was tending my horse in the fields, Ali's chief slave and four Moors arrived at Queira, and took up their lodging at the Dooty's house. My interpreter, Johnson, who suspected the nature of this visit, sent two boys to overhear the conversation, from which he learnt that they were sent to convey me back to Bubaker. The same evening two of the Moors came privately to look at my horse, and one of them proposed taking it to the Dooty's hut, but the other observed that such a precaution was unnecessary, as I could never escape upon such an animal. They then inquired where I slept, and returned to their companions.

All this was like a stroke of thunder to me, for I dreaded nothing so much as confinement again among the Moors, from whose barbarity I had nothing but death to expect. I therefore determined to set off immediately for Bambarra, a measure which I thought offered almost the only chance of saving my life, and gaining the object of my mission. I communicated the design to Johnson, who, although he applauded my resolution, was so far from showing any inclination to accompany me, that he solemnly protested he would rather forfeit his wages than go any farther. He told me that Daman had agreed to give him half the price of a slave for his service, to assist in conducting a coffle of slaves to Gambia, and that he was determined to embrace the opportunity of returning to his wife and family.

Having no hopes therefore of persuading him to accompany me, I resolved to proceed by myself. About midnight I got my clothes in readiness, which consisted of two shirts, two pair of trousers, two pocket-handkerchiefs, an upper and under waistcoat, a hat, and a pair of half boots; these, with a cloak, constituted my whole wardrobe. And I had not one single bead, nor any other article of value in my possession, to purchase victuals for myself, or corn for my horse.

About daybreak, Johnson, who had been listening to the Moors all night, came and whispered to me that they were asleep. The awful crisis was now arrived when I was again either to taste the blessing of freedom, or languish out my days in captivity. A cold sweat moistened my forehead as I thought on the dreadful alternative, and reflected that, one way or the other, my fate must be decided in the course of the ensuing day. But to deliberate was to lose the only chance of escaping. So taking up my bundle, I stepped gently over the Negroes, who were sleeping in the open air, and having mounted my horse, I bade Johnson farewell, desiring him to take particular care of the papers I had intrusted him with, and inform my friends in Gambia that he had left me in good health on my way to Bambarra.

I proceeded with great caution, surveying each bush, and frequently listening and looking behind me for the Moorish horsemen, until I was about a mile from the town, when I was surprised to find myself in the neighbourhood of a korree belonging to the Moors. The shepherds followed me for about a mile, hooting and throwing stones after me; and when I was out of their reach, and had began to indulge the pleasing hopes of escaping, I was again greatly alarmed to hear somebody halloo behind me, and looking back, I saw three Moors on horseback coming after me at full speed, whooping and brandishing their double-barrelled guns. I knew it was in vain to think of escaping, and therefore turned back and met them, when two of them caught hold of my bridle, one on each side, and the third, presenting his musket, told me I must go back to Ali.

When the human mind has for some time been fluctuating between hope and despair, tortured with anxiety, and hurried from one extreme to another, it affords a sort of gloomy relief to know the worst that can possibly happen; such was my situation. An indifference about life, and all its enjoyments, had completely benumbed my faculties, and I rode back with the Moors with apparent unconcern. But a change took place much sooner than I had any reason to expect. In passing through some thick bushes, one of the Moors ordered me to untie my bundle, and show them the contents. Having examined the different articles, they found nothing worth taking except my cloak, which they considered as a very valuable acquisition; and one of them pulling it from me, wrapped it about himself. This cloak had been of great use to me; it served to cover me from the rains in the day, and to protect me from the mosquitoes in the night; I therefore earnestly begged him to return it, and followed him some little way to obtain it, but, without paying any attention to my request, he and one of his companions rode off with their prize. When I attempted to follow them, the third, who had remained with me, struck my horse over the head, and presenting his musket, told me I should proceed no further.

I now perceived that these men had not been sent by any authority to apprehend me, but had pursued me solely in the view to rob and plunder me. Turning my horse's head, therefore, once more towards the east, and observing the Moor follow the track of his confederates, I congratulated myself on having escaped with my life, though in great distress, from such a horde of barbarians.

I was no sooner out of sight of the Moor, than I struck into the woods, to prevent being pursued, and kept pushing on with all possible speed, until I found myself near some high rocks, which I remembered to have seen in my former route from Queira to Deena; and directing my course a little to the northward, I fortunately fell in with the path.

CHAPTER XIV

The Author feels great joy at his deliverance, and proceeds through the wilderness, but finds his situation very deplorable—Suffers greatly from thirst, and faints on the sand—Recovers, and makes another effort to push forward—Is providentially relieved by a fall of rain—Arrives at a Foulah village, where he is refused relief by the Dooty, but obtains food from a poor woman—Continues his journey through the wilderness, and the next day lights on another Foulah village, where he is hospitably received by one of the shepherds—Arrives on the third day at a Negro town called Wawra, tributary to the king of Bambarra.

It is impossible to describe the joy that arose in my mind when I looked around and concluded that I was out of danger. I felt like one recovered from sickness; I breathed freer; I found unusual lightness in my limbs; even the desert looked pleasant, and I dreaded nothing so much as falling in with some wandering parties of Moors, who might convey me back to the land of thieves and murderers from which I had just escaped.

I soon became sensible, however, that my situation was very deplorable, for I had no means of procuring food, nor prospect of finding water. About ten o'clock, perceiving a herd of goats feeding close to the road, I took a circuitous route to avoid being seen, and continued travelling through the wilderness, directing my course, by compass, nearly east-south-east, in order to reach as soon as possible some town or village of the kingdom of Bambarra.

A little after noon, when the burning heat of the sun was reflected with double violence from the hot sand, and the distant ridges of the hills, seen through the ascending vapour, seemed to wave and fluctuate like the unsettled sea, I became faint with thirst, and climbed a tree in hopes of seeing distant smoke, or some other appearance of a human habitation, but in vain ; nothing appeared all around but thick underwood, and hillocks of white sand.

About four o'clock, I came suddenly upon a large herd of goats, and pulling my horse into a bush, I watched to observe if the keepers were Moors or Negroes. In a little time I perceived two Moorish boys, and with some difficulty persuaded them to approach me. They informed me that the herd belonged to Ali, and that they were going to Deena, where the water was more plentiful, and where they intended to stay until the rain had filled the pools in the Desert. They showed me their empty water-skins, and told me that they had seen no water in the woods. This account afforded me but little consolation ; however, it was in vain to repine, and I pushed on as fast as possible, in hopes of reaching some watering place in the course of the night. My thirst was by this time become insufferable ; my mouth was parched and inflamed ; a sudden dimness would frequently come over my eyes, with other symptoms of fainting ; and my horse being very much fatigued, I began seriously to apprehend that I should perish of thirst. To relieve the burning pain in my mouth and throat, I chewed the leaves of different shrubs, but found them all bitter, and of no service.

A little before sunset, having reached the top of a gentle rising, I climbed a high tree, from the topmost branches of which I cast a melancholy look over the barren wilderness, but without discovering the most distant trace of a human dwelling. The same dismal uniformity of shrubs and sand everywhere presented itself, and the horizon was as level and uninterrupted as that of the sea.

Descending from the tree, I found my horse devouring the stubble and brushwood with great avidity ; and as I was now too faint to attempt walking, and my horse too much fatigued to carry me, I thought it but an act of humanity, and perhaps the last I should ever have it in my power to perform, to take off his bridle and let him shift for himself ; in doing which I was suddenly affected with sickness and giddiness, and falling upon the sand, felt as if the hour of death was fast approaching. " Here then (thought I), after a short but ineffectual struggle, terminate all my hopes of being useful in my day and generation; here must the short span of my life come to an end." I cast (as I believed), a last look on the surrounding scene, and whilst I reflected on the awful change that was about to take place, this world, with its enjoyments, seemed to vanish from my recollection. Nature, however, at length resumed its functions; and on recovering my senses, I found myself stretched upon the sand, with the bridle still in my hand, and the sun just sinking behind the trees. I now summoned all my resolution, and determined to make another effort to prolong my existence. And as the evening was somewhat cool, I resolved to travel as far as my limbs would carry me, in hopes of reaching (my only resource) a watering place. With this view, I put the bridle on my horse, and driving him before me, went slowly along for about an hour, when I perceived some lightning from the north-east, a most delightful sight, for it promised rain. The darkness and lightning increased very rapidly, and in less than an hour I heard the wind roaring among the bushes. I had already opened my mouth to receive the refreshing drops which I expected; but I was instantly covered with a cloud of sand, driven with such force by the wind, as to give a very disagreeable sensation to my face and arms, and I was obliged to mount my horse, and stop under a bush to prevent being suffocated. The sand continued to fly in amazing quantities for near an hour, after which I again set forward, and travelled with difficulty until ten o'clock. About this time I was agreeably surprised by some very vivid flashes of lightning, followed by a few heavy drops of rain. In a little time the sand ceased to fly, and I alighted and spread out all my clean clothes to collect the rain, which at length I saw would certainly fall. For more than an hour it rained plentifully, and I quenched my thirst by wringing and sucking my clothes.

There being no moon, it was remarkably dark, so that I was obliged to lead my horse, and direct my way by the compass, which the lightning enabled me to observe. In this manner I travelled, with tolerable expedition, until past midnight; when the lightning becoming more distant, I was under the necessity of groping along, to the no small danger of my hands and eyes. About two o'clock my horse started at something, and looking round, I was not a little surprised to see a light at a short distance among the trees, and supposing it to be a town, I groped along the sand in hopes of finding corn-stalks, cotton, or other appearances of cultivation, but found none. As I approached, I perceived a number of other lights in different places, and began to suspect that I had fallen upon a party of Moors. However, in my present situation, I was resolved to see who they were, if I could do it with safety. I accordingly led my horse cautiously towards the light, and heard by the lowing of the cattle, and the clamorous tongues of the herdsmen, that it was a watering place, and most likely belonged to the Moors. Delightful as the sound of the human voice was to me, I resolved once more to strike into the woods, and rather run the risk of perishing of hunger than trust myself again in their hands; but being still thirsty, and dreading the approach of the burning day, I thought it prudent to search for the wells, which I expected to find at no great distance. In this pursuit, I inadvertently approached so near to one of the tents as to be perceived by a woman, who immediately screamed out. Two people came running to her assistance from some of the neighbouring tents, and passed so very near to me that I thought I was discovered, and hastened again into the woods.

About a mile from this place, I heard a loud and confused noise somewhere to the right of my course, and in a short time was happy to find it was the croaking of frogs, which was heavenly music to my ears. I followed the sound, and at daybreak arrived at some shallow muddy pools, so full of frogs, that it was difficult to discern the water. The noise they made frightened my horse, and I was obliged to keep them quiet by beating the water with a branch until he had drank. Having here quenched my thirst, I ascended a tree, and the morning being calm, I soon perceived the smoke of the watering place which I had passed in the night; and observed another pillar of smoke east-south-east, distant twelve or fourteen miles. Towards this I directed my route, and reached the cultivated ground a little before eleven o'clock, where, seeing a number of Negroes at work planting corn, I inquired the name of the town, and was informed that it was a Foulah village, belonging to Ali, called Shrilla. I had now some doubts about entering it; but my horse being very much fatigued, and the day growing hot, not to mention the pangs of hunger which began to assail me, I resolved to venture, and accordingly rode up to the Dooty's house, where I was unfortunately denied admittance, and could not obtain even a handful of corn either for myself or horse. Turning from this inhospitable door, I rode slowly out of the town, and perceiving some low scattered huts without the walls, I directed my route towards them; knowing that in Africa, as well as in Europe, hospitality does not always prefer the highest dwellings. At the door of one of these huts, an old motherly-looking woman sat, spinning cotton; I made signs to her that I was hungry, and inquired if she had any victuals with her in the hut. She immediately laid down her distaff, and desired me, in Arabic, to come in. When I had seated myself upon the floor, she set before me a dish of kouskous, that had been left the preceding night, of which I made a tolerable meal; and in return for this kindness, I gave her one of my pocket-handkerchiefs; begging at the same time, a little corn for my horse, which she readily brought me.

Overcome with joy at so unexpected a deliverance, I lifted up my eyes to heaven, and whilst my heart swelled with gratitude, I returned thanks to that gracious and bountiful Being, whose power had supported me under so many dangers, and had now spread for me a table in the wilderness.

Whilst my horse was feeding, the people began to assemble, and one of them whispered something to my hostess which very much excited her surprise. Though I was not well acquainted with the Foulah language, I soon discovered that some of the men wished to apprehend and carry me back to Ali, in hopes, I suppose, of receiving a reward. I therefore tied up the corn; and lest any one should suspect I had ran away from the Moors, I took a northerly direction, and went cheerfully along, driving my horse before me, followed by all the boys and girls of the town. When I had travelled about two miles, and got quit of all my troublesome attendants, I struck again into the woods and took shelter under a large tree, where I found it necessary to rest myself; a bundle of twigs serving me for a bed, and my saddle for a pillow.

I was awakened about two o'clock by three Foulahs, who, taking me for a Moor, pointed to the sun, and told me it was time to pray. Without entering into conversation with them, I saddled my horse and continued my journey. I travelled over a level, but more fertile country than I had seen for some time, until sunset, when, coming to a path that took a southerly direction, I followed it until midnight, at which time I arrived at a small pool of rain-water, and the wood being open, I determined to rest by it for the night. Having given my horse the remainder of the corn, I made my bed as formerly; but the mosquitoes and flies from the pool prevented sleep for some time, and I was twice disturbed in the night by wild beasts, which came very near, and whose howlings kept the horse in continual terror.

July 4th.—At daybreak I pursued my course through the woods as formerly; saw numbers of antelopes, wild hogs, and ostriches; but the soil was more hilly, and not so fertile as I had found it the preceding day. About eleven o'clock I ascended an eminence, where I climbed a tree, and discovered, at about eight miles' distance, an open part of the country, with several red spots, which I concluded were cultivated land; and directing my course that way, came to the precincts of a watering place about one o'clock. From the appearance of the place, I judged it to belong to the Foulahs, and was hopeful that I should meet a better reception than I had experienced at Shrilla. In this I was not deceived; for one of the shepherds

invited me to come into his tent, and partake of some
dates. This was one of those low Foulah tents in which
there is room just sufficient to sit upright, and in which
the family, the furniture, etc., seem huddled together like
so many articles in a chest. When I had crept upon my
hands and knees into this humble habitation, I found that
it contained a woman and three children, who, together
with the shepherd and myself, completely occupied the
floor. A dish of boiled corn and dates was produced, and
the master of the family, as is customary in this part of
the country, first tasted himself, and then desired me to
follow his example. Whilst I was eating, the children
kept their eyes fixed upon me ; and no sooner did the
shepherd pronounce the word *Nazarani*, than they began
to cry, and their mother crept slowly towards the door, out
of which she sprang like a greyhound, and was instantly
followed by her children, so frightened were they at the
very name of a Christian, that no entreaties could induce
them to approach the tent. Here I purchased some corn
for my horse in exchange for some brass buttons ; and
having thanked the shepherd for his hospitality, struck
again into the woods. At sunset, I came to a road that
took the direction for Bambarra, and resolved to follow it
for the night ; but about eight o'clock, hearing some people
coming from the southward, I thought it prudent to hide
myself among some thick bushes near the road. As these
thickets are generally full of wild beasts, I found my
situation rather unpleasant ; sitting in the dark, holding
my horse by the nose with both hands, to prevent him
from neighing, and equally afraid of the natives with
out, and the wild beasts within. My fears, however, were
soon dissipated, for the people, after looking round the
thicket, and perceiving nothing, went away ; and I hastened
to the more open parts of the wood, where I pursued my
journey E.S.E. until midnight, when the joyful cry of frogs
induced me once more to deviate a little from my route,
in order to quench my thirst. Having accomplished this
from a large pool of rain-water, I sought for an open place,
with a single tree in the midst, under which I made my

bed for the night. I was disturbed by some wolves towards morning, which induced me to set forward a little before day; and having passed a small village called Wassalita, I came about ten o'clock (July 5th), to a Negro town called Wawra, which properly belongs to Kaarta, but was at this time tributary to Mansong, king of Bambarra.

CHAPTER XV

The Author proceeds to Wassiboo—Is joined by some fugitive
Kaartans, who accompany him in his route through Bambarra—
Discovers the Niger—Some account of Sego, the capital of Bambarra—Mansong, the king, refuses to see the Author, but sends
him a present—Great hospitality of a Negro woman.

WAWRA is a small town surrounded with high walls, and
inhabited by a mixture of Mandingoes and Foulahs. The
inhabitants employ themselves chiefly in cultivating corn,
which they exchange with the Moors for salt. Here, being
in security from the Moors, and very much fatigued, I
resolved to rest myself, and meeting with a hearty welcome
from the Dooty, whose name was Flancharee, I laid myself
down upon a bullock's hide, and slept soundly for about
two hours. The curiosity of the people would not allow
me to sleep any longer. They had seen my saddle and
bridle, and were assembled in great number to learn who
I was, and whence I came. Some were of opinion that
I was an Arab; others insisted that I was some Moorish
Sultan; and they continued to debate the matter with such
warmth, that the noise awoke me. The Dooty (who had
formerly been at Gambia) at last interposed in my behalf,
and assured them that I was certainly a white man; but
he was convinced from my appearance that I was a very
poor one.

In the course of the day, several women, hearing that
I was going to Sego, came and begged me to inquire of
Mansong, the king, what was become of their children.
One woman in particular, told me that her son's name
was Mamadee; that he was no heathen, but prayed to
God morning and evening, and had been taken from her
about three years ago, by Mansong's army: since which
she had never heard of him. She said she often dreamed
about him; and begged me, if I should see him, either

in Bambarra, or in my own country, to tell him that his mother and sister were still alive. In the afternoon the Dooty examined the contents of the leather bag, in which I had packed up my clothes; but finding nothing that was worth taking, he returned it, and told me to depart in the morning.

July 6th.—It rained very much in the night, and at daylight I departed, in company with a Negro, who was going to a town called Dingyee for corn; but we had not proceeded above a mile, before the ass upon which he rode kicked him off, and he returned, leaving me to prosecute the journey by myself.

I reached Dingyee about noon; but the Dooty and most of the inhabitants had gone into the fields to cultivate corn. An old Foulah, observing me wandering about the town, desired me to come to his hut, where I was well entertained; and the Dooty, when he returned, sent me some victuals for myself, and corn for my horse.

July 7th.—In the morning, when I was about to depart, my landlord, with a great deal of diffidence, begged me to give him a lock of my hair. He had been told, he said, that white men's hair made a saphie, that would give to the possessor all the knowledge of white men. I had never before heard of so simple a mode of education, but instantly complied with the request; and my landlord's thirst for learning was such, that, with cutting and pulling, he cropped one side of my head pretty closely; and would have done the same with the other, had I not signified my disapprobation by putting on my hat, and assuring him, that I wished to reserve some of this precious merchandise for a future occasion.

I reached a small town called Wassiboo, about twelve o'clock, where I was obliged to stop until an opportunity should offer of procuring a guide to Satilé, which is distant a very long day's journey, through woods without any beaten path. I accordingly took up my residence at the Dooty's house, where I staid four days; during which time I amused myself by going to the fields with the family to plant corn. Cultivation is carried on here on a very extensive scale; and, as the natives themselves express it, "hunger is never known." In cultivating the soil, the men and women work together. They use a large sharp hoe, much superior to that used in Gambia; but they are obliged, for fear of the Moors, to carry their arms with them to the field. The master, with the handle of his spear, marks the field into regular plats, one of which is assigned to every three slaves.

On the evening of the 11th, eight of the fugitive Kaartans arrived at Wassiboo. They had found it impossible to live under the tyrannical government of the Moors, and were going to transfer their allegiance to the king of Bambarra. They offered to take me along with them as far as Satilé, and I accepted the offer.

July 12*th.*—At daybreak we set out, and travelled with uncommon expedition until sunset: we stopped only twice in the course of the day, once at a watering place in the woods, and another time at the ruins of a town, formerly belonging to Daisy, called *Illa-Compe* (the corn town). When we arrived in the neighbourhood of Satilé, the people who were employed in the corn fields, seeing so many horsemen, took us for a party of Moors, and ran screaming away from us. The whole town was instantly alarmed, and the slaves were seen in every direction driving the cattle and horses towards the town. It was in vain that one of our company galloped up to undeceive them: it only frightened them the more; and when we arrived at the town, we found the gates shut and the people all under arms. After a long parley we were permitted to enter; and as there was every appearance of a heavy tornado, the Dooty allowed us to sleep in his baloon, and gave us each a bullock's hide for a bed.

July 13*th.*—Early in the morning we again set forward. The roads were wet and slippery; but the country was very beautiful, abounding with rivulets, which were increased by the rain into rapid streams. About ten o'clock we came to the ruins of a village, which had been destroyed by war about six months before; and in order to prevent any town from being built there in future, the large Bentang tree, under which the natives spent the day, had been burned down, the wells filled up, and everything that could make the spot desirable completely destroyed.

About noon my horse was so much fatigued that I could not keep up with my companions; I therefore dismounted, and desired them to ride on, telling them that I would follow as soon as my horse had rested a little. But I found them unwilling to leave me. The lions, they said, were very numerous in those parts, and though they might not so readily attack a body of people, they would soon find out an individual. It was therefore agreed that one of the company should stay with me to assist in driving my horse, while the others passed on to Galloo to procure lodgings, and collect grass for the horses before night. Accompanied by this worthy Negro, I drove my horse before me, until about four o'clock, when we came in sight of Galloo, a considerable town, standing in a fertile and beautiful valley surrounded with high rocks.

As my companions had thoughts of settling in this neighbourhood, they had a fine sheep given them by the Dooty; and I was fortunate enough to procure plenty of corn for my horse. Here they blow upon elephants' teeth when they announce evening prayers, in the same manner as at Kemmoo.

Early next morning (July 14th), having first returned many thanks to our landlord for his hospitality, while my fellow-travellers offered up their prayers that he might never want, we set forward, and about three o'clock arrived at Moorja, a large town, famous for its trade in salt, which the Moors bring here in great quantities to exchange for corn and cotton cloth. As most of the people here are Mahomedans, it is not allowed to the Kafirs to drink beer, which they call *Neo-dollo* (corn spirit), except in certain houses. In one of these I saw about twenty people sitting round large vessels of this beer with the greatest conviviality, many of them in a state of intoxication. As corn is plentiful, the inhabitants are very liberal to strangers. I believe we had as much corn and milk sent us by different people as would have been sufficient for three times our number;

and though we remained here two days, we experienced no diminution of their hospitality.

On the morning of the 16th we again set forward, accompanied by a coffle of fourteen asses, loaded with salt, bound for Sansanding. The road was particularly romantic, between two rocky hills; but the Moors sometimes lie in wait here to plunder strangers. As soon as we had reached the open country, the master of the salt coffle thanked us for having staid with him so long, and now desired us to ride on. The sun was almost set before we reached Datliboo. In the evening we had a most tremendous tornado. The house in which we lodged being flat-roofed, admitted the rain in streams. The floor was soon ankle deep, the fire extinguished, and we were left to pass the night upon some bundles of firewood that happened to lie in a corner.

July 17*th*.—We departed from Datliboo, and about ten o'clock passed a large coffle returning from Sego, with corn hoes, mats, and other household utensils. At five o'clock we came to a large village, where we intended to pass the night, but the Dooty would not receive us. When we departed from this place, my horse was so much fatigued that I was under the necessity of driving him, and it was dark before we reached Fanimboo, a small village; the Dooty of which no sooner heard that I was a white man than he brought out three old muskets, and was much disappointed when he was told that I could not repair them.

July 18*th*.—We continued our journey; but, owing to a light supper the preceding night, we felt ourselves rather hungry this morning, and endeavoured to procure some corn at a village, but without success. The towns were now more numerous, and the land that is not employed in cultivation affords excellent pasturage for large herds of cattle; but owing to the great concourse of people daily going to and returning from Sego, the inhabitants are less hospitable to strangers.

My horse becoming weaker and weaker every day, was now of very little service to me; I was obliged to drive him before me for the greater part of the day, and did not reach Geosorro until eight o'clock in the evening. I found my companions wrangling with the Dooty, who had absolutely refused to give or sell them any provisions; and as none of us had tasted victuals for the last twenty-four hours, we were by no means disposed to fast another day, if we could help it. But finding our entreaties without effect, and being very much fatigued, I fell asleep, from which I was awakened, about midnight, with the joyful information, "*kinnenata*" (the victuals is come). This made the remainder of the night pass away pleasantly; and at daybreak, July 19th, we resumed our journey, proposing to stop at a village called Doolinkeaboo, for the night following. My fellow-travellers, having better horses than myself, soon left me, and I was walking barefoot, driving my horse, when I was met by a coffle of slaves, about seventy in number, coming from Sego. They were tied together by their necks with thongs of a bullock's hide, twisted like a rope; seven slaves upon a thong, and a man with a musket between every seven. Many of the slaves were ill-conditioned, and a great number of them women. In the rear came Sidi Mahomed's servant, whom I remembered to have seen at the camp of Benowm; he presently knew me, and told me that these slaves were going to Morocco, by the way of Ludamar, and the Great Desert.

In the afternoon, as I approached Doolinkeaboo, I met about twenty Moors on horseback, the owners of the slaves I had seen in the morning; they were well armed with muskets, and were very inquisitive concerning me, but not so rude as their countrymen generally are. From them I learned that Sidi Mahomed was not at Sego, but had gone to Kancaba for gold dust.

When I arrived at Doolinkeaboo, I was informed that my fellow-travellers had gone on, but my horse was so much fatigued that I could not possibly proceed after them. The Dooty of the town, at my request, gave me a draught of water, which is generally looked upon as an earnest of greater hospitality; and I had no doubt of making up for the toils of the day by a good supper and a sound sleep;

unfortunately I had neither one nor the other. The night was rainy and tempestuous, and the Dooty limited his hospitality to the draught of water.

July 20th.—In the morning I endeavoured, both by entreaties and threats, to procure some victuals from the Dooty, but in vain. I even begged some corn from one of his female slaves, as she was washing it at the well, and had the mortification to be refused. However, when the Dooty was gone to the fields, his wife sent me a handful of meal, which I mixed with water, and drank for breakfast. About eight o'clock I departed from Doolinkeaboo, and at noon stopped a few minutes at a large korree, where I had some milk given me by the Foulahs. And hearing that two Negroes were going from thence to Sego, I was happy to have their company, and we set out immediately. About four o'clock we stopped at a small village, where one of the Negroes met with an acquaintance, who invited us to a sort of public entertainment, which was conducted with more than common propriety. A dish made of sour milk and meal, called *Sinkatoo*, and beer made from their corn, was distributed with great liberality, and the women were admitted into the society—a circumstance I had never before observed in Africa. There was no compulsion, every one was at liberty to drink as he pleased; they nodded to each other when about to drink, and on setting down the calabash, commonly said *berka* (thank you). Both men and women appeared to be somewhat intoxicated, but they were far from being quarrelsome.

Departing from thence, we passed several large villages, where I was constantly taken for a Moor, and became the subject of much merriment to the Bambarrans; who seeing me drive my horse before me, laughed heartily at my appearance. He has been at Mecca, says one, you may see that by his clothes; another asked me if my horse was sick; a third wished to purchase it, etc.; so that I believe the very slaves were ashamed to be seen in my company. Just before it was dark, we took up our lodging for the night at a small village, where I procured some victuals for myself, and some corn for my horse, at the moderate price of a button, and was told that I should see the Niger (which the Negroes called Jolliba, or *the great water*) early the next day. The lions are here very numerous; the gates are shut a little after sunset, and nobody allowed to go out. The thoughts of seeing the Niger in the morning, and the troublesome buzzing of mosquitoes, prevented me from shutting my eyes during the night; and I had saddled my horse and was in readiness before daylight; but, on account of the wild beasts, we were obliged to wait until the people were stirring, and the gates opened. This happened to be a market-day at Sego, and the roads were everywhere filled with people carrying different articles to sell. We passed four large villages, and at eight o'clock saw the smoke over Sego.

As we approached the town, I was fortunate enough to overtake the fugitive Kaartans, to whose kindness I had been so much indebted in my journey through Bambarra. They readily agreed to introduce me to the king; and we rode together through some marshy ground, where, as I was anxiously looking around for the river, one of them called out, *geo affili* (see the water), and looking forwards, I saw with infinite pleasure the great object of my mission—the long sought for majestic Niger, glittering to the morning sun, as broad as the Thames at Westminster, and flowing slowly *to the eastward*. I hastened to the brink, and, having drank of the water, lifted up my fervent thanks in prayer to the Great Ruler of all things, for having thus far crowned my endeavours with success.

The circumstance of the Niger's flowing towards the east, and its collateral points, did not, however, excite my surprise; for although I had left Europe in great hesitation on this subject, and rather believed that it ran in the contrary direction, I had made such frequent inquiries during my progress, concerning this river, and received from Negroes, of different nations, such clear and decisive assurances that its general course was *towards the rising sun*, as scarce left any doubt on my mind; and more especially as I knew that Major Houghton had collected similar information in the same manner.

Sego, the capital of Bambarra, at which I had now

arrived, consists, properly speaking, of four distinct towns;
two on the northern bank of the Niger, called Sego Korro
and Sego Boo; and two on the southern bank, called Sego
Soo Korro and Sego See Korro. They are all surrounded
with high mud walls; the houses are built of clay, of a
square form, with flat roofs; some of them have two storeys,
and many of them are whitewashed. Besides these buildings, Moorish mosques are seen in every quarter; and the
streets, though narrow, are broad enough for every useful
purpose, in a country where wheel-carriages are entirely unknown. From the best inquiries I could make, I have
reason to believe that Sego contains altogether about thirty
thousand inhabitants. The king of Bambarra constantly
resides at Sego See Korro; he employs a great many slaves
in conveying people over the river, and the money they
receive (though the fare is only ten cowrie shells for each
individual) furnishes a considerable revenue to the king in
the course of a year. The canoes are of a singular construction, each of them being formed of the trunks of two
large trees, rendered concave, and joined together, not side
by side, but end ways; the junction being exactly across
the middle of the canoe; they are therefore very long
and disproportionably narrow, and have neither decks nor
masts; they are, however, very roomy; for I observed in
one of them four horses, and several people crossing over
the river. When we arrived at this ferry, with a view to
pass over to that part of the town in which the king resides,
we found a great number waiting for a passage; they looked
at me with silent wonder, and I distinguished, with concern,
many Moors among them. There were three different
places of embarkation, and the ferrymen were very diligent
and expeditious; but, from the crowd of people, I could
not immediately obtain a passage; and sat down upon the
bank of the river, to wait for a more favourable opportunity. The view of this extensive city; the numerous
canoes upon the river; the crowded population, and the
cultivated state of the surrounding country, formed altogether a prospect of civilisation and magnificence, which I
little expected to find in the bosom of Africa.

I waited more than two hours without having an opportunity of crossing the river; during which time, the people who had crossed carried information to Mansong, the king, that a white man was waiting for a passage, and was coming to see him. He immediately sent over one of his chief men, who informed me that the king could not possibly see me, until he knew what had brought me into his country; and that I must not presume to cross the river without the king's permission. He therefore advised me to lodge at a distant village, to which he pointed, for the night; and said that in the morning he would give me further instructions how to conduct myself. This was very discouraging. However, as there was no remedy, I set off for the village; where I found, to my great mortification, that no person would admit me into his house. I was regarded with astonishment and fear, and was obliged to sit all day without victuals, in the shade of a tree; and the night threatened to be very uncomfortable, for the wind rose, and there was great appearance of a heavy rain; and the wild beasts are so very numerous in the neighbourhood, that I should have been under the necessity of climbing up the tree, and resting among the branches. About sunset, however, as I was preparing to pass the night in this manner, and had turned my horse loose, that he might graze at liberty, a woman, returning from the labours of the field, stopped to observe me, and perceiving that I was weary and dejected, inquired into my situation, which I briefly explained to her; whereupon, with looks of great compassion, she took up my saddle and bridle, and told me to follow her. Having conducted me into her hut, she lighted up a lamp, spread a mat on the floor, and told me I might remain there for the night. Finding that I was very hungry, she said she would procure me something to eat. She accordingly went out, and returned in a short time with a very fine fish; which having caused to be half-broiled upon some embers, she gave me for supper. The rites of hospitality being thus performed towards a stranger in distress, my worthy benefactress (pointing to the mat, and telling me I might sleep there without apprehension) called to the female part of her family, who had stood gazing on me all the while in fixed astonishment, to resume their task of spinning cotton; in which they continued to employ themselves great part of the night. They lightened their labour by songs, one of which was composed extempore; for I was myself the subject of it. It was sung by one of the young women, the rest joining in a sort of chorus. The air was sweet and plaintive, and the words, literally translated, were these:—"The winds roared, and the rains fell. The poor white man, faint and weary, came and sat under our tree. He has no mother to bring him milk; no wife to grind his corn." *Chorus*—"Let us pity the white man; no mother has he," etc. etc. Trifling as this recital may appear to the reader, to a person in my situation, the circumstance was affecting in the highest degree. I was oppressed by such unexpected kindness; and sleep fled from my eyes. In the morning I presented my compassionate landlady with two of the four brass buttons which remained on my waistcoat; the only recom pense I could make her.

July 21st.—I continued in the village all this day in conversation with the natives, who came in crowds to see me; but was rather uneasy towards evening, to find that no message had arrived from the king; the more so as the people began to whisper, that Mansong had received some very unfavourable accounts of me from the Moors and Slatees residing at Sego; who, it seems, were exceedingly suspicious concerning the motives of my journey. I learnt that many consultations had been held with the king concerning my reception and disposal; and some of the villagers frankly told me, that I had many enemies, and must expect no favour.

July 22nd.—About eleven o'clock, a messenger arrived from the king, but he gave me very little satisfaction. He inquired particularly if I had brought any present, and seemed much disappointed when he was told that I had been robbed of everything by the Moors. When I proposed to go along with him, he told me to stop until the afternoon, when the king would send for me.

July 23rd.—In the afternoon another messenger arrived from Mansong, with a bag in his hands. He told me it was the king's pleasure that I should depart forthwith from the vicinage of Sego ; but that Mansong wishing to relieve a white man in distress, had sent me five thousand cowries,[1] to enable me to purchase provisions in the course of my journey ; the messenger added, that if my intentions were really to proceed to Jenné, he had orders to accompany me as a guide to Sansanding. I was at first puzzled to account for this behaviour of the king ; but from the conversation I had with the guide, I had afterwards reason to believe that Mansong would willingly have admitted me into his presence at Sego, but was apprehensive he might not be able to protect me against the blind and inveterate malice of the Moorish inhabitants. His conduct, therefore, was at once prudent and liberal. The circumstances under which I made my appearance at Sego, were undoubtedly such as might create in the mind of the king a well-warranted suspicion that I wished to conceal the true object of my journey. He argued probably, as my guide argued : who, when he was told that I had come from a great distance, and through many dangers, to behold the Joliba river, naturally inquired, if there were no rivers in my own country, and whether one river was not like another. Notwithstanding this, and in spite of the jealous machinations of the Moors, this benevolent prince thought it sufficient, that a white man was found in his dominions, in a condition of extreme wretchedness ; and that no other plea was necessary to entitle the sufferer to his bounty.

1 Mention has already been made of these little shells (p. 19) which pass current as money, in many parts of the East Indies, as well as Africa. In Bambarra, and the adjacent countries, where the necessaries of life are very cheap, one hundred of them would commonly purchase a day's provisions for myself and corn for my horse. I reckoned about two hundred and fifty cowries equal to one shilling.

CHAPTER XVI

Departure from Sego and arrival at Kabba—Description of the Shea, or vegetable butter tree—The Author and his guide arrive at Sansanding—Behaviour of the Moors at that place—The Author pursues his journey to the eastward—Incidents on the road—Arrives at Modiboo, and proceeds for Kea; but obliged to leave his horse by the way—Embarks at Kea in a fisherman's canoe for Moorzan; is conveyed from thence across the Niger to Silla—Determines to proceed no further eastward—Some account of the further course of the Niger, and the towns in its vicinage, towards the east.

BEING, in the manner that has been related, compelled to leave Sego, I was conducted the same evening to a village about seven miles to the eastward, with some of the inhabitants of which my guide was acquainted, and by whom we were well received.[1] He was very friendly and communicative, and spoke highly of the hospitality of his countrymen; but withal told me, that if Jenné was the place of my destination, which he seemed to have hitherto doubted, I had undertaken an enterprise of greater danger than probably I was apprised of; for, although the town of Jenné was nominally a part of the king of Bambarra's dominions, it was, in fact, he said, a city of the Moors; the leading part of the inhabitants being Bushreens, and even the governor himself, though appointed by Mansong, of the same sect. Thus was I in danger of falling a second time into the hands of men who would consider it not only justifiable, but meritorious, to destroy me; and this reflection was aggravated by the circumstance, that the danger increased as I advanced in my journey; for I learned that the places beyond Jenné were under the Moorish influence, in a still greater degree than Jenné

---

[1] I should have before observed, that I found the language of Bambarra a sort of corrupted Mandingo. After a little practice, I understood and spoke it without difficulty.

itself; and Timbuctoo, the great object of my search, altogether in possession of that savage and merciless people, who allow no Christian to live there. But I had now advanced too far to think of returning to the westward, on such vague and uncertain information, and determined to proceed; and, being accompanied by the guide, I departed from the village on the morning of the 24th. About eight o'clock we passed a large town called Kabba, situated in the midst of a beautiful and highly-cultivated country; bearing a greater resemblance to the centre of England than to what I should have supposed had been the middle of Africa. The people were everywhere employed in collecting the fruit of the shea trees, from which they prepare the vegetable butter mentioned in former parts of this work. These trees grow in great abundance all over this part of Bambarra. They are not planted by the natives, but are found growing naturally in the woods; and in clearing wood land for cultivation, every tree is cut down but the shea. The tree itself very much resembles the American oak; and the fruit, from the kernel of which, being first dried in the sun, the butter is prepared by boiling the kernel in water, has somewhat the appearance of a Spanish olive. The kernel is enveloped in a sweet pulp, under a thin green rind; and the butter produced from it, besides the advantage of its keeping the whole year without salt, is whiter, firmer, and, to my palate, of a richer flavour than the best butter I ever tasted made from cow's milk. The growth and preparation of this commodity seem to be among the first objects of African industry in this and the neighbouring states; and it constitutes a main article of their inland commerce.

We passed, in the course of the day, a great many villages, inhabited chiefly by fishermen; and in the evening about five o'clock, arrived at Sansanding, a very large town, containing, as I was told, from eight to ten thousand inhabitants. This place is much resorted to by the Moors, who bring salt from Beeroo, and beads and coral from the Mediterranean, to exchange here for gold-dust and cotton cloth. This cloth they sell to great advantage in Beeroo, and other Moorish countries, where, on account of the want of rain, no cotton is cultivated.

I desired my guide to conduct me to the house in which we were to lodge, by the most private way possible. We accordingly rode along between the town and the river, passing by a creek or harbour, in which I observed twenty large canoes, most of them fully loaded, and covered with mats to prevent the rain from injuring the goods. As we proceeded, three other canoes arrived, two with passengers and one with goods. I was happy to find that all the Negro inhabitants took me for a Moor; under which character I should probably have passed unmolested, had not a Moor, who was sitting by the river side, discovered the mistake, and setting up a loud exclamation, brought together a number of his countrymen.

When I arrived at the house of Counti Mamadi, the Dooty of the town, I was surrounded with hundreds of people, speaking a variety of different dialects, all equally unintelligible to me. At length, by the assistance of my guide, who acted as interpreter, I understood that one of the spectators pretended to have seen me at one place, and another at some other place, and a Moorish woman absolutely swore that she had kept my house three years at Gallam, on the river Senegal. It was plain that they mistook me for some other person, and I desired two of the most confident to point towards the place where they had seen me. They pointed due south; hence I think it probable that they came from Cape Coast, where they might have seen many white men. Their language was different from any I had yet heard. The Moors now assembled in great numbers; with their usual arrogance compelling the Negroes to stand at a distance. They immediately began to question me concerning my religion; but finding that I was not master of the Arabic, they sent for two men, whom they call *Ilhuidi* (Jews), in hopes that they might be able to converse with me. These Jews, in dress and appearance, very much resemble the Arabs; but though they so far conform to the religion of Mahomet as to recite, in public, prayers from the Koran, they are but little respected by the

Negroes; and even the Moors themselves allowed, that though I was a Christian, I was a better man than a Jew. They, however, insisted that, like the Jews, I must conform so far as to repeat the Mahomedan prayers; and when I attempted to waive the subject, by telling them that I could not speak Arabic, one of them, a Shereef from Tuat, in the Great Desert, started up and swore by the Prophet, that if I refused to go to the mosque he would be one that would assist in carrying me thither. And there is no doubt but this threat would have been immediately executed, had not my landlord interposed in my behalf. He told them that I was the king's stranger, and he could not see me ill treated whilst I was under his protection. He therefore advised them to let me alone for the night; assuring them that in the morning I should be sent about my business. This somewhat appeased their clamour; but they compelled me to ascend a high seat by the door of the mosque, in order that everybody might see me, for the people had assembled in such numbers as to be quite ungovernable—climbing upon the houses, and squeezing each other like the spectators at an execution. Upon this seat I remained until sunset, when I was conducted into a neat little hut, with a small court before it, the door of which Counti Mamadi shut, to prevent any person from disturbing me. But this precaution could not exclude the Moors. They climbed over the top of the mud-wall, and came in crowds into the court, in order, they said, to see me *perform my evening devotions, and eat eggs.* The former of these ceremonies I did not think proper to comply with; but I told them I had no objections to eat eggs, provided they would bring me eggs to eat. My landlord immediately brought me seven hen's eggs, and was much surprised to find that I could not eat them raw; for it seems to be a prevalent opinion among the inhabitants of the interior, that Europeans subsist almost entirely on this diet. When I had succeeded in persuading my landlord that this opinion was without foundation, and that I would gladly partake of any victuals which he might think proper to send me, he ordered a sheep to be killed, and part of it dressed for my supper. About midnight, when the Moors had left me, he paid me a visit, and with much earnestness desired me to write him a saphie. "If a Moor's saphie is good (said this hospitable old man), a white man's must needs be better." I readily furnished him with one possessed of all the virtues I could concentrate, for it contained the Lord's prayer. The pen with which it was written was made of a reed ; a little charcoal and gum-water made very tolerable ink, and a thin board answered the purpose of paper.

July 25*th*.—Early in the morning, before the Moors were assembled, I departed from Sansanding, and slept the ensuing night at a small town called Sibili ; from whence, on the day following, I reached Nyara, a large town at some distance from the river, where I halted the 27th, to have my clothes washed, and recruit my horse. The Dooty there has a very commodious house, flat-roofed, and two storeys high. He showed me some gunpowder of his own manufacturing ; and pointed out, as a great curiosity, a little brown monkey that was tied to a stake by the door, telling me that it came from a far distant country, called Kong.

July 28*th*.—I departed from Nyara and reached Nyamee about noon. This town is inhabited chiefly by Foulahs from the kingdom of Masina. The Dooty (I know not why) would not receive me, but civilly sent his son on horseback to conduct me to Modiboo, which he assured me was at no great distance.

We rode nearly in a direct line through the woods, but in general went forwards with great circumspection. I observed that my guide frequently stopped and looked under the bushes. On inquiring the reason of this caution, he told me that lions were very numerous in that part of the country, and frequently attacked people travelling through the woods. While he was speaking my horse started, and looking round I observed a large animal of the cameleopard kind standing at a little distance. The neck and fore-legs were very long ; the head was furnished with two short black horns, turning backwards ; the tail, which reached down to the ham-joint, had a tuft of hair at the end. The animal was of a mouse colour, and it trotted away from us in a very sluggish manner, moving its head from side to side, to see if we were pursuing it. Shortly after this, as we were crossing a large open plain, where there were a few scattered bushes, my guide, who was a little way before me, wheeled his horse round in a moment, calling out something in the Foulah language, which I did not understand. I inquired in Mandingo what he meant. *Wara billi billi* (a very large lion), said he, and made signs for me to ride away. But my horse was too much fatigued; so we rode slowly past the bush from which the animal had given us the alarm. Not seeing anything myself, however, I thought my guide had been mistaken, when the Foulah suddenly put his hand to his mouth, exclaiming, *Soubah an alluhi* (God preserve us!), and to my great surprise I then perceived a large red lion at a short distance from the bush, with his head couched between his fore-paws. I expected he would instantly spring upon me, and instinctively pulled my feet from my stirrups to throw myself on the ground, that my horse might become the victim rather than myself. But it is probable the lion was not hungry, for he quietly suffered us to pass, though we were fairly within his reach. My eyes were so rivetted upon this sovereign of the beasts, that I found it impossible to remove them until we were at a considerable distance. We now took a circuitous route, through some swampy ground, to avoid any more of these disagreeable rencontres. At sunset we arrived at Modiboo, a delightful village on the banks of the Niger, commanding a view of the river for many miles, both to the east and west. The small green islands (the peaceful retreat of some industrious Foulahs, whose cattle are here secure from the depredations of wild beasts) and the majestic breadth of the river, which is here much larger than at Sego, render the situation one of the most enchanting in the world. Here are caught great plenty of fish by means of long cotton nets which the natives make themselves, and use nearly in the same manner as nets are used in Europe. I observed the head of a crocodile lying upon one of the houses, which they told me had been killed by the shepherds in a swamp near the town. These animals are not uncommon in the Niger, but I believe they are not oftentimes found dangerous. They are of little account to the traveller when compared with the amazing swarms of mosquitoes, which rise from the swamps and creeks in such numbers as to harass even the most torpid of the natives; and as my clothes were now almost worn to rags, I was but ill prepared to resist their attacks. I usually passed the night without shutting my eyes, walking backwards and forwards, fanning myself with my hat. Their stings raised numerous blisters on my legs and arms, which, together with the want of rest, made me very feverish and uneasy.

July 29th.—Early in the morning my landlord, observing that I was sickly, hurried me away, sending a servant with me as a guide to Kea. But though I was little able to walk, my horse was still less able to carry me, and about six miles to the east of Modiboo, in crossing some rough clayey ground, he fell, and the united strength of the guide and myself could not place him again upon his legs. I sat down for some time beside this worn-out associate of my adventures; but finding him still unable to rise, I took off the saddle and bridle, and placed a quantity of grass before him. I surveyed the poor animal, as he lay panting on the ground, with sympathetic emotion; for I could not suppress the sad apprehension that I should myself in a short time lie down and perish in the same manner of fatigue and hunger. With this foreboding I left my poor horse, and with great reluctance followed my guide on foot along the bank of the river until about noon, when we reached Kea, which I found to be nothing more than a small fishing village. The Dooty, a surly old man, who was sitting by the gate, received me very coolly, and when I informed him of my situation, and begged his protection, told me, with great indifference, that he paid very little attention to fine speeches, and that I should not enter his house. My guide remonstrated in my favour, but to no purpose, for the Dooty remained inflexible in his determination. I knew not where to rest my wearied limbs, but was happily relieved by a fishing-canoe belonging to Silla, which was at that

moment coming down the river.   The Dooty waved to the
fisherman to come near, and desired him to take charge of
me as far as Moorzan.   The fisherman, after some hesitation, consented to carry me, and I embarked in the canoe,
in company with the fisherman, his wife, and a boy.   The
Negro who had conducted me from Modiboo now left me.
I requested him to look to my horse on his return, and
take care of him if he was still alive, which he promised
to do.

Departing from Kea, we proceeded about a mile down
the river, when the fisherman paddled the canoe to the
bank, and desired me to jump out.   Having tied the
canoe to a stake, he stripped off his clothes, and dived
for such a length of time, that I thought he had actually
drowned himself, and was surprised to see his wife behave
with so much indifference upon the occasion ; but my fears
were over when he raised up his head astern of the canoe,
and called for a rope.   With this rope he dived a second
time, and then got into the canoe, and ordered the boy to
assist him in pulling.   At length they brought up a large
basket, about ten feet in diameter, containing two fine fish,
which the fisherman (after returning the basket into the
water) immediately carried ashore, and hid in the grass.
We then went a little further down, and took up another
basket, in which was one fish.   The fisherman now left
us to carry his prizes to some neighbouring market, and
the woman and boy proceeded with me in the canoe
down the river.

About four o'clock we arrived at Moorzan, a fishing
town on the northern bank, from whence I was conveyed
across the river to Silla, a large town, where I remained
until it was quite dark, under a tree, surrounded by hundreds
of people.   But their language was very different from the
other parts of Bambarra ; and I was informed that in my
progress eastward the Bambarra tongue was but little understood, and that when I reached Jenné I should find
that the majority of the inhabitants spoke a different
language, called *Jenné Kummo* by the Negroes, and *Kalam
Soudan* by the Moors.

With a great deal of entreaty the Dooty allowed me to come into his baloon to avoid the rain, but the place was very damp, and I had a smart paroxysm of fever during the night. Worn down by sickness, exhausted with hunger and fatigue, half naked, and without any article of value by which I might procure provisions, clothes, or lodging, I began to reflect seriously on my situation. I was now convinced, by painful experience, that the obstacles to my further progress were insurmountable. The tropical rains were already set in with all their violence; the rice grounds and swamps were everywhere overflowed; and in a few days more, travelling of every kind, unless by water, would be completely obstructed. The cowries which remained of the king of Bambarra's present were not sufficient to enable me to hire a canoe for any great distance, and I had but little hopes of subsisting by charity in a country where the Moors have such influence. But, above all, I perceived that I was advancing more and more within the power of those merciless fanatics; and from my reception both at Sego and Sansanding, I was apprehensive that, in attempting to reach even Jenné (unless under the protection of some man of consequence amongst them, which I had no means of obtaining), I should sacrifice my life to no purpose, for my discoveries would perish with me. The prospect either way was gloomy. In returning to the Gambia, a journey on foot of many hundred miles presented itself to my contemplation, through regions and countries unknown. Nevertheless, this seemed to be the only alternative, for I saw inevitable destruction in attempting to proceed to the eastward. With this conviction on my mind, I hope my readers will acknowledge that I did right in going no farther. I had made every effort to execute my mission, in its fullest extent, which prudence could justify. Had there been the most distant prospect of a successful termination, neither the unavoidable hardships of the journey, nor the dangers of a second captivity, should have forced me to desist. This, however, necessity compelled me to do; and whatever may be the opinion of my general readers on this point, it affords me inexpressible satisfaction that my honourable employers have been pleased, since my return, to express their full approbation of my conduct.

Having thus brought my mind, after much doubt and perplexity, to a determination to return westward, I thought it incumbent on me, before I left Silla, to collect from the Moorish and Negro traders all the information I could concerning the further course of the Niger eastward, and the situation and extent of the kingdoms in its vicinage, and the following few notices I received from such various quarters as induce me to think they are authentic.

Two short days' journey to the eastward of Silla is the town of Jenné, which is situated on a small island in the river, and is said to contain a greater number of inhabitants than Sego itself or any other town in Bambarra. At the distance of two days more, the river spreads into a considerable lake, called *Dibbie* (or the dark lake), concerning the extent of which all the information I could obtain was, that in crossing it from west to east, the canoes lose sight of land one whole day. From this lake the water issues in many different streams, which terminate in two large branches, one whereof flows towards the north-east and the other to the east; but these branches join at Kabra, which is one day's journey to the southward of Timbuctoo, and is the port or shipping-place of that city. The tract of land which the two streams encircle is called Jinbala, and is inhabited by Negroes, and the whole distance by land from Jenné to Timbuctoo, is twelve days' journey.

From Kabra, at the distance of eleven days' journey down the stream, the river passes to the southward of Houssa, which is two days' journey distant from the river. Of the further progress of this great river, and its final exit, all the natives with whom I conversed seemed to be entirely ignorant. Their commercial pursuits seldom induce them to travel further than the cities of Timbuctoo and Houssa; and as the sole object of those journeys is the acquirement of wealth, they pay but little attention to the course of rivers, or the geography of countries. It is, however, highly probable that the Niger affords a safe and easy communication between very remote nations.   All my informants agreed, that many of the Negro merchants who arrive at Timbuctoo and Houssa from the eastward, speak a different language from that of Bambarra, or any other kingdom with which they are acquainted.   But even these merchants, it would seem, are ignorant of the termination of the river, for such of them as can speak Arabic, describe the amazing length of its course in very general terms, saying only that they believe it *runs to the world's end*.

The names of many kingdoms to the eastward of Houssa are familiar to the inhabitants of Bambarra.   I was shown quivers and arrows of very curious workmanship, which I was informed came from the kingdom of Kassina.

On the northern bank of the Niger, at a short distance from Silla, is the kingdom of Masina, which is inhabited by Foulahs.   They employ themselves there, as in other places, chiefly in pasturage, and pay an annual tribute to the king of Bambarra for the lands which they occupy.

To the north-east of Masina is situated the kingdom of Timbuctoo, the great object of European research—the capital of this kingdom being one of the principal marts for that extensive commerce which the Moors carry on with the Negroes.   The hopes of acquiring wealth in this pursuit, and zeal for propagating their religion, have filled this extensive city with Moors and Mahomedan converts; the king himself and all the chief officers of state are Moors, and they are said to be more severe and intolerant in their principles than any other of the Moorish tribes in this part of Africa.   I was informed by a venerable old Negro that when he first visited Timbuctoo, he took up his lodging at a sort of public inn, the landlord of which, when he conducted him into his hut, spread a mat on the floor, and laid a rope upon it, saying, " If you are a Mussulman, you are my friend, sit down; but if you are a Kafir, you are my slave, and with this rope I will lead you to market."   The present king of Timbuctoo is named *Abu Abrahima;* he is reported to possess immense riches.   His wives and concubines are said to be clothed in silk, and the chief officers of state live in considerable splendour. The whole expense of his government is defrayed, as I was told, by a tax upon merchandise, which is collected at the gates of the city.

The city of Houssa (the capital of a large kingdom of the same name, situated to the eastward of Timbuctoo) is another great mart for Moorish commerce. I conversed with many merchants who had visited that city, and they all agreed that it is larger and more populous than Timbuctoo. The trade, police, and government, are nearly the same in both; but in Houssa the Negroes are in greater proportion to the Moors, and have some share in the government.

Concerning the small kingdom of Jinbala, I was not able to collect much information. The soil is said to be remarkably fertile, and the whole country so full of creeks and swamps, that the Moors have hitherto been baffled in every attempt to subdue it. The inhabitants are Negroes, and some of them are said to live in considerable affluence, particularly those near the capital, which is a resting-place for such merchants as transport goods from Timbuctoo to the western parts of Africa.

To the southward of Jinbala is situated the Negro kingdom of Gotto, which is said to be of great extent. It was formerly divided into a number of petty states, which were governed by their own chiefs; but their private quarrels invited invasion from the neighbouring kingdoms. At length a politic chief, of the name of Moosee, had address enough to make them unite in hostilities against Bambarra, and on this occasion he was unanimously chosen general— the different chiefs consenting for a time to act under his command. Moosee immediately dispatched a fleet of canoes, loaded with provisions, from the banks of the lake Dibbie up the Niger, towards Jenné, and with the whole of his army pushed forwards into Bambarra. He arrived on the banks of the Niger opposite to Jenné, before the townspeople had the smallest intimation of his approach; his fleet of canoes joined him the same day, and having landed the provisions, he embarked part of his army, and

in the night took Jenné by storm.   This event so terrified
the king of Bambarra, that he sent messengers to sue for
peace, and in order to obtain it, consented to deliver to
Moosee a certain number of slaves every year, and return
everything that had been taken from the inhabitants of
Gotto.   Moosee, thus triumphant, returned to Gotto,
where he was declared king, and the capital of the country
is called by his name.

On the west of Gotto is the kingdom of Baedoo, which
was conquered by the present king of Bambarra about
seven years ago, and has continued tributary to him ever
since.

West of Baedoo is Maniana, the inhabitants of which,
according to the best information I was able to collect, are
cruel and ferocious, carrying their resentment towards their
enemies so far as never to give quarter, and even to indulge themselves with unnatural and disgusting banquets
of human flesh.

I am well aware that the accounts which the Negroes
give of their enemies ought to be received with great
caution; but I heard the same account in so many different kingdoms, and from such variety of people, whose
veracity I had no occasion to suspect, that I am disposed
to allow it some degree of credit.   The inhabitants of
Bambarra, in the course of a long and bloody war, must
have had frequent opportunities of satisfying themselves as
to the fact; and if the report had been entirely without
foundation, I cannot conceive why the term *Madummulo*
(man-eaters) should be applied exclusively to the inhabitants
of Maniana.

CHAPTER XVII

The Author returns westward—Arrives at Modiboo, and recovers his
horse—Finds great difficulty in travelling, in consequence of the
rains, and the overflowing of the river—Is informed that the king
of Bambarra had sent persons to apprehend him—Avoids Sego,
and prosecutes his journey along the banks of the Niger—Incidents
on the road—Cruelties attendant on African wars—The Author
crosses the river Frina, and arrives at Tafiara.

HAVING, for the reasons assigned in the last chapter,
determined to proceed no farther eastward than Silla, I
acquainted the Dooty with my intention of returning to
Sego, proposing to travel along the southern side of the
river; but he informed me, that from the number of creeks
and swamps on that side, it was impossible to travel by
any other route than along the northern bank; and even
that route, he said, would soon be impassable on account
of the overflowing of the river. However, as he com-
mended my determination to return westward, he agreed
to speak to some one of the fishermen to carry me over
to Moorzan. I accordingly stepped into a canoe about
eight o'clock in the morning of July 30th, and in about an
hour was landed at Moorzan. At this place I hired a
canoe for sixty cowries, and in the afternoon arrived at
Kea, where, for forty cowries more, the Dooty permitted
me to sleep in the same hut with one of his slaves. This
poor Negro, perceiving that I was sickly, and that my
clothes were very ragged, humanely lent me a large cloth
to cover me for the night.

July 31st.—The Dooty's brother being going to Modiboo,
I embraced the opportunity of accompanying him thither,
there being no beaten road. He promised to carry my
saddle, which I had left at Kea when my horse fell down
in the woods, as I now proposed to present it to the king
of Bambarra.

G 205

We departed from Kea at eight o'clock, and about a mile to the westward observed, on the bank of the river, a great number of earthen jars, piled up together. They were very neatly formed, but not glazed; and were evidently of that sort of pottery which is manufactured at Downie (a town to the west of Timbuctoo), and sold to great advantage in different parts of Bambarra. As we approached towards the jars, my companion plucked up a large handful of herbage, and threw it upon them; making signs for me to do the same, which I did. He then, with great seriousness, told me that these jars belonged to some supernatural power; that they were found in their present situation about two years ago; and as no person had claimed them, every traveller as he passed them, from respect to the invisible proprietor, threw some grass, or the branch of a tree, upon the heap, to defend the jars from the rain.

Thus conversing, we travelled in the most friendly manner, until, unfortunately, we perceived the footsteps of a lion, quite fresh in the mud, near the river side. My companion now proceeded with great circumspection; and at last, coming to some thick underwood, he insisted that I should walk before him. I endeavoured to excuse myself, by alleging that I did not know the road; but he obstinately persisted, and after a few high words and menacing looks, threw down the saddle and went away. This very much disconcerted me; but as I had given up all hopes of obtaining a horse, I could not think of encumbering myself with the saddle; and taking off the stirrups and girths, I threw the saddle into the river. The Negro no sooner saw me throw the saddle into the water, than he came running from among the bushes where he had concealed himself, jumped into the river, and by help of his spear, brought out the saddle, and ran away with it. I continued my course along the bank; but as the wood was remarkably thick, and I had reason to believe that a lion was at no great distance, I became much alarmed, and took a long circuit through the bushes to avoid him.

About four in the afternoon I reached Modiboo, where I

found my saddle. The guide, who had got there before me, being afraid that I should inform the king of his conduct, had brought the saddle with him in a canoe.

While I was conversing with the Dooty, and remonstrating against the guide for having left me in such a situation, I heard a horse neigh in one of the huts, and the Dooty inquired with a smile if I knew who was speaking to me? He explained himself by telling me that my horse was still alive, and somewhat recovered from his fatigue; but he insisted that I should take him along with me, adding that he had once kept a Moor's horse for four months, and when the horse had recovered and got into good condition, the Moor returned and claimed it, and refused to give him any reward for his trouble.

Aug. 1st.—I departed from Modiboo, driving my horse before me, and in the afternoon reached Nyamee, where I remained three days; during which time it rained without intermission, and with such violence, that no person could venture out of doors.

Aug. 5th.—I departed from Nyamee; but the country was so deluged, that I was frequently in danger of losing the road, and had to wade across the savannas for miles together, knee deep in water. Even the corn ground, which is the driest land in the country, was so completely flooded, that my horse twice stuck fast in the mud, and was not got out without the greatest difficulty.

In the evening of the same day I arrived at Nyara, where I was well received by the Dooty; and as the 6th was rainy, I did not depart until the morning of the 7th; but the water had swelled to such a height, that in many places the road was scarcely passable; and though I waded breast deep across the swamps, I could only reach a small village called Nemaboo, where, however, for a hundred cowries, I procured from some Foulahs plenty of corn for my horse, and milk for myself.

Aug. 8th.—The difficulties I had experienced the day before, made me anxious to engage a fellow-traveller, particularly, as I was assured that, in the course of a few days, the country would be so completely overflowed as to render the road utterly impassable; but though I offered two hundred cowries for a guide, nobody would accompany me. However, on the morning following (August 9th), a Moor and his wife, riding upon two bullocks, and bound for Sego with salt, passed the village, and agreed to take me along with them; but I found them of little service, for they were wholly unacquainted with the road, and being accustomed to a sandy soil, were very bad travellers. Instead of wading before the bullocks, to feel if the ground was solid, the woman boldly entered the first swamp, riding upon the top of the load; but when she had proceeded about two hundred yards, the bullock sunk into a hole, and threw both the load and herself among the reeds. The frightened husband stood for some time seemingly petrified with horror, and suffered his wife to be almost drowned before he went to her assistance.

About sunset we reached Sibity; but the Dooty received me very coolly; and when I solicited for a guide to Sansanding, he told me his people were otherwise employed. I was shown into a damp old hut, where I passed a very uncomfortable night; for when the walls of the hut are softened by the rain, they frequently become too weak to support the weight of the roof. I heard three huts fall during the night, and was apprehensive that the hut I lodged in would be the fourth. In the morning, as I went to pull some grass for my horse, I counted fourteen huts which had fallen in this manner since the commencement of the rainy season.

It continued to rain with great violence all the 10th; and as the Dooty refused to give me any provisions, I purchased some corn, which I divided with my horse.

Aug. 11th.—The Dooty compelled me to depart from the town, and I set out for Sansanding, without any great hopes of faring better there than I had done at Sibity; for I learned from people who came to visit me, that a report prevailed, and was universally believed, that I had come to Bambarra as a spy; and as Mansong had not admitted me into his presence, the Dooties of the different towns were at liberty to treat me in what manner they pleased. From repeatedly hearing the same story, I had no doubt of the truth of it; but as there was no alternative, I determined to proceed, and a little before sunset I arrived at Sansanding. My reception was what I expected. Counti Mamadi, who had been so kind to me formerly, scarcely gave me welcome. Every one wished to shun me, and my landlord sent a person to inform me that a very unfavourable report was received from Sego concerning me, and that he wished me to depart early in the morning. About ten o'clock at night Counti Mamadi himself came privately to me, and informed me that Mansong had dispatched a canoe to Janné to bring me back; and he was afraid I should find great difficulty in going to the west country. He advised me, therefore, to depart from Sansanding before daybreak; and cautioned me against stopping at Diggani, or any town near Sego.

Aug. 12*th.*—I departed from Sansanding, and reached Kabba in the afternoon. As I approached the town, I was surprised to see several people assembled at the gate; one of whom, as I advanced, came running towards me, and taking my horse by the bridle, led me round the walls of the town; and then pointing to the west, told me to go along, or it would fare worse with me. It was in vain that I represented the danger of being benighted in the woods, exposed to the inclemency of the weather, and to the fury of wild beasts. "Go along," was all the answer; and a number of people coming up, and urging me in the same manner with great earnestness, I suspected that some of the king's messengers, who were sent in search of me, were in the town; and that these Negroes, from mere kindness, conducted me past it with a view to facilitate my escape. I accordingly took the road for Sego, with the uncomfortable prospect of passing the night on the branches of a tree. After travelling about three miles I came to a small village near the road. The Dooty was splitting sticks by the gate; but I found I could have no admittance; and when I attempted to enter, he jumped up, and with the stick he held in his hand threatened to strike me off the horse, if I presumed to advance another step.

At a little distance from this village, and farther from the road, is another small one. I conjectured that being rather out of the common route, the inhabitants might have fewer objections to give me house-room for the night ; and having crossed some corn fields, I sat down under a tree by the well. Two or three women came to draw water, and one of them, perceiving I was a stranger, inquired whither I was going. I told her I was going for Sego, but being benighted on the road, I wished to stay at the village until morning, and begged she would acquaint the Dooty with my situation. In a little time the Dooty sent for me, and permitted me to sleep in a large baloon, in one corner of which was constructed a kiln for drying the fruit of the shea trees ; it contained about half a cart-load of fruit, under which was kept up a clear wood fire. I was informed that in three days the fruit would be ready for pounding and boiling, and that the butter thus manufactured is preferable to that which is prepared from fruit dried in the sun, especially in the rainy season, when the process by insolation is always tedious, and oftentimes ineffectual.

Aug. 13*th.*—About ten o'clock I reached a small village within half a mile of Sego, where I endeavoured, but in vain, to procure some provisions. Every one seemed anxious to avoid me ; and I could plainly perceive, by the looks and behaviour of the inhabitants, that some very unfavourable accounts had been circulated concerning me. I was again informed that Mansong had sent people to apprehend me ; and the Dooty's son told me I had no time to lose if I wished to get safe out of Bambarra. I now fully saw the danger of my situation, and determined to avoid Sego altogether. I accordingly mounted my horse, and taking the road for Diggani, travelled as fast as I could until I was out of sight of the villagers, when I struck to the westward, through high grass and swampy ground. About noon I stopped under a tree to consider what course to take, for I had now no doubt but that the Moors and Slatees had misinformed the king respecting the object of my mission, and that the people were absolutely in search of me to convey me a prisoner to Sego. Sometimes I had thoughts of swimming my horse across the Niger and going to the southward for Cape Coast; but reflecting that I had ten days to travel before I should reach Kong, and afterwards an extensive country to traverse, inhabited by various nations, with whose language and manners I was totally unacquainted, I relinquished this scheme, and judged that I should better answer the purpose of my mission by proceeding to the westward along the Niger, endeavouring to ascertain how far the river was navigable in that direction. Having resolved upon this course, I proceeded accordingly, and a little before sunset arrived at a Foulah village called Sooboo, where, for two hundred cowries, I procured lodging for the night.

Aug. 14*th*.—I continued my course along the bank of the river, through a populous and well-cultivated country I passed a walled town called Kamalia,[1] without stopping; and at noon rode through a large town called Samee, where there happened to be a market, and a number of people assembled in an open place in the middle of the town, selling cattle, cloth, corn, etc. I rode through the midst of them without being much observed; every one taking me for a Moor. In the afternoon I arrived at a small village called Binni, where I agreed with the Dooty's son, for one hundred cowries, to allow me to stay for the night; but when the Dooty returned, he insisted that I should instantly leave the place; and if his wife and son had not interceded for me, I must have complied.

Aug. 15*th*.—About nine o'clock I passed a large town called Sai, which very much excited my curiosity. It is completely surrounded by two very deep trenches at about two hundred yards distant from the walls. On the top of the trenches are a number of square towers, and the whole has the appearance of a regular fortification. Inquiring into the origin of this extraordinary entrenchment, I learned from two of the townspeople the following particulars, which, if true, furnish a mournful picture of the enormities of African wars. About fifteen years ago, when the present king of Bambarra's father desolated Maniana, the Dooty of

---

[1] There is another town of this name hereafter to be mentioned.

Sai had two sons slain in battle, fighting in the king's cause. He had a third son living, and when the king demanded a further reinforcement of men, and this youth among the rest, the Dooty refused to send him. This conduct so enraged the king, that when he returned from Maniana, about the beginning of the rainy season, and found the Dooty protected by the inhabitants, he sat down before Sai with his army, and surrounded the town with the trenches I had now seen. After a siege of two months, the townspeople became involved in all the horrors of famine ; and whilst the king's army were feasting in their trenches, they saw, with pleasure, the miserable inhabitants of Sai devour the leaves and bark of the Bentang tree that stood in the middle of the town. Finding, however, that the besieged would sooner perish than surrender, the king had recourse to treachery. He promised, that if they would open the gates, no person should be put to death, nor suffer any injury but the Dooty alone. The poor old man determined to sacrifice himself for the sake of his fellow-citizens, and immediately walked over to the king's army, where he was put to death. His son, in attempting to escape, was caught and massacred in the trenches, and the rest of the townspeople were carried away captives, and sold as slaves to the different Negro traders.

About noon I came to the village of Kaimoo, situated upon the bank of the river ; and as the corn I had purchased at Sibili was exhausted, I endeavoured to purchase a fresh supply ; but was informed that corn was become very scarce all over the country ; and though I offered fifty cowries for a small quantity, no person would sell me any. As I was about to depart, however, one of the villagers (who probably mistook me for a Moorish shereef) brought me some as a present, only desiring me in return to bestow my blessing upon him, which I did in plain English, and he received it with a thousand acknowledgments. Of this present I made my dinner, and it was the third successive day that I had subsisted entirely upon raw corn.

In the evening I arrived at a small village called Song, the surly inhabitants of which would not receive me, nor so much as permit me to enter the gate; but as lions were very numerous in this neighbourhood, and I had frequently, in the course of the day, seen the impression of their feet on the road, I resolved to stay in the vicinity of the village. Having collected some grass for my horse, I accordingly lay down under a tree by the gate. About ten o'clock I heard the hollow roar of a lion at no great distance, and attempted to open the gate; but the people from within told me, that no person must attempt to enter the gate without the Dooty's permission. I begged them to inform the Dooty that a lion was approaching the village, and I hoped he would allow me to come within the gate. I waited for an answer to this message with great anxiety : for the lion kept prowling round the village, and once advanced so very near me, that I heard him rustling among the grass, and climbed the tree for safety. About midnight the Dooty with some of his people opened the gate, and desired me to come in. They were convinced, they said, that I was not a Moor, for no Moor ever waited any time at the gate of a village, without cursing the inhabitants.

Aug. 16*th*.—About ten o'clock I passed a considerable town, with a mosque, called Jabbe. Here the country begins to rise into hills, and I could see the summits of high mountains to the westward. I had very disagreeable travelling all this day on account of the swampiness of the roads; for the river was now risen to such a height, as to overflow great part of the flat land on both sides, and from the muddiness of the water, it was difficult to discern its depth. In crossing one of these swamps, a little to the westward of a town called Gangu, my horse being up to the belly in water, slipt suddenly into a deep pit, and was almost drowned before he could disengage his feet from the stiff clay at the bottom. Indeed both the horse and its rider were so completely covered with mud, that in passing the village of Callimana, the people compared us to two dirty elephants. About noon I stopped at a small village near Yamina, where I purchased some corn, and dried my papers and clothes.

The town of Yamina, at a distance, has a very fine

appearance. It covers nearly the same extent of ground as Sansanding; but having been plundered by Daisy, king of Kaarta, about four years ago, it has not yet resumed its former prosperity—nearly one half of the town being nothing but a heap of ruins: however, it is still a considerable place, and is so much frequented by the Moors, that I did not think it safe to lodge in it; but, in order to satisfy myself respecting its population and extent, I resolved to ride through it; in doing which, I observed a great many Moors sitting upon the Bentangs, and other places of public resort. Everybody looked at me with astonishment; but as I rode briskly along, they had no time to ask questions.

I arrived in the evening at Farra, a walled village, where, without much difficulty, I procured a lodging for the night.

Aug. 17*th.*—Early in the morning I pursued my journey, and at eight o'clock passed a considerable town called Balaba; after which the road quits the plain, and stretches along the side of the hill. I passed in the course of this day the ruins of three towns; the inhabitants of which were all carried away by Daisy, king of Kaarta, on the same day that he took and plundered Yamina. Near one of these ruins I climbed a tamarind tree, but found the fruit quite green and sour, and the prospect of the country was by no means inviting; for the high grass and bushes seemed completely to obstruct the road, and the low lands were all so flooded by the river, that the Niger had the appearance of an extensive lake. In the evening I arrived at Kanika, where the Dooty, who was sitting upon an elephant's hide at the gate, received me kindly; and gave me for supper some milk and meal, which I considered (as to a person in my situation it really was) a very great luxury.

Aug. 18*th.*—By mistake I took the wrong road, and did not discover my error until I had travelled near four miles; when coming to an eminence, I observed the Niger considerably to the left. Directing my course towards it, I travelled through long grass and bushes, with great difficulty, until two o'clock in the afternoon; when I came to a comparatively small, but very rapid river, which I took at first for a creek, or one of the streams of the Niger. However, after I had examined it with more attention, I was convinced that it was a distinct river; and as the road evidently crossed it (for I could see the pathway on the opposite side), I sat down upon the bank, in hopes that some traveller might arrive, who would give me the necessary information concerning the fording place; for the banks were so covered with reeds and bushes, that it would have been almost impossible to land on the other side, except at the pathway; which, on account of the rapidity of the stream, it seemed very difficult to reach. No traveller, however, arriving, and there being a great appearance of rain, I examined the grass and bushes, for some way up the bank, and determined upon entering the river considerably above the pathway, in order to reach the other side before the stream had swept me too far down.   With this view I fastened my clothes upon the saddle, and was standing up to the neck in water, pulling my horse by the bridle to make him follow me, when a man came accidentally to the place, and seeing me in the water, called to me with great vehemence to come out. The alligators, he said, would devour both me and my horse, if we attempted to swim over.   When I had got out, the stranger, who had never before seen a European, seemed wonderfully surprised.   He twice put his hand to his mouth, exclaiming in a low tone of voice, " God preserve me ! who is this ? " but when he heard me speak the Bambarra tongue, and found that I was going the same way as himself, he promised to assist me in crossing the river; the name of which he told me was Frina.   He then went a little way along the bank, and called to some person, who answered from the other side.   In a short time, a canoe with two boys came paddling from among the reeds ; these boys agreed, for fifty cowries, to transport me and my horse over the river, which was effected without much difficulty ; and I arrived in the evening at Taffara, a walled town, and soon discovered that the language of the natives was improved, from the corrupted dialect of Bambarra, to the pure Mandingo.

CHAPTER XVIII

Inhospitable reception at Taffara—A Negro funeral at Sooha—The Author continues his route through several villages along the banks of the Niger, until he comes to Koolikorro—Supports himself by writing saphies—Reaches Marraboo—Loses the road, and after many difficulties arrives at Bammakoo—Takes the road for Sibidooloo—Meets with great kindness at a village called Kooma—Is afterwards robbed, stripped, and plundered by banditti—The Author's resource and consolation under exquisite distress—He arrives in safety at Sibidooloo.

On my arrival at Taffara, I inquired for the Dooty, but was informed that he had died a few days before my arrival, and that there was, at that moment, a meeting of the chief men for electing another; there being some dispute about the succession. It was probably owing to the unsettled state of the town, that I experienced such a want of hospitality in it; for though I informed the inhabitants that I should only remain with them for one night, and assured them that Mansong had given me some cowries to pay for my lodging, yet no person invited me to come in; and I was forced to sit alone under the Bentang tree, exposed to the rain and wind of a tornado, which lasted with great violence until midnight. At this time the stranger who had assisted me in crossing the river paid me a visit, and observing that I had not found a lodging, invited me to take part of his supper, which he had brought to the door of his hut; for being a guest himself, he could not, without his landlord's consent, invite me to come in. After this, I slept upon some wet grass in the corner of a court. My horse fared still worse than myself; the corn I had purchased being all expended, and I could not procure a supply.

Aug. 20th.—I passed the town of Jaba, and stopped a few minutes at a village called Somino, where I begged and obtained some coarse food, which the natives prepare from the husks of corn, and call *Boo*. About two o'clock I came to the village of Sooha, and endeavoured to purchase some corn from the Dooty, who was sitting by the gate, but without success. I then requested a little food by way of charity, but was told he had none to spare. Whilst I was examining the countenance of this inhospitable old man, and endeavouring to find out the cause of the sullen discontent which was visible in his eye, he called to a slave who was working in the corn field at a little distance, and ordered him to bring his hoe along with him. The Dooty then told him to dig a hole in the ground; pointing to a spot at no great distance. The slave, with his hoe, began to dig a pit in the earth; and the Dooty, who appeared to be a man of a very fretful disposition, kept muttering and talking to himself until the pit was almost finished, when he repeatedly pronounced the words *dankatoo* (good for nothing), *jankra lemen* (a real plague); which expressions I thought could be applied to nobody but myself; and as the pit had very much the appearance of a grave, I thought it prudent to mount my horse, and was about to decamp, when the slave, who had before gone into the village, to my surprise, returned with the corpse of a boy about nine or ten years of age, quite naked. The Negro carried the body by a leg and an arm, and threw it into the pit with a savage indifference which I had never before seen. As he covered the body with earth, the Dooty often expressed himself, *naphula attiniata* (money lost), whence I concluded that the boy had been one of his slaves.

Departing from this shocking scene, I travelled by the side of the river until sunset, when I came to Koolikorro, a considerable town, and a great market for salt. Here I took up my lodging at the house of a Bambarran, who had formerly been the slave of a Moor, and in that character had travelled to Aoran, Towdinni, and many other places in the Great Desert; but turning Mussulman, and his master dying at Jenné, he obtained his freedom, and settled at this place, where he carries on a considerable trade in salt, cotton cloth, etc. His knowledge of the world has not lessened that superstitious confidence in saphies and charms which he had imbibed in his earlier years; for when he heard that I was a Christian, he immediately thought of procuring a saphie, and for this purpose brought out his *walha*, or writing-board, assuring me that he would dress me a supper of rice if I would write him a saphie to protect him from wicked men. The proposal was of too great consequence to me to be refused; I therefore wrote the board full from top to bottom on both sides; and my landlord, to be certain of having the whole force of the charm, washed the writing from the board into a calabash with a little water, and having said a few prayers over it, drank this powerful draught: after which, lest a single word should escape, he licked the board until it was quite dry. A saphie writer was a man of too great consequence to be long concealed; the important information was carried to the Dooty, who sent his son with half a sheet of writing paper, desiring me to write him a *naphula saphie* (a charm to procure wealth). He brought me, as a present, some meal and milk; and when I had finished the saphie, and read it to him with an audible voice, he seemed highly satisfied with his bargain, and promised to bring me in the morning some milk for my breakfast. When I had finished my supper of rice and salt, I laid myself down upon a bullock's hide, and slept very quietly until morning; this being the first good meal and refreshing sleep that I had enjoyed for a long time.

Aug. 21st.—At daybreak I departed from Koolikorro, and about noon passed the villages of Kayoo and Toolumbo. In the afternoon I arrived at Marraboo, a large town, and like Koolikorro, famous for its trade in salt. I was conducted to the house of a Kaartan, of the tribe of Jower, by whom I was well received. This man had acquired a considerable property in the slave trade, and from his hospitality to strangers, was called by way of pre-eminence *Jattee* (the landlord), and his house was a sort of public inn for all travellers. Those who had money were well lodged, for they always made him some return for his kindness; but those who had nothing to give were content to accept whatever he thought proper; and as I could not rank myself among the monied men, I was happy to take up my lodging in the same hut with seven poor fellows who had come from Kancaba in a canoe. But our landlord sent us some victuals.

Aug. 22nd.—One of the landlord's servants went with me a little way from the town to show me what road to take; but whether from ignorance or design, I know not, he directed me wrong; and I did not discover my mistake until the day was far advanced; when, coming to a deep creek, I had some thoughts of turning back; but as by that means I foresaw that I could not possibly reach Bammakoo before night, I resolved to cross it; and leading my horse close to the brink, I went behind him, and pushed him headlong into the water; and then taking the bridle in my teeth, swam over to the other side. This was the third creek I had crossed in this manner, since I had left Sego; but having secured my notes and memorandums in the crown of my hat, I received little or no inconvenience from such adventures. The rain and heavy dew kept my clothes constantly wet; and the roads being very deep and full of mud, such a washing was sometimes pleasant, and often-times necessary. I continued travelling through high grass without any beaten road, and about noon came to the river, the banks of which are here very rocky, and the force and roar of the water were very great. The king of Bambarra's canoes, however, frequently pass these rapids, by keeping close to the bank; persons being stationed on the shore with ropes fastened to the canoe, while others push it forward with long poles. At this time, however, it would, I think, have been a matter of great difficulty for any European boat to have crossed the stream. About four o'clock in the afternoon, having altered my course from the river towards the mountains, I came to a small pathway, which led to a village called Frookaboo, where I slept.

Aug. 23rd.—Early in the morning I set out for Bammakoo, at which place I arrived about five o'clock in the afternoon. I had heard Bammakoo much talked of as a great market for salt, and I felt rather disappointed to find it only a middling town, not quite so large as Marraboo; however, the smallness of its size is more than compensated by the riches of its inhabitants; for when the Moors bring their salt through Kaarta or Bambarra, they constantly rest a few days at this place; and the Negro merchants here, who are well acquainted with the value of salt in different kingdoms, frequently purchase by wholesale, and retail it to great advantage. Here I lodged at the house of a Serawoolli Negro, and was visited by a number of Moors. They spoke very good Mandingo, and were more civil to me than their countrymen had been. One of them had travelled to Rio Grande, and spoke very highly of the Christians. He sent me in the evening some boiled rice and milk. I now endeavoured to procure information concerning my route to the westward, from a slave merchant who had resided some years on the Gambia. He gave me some imperfect account of the distance, and enumerated the names of a great many places that lay in the way; but withal told me that the road was impassable at this season of the year; he was even afraid, he said, that I should find great difficulty in proceeding any farther; as the road crossed the Joliba at a town about half a day's journey to the westward of Bammakoo; and there being no canoes at that place large enough to receive my horse, I could not possibly get him over for some months to come. This was an obstruction of a very serious nature; but as I had no money to maintain myself even for a few days, I resolved to push on, and if I could not convey my horse across the river, to abandon him, and swim over myself. In thoughts of this nature I passed the night, and in the morning consulted with my landlord how I should surmount the present difficulty. He informed me that one road still remained, which was indeed very rocky, and scarcely passable for horses; but that if I had a proper guide over the hills to a town called Sibidooloo, he had no doubt, but with patience and caution, I might travel forwards through Manding. I immediately applied to the Dooty, and was informed that a *Jilli Kea* (singing man) was about to depart for Sibidooloo, and would show me the road over the hills. With

this man, who undertook to be my conductor, I travelled
up a rocky glen about two miles, when we came to a small
village; and here my musical fellow-traveller found out
that he had brought me the wrong road. He told me that
the horse-road lay on the other side of the hill, and throwing his drum upon his back, mounted up the rocks, where
indeed no horse could follow him, leaving me to admire
his agility, and trace out a road for myself. As I found
it impossible to proceed, I rode back to the level ground,
and directing my course to the eastward, came about noon
to another glen, and discovered a path on which I observed
the marks of horses' feet; following this path, I came in a
short time to some shepherds' huts, where I was informed
that I was in the right road, but that I could not possibly
reach Sibidooloo before night. Soon after this I gained
the summit of a hill, from whence I had an extensive view
of the country. Towards the south-east appeared some
very distant mountains, which I had formerly seen from an
eminence near Marraboo, where the people informed me
that these mountains were situated in a large and powerful
kingdom called Kong; the sovereign of which could raise
a much greater army than the king of Bambarra. Upon
this height the soil is shallow; the rocks are ironstone and
schistus, with detached pieces of white quartz.

A little before sunset, I descended on the north-west side
of this ridge of hills; and as I was looking about for a convenient tree under which to pass the night (for I had no
hopes of reaching any town), I descended into a delightful
valley, and soon afterwards arrived at a romantic village
called Kooma. This village is surrounded by a high wall,
and is the sole property of a Mandingo merchant, who fled
hither with his family during a former war. The adjacent
fields yield him plenty of corn, his cattle roam at large in
the valley, and the rocky hills secure him from the depredations of war. In this obscure retreat he is seldom visited
by strangers; but whenever this happens, he makes the
weary traveller welcome. I soon found myself surrounded
by a circle of the harmless villagers. They asked me a
thousand questions about my country; and, in return for

my information, brought corn and milk for myself, and grass for my horse; kindled a fire in the hut where I was to sleep, and appeared very anxious to serve me.

Aug. 25*th.*—I departed from Kooma, accompanied by two shepherds, who were going towards Sibidooloo. The road was very steep and rocky, and as my horse had hurt his feet much in coming from Bammakoo, he travelled slowly and with great difficulty; for in many places the ascent was so sharp, and the declivities so great, that if he had made one false step, he must inevitably have been dashed to pieces. The shepherds being anxious to proceed, gave themselves little trouble about me or my horse, and kept walking on at a considerable distance. It was about eleven o'clock, as I stopped to drink a little water at a rivulet (my companions being nearly a quarter of a mile before me), that I heard some people calling to each other, and presently a loud screaming, as from a person in great distress. I immediately conjectured that a lion had taken one of the shepherds, and mounted my horse to have a better view of what had happened. The noise, however, ceased; and I rode slowly towards the place from whence I thought it had proceeded, calling out, but without receiving any answer. In a little time, however, I perceived one of the shepherds lying among the long grass near the road; and though I could see no blood upon him, I concluded he was dead. But when I came close to him, he whispered me to stop; telling me that a party of armed men had seized upon his companion, and shot two arrows at himself as he was making his escape. I stopped to consider what course to take, and looking round, saw at a little distance a man sitting on the stump of a tree; I distinguished also the heads of six or seven more, sitting among the grass, with muskets in their hands. I had now no hopes of escaping, and therefore determined to ride forward towards them. As I approached them, I was in hopes they were elephant hunters; and by way of opening the conversation, inquired if they had shot anything; but without returning an answer, one of them ordered me to dismount; and then, as if recollecting himself, waved with his hand for me to proceed. I accordingly rode past, and had with some difficulty crossed a deep rivulet, when I heard somebody holloa; and looking behind, saw those I had taken for elephant hunters running after me, and calling out to me to turn back. I stopped until they were all come up; when they informed me that the king of the Foulahs had sent them on purpose to bring me, my horse, and everything that belonged to me, to Fooladoo, and that therefore I must turn back, and go along with them. Without hesitating a moment, I turned round and followed them, and we travelled together near a quarter of a mile without exchanging a word; when coming to a dark place of the wood, one of them said, in the Mandingo language, "This will do;" and immediately snatched my hat from my head. Though I was by no means free of apprehension, yet I resolved to show as few signs of fear as possible, and therefore told them, that unless my hat was returned to me, I should proceed no further. But before I had time to receive an answer, another drew his knife, and seizing upon a metal button which remained upon my waistcoat, cut it off, and put it into his pocket. Their intentions were now obvious; and I thought that the easier they were permitted to rob me of everything, the less I had to fear. I therefore allowed them to search my pockets without resistance, and examine every part of my apparel, which they did with the most scrupulous exactness. But observing that I had one waistcoat under another, they insisted that I should cast them both off; and at last, to make sure work, stripped me quite naked. Even my half boots (though the sole of one of them was tied on to my foot with a broken bridle rein) were minutely inspected. Whilst they were examining the plunder, I begged them, with great earnestness, to return my pocket compass; but when I pointed it out to them, as it was lying on the ground, one of the banditti, thinking I was about to take it up, cocked his musket, and swore that he would lay me dead on the spot if I presumed to put my hand upon it. After this, some of them went away with my horse, and the remainder stood considering whether they should leave me quite naked, or allow me something to shelter me from the sun.   Humanity at last prevailed; they returned me the worst of the two shirts, and a pair of trousers; and, as they went away, one of them threw back my hat, in the crown of which I kept my memorandums; and this was probably the reason they did not wish to keep it.   After they were gone, I sat for some time looking around me with amazement and terror.   Whichever way I turned, nothing appeared but danger and difficulty.   I saw myself in the midst of a vast wilderness in the depth of the rainy season, naked and alone; surrounded by savage animals, and men still more savage.   I was five hundred miles from the nearest European settlement.   All these circumstances crowded at once on my recollection; and I confess that my spirits began to fail me.   I considered my fate as certain, and that I had no alternative, but to lie down and perish.   The influence of religion, however, aided and supported me.   I reflected that no human prudence or foresight could possibly have averted my present sufferings.   I was indeed a stranger in a strange land, yet I was still under the protecting eye of that Providence who has condescended to call himself the stranger's friend.   At this moment, painful as my reflections were, the extraordinary beauty of a small moss, in fructification, irresistibly caught my eye.   I mention this to show from what trifling circumstances the mind will sometimes derive consolation; for though the whole plant was not larger than the top of one of my fingers, I could not contemplate the delicate conformation of its roots, leaves, and capsula, without admiration.   Can that Being (thought I) who planted, watered, and brought to perfection, in this obscure part of the world, a thing which appears of so small importance, look with unconcern upon the situation and sufferings of creatures formed after His own image?—surely not!   Reflections like these would not allow me to despair. I started up, and disregarding both hunger and fatigue, travelled forwards, assured that relief was at hand; and I was not disappointed.   In a short time I came to a small village, at the entrance of which I overtook the two shepherds who had come with me from Kooma.   They were much surprised to see me; for they said they never doubted that the Foulahs, when they had robbed, had murdered me. Departing from this village, we travelled over several rocky ridges, and at sunset arrived at Sibidooloo, the frontier town of the kingdom of Manding.

CHAPTER XIX

Government of Manding—The Author's reception by the Mansa, or chief man of Sibidooloo, who takes measures for the recovery of his horse and effects—The Author removes to Wonda—Great scarcity, and its afflicting consequences—The Author recovers his horse and clothes—Presents his horse to the Mansa; and prosecutes his journey to Kamalia—Some account of that town—The Author's kind reception by Karfa Taura, a Slatee, who proposes to go to the Gambia in the next dry season with a caravan of slaves—The Author's sickness, and determination to remain and accompany Karfa.

THE town of Sibidooloo is situated in a fertile valley, surrounded with high rocky hills. It is scarcely accessible for horses, and during the frequent wars between the Bambarrans, Foulahs, and Mandingoes, has never once been plundered by an enemy. When I entered the town, the people gathered round me, and followed me into the baloon, where I was presented to the Dooty or chief man, who is here called Mansa, which usually signifies king. Nevertheless, it appeared to me that the government of Manding was a sort of republic, or rather an oligarchy—every town having a particular Mansa, and the chief power of the state, in the last resort, being lodged in the assembly of the whole body. I related to the Mansa the circumstances of my having been robbed of my horse and apparel; and my story was confirmed by the two shepherds. He continued smoking his pipe all the time I was speaking; but I had no sooner finished, than, taking his pipe from his mouth and tossing up the sleeve of his coat, with an indignant air, "Sit down," said he, "you shall have everything restored to you—I have sworn it;"—and then turning to an attendant, "Give the white man," said he, "a draught of water; and with the first light of the morning go over the hills, and inform the Dooty of Bammakoo that a poor white man, the king of Bambarra's stranger, has been robbed by the king of Fooladoo's people."

I little expected, in my forlorn condition, to meet with a man who could thus feel for my sufferings. I heartily thanked the Mansa for his kindness, and accepted his invitation to remain with him until the return of the messenger. I was conducted into a hut, and had some victuals sent me; but the crowd of people which assembled to see me, all of whom commiserated my misfortunes, and vented imprecations against the Foulahs, prevented me from sleeping until past midnight. Two days I remained without hearing any intelligence of my horse or clothes; and as there was at this time a great scarcity of provisions, approaching even to famine, all over this part of the country, I was unwilling to trespass any further on the Mansa's generosity, and begged permission to depart to the next village. Finding me very anxious to proceed, he told me that I might go as far as a town called Wonda, where he hoped I would remain a few days, until I heard some account of my horse, etc.

I departed accordingly on the next morning, the 28th, and stopped at some small villages for refreshment. I was presented at one of them with a dish which I had never before seen. It was composed of the blossoms or *antheræ* of the maize, stewed in milk and water. It is eaten only in time of great scarcity. On the 30th, about noon, I arrived at Wonda, a small town with a mosque, and surrounded by a high wall. The Mansa, who was a Mahomedan, acted in two capacities—as chief magistrate of the town, and schoolmaster to the children. He kept his school in an open shed, where I was desired to take up my lodging, until some account should arrive from Sibidooloo concerning my horse and clothes; for though the horse was of little use to me, yet the few clothes were essential. The little raiment upon me could neither protect me from the sun by day, nor the dews and mosquitoes by night; indeed, my shirt was not only worn thin, like a piece of muslin, but withal was so very dirty, that I was happy to embrace an opportunity of washing it; which having done, and spread it upon a bush, I sat down naked, in the shade, until it was dry.

Ever since the commencement of the rainy season, my health had been greatly on the decline. I had often been affected with slight paroxysms of fever; and from the time of leaving Bammakoo, the symptoms had considerably increased. As I was sitting in the manner described, the fever returned with such violence that it very much alarmed me; the more so, as I had no medicine to stop its progress, nor any hope of obtaining that care and attention which my situation required.

I remained at Wonda nine days, during which time I experienced the regular return of the fever every day. And though I endeavoured as much as possible to conceal my distress from my landlord, and frequently lay down the whole day, out of his sight, in a corn field, conscious how burdensome I was to him and his family in a time of such great scarcity; yet I found that he was apprised of my situation; and one morning, as I feigned to be asleep by the fire, he observed to his wife that they were likely to find me a very troublesome and chargeable guest, for that, in my present sickly state, they should be obliged, for the sake of their good name, to maintain me until I recovered or died.

The scarcity of provisions was certainly felt at this time most severely by the poor people, as the following circumstance most painfully convinced me. Every evening during my stay I observed five or six women come to the Mansa's house, and receive each of them a certain quantity of corn. As I knew how valuable this article was at this juncture, I inquired of the Mansa whether he maintained these poor women from pure bounty, or expected a return when the harvest should be gathered in. "Observe that boy," said he (pointing to a fine child about five years of age); "his mother has sold him to me for forty days' provision for herself and the rest of her family. I have bought another boy in the same manner." Good God, thought I, what must a mother suffer before she sells her own child! I could not get this melancholy subject out of my mind, and the next night, when the women returned for their allowance, I desired the boy to point out to me his mother, which he did. She was much emaciated, but had nothing cruel or savage in her countenance; and when she had received her corn, she came and talked to her son with as much cheerfulness as if he had still been under her care.

Sept. 6th.—Two people arrived from Sibidooloo, bringing with them my horse and clothes; but I found that my pocket compass was broken to pieces. This was a great loss, which I could not repair.

Sept. 7th.—As my horse was grazing near the brink of a well, the ground gave way, and he fell in. The well was about ten feet diameter, and so very deep, that when I saw my horse snorting in the water, I thought it was impossible to save him. The inhabitants of the village, however, immediately assembled, and having tied together a number of withes,[1] they lowered a man down into the well, who fastened those withes round the body of the horse; and the people, having first drawn up the man, took hold of the withes, and to my surprise pulled the horse out with the greatest facility. The poor animal was now reduced to a mere skeleton, and the roads were scarcely passable, being either very rocky, or else full of mud and water; I therefore found it impracticable to travel with him any farther, and was happy to leave him in the hands of one who I thought would take care of him. I accordingly presented him to my landlord, and desired him to send my saddle and bridle as a present to the Mansa of Sibidooloo, being the only return I could make him for having taken so much trouble in procuring my horse and clothes.

I now thought it necessary, sick as I was, to take leave of my hospitable landlord. On the morning of Sept. 8th, when I was about to depart, he presented me with his spear as a token of remembrance, and a leather bag to contain my clothes. Having converted my half-boots into sandals, I travelled with more ease, and slept that night at a village called Ballanti. On the 9th I reached Nemacoo; but the Mansa of the village thought fit to

[1] From a plant called *kabba*, that climbs like a vine upon the trees.

make me sup upon the cameleon's dish.   By way of
apology, however, he assured me the next morning that
the scarcity of corn was such that he could not possibly
allow me any.   I could not accuse him of unkindness, as
all the people actually appeared to be starving.

Sept. 10*th.*—It rained hard all day, and the people kept
themselves in their huts.   In the afternoon I was visited
by a Negro, named Modi Lemina Taura, a great trader,
who suspecting my distress, brought me some victuals,
and promised to conduct me to his house at Kinyeto the
day following.

Sept. 11*th.*—I departed from Nemacoo, and arrived at
Kinyeto in the evening; but having hurt my ankle in the
way, it swelled and inflamed so much that I could neither
walk, nor set my foot to the ground the next day, without
great pain.   My landlord observing this, kindly invited me
to stop with him a few days; and I accordingly remained
at his house until the 14th; by which time I felt much
relieved, and could walk with the help of a staff.   I now
set out, thanking my landlord for his great care and attention : and being accompanied by a young man, who was
travelling the same way, I proceeded for Jerijang, a beautiful and well-cultivated district, the Mansa of which is
reckoned the most powerful chief of any in Manding.

On the 15th, I reached Dosita, a large town, where I
staid one day on account of the rain; but continued very
sickly, and was slightly delirious in the night.   On the 17th,
I set out for Mansia, a considerable town, where small
quantities of gold are collected.   The road led over a
high rocky hill, and my strength and spirits were so much
exhausted, that before I could reach the top of the hill
I was forced to lie down three times, being very faint and
sickly.   I reached Mansia in the afternoon.   The Mansa
of this town had the character of being very inhospitable;
he, however, sent me a little corn for my supper, but
demanded something in return; and when I assured him
that I had nothing of value in my possession, he told me
(as if in jest) that my white skin should not defend me if
I told him lies.   He then showed me the hut wherein I

was to sleep, but took away my spear, saying that it would be returned to me in the morning. This trifling circumstance, when joined to the character I had heard of the man, made me rather suspicious of him; and I privately desired one of the inhabitants of the place, who had a bow and quiver, to sleep in the same hut with me. About midnight, I heard somebody approach the door, and observing the moonlight strike suddenly into the hut, I started up, and saw a man stepping cautiously over the threshold. I immediately snatched up the Negro's bow and quiver, the rattling of which made the man withdraw; and my companion looking out, assured me that it was the Mansa himself, and advised me to keep awake until the morning. I closed the door, and placed a large piece of wood behind it, and was wondering at this unexpected visit, when somebody pressed so hard against the door, that the Negro could scarcely keep it shut. But when I called to him to open the door, the intruder ran off as before.

Sept. 16*th.*—As soon as it was light, the Negro, at my request, went to the Mansa's house, and brought away my spear. He told me that the Mansa was asleep; and lest this inhospitable chief should devise means to detain me, he advised me to set out before he was awake, which I immediately did; and about two o'clock reached Kamalia, a small town, situated at the bottom of some rocky hills, where the inhabitants collect gold in considerable quantities. The Bushreens here live apart from the Kafirs, and have built their huts in a scattered manner at a short distance from the town. They have a place set apart for performing their devotions in, to which they give the name of *missura* or mosque; but it is in fact nothing more than a square piece of ground made level, and surrounded with the trunks of trees, having a small projection towards the east, where the Marraboo, or priest, stands, when he calls the people to prayers. Mosques of this construction are very common among the converted Negroes; but, having neither walls nor roof, they can only be used in fine weather. When it rains, the Bushreens perform their devotions in their huts.

On my arrival at Kamalia, I was conducted to the house

of a Bushreen named Karfa Taura, the brother of him to whose hospitality I was indebted at Kinyeto. He was collecting a coffle of slaves, with a view to sell them to the Europeans on the Gambia, as soon as the rains should be over. I found him sitting in his baloon surrounded by several Slatees, who proposed to join the coffle. He was reading to them from an Arabic book, and inquired, with a smile, if I understood it? Being answered in the negative, he desired one of the Slatees to fetch the little curious book, which had been brought from the west country. On opening this small volume, I was surprised and delighted to find it our *Book of Common Prayer;* and Karfa expressed great joy to hear that I could read it; for some of the Slatees, who had seen the Europeans upon the coast, observing the colour of my skin (which was now become very yellow from sickness), my long beard, ragged clothes, and extreme poverty, were unwilling to admit that I was a white man, and told Karfa, that they suspected I was some Arab in disguise. Karfa, however, perceiving that I could read this book, had no doubt concerning me, and kindly promised me every assistance in his power. At the same time he informed me, that it was impossible to cross the Jallonka wilderness for many months yet to come, as no less than eight rapid rivers, he said, lay in the way. He added, that he intended to set out himself for Gambia as soon as the rivers were fordable, and the grass burnt, and advised me to stay and accompany him. He remarked, that when a caravan of the natives could not travel through the country, it was idle for a single white man to attempt it. I readily admitted that such an attempt was an act of rashness; but I assured him that I had now no alternative, for having no money to support myself, I must either beg my subsistence, by travelling from place to place, or perish for want. Karfa now looked at me with great earnestness, and inquired if I could eat the common victuals of the country —assuring me he had never before seen a white man. He added, that if I would remain with him until the rains were over, he would give me plenty of victuals in the meantime, and a hut to sleep in; and that after he had conducted me

A View of Kamalia

in safety to the Gambia, I might then make him what
return I thought proper. I asked him if the value of one
prime slave would satisfy him. He answered in the affirmative, and immediately ordered one of the huts to be
swept for my accommodation. Thus was I delivered by the
friendly care of this benevolent Negro from a situation truly
deplorable. Distress and famine pressed hard upon me;
I had before me the gloomy wilds of Jallonkadoo, where
the traveller sees no habitation for five successive days. I
had observed at a distance the rapid course of the river
Kokoro. I had almost marked out the place where I
was doomed, I thought, to perish, when this friendly Negro
stretched out his hospitable hand for my relief.

In the hut which was appropriated for me, I was provided with a mat to sleep on, an earthen jar for holding
water, and a small calabash to drink out of; and Karfa
sent me from his own dwelling two meals a day, and
ordered his slaves to supply me with firewood and water.
But I found that neither the kindness of Karfa, nor any
sort of accommodation, could put a stop to the fever which
weakened me, and which became every day more alarming.
I endeavoured as much as possible to conceal my distress;
but on the third day after my arrival, as I was going with
Karfa to visit some of his friends, I found myself so faint
that I could scarcely walk, and before we reached the place,
I staggered and fell into a pit from which the clay had been
taken to build one of the huts. Karfa endeavoured to console me with the hopes of a speedy recovery, assuring me,
that if I would not walk out in the wet, I should soon be
well. I determined to follow his advice, and confine myself
to my hut; but was still tormented with the fever, and my
health continued to be in a very precarious state for five
ensuing weeks. Sometimes I could crawl out of the hut,
and sit a few hours in the open air; at other times I was
unable to rise, and passed the lingering hours in a very
gloomy and solitary manner. I was seldom visited by any
person except my benevolent landlord, who came daily to
inquire after my health. When the rains became less
frequent, and the country began to grow dry, the fever left

me, but in so debilitated a condition that I could scarcely stand upright, and it was with great difficulty that I could carry my mat to the shade of a tamarind tree at a short distance, to enjoy the refreshing smell of the corn fields, and delight my eyes with a prospect of the country. I had the pleasure at length to find myself in a state of convalescence, towards which the benevolent and simple manners of the Negroes, and the perusal of Karfa's little volume, greatly contributed.

In the meantime, many of the Slatees who resided at Kamalia having spent all their money, and become in a great measure dependent upon Karfa's hospitality, beheld me with an eye of envy, and invented many ridiculous and trifling stories to lessen me in Karfa's esteem. And in the beginning of December, a Serawoolli Slatee, with five slaves, arrived from Sego. This man, too, spread a number of malicious reports concerning me ; but Karfa paid no attention to them, and continued to show me the same kindness as formerly. As I was one day conversing with the slaves which this Slatee had brought, one of them begged me to give him some victuals. I told him I was a stranger, and had none to give. He replied, " I gave *you* victuals when you was hungry. Have you forgot the man who brought you milk at Karankalla ? But (added he, with a sigh) *the irons were not then upon my legs !* " I immediately recollected him, and begged some ground nuts from Karfa to give him as a return for his former kindness. He told me that he had been taken by the Bambarrans the day after the battle at Joka, and sent to Sego, where he had been purchased by his present master, who was carrying him down to Kajaaga. Three more of these slaves were from Kaarta, and one from Wassela, all of them prisoners of war. They stopped four days at Kamalia, and were then taken to Bala, where they remained until the river Kokoro was fordable, and the grass burnt.

In the beginning of December, Karfa proposed to complete his purchase of slaves, and for this purpose collected all the debts which were owing to him in his own country. And on the 19th, being accompanied by three Slatees, he

departed for Kancaba, a large town on the banks of the
Niger, and a great slave-market.   Most of the slaves who
are sold at Kancaba come from Bambarra; for Mansong,
to avoid the expense and danger of keeping all his prisoners
at Sego, commonly sends them in small parties to be sold
at the different trading towns; and as Kancaba is much
resorted to by merchants, it is always well supplied with
slaves, which are sent thither up the Niger in canoes.
When Karfa departed from Kamalia, he proposed to return
in the course of a month, and during his absence I was
left to the care of a good old Bushreen who acted as
schoolmaster to the young people of Kamalia.

Being now left alone, and at leisure to indulge my own
reflections, it was an opportunity not to be neglected of
augmenting and extending the observations I had already
made on the climate and productions of the country, and
of acquiring a more perfect knowledge of the natives, than
it was possible for me to obtain in the course of a transient
and perilous journey through the country.   I endeavoured
likewise to collect all the information I could concerning
those important branches of African commerce, the trade
for gold, ivory, and slaves.   Such was my employment
during the remainder of my stay at Kamalia; and I shall
now proceed to lay before my readers the result of my
researches and inquiries, avoiding, as far as I can, a repetition of those circumstances and observations which were
related, as occasion arose, in the narrative of my journey.

CHAPTER XX

Of the climate and seasons—Winds—Vegetable productions—Population—General observations on the character and disposition of
the Mandingoes ; and a summary account of their manners and
habits of life, their marriages, etc.

THE whole of my route, both in going and returning,
having been confined to a tract of country bounded nearly
by the 12th and 15th parallels of latitude, the reader must
imagine that I found the climate in most places extremely
hot; but nowhere did I feel the heat so intense and
oppressive as in the camp at Benowm, of which mention
has been made in a former place. In some parts, where
the country ascends into hills, the air is at all times comparatively cool; yet none of the districts which I traversed
could properly be called mountainous. About the middle
of June, the hot and sultry atmosphere is agitated by violent
gusts of wind (called *tornadoes*), accompanied with thunder
and rain. These usher in what is denominated the *rainy
season*, which continues until the month of November.
During this time the diurnal rains are very heavy, and the
prevailing winds are from the south-west. The termination
of the rainy season is likewise attended with violent tornadoes; after which, the wind shifts to the north-east, and
continues to blow from that quarter during the rest of
the year.

When the wind sets in from the north-east it produces a
wonderful change in the face of the country. The grass
soon becomes dry and withered; the rivers subside very
rapidly, and many of the trees shed their leaves. About
this period is commonly felt the *harmattan*, a dry and
parching wind, blowing from the north-east, and accompanied by a thick smoky haze, through which the sun
appears of a dull red colour. This wind, in passing over

the great desert of Sahara, acquires a very strong attraction for humidity, and parches up everything exposed to its current. It is, however, reckoned very salutary, particularly to Europeans, who generally recover their health during its continuance. I experienced immediate relief from sickness, both at Dr. Laidley's and at Kamalia, during the *harmattan*. Indeed, the air, during the rainy season, is so loaded with moisture, that clothes, shoes, trunks, and everything that is not close to the fire, become damp and mouldy, and the inhabitants may be said to live in a sort of vapour bath; but this dry wind braces up the solids, which were before relaxed, gives a cheerful flow of spirits, and is even pleasant to respiration. Its ill effects are, that it produces chaps in the lips, and afflicts many of the natives with sore eyes.

Whenever the grass is sufficiently dry, the Negroes set it on fire; but in Ludamar, and other Moorish countries, this practice is not allowed; for it is upon the withered stubble that the Moors feed their cattle until the return of the rains. The burning the grass in Manding exhibits a scene of terrific grandeur. In the middle of the night I could see the plains and mountains, as far as my eye could reach, variegated with lines of fire, and the light reflected on the sky made the heavens appear in a blaze. In the day-time pillars of smoke were seen in every direction; while the birds of prey were observed hovering round the conflagration, and pouncing down upon the snakes, lizards, and other reptiles, which attempted to escape from the flames. This annual burning is soon followed by a fresh and sweet verdure, and the country is thereby rendered more healthful and pleasant.

Of the most remarkable and important of the vegetable productions mention has already been made, and they are nearly the same in all the districts through which I passed. It is observable, however, that although many species of the edible roots which grow in the West India Islands are found in Africa, yet I never saw, in any part of my journey, either the sugar-cane, the coffee, or the cocoa tree; nor could I learn on inquiry that they were known to the natives. The pine-apple, and the thousand other delicious fruits which the industry of civilised man (improving the bounties of nature) has brought to such great perfection in the tropical climates of America, are here equally unknown. I observed, indeed, a few orange and banana trees near the mouth of the Gambia; but whether they were indigenous, or were formerly planted there by some of the white traders, I could not positively learn. I suspect that they were originally introduced by the Portuguese.

Concerning property in the soil, it appeared to me that the lands in native woods were considered as belonging to the king, or (where the government was not monarchical) to the state. When any individual of free condition had the means of cultivating more land than he actually possessed, he applied to the chief man of the district, who allowed him an extension of territory, on condition of forfeiture if the lands were not brought into cultivation by a given period. The condition being fulfilled, the soil became vested in the possessor; and for aught that appeared to me, descended to his heirs.

The population, however, considering the extent and fertility of the soil, and the ease with which lands are obtained, is not very great in the countries which I visited. I found many extensive and beautiful districts, entirely destitute of inhabitants; and, in general, the borders of the different kingdoms were either very thinly peopled, or entirely deserted. Many places are likewise unfavourable to population, from being unhealthful. The swampy banks of the Gambia, the Senegal, and other rivers towards the coast, are of this description. Perhaps it is on this account chiefly that the interior countries abound more with inhabitants than the maritime districts; for all the Negro nations that fell under my observation, though divided into a number of petty independent states, subsist chiefly by the same means, live nearly in the same temperature, and possess a wonderful similarity of disposition. The Mandingoes, in particular, are a very gentle race; cheerful in their dispositions, inquisitive, credulous, simple, and fond of flattery. Perhaps the most prominent defect in their character was that insurmountable propensity which the reader must have observed to prevail in all classes of them, to steal from me the few effects I was possessed of. For this part of their conduct no complete justification can be offered, because theft is a crime in their own estimation; and it must be observed that they are not habitually and generally guilty of it towards each other. This, however, is an important circumstance in mitigation; and before we pronounce them a more depraved people than any other, it were well to consider whether the lower order of people in any part of Europe would have acted, under similar circumstances, with greater honesty towards a stranger, than the Negroes acted towards me. It must not be forgotten that the laws of the country afforded me no protection; that every one was at liberty to rob me with impunity; and finally, that some part of my effects were of as great value, in the estimation of the Negroes, as pearls and diamonds would have been in the eyes of a European. Let us suppose a black merchant of Hindostan to have found his way into the centre of England, with a box of jewels at his back, and that the laws of the kingdom afforded him no security; in such a case, the wonder would be, not that the stranger was robbed of any part of his riches, but that any part was left for a second depredator. Such, on sober reflection, is the judgment I have formed concerning the pilfering disposition of the Mandingo Negroes towards myself. Notwithstanding I was so great a sufferer by it, I do not consider that their natural sense of justice was perverted or extinguished; it was overpowered only for the moment by the strength of a temptation which it required no common virtue to resist.

On the other hand, as some counterbalance to this depravity in their nature—allowing it to be such—it is impossible for me to forget the disinterested charity and tender solicitude with which many of these poor heathens (from the sovereign of Sego to the poor women who received me at different times into their cottages when I was perishing of hunger) sympathised with me in my sufferings, relieved my distresses, and contributed to my safety. This acknowledgment, however, is perhaps more particularly due to the female part of the nation. Among the men, as the reader must have seen, my reception, though generally kind, was sometimes otherwise. It varied according to the various tempers of those to whom I made application. The hardness of avarice in some, and the blindness of bigotry in others, had closed up the avenues to compassion; but I do not recollect a single instance of hardheartedness towards me in the women. In all my wanderings and wretchedness, I found them uniformly kind and compassionate; and I can truly say, as my predecessor Mr. Ledyard has eloquently said before me :—" To a woman, I never addressed myself in the language of decency and friendship, without receiving a decent and friendly answer. If I was hungry or thirsty, wet or sick, they did not hesitate, like the men, to perform a generous action. In so free and so kind a manner did they contribute to my relief, that if I was dry I drank the sweetest draught, and if hungry I ate the coarsest morsel with a double relish."

It is surely reasonable to suppose that the soft and amiable sympathy of nature, which was thus spontaneously manifested towards me in my distress, is displayed by these poor people, as occasion requires, much more strongly towards persons of their own nation and neighbourhood, and especially when the objects of their compassion are endeared to them by the ties of consanguinity. Accordingly, the maternal affection (neither suppressed by the restraints, nor diverted by the solicitudes of civilised life) is everywhere conspicuous among them, and creates a correspondent return of tenderness in the child. An illustration of this has been given in page 35. "Strike me," said my attendant, "but do not curse my mother." The same sentiment I found universally to prevail, and observed in all parts of Africa that the greatest affront which could be offered to a Negro was to reflect on her who gave him birth.

It is not strange that this sense of filial duty and affection among the Negroes should be less ardent towards the father than the mother. The system of polygamy, while it weakens the father's attachment, by dividing it among the children of different wives, concentrates all the mother's jealous tenderness to one point—the protection of her own offspring. I perceived with great satisfaction, too, that the maternal solicitude extended not only to the growth and security of the person, but also, in a certain degree, to the improvement of the mind of the infant; for one of the first lessons in which the Mandingo women instruct their children, is *the practice of truth.* The reader will probably recollect the case of the unhappy mother, whose son was murdered by the Moorish banditti at Funingkedy, p. 77. Her only consolation in her uttermost distress, was the reflection that the poor boy, in the course of his blameless life, *had never told a lie.* Such testimony from a fond mother, on such an occasion, must have operated powerfully on the youthful part of the surrounding spectators. It was at once a tribute of praise to the deceased, and a lesson to the living.

The Negro women suckle their children until they are able to walk of themselves. Three years' nursing is not uncommon; and during this period the husband devotes his whole attention to his other wives. To this practice it is owing, I presume, that the family of each wife is seldom very numerous. Few women have more than five or six children. As soon as an infant is able to walk, it is permitted to run about with great freedom. The mother is not over solicitous to preserve it from slight falls and other trifling accidents. A little practice soon enables the child to take care of itself, and experience acts the part of a nurse. As they advance in life, the girls are taught to spin cotton, and to beat corn, and are instructed in other domestic duties; and the boys are employed in the labours of the field. Both sexes, whether Bushreens or Kafirs, on attaining the age of puberty, are circumcised. This painful operation is not considered by the Kafirs so much in the light of a religious ceremony, as a matter of convenience and utility. They have, indeed, a superstitious notion that it contributes to render the marriage state prolific. The operation is performed upon several young people at the same time; all of whom are exempted from every sort of

labour for two months afterwards.   During this period
they form a society called *Solimana*.   They visit the towns
and villages in the neighbourhood, where they dance and
sing, and are well treated by the inhabitants.   I had frequently, in the course of my journey, observed parties of
this description, but they were all males.   I had, however,
an opportunity of seeing a female *Solimana*, at Kamalia.

In the course of the celebration, it frequently happens that
some of the young women get married.   If a man takes a
fancy to any one of them, it is not considered as absolutely
necessary that he should make an overture to the girl herself.   The first object is to agree with the parents concerning
the recompense to be given them for the loss of the company
and services of their daughter.   The value of two slaves is
a common price, unless the girl is thought very handsome,
in which case the parents will raise their demand very considerably.   If the lover is rich enough, and willing to give
the sum demanded, he then communicates his wishes to
the damsel; but her consent is by no means necessary to
the match; for if the parents agree to it, and eat a few
kolla-nuts, which are presented by the suitor as an earnest
of the bargain, the young lady must either have the man of
their choice or continue unmarried, for she cannot afterwards be given to another.   If the parents should attempt
it, the lover is then authorised, by the laws of the country,
to seize upon the girl as his slave.   When the day for
celebrating the nuptials is fixed on, a select number of
people are invited to be present at the wedding; a bullock
or goat is killed, and great plenty of victuals dressed for
the occasion.   As soon as it is dark, the bride is conducted
into a hut, where a company of matrons assist in arranging
the wedding-dress, which is always white cotton, and is put
on in such a manner as to conceal the bride from head to
foot.   Thus arrayed, she is seated upon a mat in the middle
of the floor, and the old women place themselves in a circle
round her.   They then give her a series of instructions,
and point out, with great propriety, what ought to be her
future conduct in life.   This scene of instruction, however,
is frequently interrupted by girls, who amuse the company

with songs and dances, which are rather more remarkable for their gaiety than delicacy. While the bride remains within the hut with the women, the bridegroom devotes his attention to the guests of both sexes, who assemble without doors, and by distributing among them small presents of kolla-nuts, and seeing that every one partakes of the good cheer which is provided, he contributes much to the general hilarity of the evening. When supper is ended, the company spend the remainder of the night in singing and dancing, and seldom separate until daybreak. About midnight, the bride is privately conducted by the women into the hut which is to be her future residence; and the bridegroom, upon a signal given, retires from his company. The new-married couple, however, are always disturbed towards morning by the women, who assemble to inspect the nuptial sheet (according to the manners of the ancient Hebrews, as recorded in Scripture), and dance round it. This ceremony is thought indispensably necessary, nor is the marriage considered as valid without it.

The Negroes, as hath been frequently observed, whether Mahomedan or Pagan, allow a plurality of wives. The Mahomedans alone are by their religion confined to four; and as the husband commonly pays a great price for each, he requires from all of them the utmost deference and submission, and treats them more like hired servants than companions. They have, however, the management of domestic affairs, and each in rotation is mistress of the household, and has the care of dressing the victuals, overlooking the female slaves, etc. But though the African husbands are possessed of great authority over their wives, I did not observe that in general they treat them with cruelty, neither did I perceive that mean jealousy in their dispositions, which is so prevalent among the Moors. They permit their wives to partake of all public diversions, and this indulgence is seldom abused; for though the Negro women are very cheerful and frank in their behaviour, they are by no means given to intrigue. I believe that instances of conjugal infidelity are not common. When the wives quarrel among themselves, a circumstance which, from the nature of their situation, must frequently happen, the husband decides between them, and sometimes finds it necessary to administer a little corporal chastisement before tranquillity can be restored. But if any one of the ladies complains to the chief of the town that her husband has unjustly punished her, and shown an undue partiality to some other of his wives, the affair is brought to a public trial. In these *palavers*, however, which are conducted chiefly by married men, I was informed that the complaint of the wife is not always considered in a very serious light, and the complainant herself is sometimes convicted of strife and contention, and left without remedy. If she murmurs at the decision of the court, the magic rod of *Mumbo Jumbo* soon puts an end to the business.

The children of the Mandingoes are not always named after their relations, but frequently in consequence of some remarkable occurrence. Thus, my landlord at Kamalia was called *Karfa*, a word signifying *to replace ;* because he was born shortly after the death of one of his brothers. Other names are descriptive of good or bad qualities, as *Modi*, "a good man ;" *Fadibba*, "father of the town," etc. ; indeed the very names of their towns have something descriptive in them, as *Sibidooloo*, "the town of ciboa trees ;" *Kenneyeto*, "victuals here ;" *Dosita*, "lift your spoon." Others seem to be given by way of reproach, as *Bammakoo*, "wash a crocodile ;" *Karankalla*, "no cup to drink from," etc. A child is named when it is seven or eight days old. The ceremony commences by shaving the infant's head; and a dish called *Dega*, made of pounded corn and sour milk, is prepared for the guests. If the parents are rich, a sheep or goat is commonly added. The feast is called *Ding koon lee*, "the child's head shaving." During my stay at Kamalia I was present at four different feasts of this kind, and the ceremony was the same in each, whether the child belonged to a Bushreen or a Kafir. The schoolmaster, who officiated as priest on these occasions, and who is necessarily a Bushreen, first said a long prayer over the *dega*, during which every person present took hold of the brim of the calabash with his right hand. After this the schoolmaster took the child in his arms, and said a second prayer, in which he repeatedly solicited the blessing of God upon the child, and upon all the company. When this prayer was ended, he whispered a few sentences in the child's ear, and spat three times in its face, after which he pronounced its name aloud, and returned the infant to the mother. This part of the ceremony being ended, the father of the child divided the *dega* into a number of balls, one of which he distributed to every person present. And inquiry was then made if any person in the town was dangerously sick—it being usual in such cases to send the party a large portion of the *dega*, which is thought to possess great medical virtues.[1]

Among the Negroes every individual, besides his own proper name, has likewise a *kontong*, or surname, to denote the family or clan to which he belongs. Some of these families are very numerous and powerful. It is impossible to enumerate the various *kontongs* which are found in different parts of the country, though the knowledge of many of them is of great service to the traveller; for as every Negro plumes himself upon the importance or the antiquity of his clan, he is much flattered when he is addressed by his *kontong*.

Salutations among the Negroes to each other, when they meet, are always observed; but those in most general use among the Kafirs are *Abbe paeretto—E ning seni—Anawari*, etc., all of which have nearly the same meaning, and signify, *are you well?* or to that effect. There are likewise salutations which are used at different times of the day, as *E ning somo*, good morning, etc. The general answer to all salutations is to repeat the *kontong* of the person who salutes, or else to repeat the salutation itself, first pronouncing the word *marhaba*, my friend.

---

[1] Soon after baptism, the children are marked in different parts of the skin, in a manner resembling what is called *tattooing* in the South Sea Islands.

CHAPTER XXI

The account of the Mandingoes continued—Their notions in respect
of the pla etary bodies, and the figure of the earth—Their religious
opinions and belief in a future state—Their diseases and methods
of treatment—Their funeral ceremonies, amusements, occupations,
diet, arts, manufactures, etc.

THE Mandingoes, and, I believe, the Negroes in general,
have no artificial method of dividing time. They calculate
the years by the number of *rainy seasons*. They portion
the year into *moons*, and reckon the days by so many
suns. The day they divide into morning, mid-day, and
evening ; and further subdivide it, when necessary, by
pointing to the sun's place in the heavens. I frequently
inquired of some of them what became of the sun during
the night, and whether we should see the same sun or
a different one in the morning ; but I found that they
considered the question as very childish. The subject
appeared to them as placed beyond the reach of human
investigation ; they had never indulged a conjecture, nor
formed any hypothesis about the matter. The moon, by
varying her form, has more attracted their attention. On
the first appearance of the new moon, which they look
upon to be newly created, the Pagan natives, as well as
Mahomedans, say a short prayer ; and this seems to be
the only visible adoration which the Kafirs offer to the
Supreme Being. This prayer is pronounced in a whisper—
the party holding up his hands before his face ; its purport
(as I have been assured by many different people) is to
return thanks to God for His kindness through the existence of the past moon, and to solicit a continuation of His
favour during that of the new one. At the conclusion,
they spit upon their hands, and rub them over their faces.
This seems to be nearly the same ceremony which prevailed among the heathens in the days of Job.[1]

[1] Chapter xxxi. verses 26, 27, 28.

Great attention, however, is paid to the changes of this luminary, in its monthly course; and it is thought very unlucky to begin a journey or any other work of consequence, in the last quarter. An eclipse, whether of the sun or moon, is supposed to be effected by witchcraft. The stars are very little regarded; and the whole study of astronomy appears to them as a useless pursuit, and attended to by such persons only as deal in magic.

Their notions of geography are equally puerile. They imagine that the world is an extended plain, the termination of which no eye has discovered—it being, they say, overhung with clouds and darkness. They describe the sea as a large river of salt water, on the further shore of which is situated a country called *Tobaubo doo*—"the land of the white people." At a distance from Tobaubo doo, they describe another country, which they allege is inhabited by cannibals of gigantic size, called *Koomi*. This country they call *Jong sang doo*—"the land where the slaves are sold." But of all countries in the world their own appears to them as the best, and their own people as the happiest; and they pity the fate of other nations, who have been placed by Providence in less fertile and less fortunate districts.

Some of the religious opinions of the Negroes, though blended with the weakest credulity and superstition, are not unworthy of attention. I have conversed with all ranks and conditions upon the subject of their faith, and can pronounce, without the smallest shadow of doubt, that the belief of one God, and of a future state of reward and punishment, is entire and universal among them. It is remarkable, however, that, except on the appearance of a new moon, as before related, the Pagan natives do not think it necessary to offer up prayers and supplications to the Almighty. They represent the Deity, indeed, as the creator and preserver of all things; but in general they consider him as a being so remote, and of so exalted a nature, that it is idle to imagine the feeble supplications of wretched mortals can reverse the decrees, and change the purposes of unerring Wisdom. If they are asked, for what reason then do they offer up a prayer on the appearance of the

new moon; the answer is, that custom has made it necessary; they do it because their fathers did it before them.
Such is the blindness of unassisted nature! The concerns
of this world, they believe, are committed by the Almighty
to the superintendence and direction of subordinate spirits,
over whom they suppose that certain magical ceremonies
have great influence. A white fowl suspended to the
branch of a particular tree, a snake's head, or a few handfuls
of fruit, are offerings which ignorance and superstition frequently present, to deprecate the wrath or to conciliate the
favour, of these tutelary agents. But it is not often that the
Negroes make their religious opinions the subject of conversation. When interrogated, in particular, concerning
their ideas of a future state, they express themselves with
great reverence, but endeavour to shorten the discussion
by observing—*mo o mo inta allo*, "no man knows anything
about it." They are content, they say, to follow the pre-
cepts and examples of their forefathers, through the various
vicissitudes of life; and when this world presents no objects
of enjoyment or comfort, they seem to look with anxiety
towards another, which they believe will be better suited
to their natures, but concerning which they are far from
indulging vain and delusive conjectures.

The Mandingoes seldom attain extreme old age. At
forty, most of them become grey-haired, and covered with
wrinkles; and but few of them survive the age of fifty-five
or sixty. They calculate the years of their lives, as I have
already observed, by the number of rainy seasons (there
being but one such in the year); and distinguish each year
by a particular name, founded on some remarkable occurrence which happened in that year. Thus they say the
year of the *Farbanna war*; the year of the *Kaarta war*;
the year on which *Gadou was plundered, etc. etc.*; and I
have no doubt that the year 1796 will in many places be
distinguished by the name of *Tobaubo tambi sang*, "the
year the white man passed;" as such an occurrence would
naturally form an epoch in their traditional history.

But notwithstanding that longevity is uncommon among
them, it appeared to me that their diseases are but few in

number. Their simple diet, and active way of life, preserve them from many of those disorders which embitter the days of luxury and idleness. Fevers and fluxes are the most common and the most fatal. For these, they generally apply saphies to different parts of the body, and perform a great many other superstitious ceremonies; some of which are, indeed, well calculated to inspire the patient with the hope of recovery, and divert his mind from brooding over his own danger. But I have sometimes observed among them a more systematic mode of treatment. On the first attack of a fever, when the patient complains of cold, he is frequently placed in a sort of vapour; this is done by spreading branches of the *Nauclea orientalis* upon hot wood embers, and laying the patient upon them, wrapped up in a large cotton cloth. Water is then sprinkled upon the branches, which, descending to the hot embers, soon covers the patient with a cloud of vapour, in which he is allowed to remain until the embers are almost extinguished. This practice commonly produces a profuse perspiration, and wonderfully relieves the sufferer.

For the dysentery, they use the bark of different trees reduced to powder, and mixed with the patient's food; but this practice is in general very unsuccessful.

The other diseases which prevail among the Negroes are the *yaws*, the *elephantiasis*, and a *leprosy* of the very worst kind. This last mentioned complaint appears, at the beginning, in scurfy spots upon different parts of the body, which finally settle upon the hands or feet, where the skin becomes withered, and cracks in many places. At length, the ends of the fingers swell and ulcerate; the discharge is acrid and foetid; the nails drop off, and the bones of the fingers become carious, and separate at the joints. In this manner the disease continues to spread, frequently until the patient loses all his fingers and toes. Even the hands and feet are sometimes destroyed by this inveterate malady, to which the Negroes give the name of *balla jou*, " incurable."

The *Guinea worm* is likewise very common in certain places, especially at the commencement of the rainy season.

The Negroes attribute this disease, which has been described by many writers, to bad water; and allege that the people who drink from wells are more subject to it than those who drink from streams.   To the same cause they attribute the swelling of the glands of the neck (goîtres), which are very common in some parts of Bambarra.   I observed also, in the interior countries, a few instances of simple gonorrhœa ; but never the confirmed lues.   On the whole, it appeared to me that the Negroes are better surgeons than physicians. I found them very successful in their management of fractures and dislocations, and their splints and bandages are simple, and easily removed.   The patient is laid upon a soft mat, and the fractured limb is frequently bathed with cold water.   All abscesses they open with the actual cautery ; and the dressings are composed of either soft leaves, Shea butter, or cow's dung, as the case seems, in their judgment, to require.   Towards the coast, where a supply of European lancets can be procured, they some-times perform phlebotomy ; and in cases of local inflamma-tion, a curious sort of cupping is practised.   This operation is performed by making incisions in the part, and applying to it a bullock's horn, with a small hole in the end.   The operator then takes a piece of bees-wax in his mouth, and putting his lips to the hole extracts the air from the horn ; and by a dexterous use of his tongue, stops up the hole with the wax.   This method is found to answer the purpose, and in general produces a plentiful discharge.

When a person of consequence dies, the relations and neighbours meet together, and manifest their sorrow by loud and dismal howlings.   A bullock or goat is killed for such persons as come to assist at the funeral, which generally takes place in the evening of the same day on which the party died.   The Negroes have no appropriate burial places, and frequently dig the grave in the floor of the deceased's hut, or in the shade of a favourite tree.   The body is dressed in white cotton, and wrapped up in a mat. It is carried to the grave, in the dusk of the evening, by the relations.   If the grave is without the walls of the town, a number of prickly bushes are laid upon it, to prevent the wolves from digging up the body; but I never observed that any stone was placed over the grave, as a monument or memorial.

Hitherto I have considered the Negroes chiefly in a moral light, and confined myself to the most prominent features in their mental character. Their domestic amusements, occupations, and diet, their arts and manufactures, with some other subordinate objects, are now to be noticed.

Of their music and dances, some account has incidently been given in different parts of my journal. On the first of these heads, I have now to add a list of their musical instruments, the principal of which are the *koonting*, a sort of guitar with three strings; the *korro*, a large harp with eighteen strings; the *simbing*, a small harp with seven strings; the *balafou*, an instrument composed of twenty pieces of hard wood of different lengths, with the shells of gourds hung underneath, to increase the sound; the *tang-tang*, a drum, open at the lower end; and lastly, the *tabala*, a large drum, commonly used to spread an alarm through the country. Besides these, they make use of small flutes, bowstrings, elephants' teeth, and bells; and at all their dances and concerts, *clapping of hands* appears to constitute a necessary part of the chorus.

With the love of music is naturally connected a taste for poetry: and fortunately for the poets of Africa, they are in a great measure exempted from that neglect and indigence which, in more polished countries, commonly attend the votaries of the Muses. They consist of two classes; the most numerous are the *singing men*, called *Jilli kea*, mentioned in a former part of my narrative. One or more of these may be found in every town. They sing extempore songs, in honour of their chief men, or any other persons who are willing to give "solid pudding for empty praise." But a nobler part of their office is to recite the historical events of their country; hence, in war, they accompany the soldiers to the field, in order, by reciting the great actions of their ancestors, to awaken in them a spirit of glorious emulation. The other class are devotees of the Mahomedan faith, who travel about the country, singing devout hymns and performing religious ceremonies, to conciliate the favour of the Almighty, either in averting calamity, or insuring success to any enterprise. Both descriptions of these itinerant bards are much employed and respected by the people, and very liberal contributions are made for them.

The usual diet of the Negroes is somewhat different in different districts. In general, the people of free condition breakfast about daybreak, upon gruel made of meal and water, with a little of the fruit of the tamarind to give it an acid taste. About two o'clock in the afternoon, a sort of hasty pudding, with a little Shea butter, is the common meal; but the supper constitutes the principal repast, and is seldom ready before midnight. This consists almost universally of kouskous, with a small portion of animal food, or Shea butter, mixed with it. In eating, the Kafirs, as well as Mahomedans, use the right hand only.

The beverages of the Pagan Negroes are beer and mead; of each of which they frequently drink to excess. The Mahomedan converts drink nothing but water. The natives of all descriptions take snuff and smoke tobacco. Their pipes are made of wood, with an earthen bowl of curious workmanship. But in the interior countries, the greatest of all luxuries is salt. It would appear strange to a European to see a child suck a piece of rock-salt as if it were sugar. This, however, I have frequently seen; although, in the inland parts, the poorer class of inhabitants are so very rarely indulged with this precious article, that to say *a man eats salt with his victuals* is the same as saying *he is a rich man.* I have myself suffered great inconvenience from the scarcity of this article. The long use of vegetable food creates so painful a longing for salt, that no words can sufficiently describe it.

The Negroes in general, and the Mandingoes in particular, are considered by the whites on the coast as an indolent and inactive people, I think without reason. The nature of the climate is, indeed, unfavourable to great exertion; but surely a people cannot justly be denominated habitually indolent, whose wants are supplied, not by the spontaneous productions of nature, but by their own exertions. Few people work harder, when occasion requires, than the Mandingoes; but not having many opportunities of turning to advantage the superfluous produce of their labour, they are content with cultivating as much ground only as is necessary for their own support. The labours of the field give them pretty full employment during the rains; and in the dry season, the people who live in the vicinity of large rivers employ themselves chiefly in fishing. The fish are taken in wicker baskets, or with small cotton nets, and are preserved by being first dried in the sun, and afterwards rubbed with Shea butter to prevent them from contracting fresh moisture. Others of the natives employ themselves in hunting. Their weapons are bows and arrows; but the arrows in common use are not poisoned.[1] They are very dexterous marksmen, and will hit a lizard on a tree, or any other small object, at an amazing distance. They likewise kill Guinea-fowls, partridges, and pigeons, but never on the wing. While the men are occupied in these pursuits, the women are very diligent in manufacturing cotton cloth. They prepare the cotton for spinning by laying it, in small quantities at a time, upon a smooth stone or piece of wood, and rolling the seeds out with a thick iron spindle, and they spin it with the distaff. The thread is not fine, but well twisted, and makes a very durable cloth. A woman with common diligence will spin from six to nine garments of this cloth in one year, which, according to its fineness, will sell for a minkalli and a half or two minkallies each.[2] The weaving is performed by the men. The loom is made exactly upon the same principle as that of Europe; but so small and narrow that the web is seldom more than four inches broad. The shuttle is of the

[1] Poisoned arrows are used chiefly in war. The poison, which is said to be very deadly, is prepared from a shrub called *koona* (a species of *echites*), which is very common in the woods. The leaves of this shrub, when boiled with a small quantity of water, yield a thick black juice, into which the Negroes dip a cotton thread; this thread they fasten round the iron of the arrow in such a manner that it is almost impossible to extract the arrow, when it has sunk beyond the barbs, without leaving the iron point and the poisoned thread in the wound.

[2] A minkalli is a quantity of gold nearly equal in value to ten shillings sterling.

common construction; but as the thread is coarse, the chamber is somewhat larger than the European.

The women dye this cloth of a rich and lasting blue colour, by the following simple process. The leaves of the indigo, when fresh gathered, are pounded in a wooden mortar, and mixed in a large earthen jar with a strong lye of wood ashes. Chamber-lye is sometimes added. The cloth is steeped in this mixture, and allowed to remain until it has acquired the proper shade. In Kaarta and Ludamar, where the indigo is not plentiful, they collect the leaves, and dry them in the sun; and when they wish to use them they reduce a sufficient quantity to powder, and mix it with the lye, as before mentioned. Either way, the colour is very beautiful, with a fine purple gloss, and equal, in my opinion, to the best Indian or European blue. This cloth is cut into various pieces, and sewed into garments with needles of the natives' own making.

As the arts of weaving, dyeing, sewing, etc., may easily be acquired, those who exercise them are not considered in Africa as following any particular profession, for almost every slave can weave, and every boy can sew. The only artists which are distinctly acknowledged as such by the Negroes, and who value themselves on exercising appropriate and peculiar trades, are the manufacturers of *leather* and of *iron*. The first of these are called *Karrankea* (or, as the word is sometimes pronounced, *Gaungay*). They are to be found in almost every town, and they frequently travel through the country in the exercise of their calling. They tan and dress leather with very great expedition, by steeping the hide first in a mixture of wood ashes and water, until it parts with the hair, and afterwards by using the pounded leaves of a tree called *goo* as an astringent. They are at great pains to render the hide as soft and pliant as possible, by rubbing it frequently between their hands, and beating it upon a stone. The hides of bullocks are converted chiefly into sandals, and therefore require less care in dressing than the skins of sheep and goats, which are used for covering quivers and saphies, and in making sheaths for swords and knives, belts, pockets, and a variety of ornaments. These skins are commonly dyed of a red or yellow colour; the red by means of millet stalks reduced to powder, and the yellow by the root of a plant, the name of which I have forgotten.

The manufacturers in iron are not so numerous as the *Karrankeas;* but they appear to have studied their business with equal diligence. The Negroes on the coast being cheaply supplied with iron from the European traders, never attempt the manufacturing of this article themselves; but in the inland parts, the natives smelt this useful metal in such quantities, as not only to supply themselves from it with all necessary weapons and instruments, but even to make it an article of commerce with some of the neighbouring states. During my stay at Kamalia, there was a smelting furnace at a short distance from the hut where I lodged, and the owner and his workmen made no secret about the manner of conducting the operation, and readily allowed me to examine the furnace, and assist them in breaking the ironstone. The furnace was a circular tower of clay, about ten feet high and three in diameter, surrounded in two places with withes, to prevent the clay from cracking and falling to pieces by the violence of the heat. Round the lower part, on a level with the ground (but not so low as the bottom of the furnace, which was somewhat concave), were made seven openings, into every one of which were placed three tubes of clay, and the openings again plastered up in such a manner that no air could enter the furnace but through the tubes, by the opening and shutting of which they regulated the fire. These tubes were formed by plastering a mixture of clay and grass round a smooth roller of wood, which, as soon as the clay began to harden, was withdrawn, and the tube left to dry in the sun. The ironstone which I saw was very heavy, and of a dull red colour, with greyish specks; it was broken into pieces about the size of a hen's egg. A bundle of dry wood was first put into the furnace, and covered with a considerable quantity of charcoal, which was brought ready burnt from the woods. Over this was laid a stratum of ironstone, and then another of charcoal, and so on, until the furnace was quite full. The fire was applied through one of the tubes, and blown for some time with bellows made of goats' skins. The operation went on very slowly at first, and it was some hours before the flame appeared above the furnace; but after this it burnt with great violence all the first night, and the people who attended put in at times more charcoal. On the day following the fire was not so fierce, and on the second night some of the tubes were withdrawn, and the air allowed to have freer access to the furnace; but the heat was still very great, and a bluish flame rose some feet above the top of the furnace. On the third day from the commencement of the operation, all the tubes were taken out, the ends of many of them being vitrified with the heat; but the metal was not removed until some days afterwards, when the whole was perfectly cool. Part of the furnace was then taken down, and the iron appeared in the form of a large irregular mass, with pieces of charcoal adhering to it. It was sonorous; and when any portion was broken off, the fracture exhibited a granulated appearance, like broken steel. The owner informed me that many parts of this cake were useless, but still there was good iron enough to repay him for his trouble. This iron, or rather steel, is formed into various instruments, by being repeatedly heated in a forge, the heat of which is urged by a pair of double bellows, of a very simple construction, being made of two goats' skins, the tubes from which unite before they enter the forge, and supply a constant and very regular blast. The hammer, forceps, and anvil, are all very simple, and the workmanship (particularly in the formation of knives and spears), is not destitute of merit. The iron, indeed, is hard and brittle, and requires much labour before it can be made to answer the purpose.

Most of the African blacksmiths are acquainted also with the method of smelting gold, in which process they use an alkaline salt, obtained from a lye of burnt corn-stalks evaporated to dryness. They likewise draw the gold into wire, and form it into a variety of ornaments, some of which are executed with a great deal of taste and ingenuity.

Such is the chief information I obtained concerning the present state of arts and manufactures in those regions of Africa which I explored in my journey. I might add, though it is scarce worthy of observation, that in Bambarra and Kaarta, the natives make very beautiful baskets, hats, and other articles, both for use and ornament, from *rushes*, which they stain of different colours, and they contrive also to cover their calabashes with interwoven cane, dyed in the same manner.

In all the laborious occupations above described, the master and his slaves work together, without any distinction of superiority. Hired servants, by which I mean persons of free condition, voluntarily working for pay, are unknown in Africa ; and this observation naturally leads me to consider the condition of the slaves, and the various means by which they are reduced to so miserable a state of servitude. This unfortunate class are found, I believe, in all parts of this extensive country, and constitute a considerable branch of commerce with the states on the Mediterranean, as well as with the nations of Europe.

CHAPTER XXII

Observations concerning the State and Sources of Slavery in Africa.

A STATE of subordination and certain inequalities of rank and condition, are inevitable in every stage of civil society; but when this subordination is carried to so great a length, that the persons and services of one part of the community are entirely at the disposal of another part, it may then be denominated a state of slavery; and in this condition of life, a great body of the Negro inhabitants of Africa have continued from the most early period of their history, with this aggravation, that their children are born to no other inheritance.

The slaves in Africa, I suppose, are nearly in the proportion of three to one to the free men. They claim no reward for their services except food and clothing, and are treated with kindness or severity, according to the good or bad disposition of their masters. Custom, however, has established certain rules with regard to the treatment of slaves, which it is thought dishonourable to violate. Thus, the domestic slaves, or such as are born in a man's own house, are treated with more lenity than those which are purchased with money. The authority of the master over the domestic slave, as I have elsewhere observed, extends only to reasonable correction; for the master cannot sell his domestic without having first brought him to a public trial before the chief men of the place.[1] But these restrictions on the power of the master extend not to the case of prisoners

[1] In time of famine, the master is permitted to sell one or more of his domestics, to purchase provisions for his family; and in case of the master's insolvency, the domestic slaves are sometimes seized upon by the creditors, and if the master cannot redeem them, they are liable to be sold for payment of his debts. These are the only cases that I recollect, in which the domestic slaves are liable to be sold, without any misconduct or demerit of their own.

taken in war, nor to that of slaves purchased with money. All these unfortunate beings are considered as strangers and foreigners, who have no right to the protection of the law, and may be treated with severity, or sold to a stranger, according to the pleasure of their owners. There are, indeed, regular markets, where slaves of this description are bought and sold; and the value of a slave in the eye of an African purchaser, increases in proportion to his distance from his native kingdom; for when slaves are only a few days' journey from the place of their nativity, they frequently effect their escape; but when one or more kingdoms intervene, escape being more difficult, they are more readily reconciled to their situation. On this account, the unhappy slave is frequently transferred from one dealer to another, until he has lost all hopes of returning to his native kingdom. The slaves which are purchased by the Europeans on the coast are chiefly of this description; a few of them are collected in the petty wars, hereafter to be described, which take place near the coast; but by far the greater number are brought down in large caravans from the inland countries, of which many are unknown even by name to the Europeans. The slaves which are thus brought from the interior may be divided into two distinct classes; *first*, such as were slaves from their birth, having been born of enslaved mothers; *secondly*, such as were born free, but who afterwards, by whatever means, became slaves. Those of the first description are by far the most numerous; for prisoners taken in war (at least such as are taken in open and declared war, when one kingdom avows hostilities against another), are generally of this description. The comparatively small proportion of free people to the enslaved throughout Africa has already been noticed; and it must be observed, that men of free condition have many advantages over the slaves, even in war time. They are in general better armed and well mounted, and can either fight or escape with some hopes of success; but the slaves who have only their spears and bows, and of whom great numbers are loaded with baggage, become an easy prey. Thus, when Mansong, king of

Bambarra, made war upon Kaarta (as I have related in a former chapter), he took in one day nine hundred prisoners, of which number not more than seventy were free men. This account I received from Daman Jumma, who had thirty slaves at Kemmoo, all of whom were made prisoners by Mansong. Again, when a free man is taken prisoner, his friends will sometimes ransom him by giving two slaves in exchange; but when a slave is taken, he has no hopes of such redemption. To these disadvantages, it is to be added that the Slatees, who purchase slaves in the interior countries, and carry them down to the coast for sale, constantly prefer such as have been in that condition of life from their infancy, well knowing that these have been accustomed to hunger and fatigue, and are better able to sustain the hardships of a long and painful journey than free men; and on their reaching the coast, if no opportunity offers of selling them to advantage, they can easily be made to maintain themselves by their labour, neither are they so apt to attempt making their escape as those who have once tasted the blessings of freedom.

Slaves of the second description generally become such by one or other of the following causes :—1. *Captivity ;* 2. *Famine ;* 3. *Insolvency ;* 4. *Crimes.* A free man may, by the established customs of Africa, become a slave by being taken in war. War is, of all others, the most productive source, and was probably the origin of slavery; for when one nation had taken from another a greater number of captives than could be exchanged on equal terms, it is natural to suppose that the conquerors, finding it inconvenient to maintain their prisoners, would compel them to labour; at first, perhaps, only for their own support, but afterwards to support their masters. Be this as it may, it is a known fact, that prisoners of war in Africa are the slaves of the conquerors; and when the weak or unsuccessful warrior begs for mercy beneath the uplifted spear of his opponent, he gives up at the same time his claim to liberty, and purchases his life at the expense of his freedom.

In a country divided into a thousand petty states, mostly independent and jealous of each other, where every free man is accustomed to arms and fond of military achievements; where the youth, who has practised the bow and spear from his infancy, longs for nothing so much as an opportunity to display his valour, it is natural to imagine that wars frequently originate from very frivolous provocation. When one nation is more powerful than another, a pretext is seldom wanting for commencing hostilities. Thus the war between Kajaaga and Kasson was occasioned by the detention of a fugitive slave; that between Bambarra and Kaarta by the loss of a few cattle. Other cases of the same nature perpetually occur, in which the folly or mad ambition of their princes, and the zeal of their religious enthusiasts, give full employment to the scythe of desolation.

The wars of Africa are of two kinds, which are distinguished by different appellations; that species which bears the greatest resemblance to our European contests, is denominated *killi*, a word signifying "to call out," because such wars are openly avowed and previously declared. Wars of this description in Africa commonly terminate, however, in the course of a single campaign. A battle is fought, the vanquished seldom think of rallying again; the whole inhabitants become panic-struck, and the conquerors have only to bind the slaves, and carry off their plunder and their victims. Such of the prisoners as, through age or infirmity, are unable to endure fatigue, or are found unfit for sale, are considered as useless, and I have no doubt are frequently put to death. The same fate commonly awaits a chief, or any other person who has taken a very distinguished part in the war. And here it may be observed that, notwithstanding this exterminating system, it is surprising to behold how soon an African town is rebuilt and repeopled. The circumstance arises probably from this, that their pitched battles are few, the weakest know their own situation, and seek safety in flight. When their country has been desolated, and their ruined towns and villages deserted by the enemy, such of the inhabitants as have escaped the *sword* and the *chain*, generally return, though with cautious steps, to the place of their nativity; for it seems to be the universal wish of mankind to spend the evening of their days where they passed their infancy. The poor Negro feels this desire in its full force. To him no water is sweet but what is drawn from his own well, and no tree has so cool and pleasant a shade as the *tabba* tree[1] of his native village. When war compels him to abandon the delightful spot in which he first drew his breath, and seek for safety in some other kingdom, his time is spent in talking about the country of his ancestors; and no sooner is peace restored, than he turns his back upon the land of strangers, rebuilds with haste his fallen walls, and exults to see the smoke ascend from his native village.

The other species of African warfare is distinguished by the appellation of *tegria*, "plundering or stealing." It arises from a sort of hereditary feud which the inhabitants of one nation or district bear towards another. No immediate cause of hostility is assigned, or notice of attack given; but the inhabitants of each watch every opportunity to plunder and distress the objects of their animosity by predatory excursions. These are very common, particularly about the beginning of the dry season, when the labour of the harvest is over, and provisions are plentiful. Schemes of vengeance are then meditated. The chief man surveys the number and activity of his vassals, as they brandish their spears at festivals, and, elated with his own importance, turns his whole thoughts towards revenging some depredation or insult, which either he or his ancestors may have received from a neighbouring state.

Wars of this description are generally conducted with great secrecy. A few resolute individuals, headed by some person of enterprise and courage, march quietly through the woods, surprise in the night some unprotected village, and carry off the inhabitants and their effects before their neighbours can come to their assistance. One morning, during my stay at Kamalia, we were all much alarmed by a party of this kind. The king of Fooladoo's son, with five hundred horsemen, passed secretly through the woods, a little to the southward of Kamalia, and on the morning

[1] This is a large spreading tree (a species of *sterculia*) under which the Bentang is commonly placed.

following plundered three towns belonging to Madigai, a powerful chief in Jallonkadoo.

The success of this expedition encouraged the governor of Bangassi, a town in Fooladoo, to make a second inroad upon another part of the same country. Having assembled about two hundred of his people, he passed the river Kokoro in the night, and carried off a great number of prisoners. Several of the inhabitants who had escaped these attacks, were afterwards seized by the Mandingoes as they wandered about in the woods, or concealed themselves in the glens and strong places of the mountains.

These plundering excursions always produce speedy retaliation; and when large parties cannot be collected for this purpose, a few friends will combine together, and advance into the enemy's country, with a view to plunder, or carry off the inhabitants. A single individual has been known to take his bow and quiver, and proceed in like manner. Such an attempt is doubtless in him an act of rashness; but when it is considered that in one of these predatory wars, he has probably been deprived of his child, or his nearest relation, his situation will rather call for pity than censure. The poor sufferer, urged on by the feelings of domestic or paternal attachment, and the ardour of revenge, conceals himself among the bushes, until some young or unarmed person passes by. He then, tiger-like, springs upon his prey, drags his victim into the thicket, and in the night carries him off as a slave.

When a Negro has, by means like these, once fallen into the hands of his enemies, he is either retained as the slave of his conqueror, or bartered into a distant kingdom; for an African, when he has once subdued his enemy, will seldom give him an opportunity of lifting up his hand against him at a future period. A conqueror commonly disposes of his captives according to the rank which they held in their native kingdom. Such of the domestic slaves as appear to be of a mild disposition, and particularly the young women, are retained as his own slaves. Others that display marks of discontent are disposed of in a distant country, and such of the free men or slaves as have taken an active part in the war, are either sold to the Slatees, or put to death.   War, therefore, is certainly the most general and most productive source of slavery, and the desolations of war often (but not always) produce the second cause of slavery, *famine*, in which case a free man becomes a slave to avoid a greater calamity.

Perhaps, by a philosophic and reflecting mind, death itself would scarcely be considered as a greater calamity than slavery; but the poor Negro, when fainting with hunger, thinks like Esau of old : "*Behold I am at the point to die, and what profit shall this birthright do to me?*" There are many instances of free men voluntarily surrendering up their liberty to save their lives.   During a great scarcity, which lasted for three years, in the countries of the Gambia, great numbers of people became slaves in this manner.   Dr. Laidley assured me, that at that time many free men came and begged with great earnestness *to be put upon his slave-chain*, to save them from perishing of hunger. Large families are very often exposed to absolute want; and as the parents have almost unlimited authority over their children, it frequently happens, in all parts of Africa, that some of the latter are sold to purchase provisions for the rest of the family.   When I was at Jarra, Daman Jumma pointed out to me three young slaves which he had purchased in this manner.   I have already related another instance which I saw at Wonda, and I was informed that in Fooladoo, at that time, it was a very common practice.

The third cause of slavery is *insolvency*.   Of all the offences (if insolvency may be so called) to which the laws of Africa have affixed the punishment of slavery, this is the most common.   A Negro trader commonly contracts debts on some mercantile speculation, either from his neighbours, to purchase such articles as will sell to advantage in a distant market, or from the European traders on the coast—payment to be made in a given time.   In both cases the situation of the adventurer is exactly the same. If he succeeds he may secure an independency.   If he is unsuccessful, his person and services are at the disposal of another, for in Africa not only the effects of the insolvent, but even the insolvent himself, is sold to satisfy the lawful demands of his creditors.[1]

The fourth cause above enumerated is *the commission of crimes, on which the laws of the country affix slavery as a punishment.* In Africa, the only offences of this class are murder, adultery, and witchcraft; and I am happy to say that they did not appear to me to be common. In cases of murder, I was informed that the nearest relation of the deceased had it in his power, after conviction, either to kill the offender with his own hand, or sell him into slavery. When adultery occurs, it is generally left to the option of the person injured, either to sell the culprit, or accept such a ransom for him as he may think equivalent to the injury he has sustained. By witchcraft is meant pretended magic, by which the lives or healths of persons are affected; in other words, it is the administering of poison. No trial for this offence, however, came under my observation while I was in Africa, and I therefore suppose that the crime and its punishment occur but very seldom.

When a free man has become a slave by any one of the causes before mentioned, he generally continues so for life, and his children (if they are born of an enslaved mother) are brought up in the same state of servitude. There are, however, a few instances of slaves obtaining their freedom, and sometimes even with the consent of their masters; as by performing some singular piece of service, or by going to battle, and bringing home two slaves as a ransom ; but the common way of regaining freedom is by escape; and when slaves have once set their minds on running away,

[1] When a Negro takes up goods on credit from any of the Europeans on the coast, and does not make payment at the time appointed, the European is authorised, by the laws of the country, to seize upon the debtor himself, if he can find him ; or, if he cannot be found, on any person of his family ; or, in the last resort, on *any native of the same kingdom.* The person thus seized on is detained, while his friends are sent in quest of the debtor. When he is found, a meeting is called of the chief people of the place, and the debtor is compelled to ransom his friend by fulfilling his engagements. If he is unable to do this, his person is immediately secured and sent down to the coast, and the other released. If the debtor cannot be found, the person seized on is obliged to pay double the amount of the debt, or is himself sold into slavery. I was given to understand, however, that this part of the law is seldom enforced.

they often succeed.   Some of them will wait for years before an opportunity presents itself, and during that period show no signs of discontent.   In general, it may be remarked, that slaves who come from a hilly country, and have been much accustomed to hunting and travel, are more apt to attempt their escape than such as are born in a flat country, and have been employed in cultivating the land.

Such are the general outlines of that system of slavery which prevails in Africa, and it is evident, from its nature and extent, that it is a system of no modern date.   It probably had its origin in the remote ages of antiquity, before the Mahomedans explored a path across the desert. How far it is maintained and supported by the slave traffic, which for two hundred years the nations of Europe have carried on with the natives of the coast, it is neither within my province nor in my power to explain.   If my senti-ments should be required concerning the effect which a discontinuance of that commerce would produce on the manners of the natives, I should have no hesitation in observing, that, in the present unenlightened state of their minds, my opinion is, the effect would neither be so exten-sive or beneficial as many wise and worthy persons fondly expect.

CHAPTER XXIII

Of gold dust, and the manner in which it is collected—Process of washing it—Its value in Africa—Of Ivory—Surprise of the Negroes at the eagerness of the Europeans for this commodity —Scattered teeth frequently picked up in the woods—Mode of hunting the elephant—Some reflections on the unimproved state of the country, etc.

THOSE valuable commodities, gold and ivory (the next objects of our inquiry) have probably been found in Africa from the first ages of the world. They are reckoned among its most important productions in the earliest records of its history.

It has been observed, that gold is seldom or never discovered, except in *mountainous* and *barren* countries; nature, it is said, thus making amends in one way for her penuriousness in the other. This, however, is not wholly true. Gold is found in considerable quantities throughout every part of Manding— a country which is indeed hilly, but cannot properly be called *mountainous*, much less *barren*. It is also found in great plenty in Jallonkadoo (particularly about Boori), another hilly, but by no means an infertile country. It is remarkable that in the place last mentioned (Boori), which is situated about four days' journey to the south-west of Kamalia, the salt market is often supplied, at the same time, with rock-salt from the Great Desert, and sea-salt from the Rio-Grande; the price of each, at this distance from its source, being nearly the same; and the dealers in each, whether Moors from the north, or Negroes from the west, are invited thither by the same motives—that of bartering their salt for gold.

The gold of Manding, so far as I could learn, is never found in any matrix or vein, but always in small grains, nearly in a pure state, from the size of a pin's head to that of a pea, scattered through a large body of sand or clay;

and in this state it is called by the Mandingoes *sanoo munko*, "gold powder." It is, however, extremely probable, by what I could learn of the situation of the ground, that most of it has originally been washed down by repeated torrents from the neighbouring hills. The manner in which it is collected is nearly as follows :—

About the beginning of December, when the harvest is over, and the streams and torrents have greatly subsided, the Mansa, or chief man of the town, appoints a day to begin *sanoo koo*, "gold washing ;" and the women are sure to have themselves in readiness by the time appointed. A hoe, or spade, for digging up the sand, two or three calabashes for washing it in, and a few quills for containing the gold dust, are all the implements necessary for the purpose. On the morning of their departure, a bullock is killed for the first day's entertainment, and a number of prayers and charms are used to ensure success ; for a failure on that day is thought a bad omen. The Mansa of Kamalia, with fourteen of his people, were, I remember, so much disappointed in their first day's washing, that very few of them had resolution to persevere, and the few that did had but very indifferent success, which, indeed, is not much to be wondered at, for instead of opening some untried place, they continued to dig and wash in the same spot where they had dug and washed for years, and where, of course, but few large grains could be left.

The washing the sands of the streams is by far the easiest way of obtaining the gold dust ; but in most places the sands have been so narrowly searched before, that unless the stream takes some new course, the gold is found but in small quantities. While some of the party are busied in washing the sands, others employ themselves farther up the torrent, where the rapidity of the stream has carried away all the clay, sand, etc., and left nothing but small pebbles. The search among these is a very troublesome task. I have seen women who have had the skin worn off the tops of their fingers in this employment. Sometimes, however, they are rewarded by finding pieces of gold, which they call *sanoo birro*, "gold stones," that amply repay them for

their trouble. A woman and her daughter, inhabitants of
Kamalia, found in one day two pieces of this kind; one
of five drachms, and the other of three drachms weight.
But the most certain and profitable mode of washing is
practised in the height of the dry season by digging a deep
pit, like a draw-well, near some hill which has previously
been discovered to contain gold. The pit is dug with
small spades or corn hoes, and the earth is drawn up in
large calabashes. As the Negroes dig through the different
strata of clay or sand, a calabash or two of each is washed,
by way of experiment; and in this manner the labourers
proceed, until they come to a stratum containing gold, or
until they are obstructed by rocks or inundated by water.
In general, when they come to a stratum of fine reddish
sand, with small black specks therein, they find gold in
some proportion or other, and send up large calabashes
full of the sand, for the women to wash; for though the
pit is dug by the men, the gold is always washed by the
women, who are accustomed from their infancy to a similar
operation, in separating the husks of corn from the meal.

As I never descended into any of these pits, I cannot
say in what manner they are worked under ground. Indeed, the situation in which I was placed, made it necessary for me to be cautious not to incur the suspicion of
the natives, by examining too far into the riches of their
country; but the manner of separating the gold from the
sand is very simple, and is frequently performed by the
women in the middle of the town; for when the searchers
return from the valleys in the evening, they commonly
bring with them each a calabash or two of sand, to be
washed by such of the females as remain at home. The
operation is simply as follows:—

A portion of sand or clay (for gold is sometimes found
in a brown coloured clay), is put into a large calabash, and
mixed with a sufficient quantity of water. The woman
whose office it is, then shakes the calabash in such a
manner as to mix the sand and water together, and give
the whole a rotatory motion, at first gently, but afterwards
more quick, until a small portion of sand and water, at

every revolution, flies over the brim of the calabash.   The sand thus separated is only the coarsest particles, mixed with a little muddy water.   After the operation has been continued for some time, the sand is allowed to subside, and the water poured off; a portion of coarse sand, which is now uppermost in the calabash, is removed by the hand, and fresh water being added, the operation is repeated until the water comes off almost pure.   The woman now takes a second calabash, and shakes the sand and water gently from the one to the other, reserving that portion of sand which is next the bottom of the calabash, and which is most likely to contain the gold.   This small quantity is mixed with some pure water, and being moved about in the calabash, is carefully examined.   If a few particles of gold are picked out, the contents of the other calabash are examined in the same manner; but, in general, the party is well contented if she can obtain three or four grains from the contents of both calabashes.   Some women, how-ever, by long practice, become so well acquainted with the nature of the sand, and the mode of washing it, that they will collect gold where others cannot find a single particle. The gold dust is kept in quills, stopped up with cotton; and the washers are fond of displaying a number of these quills in their hair.   Generally speaking, if a person uses common diligence in a proper soil, it is supposed that as much gold may be collected by him in the course of the dry season as is equal to the value of two slaves. Thus simple is the process by which the Negroes obtain gold in Manding; and it is evident from this account, that the country contains a considerable portion of this precious metal, for many of the smaller particles must necessarily escape the observation of the naked eye; and as the natives generally search the sands of streams at a considerable distance from the hills, and consequently far removed from the mines where the gold was originally produced, the labourers are sometimes but ill paid for their trouble.   Minute particles only of this heavy metal can be carried by the current to any considerable distance; the larger must remain deposited near the original source from whence they came. Were the gold-bearing streams to be traced to their fountains, and the hills from whence they spring properly examined, the sand in which the gold is there deposited would no doubt be found to contain particles of a much larger size,[1] and even the small grains might be collected to considerable advantage by the use of quicksilver, and other improvements, with which the natives are at present unacquainted.

Part of this gold is converted into ornaments for the women; but, in general, these ornaments are more to be admired for their weight than their workmanship. They are massy and inconvenient, particularly the ear-rings, which are commonly so heavy as to pull down and lacerate the lobe of the ear; to avoid which they are supported by a thong of red leather, which passes over the crown of the head from one ear to the other. The necklace displays greater fancy : and the proper arrangement of the different beads and plates of gold is the great criterion of taste and elegance. When a lady of consequence is in full dress, her gold ornaments may be worth altogether from fifty to eighty pounds sterling.

A small quantity of gold is likewise employed by the Slatees, in defraying the expenses of their journeys to and from the coast; but by far the greater proportion is annually carried away by the Moors in exchange for salt and other merchandise. During my stay at Kamalia, the gold collected by the different traders at that place, for salt alone, was nearly equal to one hundred and ninety-eight pounds sterling; and as Kamalia is but a small town, and not much resorted to by the trading Moors, this quantity must have borne a very small proportion to the gold collected at Kancaba, Kancaree, and some other large towns. The value of salt in this part of Africa is very great. One slab, about

---

[1] I am informed that the gold mine, as it is called, in Wicklow, in Ireland, which was discovered in the year 1795, is near the top, and upon the steep slope of a mountain. Here pieces of gold of several ounces weight were frequently found. What would have been gold dust two miles below, was here golden gravel—that is, each grain was like a small pebble in size, and one piece was found which weighed nearly twenty-two ounces troy.

two feet and a half in length, fourteen inches in breadth, and two inches in thickness, will sometimes sell for about two pounds ten shillings sterling, and from one pound fifteen shillings to two pounds may be considered as the common price. Four of these slabs are considered as a load for an ass, and six for a bullock. The value of European merchandise in Manding varies very much, according to the supply from the coast, or the dread of war in the country ; but the return for such articles is commonly made in slaves. The price of a prime slave when I was at Kamalia, was from *nine* to *twelve* minkallies, and European commodities had then nearly the following value—

18 gun flints,	
48 leaves of tobacco,	one minkalli.
20 charges of gunpowder,	
A cutlass,	

A musket from three to four minkallies.

The produce of the country, and the different necessaries of life, when exchanged for gold, sold as follows :—

Common provisions for one day, the weight of one *teelee-kissi* (a black bean, six of which make the weight of one minkalli) — a chicken, one teelee-kissi — a sheep, three teelee-kissi—a bullock, one minkalli—a horse, from ten to seventeen minkallies.

The Negroes weigh the gold in small balances, which they always carry about them.   They make no difference in point of value, between gold dust and wrought gold.   In bartering one article for another, the person who receives the gold, always weighs it with his own teelee-kissi.   These beans are sometimes fraudulently soaked in Shea-butter, to make them heavy ; and I once saw a pebble ground exactly into the form of one of them ; but such practices are not very common.

Having now related the substance of what occurs to my recollection concerning the African mode of obtaining gold from the earth, and its value in barter, I proceed to the next article, of which I proposed to treat, namely *ivory.*

Nothing creates a greater surprise among the Negroes on the sea coast, than the eagerness displayed by the European traders to procure elephants' teeth; it being exceedingly difficult to make them comprehend to what use it is applied. Although they are shown knives with ivory hafts, combs, and toys of the same material, and are convinced that the ivory thus manufactured was originally parts of a tooth, they are not satisfied. They suspect that this commodity is more frequently converted in Europe to purposes of far greater importance; the true nature of which is studiously concealed from them, lest the price of ivory should be enhanced. They cannot, they say, easily persuade themselves, that ships would be built, and voyages undertaken, to procure an article which had no other value than that of furnishing handles to knives, etc., when pieces of wood would answer the purpose equally well.

Elephants are very numerous in the interior of Africa, but they appear to be a distinct species from those found in Asia. Blumenbach, in his figures of objects of natural history, has given good drawings of a grinder of each; and the variation is evident. M. Cuvier also has given in the *Magazin Encyclopedique*, a clear account of the difference between them. As I never examined the Asiatic elephant, I have chosen rather to refer to those writers, than advance this as an opinion of my own. It has been said that the African elephant is of a less docile nature than the Asiatic, and incapable of being tamed. The Negroes certainly do not at present tame them; but when we consider that the Carthaginians had always tame elephants in their armies, and actually transported some of them to Italy in the course of the Punic wars, it seems more likely that they should have possessed the art of taming their own elephants, than have submitted to the expense of bringing such vast animals from Asia. Perhaps the barbarous practice of hunting the African elephants for the sake of their teeth, has rendered them more untractable and savage than they were found to be in former times.

The greater part of the ivory which is sold on the Gambia and Senegal rivers is brought from the interior country.

The lands towards the coast are too swampy, and too much intersected with creeks and rivers, for so bulky an animal as the elephant to travel through, without being discovered; and when once the natives discern the marks of his feet in the earth, the whole village is up in arms. The thoughts of feasting on his flesh, making sandals of his hide, and selling the teeth to the Europeans, inspire every one with courage; and the animal seldom escapes from his pursuers; but in the plains of Bambarra and Kaarta, and the extensive wilds of Jallonkadoo, the elephants are very numerous; and, from the great scarcity of gunpowder in those districts, they are less annoyed by the natives.

Scattered teeth are frequently picked up in the woods, and travellers are very diligent in looking for them. It is a common practice with the elephant to thrust his teeth under the roots of such shrubs and bushes as grow in the more dry and elevated parts of the country where the soil is shallow. These bushes he easily overturns, and feeds on the roots, which are in general more tender and juicy than the hard woody branches or the foliage; but when the teeth are partly decayed by age, and the roots more firmly fixed, the great exertions of the animal in this practice frequently causes them to break short. At Kamalia I saw two teeth, one a very large one, which were found in the woods, and which were evidently broken off in this manner. Indeed, it is difficult otherwise to account for such a large proportion of broken ivory as is daily offered for sale at the different factories; for when the elephant is killed in hunting. unless he dashes himself over a precipice, the teeth are always extracted entire.

There are certain seasons of the year when the elephants collect into large herds, and traverse the country in quest of food or water; and as all that part of the country to the north of the Niger is destitute of rivers, whenever the pools in the woods are dried up, the elephants approach towards the banks of that river. Here they continue until the commencement. of the rainy season, in the months of June or July; and during this time they are much hunted by such of the Bambarrans as have gunpowder to spare. The elephant-hunters seldom go out singly; a party of four or five join together; and having each furnished himself with powder and ball, and a quantity of corn-meal in a leather bag, sufficient for five or six days' provision, they enter the most unfrequented parts of the wood, and examine with great care everything that can lead to the discovery of the elephants.   In this pursuit, notwithstanding the bulk of the animal, very great nicety of observation is required.   The broken branches, the scattered dung of the animal, and the marks of his feet, are carefully inspected; and many of the hunters have, by long experience and attentive observation, become so expert in their search, that as soon as they observe the footmarks of an elephant, they will tell almost to a certainty at what time it passed, and at what distance it will be found.

When they discover a herd of elephants, they follow them at a distance, until they perceive some one stray from the rest, and come into such a situation as to be fired at with advantage.   The hunters then approach with great caution, creeping amongst the long grass until they have got near enough to be sure of their aim.   They then discharge all their pieces at once, and throw themselves on their faces among the grass.   The wounded elephant immediately applies his trunk to the different wounds, but being unable to extract the balls, and seeing nobody near him, becomes quite furious, and runs about amongst the bushes, until by fatigue and loss of blood he has exhausted himself, and affords the hunters an opportunity of firing a second time at him, by which he is generally brought to the ground.

The skin is now taken off, and extended on the ground with pegs to dry; and such parts of the flesh as are most esteemed, are cut up into thin slices and dried in the sun, to serve for provisions on some future occasion.   The teeth are struck out with a light hatchet, which the hunters always carry along with them; not only for that purpose, but also to enable them to cut down such trees as contain honey; for though they carry with them only five or six days' provisions, they will remain in the woods for months if they are successful, and support themselves upon the flesh of such elephants as they kill, and wild honey.

The ivory thus collected is seldom brought down to the coast by the hunters themselves. They dispose of it to the itinerant merchants, who come annually from the coast with arms and ammunition to purchase this valuable commodity. Some of these merchants will collect ivory in the course of one season, sufficient to load four or five asses. A great quantity of ivory is likewise brought from the interior by the slave coffles; there are, however, some Slatees of the Mahomedan persuasion, who, from motives of religion, will not deal in ivory, nor eat of the flesh of the elephant, unless it has been killed with a spear.

The quantity of ivory collected in this part of Africa is not so great, nor are the teeth in general so large as in the countries nearer the line; few of them weigh more than eighty or one hundred pounds; and upon an average, a bar of European merchandise may be reckoned as the price of a pound of ivory.

I have now, I trust, in this and the preceding chapters, explained with sufficient minuteness the nature and extent of the commercial connection which at present prevails, and has long subsisted, between the Negro natives of those parts of Africa which I visited, and the nations of Europe; and it appears that slaves, gold, and ivory, together with the few articles enumerated in the beginning of my work, viz., bees-wax and honey, hides, gums, and dye-woods, constitute the whole catalogue of exportable commodities. Other productions, however, have been incidentally noticed as the growth of Africa; such as grain of different kinds, tobacco, indigo, cotton-wool, and perhaps a few others; but all of these (which can only be obtained by cultivation and labour), the natives raise sufficient only for their own immediate expenditure; nor under the present system of their laws, manners, trade, and government, can anything farther be expected from them. It cannot, however, admit of a doubt, that all the rich and valuable productions, both of the East and West Indies, might easily be naturalised and brought to the utmost perfection in the tropical parts of this immense continent. Nothing is wanting to this end but example, to enlighten the minds of the natives, and instruction, to enable them to direct their industry to proper objects. It was not possible for me to behold the wonderful fertility of the soil, the vast herds of cattle, proper both for labour and food, and a variety of other circumstances favourable to colonisation and agriculture— and reflect, withal, on the means which presented themselves of a vast inland navigation, without lamenting that a country so abundantly gifted and favoured by nature, should remain in its present savage and neglected state. Much more did I lament that a people of manners and disposition so gentle and benevolent, should either be left as they now are, immersed in the gross and uncomfortable blindness of pagan superstition, or permitted to become converts to a system of bigotry and fanaticism, which, without enlightening the mind, often debases the heart. On this subject many observations might be made; but the reader will probably think that I have already digressed too largely, and I now, therefore, return to my situation at Kamalia.

CHAPTER XXIV

Transactions at Kamalia resumed—Arabic manuscripts in use among the Mahomedan Negroes—Reflections concerning the conversion and education of the Negro children—Return of the Author's benefactor, Karfa—Further account of the purchase and treatment of slaves—Fast of Rhamadan, how observed by the Negroes—Author's anxiety for the day of departure—The caravan sets out —Account of it on its departure, and proceedings on the road until its arrival at Kinytakooro.

THE schoolmaster, to whose care I was entrusted during the absence of Karfa, was a man of a mild disposition and gentle manners; his name was Fankooma; and although he himself adhered strictly to the religion of Mahomet, he was by no means intolerant in his principles towards others who differed from him. He spent much of his time in reading; and teaching appeared to be his pleasure, as well as employment. His school consisted of seventeen boys, most of whom were sons of Kafirs, and two girls, one of whom was Karfa's own daughter. The girls received their instructions in the day-time, but the boys always had their lessons by the light of a large fire before daybreak, and again late in the evening; for being considered, during their scholarship, as the domestic slaves of the master, they were employed in planting corn, bringing fire-wood, and in other servile offices through the day.

Exclusive of the Koran, and a book or two of commentaries thereon, the schoolmaster possessed a variety of manuscripts, which had partly been purchased from the trading Moors, and partly borrowed from Bushreens in the neighbourhood, and copied with great care. Other manuscripts had been produced to me at different places in the course of my journey, and on recounting those I had before seen, and those which were now shown to me, and interrogating the schoolmaster on the subject, I discovered that the Negroes are in possession (among others) of an Arabic version of the Pentateuch of Moses, which they call *Taureta la Moosa.* This is so highly esteemed, that it is often sold for the value of one prime slave. They have likewise a version of the Psalms of David (*Zabora Dawidi*). And, lastly, the book of Isaiah, which they call *Lingeeli la Isa*, and it is in very high esteem. I suspect, indeed, that in all these copies, there are interpolations of some of the peculiar tenets of Mahomet; for I could distinguish in many passages the name of the Prophet. It is possible, however, that this circumstance might otherwise have been accounted for, if my knowledge of the Arabic had been more extensive. By means of those books, many of the converted Negroes have acquired an acquaintance with some of the remarkable events recorded in the Old Testament. The account of our first parents; the death of Abel; the deluge; the lives of Abraham, Isaac, and Jacob; the story of Joseph and his brethren; the history of Moses, David, Solomon, etc. All these have been related to me in the Mandingo language, with tolerable exactness, by different people, and my surprise was not greater on hearing these accounts from the lips of the Negroes, than theirs, on finding that I was already acquainted with them; for although the Negroes in general have a very great idea of the wealth and power of the Europeans, I am afraid that the Mahomedan converts among them think but very lightly of our superior attainments in religious knowledge. The white traders in the maritime districts take no pains to counteract this unhappy prejudice; always performing their own devotions in secret, and seldom condescending to converse with the Negroes in a friendly and instructive manner. To me, therefore, it was not so much the subject of wonder as matter of regret, to observe, that while the superstition of Mahomet has, in this manner, scattered a few faint beams of learning among these poor people, the precious light of Christianity is altogether excluded. I could not but lament that, although the coast of Africa has now been known and frequented by the Europeans for more than two hundred years, yet the Negroes still remain entire strangers to the doctrines of our holy religion. We are anxious to draw from obscurity the opinions and records of antiquity, the beauties of Arabian and Asiatic literature, etc.; but while our libraries are thus stored with the learning of various countries, we distribute, with a parsimonious hand, the blessings of religious truth to the benighted nations of the earth. The natives of Asia derive but little advantage in this respect from an intercourse with us; and even the poor Africans, whom we affect to consider as barbarians, look upon us, I fear, as little better than a race of formidable but ignorant heathens. When I produced Richardson's Arabic Grammar to some Slatees on the Gambia, they were astonished to think that any European should understand and write the sacred language of their religion. At first they suspected that it might have been written by some of the slaves carried from the coast; but on a closer examination, they were satisfied that no Bushreen could write such beautiful Arabic; and one of them offered to give me an ass, and sixteen bars of goods, if I would part with the book. Perhaps, a short and easy introduction to Christianity, such as is found in some of the catechisms for children, elegantly printed in Arabic, and distributed on different parts of the coast, might have a wonderful effect. The expense would be but trifling; curiosity would induce many to read it; and the evident superiority which it would possess over their present manuscripts, both in point of elegance and cheapness, might at last obtain it a place among the school-books of Africa.

The reflections which I have thus ventured to submit to my readers on this important subject, naturally suggested themselves to my mind on perceiving the encouragement which was thus given to learning (such as it is) in many parts of Africa. I have observed that the pupils at Kamalia were, most of them, the children of Pagans; their parents, therefore, could have had no predilection for the doctrines of Mahomet. Their aim was their children's improvement; and if a more enlightened system had presented itself, it would probably have been preferred. The children, too, wanted not a spirit of emulation, which it is the aim of the tutor to encourage. When any one of them has read through the Koran, and performed a certain number of public prayers, a feast is prepared by the schoolmaster, and the scholar undergoes an examination, or (in European terms) *takes out his degree.* I attended at three different inaugurations of this sort, and heard with pleasure the distinct and intelligent answers which the scholars frequently gave to the Bushreens who assembled on those occasions, and acted as examiners. When the Bushreens had satisfied themselves respecting the learning and abilities of the scholar, the last page of the Koran was put into his hand, and he was desired to read it aloud; after the boy had finished this lesson, he pressed the paper against his forehead, and pronounced the word *Amen;* upon which all the Bushreens rose, and shaking him cordially by the hand, bestowed upon him the title of Bushreen.

When a scholar has undergone this examination, his parents are informed that he has completed his education, and that it is incumbent on them to redeem their son, by giving to the schoolmaster a slave, or the price of a slave, in exchange, which is always done, if the parents can afford to do it; if not, the boy remains the domestic slave of the schoolmaster until he can, by his own industry, collect goods sufficient to ransom himself.

About a week after the departure of Karfa, three Moors arrived at Kamalia, with a considerable quantity of salt and other merchandise, which they had obtained on credit from a merchant of Fezzan, who had lately arrived at Kancaba. Their engagement was to pay him his price when the goods were sold, which they expected would be in the course of a month. Being rigid Bushreens, they were accommodated with two of Karfa's huts, and sold their goods to very great advantage.

On the 24th of January, Karfa returned to Kamalia with a number of people, and thirteen prime slaves which he had purchased. He likewise brought with him a young girl whom he had married at Kancaba, as his fourth wife, and had given her parents three prime slaves for her.   She was kindly received at the door of the baloon by Karfa's other wives, who conducted their new acquaintance and co-partner into one of the best huts, which they had caused to be swept and whitewashed on purpose to receive her.[1]

My clothes were by this time become so very ragged, that I was almost ashamed to appear out of doors ; but Karfa, on the day after his arrival, generously presented me with such a garment and trousers as are commonly worn in the country.

The slaves which Karfa had brought with him were all of them prisoners of war ; they had been taken by the Bam-barran army in the kingdoms of Wassela and Kaarta, and carried to Sego, where some of them had remained three years in irons.   From Sego they were sent, in company with a number of other captives, up the Niger in two large canoes, and offered for sale at Yamina, Bammakoo, and Kancaba, at which places the greater number of the captives were bartered for gold dust, and the remainder sent forward to Kankaree.

Eleven of them confessed to me that they had been slaves from their infancy ; but the other two refused to give any account of their former condition.   They were all very inquisitive ; but they viewed me at first with looks of horror, and repeatedly asked if my countrymen were cannibals. They were very desirous to know what became of the slaves after they had crossed the salt water.   I told them that they were employed in cultivating the land, but they would not believe me ; and one of them, putting his hand upon the ground, said, with great simplicity, " Have you really got such ground as this to set your feet upon ? "   A deeply-rooted idea that the whites purchase Negroes for the pur-pose of devouring them, or of selling them to others, that they may be devoured hereafter, naturally makes the slaves contemplate a journey towards the coast with great terror, insomuch that the Slatees are forced to keep them con-stantly in irons, and watch them very closely to prevent

---

[1] The Negroes whitewash their huts with a mixture of bone ashes and water, to which is commonly added a little gum.

their escape. They are commonly secured by putting the right leg of one and the left of another into the same pair of fetters. By supporting the fetters with a string, they can walk, though very slowly. Every four slaves are likewise fastened together by the necks with a strong rope of twisted thongs; and in the night an additional pair of fetters is put on their hands, and sometimes a light iron chain passed round their necks.

Such of them as evince marks of discontent, are secured in a different manner. A thick billet of wood is cut about three feet long, and a smooth notch being made upon one side of it, the ankle of the slave is bolted to the smooth part by means of a strong iron staple, one prong of which passes on each side of the ankle. All these fetters and bolts are made from native iron; in the present case they were put on by the blacksmith as soon as the slaves arrived from Kancaba, and were not taken off until the morning on which the coffle departed for Gambia.

In other respects, the treatment of the slaves during their stay at Kamalia was far from being harsh or cruel. They were led out in their fetters every morning to the shade of the tamarind tree, where they were encouraged to play at games of hazard, and sing diverting songs, to keep up their spirits; for though some of them sustained the hardships of their situation with amazing fortitude, the greater part were very much dejected, and would sit all day in a sort of sullen melancholy, with their eyes fixed upon the ground. In the evening their irons were examined and their hand fetters put on, after which they were conducted into two large huts, where they were guarded during the night by Karfa's domestic slaves. But notwithstanding all this, about a week after their arrival, one of the slaves had the address to procure a small knife, with which he opened the rings of his fetters, cut the rope, and made his escape; more of them would probably have got off had they assisted each other; but the slave no sooner found himself at liberty than he refused to stop and assist in breaking the chain which was fastened round the necks of his companions.

As all the Slatees and slaves belonging to the coffle

were now assembled, either at Kamalia or some of the neighbouring villages, it might have been expected that we should have set out immediately for Gambia; but though the day of our departure was frequently fixed, it was always found expedient to change it. Some of the people had not prepared their dry provisions; others had gone to visit their relations, or collect some trifling debts; and, last of all, it was necessary to consult whether the day would be a lucky one. On account of one of these, or other such causes, our departure was put off day after day until the month of February was far advanced, after which all the Slatees agreed to remain in their present quarters until the *fast moon was over*. And here I may remark, that loss of time is an object of no great importance in the eyes of a Negro. If he has anything of consequence to perform, it is a matter of indifference to him whether he does it to-day or to-morrow, or a month or two hence; so long as he can spend the present moment with any degree of comfort, he gives himself very little concern about the future.

The fast of Rhamadan was observed with great strictness by all the Bushreens; but instead of compelling me to follow their example, as the Moors did on a similar occasion, Karfa told me I was at liberty to pursue my own inclination. In order, however, to manifest a respect for their religious opinions, I voluntarily fasted three days, which was thought sufficient to screen me from the reproachful epithet of Kafir. During the fast, all the Slatees belonging to the coffle assembled every morning in Karfa's house, where the schoolmaster read to them some religious lesson from a large folio volume, the author of which was an Arab, of the name of *Sheiffa*. In the evening, such of the women as had embraced Mahomedanism assembled and said their prayers publicly at the Misura. They were all dressed in white, and went through the different prostrations prescribed by their religion with becoming solemnity. Indeed, during the whole fast of Rhamadan, the Negroes behaved themselves with the greatest meekness and humility, forming a striking contrast to the savage intolerance and brutal bigotry which at this period characterise the Moors.

When the fast month was almost at an end, the Bushreens assembled at the Misura, to watch for the appearance of the new moon; but the evening being rather cloudy, they were for some time disappointed, and a number of them had gone home with a resolution to fast another day, when on a sudden this delightful object showed her sharp horns from behind a cloud, and was welcomed with the clapping of hands, beating of drums, firing muskets, and other marks of rejoicing. As this moon is reckoned extremely lucky, Karfa gave orders that all the people belonging to the coffle should immediately pack up their dry provisions, and hold themselves in readiness; and on the 16th of April, the Slatees held a consultation, and fixed on the 19th of the same month as the day on which the coffle should depart from Kamalia. This resolution freed me from much uneasiness; for our departure had already been so long deferred, that I was apprehensive it might still be put off until the commencement of the rainy season; and although Karfa behaved towards me with the greatest kindness, I found my situation very unpleasant. The Slatees were unfriendly to me, and the trading Moors, who were at this time at Kamalia, continued to plot mischief against me from the first day of their arrival. Under these circumstances, I reflected that my life in a great measure depended on the good opinion of an individual who was daily hearing malicious stories concerning the Europeans; and I could hardly expect that he would always judge with impartiality between me and his countrymen. Time had, indeed, reconciled me, in some degree, to their mode of life, and a smoky hut or a scanty supper gave me no great uneasiness; but I became at last wearied out with a constant state of alarm and anxiety, and felt a painful longing for the manifold blessings of civilised society.

On the morning of the 17th, a circumstance occurred which wrought a considerable change in my favour. The three trading Moors who had lodged under Karfa's protection ever since their arrival at Kamalia, and had gained the esteem of all the Bushreens by an appearance of great sanctity, suddenly packed up their effects, and, without once thanking Karfa for his kindness towards them, marched over the hills to Bala. Every one was astonished at this unexpected removal, but the affair was cleared up in the evening by the arrival of the Fezzan merchant from Kancaba (mentioned in p. 243), who assured Karfa that these Moors had borrowed all their salt and goods from him, and had sent for him to come to Kamalia and receive payment When he was told that they had fled to the westward. he wiped a tear from each eye with the sleeve of his cloak and exclaimed, "These *shirrukas* (robbers) are Mahomedans, but they are not men; they have robbed me of two hundred minkallies." From this merchant I received information of the capture of our Mediterranean convoy by the French, in October 1795.

April 19th.—The long-wished for day of our departure was at length arrived, and the Slatees having taken the irons from their slaves, assembled with them at the door of Karfa's house, where the bundles were all tied up, and every one had his load assigned him. The coffle, on its departure from Kamalia, consisted of twenty-seven slaves for sale, the property of Karfa and four other Slatees; but we were afterwards joined by five at Marraboo, and three at Bala, making in all thirty-five slaves. The free men were fourteen in number, but most of them had one or two wives and some domestic slaves, and the schoolmaster, who was now upon his return for Woradoo, the place of his nativity, took with him eight of his scholars, so that the number of free people and domestic slaves amounted to thirty-eight, and the whole amount of the coffle was seventy-three. Among the free men were six Jilli keas (singing men), whose musical talents were frequently exerted either to divert our fatigue, or obtain us a welcome from strangers. When we departed from Kamalia we were followed for about half a mile by most of the inhabitants of the town, some of them crying and others shaking hands with their relations who were now about to leave them; and when we had gained a piece of rising ground, from which we had a view of Kamalia, all the people belonging to the coffle were ordered to sit down in one place, with their faces towards the west, and the townspeople were desired to sit down in another place with their faces towards Kamalia. In this situation the schoolmaster, with two of the principal Slatees, having taken their places between the two parties, pronounced a long and solemn prayer: after which they walked three times round the coffle, making an impression on the ground with the ends of their spears, and muttering something by way of charm. When this ceremony was ended, all the people belonging to the coffle sprang up, and without taking a formal farewell of their friends, set forwards. As many of the slaves had remained for years in irons, the sudden exertion of walking quick with heavy loads upon their heads, occasioned spasmodic contractions of their legs, and we had not proceeded above a mile, before it was found necessary to take two of them from the rope, and allow them to walk more slowly until we reached Marraboo, a walled village, where some people were waiting to join the coffle. Here we stopped about two hours to allow the strangers time to pack up their provisions, and then continued our route to Bala, which town we reached about four in the afternoon. The inhabitants of Bala, at this season of the year, subsist chiefly on fish, which they take in great plenty from the streams in the neighbourhood. We remained here until the afternoon of the next day, the 20th, when we proceeded to Worumbang, the frontier village of Manding towards Jallonkadoo. As we proposed shortly to enter the Jallonka wilderness, the people of this village furnished us with great plenty of provisions; and on the morning of the 21st we entered the woods to the westward of Worumbang. After having travelled some little way, a consultation was held whether we should continue our route through the wilderness, or save one day's provisions by going to Kinytakooro, a town in Jallonkadoo. After debating the matter for some time, it was agreed that we should take the road for Kinytakooro; but as that town was a long day's journey distant, it was necessary to take some refreshment. Accordingly, every person opened his provision-bag, and brought a handful or two of meal to the place where Karfa and the Slatees were sitting. When every one had brought his quota, and the whole was properly arranged in small gourd shells, the schoolmaster offered up a short prayer, the substance of which was, that God and the holy Prophet might preserve us from robbers and all bad people, that our provisions might never fail us, nor our limbs become fatigued.   This ceremony being ended, every one partook of the meal, and drank a little water; after which we set forward (rather running than walking) until we came to the river Kokoro, a branch of the Senegal, where we halted about ten minutes.   The banks of this river are very high; and from the grass and brushwood which had been left by the stream, it was evident that at this place the water had risen more than twenty feet perpendicular during the rainy season.   At this time it was only a small stream, such as would turn a mill, swarming with fish; and on account of the number of crocodiles, and the danger of being carried past the ford by the force of the stream in the rainy season, it is called *Kokoro* (dangerous). From this place we continued to travel with the greatest expedition, and in the afternoon crossed two small branches of the Kokoro.   About sunset we came in sight of Kinyta-kooro, a considerable town, nearly square, situated in the middle of a large and well-cultivated plain.   Before we entered the town we halted, until the people who had fallen behind came up.   During this day's travel, two slaves, a woman and a girl belonging to a Slatee of Bala, were so much fatigued that they could not keep up with the coffle; they were severely whipped, and dragged along until about three o'clock in the afternoon, when they were both affected with vomiting, by which it was discovered that they had *eaten clay*.   This practice is by no means uncommon amongst the Negroes; but whether it arises from a vitiated appetite, or from a settled intention to destroy themselves, I cannot affirm.   They were permitted to lie down in the woods, and three people remained with them until they had rested themselves; but they did not arrive at the town until past midnight, and were then so much exhausted that the Slatee gave up all thoughts of taking them across the woods in their present condition, and determined to return with them to Bala, and wait for another opportunity.

As this was the first town beyond the limits of Manding, greater etiquette than usual was observed. Every person was ordered to keep in his proper station, and we marched towards the town in a sort of procession, nearly as follows. In front, five or six singing men, all of them belonging to the coffle; these were followed by the other free people; then came the slaves, fastened in the usual way by a rope round their necks, four of them to a rope, and a man with a spear between each four; after them came the domestic slaves, and in the rear the women of free condition, wives of the Slatees, etc. In this manner we proceeded until we came within a hundred yards of the gate, when the singing men began a loud song, well calculated to flatter the vanity of the inhabitants, by extolling their known hospitality to strangers, and their particular friendship for the Mandingoes. When we entered the town we proceeded to the Bentang, where the people gathered round us to hear our *dentegi* (history); this was related publicly by two of the singing men; they enumerated every little circumstance which had happened to the coffle, beginning with the events of the present day, and relating everything in a backward series, until they reached Kamalia. When this history was ended, the master of the town gave them a small present, and all the people of the coffle, both free and enslaved, were invited by some person or other, and accommodated with lodging and provisions for the night.

CHAPTER XXV

The coffle crosses the Jallonka wilderness—Miserable fate of one of the female slaves—Arrives at Sooseta—Proceeds to Manna—Some account of the Jallonkas—Crosses the main stream of the Senegal —Bridge of a singular construction—Arrives at Malacotta—Remarkable conduct of the king of the Jaloffs.

WE continued at Kinytakooro until noon of the 22nd of April, when we removed to a village about seven miles to the westward, the inhabitants of which, being apprehensive of hostilities from the Foulahs of Fooladoo, were at this time employed in constructing small temporary huts among the rocks, on the side of a high hill close to the village. The situation was almost impregnable, being everywhere surrounded with high precipices, except on the eastern side, where the natives had left a pathway sufficient to allow one person at a time to ascend.   Upon the brow of the hill, immediately over this path, I observed several heaps of large loose stones, which the people told me were intended to be thrown down upon the Foulahs if they should attempt the hill.

At daybreak, on the 23rd, we departed from this village, and entered the Jallonka wilderness. We passed, in the course of the morning, the ruins of two small towns which had lately been burnt by the Foulahs.   The fire must have been very intense, for I observed that the walls of many of the huts were slightly vitrified, and appeared at a distance as if covered with a red varnish.   About ten o'clock we came to the river Wonda, which is somewhat larger than the river Kokoro ; but the stream was at this time rather muddy, which Karfa assured me was occasioned by amazing shoals of fish.   They were indeed seen in all directions, and in such abundance that I fancied the water itself tasted and smelt fishy.   As soon as we had crossed the river, Karfa gave orders that all the people of the coffle should in future keep close together and travel in their proper station; the guides and young men were accordingly placed in the van, the women and slaves in the centre, and the free men in the rear. In this order we travelled with uncommon expedition through a woody but beautiful country, interspersed with a pleasing variety of hill and dale, and abounding with partridges, guinea-fowl, and deer, until we arrived at a most romantic stream called Co-meissang. My arms and neck having been exposed to the sun during the whole day, and irritated by the rubbing of my dress in walking, were now very much inflamed and covered with blisters; and I was happy to embrace the opportunity, while the coffle rested on the bank of this river, to bathe myself in the stream. This practice, together with the cool of the evening, much diminished the inflammation About three miles to the westward of the Co-meissang we halted in a thick wood, and kindled our fires for the night. We were all by this time very much fatigued, having, as I judged, travelled this day thirty miles; but no person was heard to complain. Whilst supper was preparing, Karfa made one of the slaves break some branches from the trees for my bed. When we had finished our supper of kouskous, moistened with some boiling water, and put the slaves in irons, we all lay down to sleep; but we were frequently disturbed in the night by the howling of wild beasts, and we found the small brown ants very troublesome.

April 24th.—Before daybreak the Bushreens said their morning prayers, and most of the free people drank a little *moening* (a sort of gruel) part of which was likewise given to such of the slaves as appeared least able to sustain the fatigues of the day. One of Karfa's female slaves was very sulky, and when some gruel was offered to her, she refused to drink it. As soon as day dawned we set out, and travelled the whole morning over a wild and rocky country, by which my feet were very much bruised, and I was sadly apprehensive that I should not be able to keep up with the coffle during the day; but I was in a great measure relieved from this anxiety when I observed that others were more exhausted than myself. In particular, the woman slave

who had refused victuals in the morning began now to lag
behind, and complain dreadfully of pains in her legs.   Her
load was taken from her, and given to another slave, and
she was ordered to keep in the front of the coffle.   About
eleven o'clock, as we were resting by a small rivulet, some
of the people discovered a hive of bees in a hollow tree,
and they were proceeding to obtain the honey, when the
largest swarm I ever beheld flew out, and, attacking the
people of the coffle, made us fly in all directions.   I took
the alarm first, and I believe was the only person who
escaped with impunity.   When our enemies thought fit to
desist from pursuing us, and every person was employed in
picking out the stings he had received, it was discovered
that the poor woman above mentioned, whose name was
Nealee, was not come up; and as many of the slaves in
their retreat had left their bundles behind them, it became
necessary for some persons to return and bring them.   In
order to do this with safety, fire was set to the grass, a
considerable way to the eastward of the hive, and the wind
driving the fire furiously along, the party pushed through
the smoke, and recovered the bundles.   They likewise
brought with them poor Nealee, whom they found lying
by the rivulet.   She was very much exhausted, and had
crept to the stream, in hopes to defend herself from the
bees by throwing water over her body, but this proved
ineffectual, for she was stung in the most dreadful manner.
When the Slatees had picked out the stings as far as they
could, she was washed with water, and then rubbed with
bruised leaves; but the wretched woman obstinately refused
to proceed any farther, declaring that she would rather die
than walk another step.   As entreaties and threats were
used in vain, the whip was at length applied; and after
bearing patiently a few strokes, she started up, and walked
with tolerable expedition for four or five hours longer, when
she made an attempt to run away from the coffle, but was
so very weak that she fell down in the grass.   Though she
was unable to rise, the whip was a second time applied,
but without effect; upon which Karfa desired two of the
Slatees to place her upon the ass which carried our dry

provisions; but she could not sit erect, and the ass being very refractory, it was found impossible to carry her forward in that manner. The Slatees, however, were unwilling to abandon her, the day's journey being nearly ended; they therefore made a sort of litter of bamboo canes, upon which she was placed, and tied on it with slips of bark. This litter was carried upon the heads of two slaves, one walking before the other, and they were followed by two others, who relieved them occasionally. In this manner the woman was carried forward until it was dark, when we reached a stream of water, at the foot of a high hill called Gankaran-Kooro, and here we stopt for the night, and set about preparing our supper. As we had eaten only one handful of meal since the preceding night, and travelled all day in a hot sun, many of the slaves, who had loads upon their heads, were very much fatigued, and some of them *snapt their fingers*, which among the Negroes is a sure sign of desperation. The Slatees immediately put them all in irons; and such of them as had evinced signs of great despondency were kept apart from the rest, and had their hands tied. In the morning they were found greatly recovered.

April 25th.—At daybreak poor Nealee was awakened; but her limbs were now become so stiff and painful that she could neither walk nor stand; she was therefore lifted like a corpse upon the back of the ass, and the Slatees endeavoured to secure her in that situation, by fastening her hands together under the ass's neck, and her feet under the belly, with long slips of bark; but the ass was so very unruly, that no sort of treatment could induce him to proceed with his load; and as Nealee made no exertion to prevent herself from falling, she was quickly thrown off, and had one of her legs much bruised. Every attempt to carry her forward being thus found ineffectual, the general cry of the coffle was, *kang-tegi, kang-tegi*, "cut her throat, cut her throat," an operation I did not wish to see performed, and therefore marched onwards with the foremost of the coffle. I had not walked above a mile, when one of Karfa's domestic slaves came up to me, with poor Nealee's garment upon the end of his bow, and exclaimed, *Nealee affeeleeta* (Nealee is lost). I asked him whether the Slatees had given him the garment as a reward for cutting her throat? He replied, that Karfa and the schoolmaster would not consent to that measure, but had left her on the road, where undoubtedly she soon perished, and was probably devoured by wild beasts.

The sad fate of this wretched woman, notwithstanding the outcry before mentioned, made a strong impression on the minds of the whole coffle, and the schoolmaster fasted the whole of the ensuing day in consequence of it. We proceeded in deep silence, and soon afterwards crossed the river Furkoomah, which was about as large as the river Wonda. We now travelled with great expedition, every one being apprehensive he might otherwise meet with the fate of poor Nealee. It was, however, with great difficulty that I could keep up, although I threw away my spear, and everything that could in the least obstruct me. About noon we saw a large herd of elephants, but they suffered us to pass unmolested, and in the evening we halted near a thicket of bamboo, but found no water, so that we were forced to proceed four miles farther to a small stream, where we stopt for the night. We had marched this day, as I judged, about twenty-six miles.

April 26th.—This morning two of the schoolmaster's pupils complained much of pains in their legs, and one of the slaves walked lame, the soles of his feet being very much blistered and inflamed. We proceeded, notwithstanding, and about eleven o clock began to ascend a rocky hill called Boki-Kooro, and it was past two in the afternoon before we reached the level ground on the other side. This was the most rocky road we had yet encountered, and it hurt our feet much. In a short time we arrived at a pretty large river called Boki, which we forded; it ran smooth and clear over a bed of whinstone. About a mile to the westward of the river, we came to a road which leads to the north-east towards Gadou, and seeing the marks of many horses' feet upon the soft sand, the Slatees conjectured that a party of plunderers had lately rode that way, to fall upon some town of Gadou; and lest they should discover

upon their return that we had passed, and attempt to pursue
us by the marks of our feet, the coffle was ordered to disperse,
and travel in a loose manner through the high grass and
bushes. A little before it was dark, having crossed the
ridge of hills to the westward of the river Boki, we came to
a well called *cullong qui* (white sand well), and here we
rested for the night.

April 27th.—We departed from the well early in the
morning, and walked on with the greatest alacrity, in hopes
of reaching a town before night. The road during the
forenoon led through extensive thickets of dry bamboos.
About two o'clock we came to a stream called Nunkolo,
where we were each of us regaled with a handful of meal,
which, according to a superstitious custom, was not to be
eaten until it was first moistened with water from this
stream. About four o'clock we reached Sooseeta, a small
Jallonka village situated in the district of Kullo, which
comprehends all that tract of country lying along the banks
of the Black River, or main branch of the Senegal. These
were the first human habitations we had seen since we left
the village to the westward of Kinytakooro, having travelled
in the course of the last five days upwards of one hundred
miles. Here, after a great deal of entreaty, we were provided with huts to sleep in, but the master of the village
plainly told us that he could not give us any provisions, as
there had lately been a great scarcity in this part of the
country. He assured us that before they had gathered in
their present crops the whole inhabitants of Kullo had been
for twenty-nine days without tasting corn, during which
time they supported themselves entirely upon the yellow
powder which is found in the pods of the *nitta*. so called
by the natives, a species of mimosa, and upon the seeds
of the bamboo cane, which, when properly pounded and
dressed, taste very much like rice. As our dry provisions
were not yet exhausted, a considerable quantity of kouskous
was dressed for supper, and many of the villagers were
invited to take part of the repast; but they made a very
bad return for this kindness, for in the night they seized
upon one of the schoolmaster's boys, who had fallen asleep

under the Bentang tree, and carried him away. The boy
fortunately awoke before he was far from the village, and
setting up a loud scream, the man who carried him put his
hand upon his mouth, and ran with him into the woods;
but afterwards, understanding that he belonged to the
schoolmaster, whose place of residence is only three days'
journey distant, he thought, I suppose, that he could not
retain him as a slave without the schoolmaster's knowledge,
and therefore stripped off the boy's clothes and permitted
him to return.

April 28th.—Early in the morning we departed from
Sooseeta, and about ten o'clock came to an unwalled town
called Manna, the inhabitants of which were employed in
collecting the fruit of the nitta trees, which are very
numerous in this neighbourhood. The pods are long and
narrow, and contain a few black seeds enveloped in the fine
mealy powder before mentioned; the meal itself is of a
bright yellow colour, resembling the flour of sulphur, and
has a sweet mucilaginous taste; when eaten by itself it is
clammy, but when mixed with milk or water it constitutes
a very pleasant and nourishing article of diet.

The language of the people of Manna is the same that
is spoken all over that extensive and hilly country called
Jallonkadoo. Some of the words have a great affinity to
the Mandingo, but the natives themselves consider it as a
distinct language. Their numerals are these : One, *kidding;*
two, *fidding;* three, *sarra;* four, *nani;* five, *soolo;* six, *seni;*
seven, *soolo ma fidding;* eight, *soolo ma sarra;* nine, *soolo
ma nani;* ten, *nuff.*

The Jallonkas, like the Mandingoes, are governed by a
number of petty chiefs, who are, in a great measure, independent of each other. They have no common sovereign ;
and the chiefs are seldom upon such terms of friendship as
to assist each other even in war time. The chief of Manna,
with a number of his people, accompanied us to the banks
of the Bafing, or Black River (a principal branch of the
Senegal), which we crossed upon a bridge of bamboos, of
a very singular construction. The river at this place is
smooth and deep, and has very little current. Two tall

A View of a Bridge over the Ba-fing or Black River

trees, when tied together by the tops, are sufficiently long to reach from one side to the other; the roots resting upon the rocks, and the tops floating in the water. When a few trees have been placed in this direction, they are covered with dry bamboos, so as to form a floating bridge, with a sloping gangway at each end, where the trees rest upon the rocks. This bridge is carried away every year by the swelling of the river in the rainy season, and is constantly rebuilt by the inhabitants of Manna, who, on that account, expect a small tribute from every passenger.

In the afternoon we passed several villages, at none of which could we procure a lodging; and in the twilight we received information that two hundred Jallonkas had assembled near a town called Melo, with a view to plunder the coffle. This induced us to alter our course, and we travelled with great secrecy until midnight, when we approached a town called Koba. Before we entered the town, the names of all the people belonging to the coffle were called over, and a free man and three slaves were found to be missing. Every person immediately concluded that the slaves had murdered the free man, and made their escape. It was therefore agreed that six people should go back as far as the last village, and endeavour to find his body, or collect some information concerning the slaves. In the meantime the coffle was ordered to lie concealed in a cotton field near a large nitta tree, and nobody to speak except in a whisper. It was towards morning before the six men returned, having heard nothing of the man or the slaves. As none of us had tasted victuals for the last twenty-four hours, it was agreed that we should go into Koba, and endeavour to procure some provisions. We accordingly entered the town before it was quite day, and Karfa purchased from the chief man, for three strings of beads, a considerable quantity of ground-nuts, which we roasted and ate for breakfast; we were afterwards provided with huts, and rested here for the day.

About eleven o'clock, to our great joy and surprise, the free man and slaves, who had parted from the coffle the preceding night, entered the town. One of the slaves, it seems, had hurt his foot, and the night being very dark, they soon lost sight of the coffle. The free man, as soon as he found himself alone with the slaves, was aware of his own danger, and insisted on putting them in irons. The slaves were at first rather unwilling to submit; but when he threatened to stab them one by one with his spear, they made no further resistance, and he remained with them among the bushes until morning, when he let them out of irons, and came to the town in hopes of hearing which route the coffle had taken. The information that we received concerning the Jallonkas, who intended to rob the coffle, was this day confirmed, and we were forced to remain here until the afternoon of the 30th, when Karfa hired a number of people to protect us, and we proceeded to a village called Tinkingtang. Departing from this village on the day following, we crossed a high ridge of mountains to the west of the Black River, and travelled over a rough stony country until sunset, when we arrived at Lingicotta. a small village in the district of Woradoo. Here we shook out the last handful of meal from our dry-provision bags; this being the second day (since we crossed the Black River) that we had travelled from morning until night, without tasting one morsel of food.

May 2nd.—We departed from Lingicotta; but the slaves being very much fatigued, we halted for the night at a village about nine miles to the westward, and procured some provisions through the interest of the schoolmaster, who now sent forward a messenger to Malacotta, his native town, to inform his friends of his arrival in the country, and to desire them to provide the necessary quantity of victuals to entertain the coffle for two or three days.

May 3rd.—We set out for Malacotta, and about noon arrived at a village, near a considerable stream of water which flows to the westward. Here we determined to stop for the return of the messenger which had been sent to Malacotta the day before; and as the natives assured me there were no crocodiles in this stream, I went and bathed myself. Very few people here can swim; for they came in numbers to dissuade me from venturing into a pool, where they said the water would come over my head. About two o'clock the messenger returned from Malacotta, and the schoolmaster's elder brother being impatient to see him, came along with the messenger to meet him at this village. The interview between the two brothers, who had not seen each other for nine years, was very natural and affecting. They fell upon each other's neck, and it was some time before either of them could speak. At length when the schoolmaster had a little recovered himself, he took his brother by the hand, and turning round— "This is the man," said he, pointing to Karfa, "who has been my father in Manding; I would have pointed him out sooner to you, but my heart was too full."

We reached Malacotta in the evening, where we were well received. This is an unwalled town; the huts for the most part are made of split cane, twisted into a sort of wicker-work, and plastered over with mud. Here we remained three days, and were each day presented with a bullock from the schoolmaster; we were likewise well entertained by the townspeople, who appear to be very active and industrious. They make very good soap by boiling ground-nuts in water, and then adding a lye of wood ashes. They likewise manufacture excellent iron, which they carry to Bondou to barter for salt. A party of the townspeople had lately returned from a trading expedition of this kind, and brought information concerning a war between Almami Abdulkader, king of Foota Torra, and Damel, king of the Jaloffs. The events of this war soon became a favourite subject with the singing men, and the common topic of conversation in all the kingdoms bordering upon the Senegal and Gambia; and as the account is somewhat singular, I shall here abridge it for the reader's information. The king of Foota Torra, inflamed with a zeal for propagating his religion, had sent an embassy to Damel, similar to that which he had sent to Kasson, as related in page 59. The ambassador, on the present occasion, was accompanied by two of the principal Bushreens, who carried each a large knife, fixed on the top of a long pole. As soon as he had procured admission into the presence of Damel, and announced the pleasure of his sovereign, he ordered the Bushreens to present the emblems of his mission. The two knives were accordingly laid before Damel, and the ambassador explained himself as follows :—" With this knife," said he, " Abdulkader will condescend to shave the head of Damel, if Damel will embrace the Mahomedan faith ; and with this other knife, Abdulkader will cut the throat of Damel, if Damel refuses to embrace it ; take your choice." Damel coolly told the ambassador that he had no choice to make ; he neither chose to have his head shaved nor his throat cut ; and with this answer the ambassador was civilly dismissed. Abdulkader took his measures accordingly, and with a powerful army invaded Damel's country. The inhabitants of the towns and villages filled up their wells, destroyed their provisions, carried off their effects, and abandoned their dwellings as he approached. By this means he was led on from place to place, until he had advanced three days' journey into the country of the Jaloffs. He had, indeed, met with no opposition ; but his army had suffered so much from the scarcity of water, that several of his men had died by the way. This induced him to direct his march towards a watering place in the woods, where his men having quenched their thirst, and being overcome with fatigue, lay down carelessly to sleep among the bushes. In this situation they were attacked by Damel before daybreak, and completely routed. Many of them were trampled to death as they lay asleep by the Jaloff horses ; others were killed in attempting to make their escape ; and a still greater number were taken prisoners. Among the latter was Abdulkader himself. This ambitious or rather frantic prince, who, but a month before, had sent the threatening message to Damel, was now himself led into his presence a miserable captive. The behaviour of Damel on this occasion is never mentioned by the singing men but in terms of the highest approbation ; and it was indeed so extraordinary in an African prince, that the reader may find it difficult to

give credit to the recital. When his royal prisoner was
brought before him in irons, and thrown upon the ground,
the magnanimous Damel, instead of setting his foot upon
his neck, and stabbing him with his spear, according
to custom in such cases, addressed him as follows:—
"Abdulkader, answer me this question:—If the chance
of war had placed me in your situation, and you in
mine, how would you have treated me?" "I would
have thrust my spear into your heart," returned Abdulkader with great firmness; "and I know that a similar
fate awaits me." "Not so," said Damel; "my spear is
indeed red with the blood of your subjects killed in
battle, and I could now give it a deeper stain by dipping
it in your own; but this would not build up my towns,
nor bring to life the thousands who fell in the woods. I
will not, therefore, kill you in cold blood, but I will retain
you as my slave, until I perceive that your presence in
your own kingdom will be no longer dangerous to your
neighbours, and then I will consider of the proper way
of disposing of you." Abdulkader was accordingly retained, and worked as a slave for three months; at the
end of which period, Damel listened to the solicitations
of the inhabitants of Foota Torra, and restored to them
their king. Strange as this story may appear, I have no
doubt of the truth of it; it was told me at Malacotta
by the Negroes; it was afterwards related to me by the
Europeans on the Gambia; by some of the French at
Goree; and confirmed by nine slaves, who were taken
prisoners along with Abdulkader, by the watering place
in the woods, and carried in the same ship with me to
the West Indies.

CHAPTER XXVI

The caravan proceeds to Konkadoo, and crosses the Falemé River—
Its arrival at Baniserile, Kirwani, and Tambacunda—Incidents
on the road—A matrimonial case—The caravan proceeds through
many towns and villages, and arrives at length on the banks of
the Gambia—Passes through Medina, the capital of Woolli, and
finally stops at Jindey—The Author, accompanied by Karfa, proceeds to Pisania—Various occurrences previous to his departure
from Africa—Takes his passage in an American ship—Short
account of his voyage to Great Britain by way of the West Indies.

On the 7th of May we departed from Malacotta, and
having crossed the *Ba lee*, "Honey River," a branch
of the Senegal, we arrived in the evening at a walled
town called Bintingala, where we rested two days.   From
thence, in one day more, we proceeded to Dindikoo, a
small town situated at the bottom of a high ridge of
hills, from which this district is named *Konkadoo*, "the
country of mountains."   These hills are very productive
of gold.   I was shown a small quantity of this metal
which had been lately collected; the grains were about
the usual size, but much flatter than those of Manding,
and were found in white quartz, which had been broken
to pieces by hammers.   At this town I met with a Negro,
whose hair and skin were of a dull white colour.   He was
of that sort which are called in the Spanish West Indies
Albinos, or white Negroes.   The skin is cadaverous and
unsightly, and the natives considered this complexion (I
believe truly) as the effect of disease.

May 11th.—At daybreak we departed from Dindikoo,
and after a toilsome day's travel arrived in the evening
at Satadoo, the capital of a district of the same name.
This town was formerly of considerable extent; but many
families had left it in consequence of the predatory in-
cursions of the Foulahs of Foota Jalla, who made it a

practice to come secretly through the woods and carry off people from the corn fields, and even from the wells near the town. In the afternoon of the 12th, we crossed the Falemé River, the same which I had formerly crossed at Bondou in my journey eastward. This river, at this season of the year, is easily forded at this place, the stream being only about two feet deep. The water is very pure, and flows rapidly over a bed of sand and gravel. We lodged for the night at a small village called Medina, the sole property of a Mandingo merchant, who, by a long intercourse with Europeans, has been induced to adopt some of their customs. His victuals were served up in pewter dishes, and even his houses were built after the fashion of the English houses on the Gambia.

May 13*th*.—In the morning, as we were preparing to depart, a coffle of slaves belonging to some Serawoolli traders, crossed the river, and agreed to proceed with us to Baniserile, the capital of Dentila, a very long day's journey from this place. We accordingly set out together, and travelled with great expedition through the woods until noon, when one of the Serawoolli slaves dropt the load from his head, for which he was smartly whipped. The load was replaced, but he had not proceeded above a mile before he let it fall a second time, for which he received the same punishment. After this he travelled in great pain until about two o'clock, when we stopt to breathe a little by a pool of water, the day being remarkably hot. The poor slave was now so completely exhausted, that his master was obliged to release him from the rope, for he lay motionless on the ground. A Serawoolli, therefore, undertook to remain with him, and endeavour to bring him to the town during the cool of the night. In the meanwhile we continued our route, and after a very hard day's travel, arrived at Baniserile late in the evening.

One of our Slatees was a native of this place, from which he had been absent three years. This man invited me to go with him to his house, at the gate of which his friends met him with many expressions of joy—shaking hands with him, embracing him, and singing and dancing before him. As soon as he had seated himself upon a mat by the threshold of his door, a young woman (his intended bride) brought a little water in a calabash, and kneeling down before him, desired him to wash his hands; when he had done this, the girl, with a tear of joy sparkling in her eyes, drank the water—this being considered the greatest proof she could give him of her fidelity and attachment. About eight o'clock the same evening, the Serawoolli, who had been left in the woods to take care of the fatigued slave, returned and told us that he was dead; the general opinion, however, was that he himself had killed him, or left him to perish on the road, for the Serawoollies are said to be infinitely more cruel in their treatment of slaves than the Mandingoes. We remained at Baniserile two days, in order to purchase native iron, Shea butter, and some other articles for sale on the Gambia; and here the Slatee who had invited me to his house, and who possessed three slaves, part of the coffle, having obtained information that the price on the coast was very low, determined to separate from us, and remain with his slaves where he was, until an opportunity should offer of disposing of them to advantage, giving us to understand that he should complete his nuptials with the young woman before mentioned, in the meantime.

May 16*th*.—We departed from Baniserile, and travelled through thick woods until noon, when we saw at a distance the town of Julifunda, but did not approach it, as we proposed to rest for the night at a large town called Kirwani, which we reached about four o'clock in the afternoon. This town stands in a valley, and the country, for more than a mile round it, is cleared of wood, and well cultivated. The inhabitants appear to be very active and industrious, and seemed to have carried the system of agriculture to some degree of perfection, for they collect the dung of their cattle into large heaps during the dry season, for the purpose of manuring their land with it at the proper time. I saw nothing like this in any other part of Africa.

Near the town are several smelting furnaces, from which the natives obtain very good iron. They afterwards hammer the metal into small bars, about a foot in length and two inches in breadth, one of which bars is sufficient to make two Mandingo corn hoes. On the morning after our arrival, we were visited by a Slatee of this place, who informed Karfa that among some slaves he had lately purchased, was a native of Foota Jalla, and as that country was at no great distance, he could not safely employ him in the labours of the field, lest he should effect his escape. The Slatee was therefore desirous of exchanging this slave for one of Karfa's, and offered some cloth and Shea butter to induce Karfa to comply with the proposal, which was accepted. The Slatee thereupon sent a boy to order the slave in question to bring him a few ground-nuts. The poor creature soon afterwards entered the court in which we were sitting, having no suspicion of what was negotiating, until the master caused the gate to be shut, and told him to sit down. The slave now saw his danger, and, perceiving the gate to be shut upon him, threw down the nuts, and jumped over the fence. He was immediately pursued and overtaken by the Slatees, who brought him back, and secured him in irons, after which one of Karfa's slaves was released and delivered in exchange. The unfortunate captive was at first very much dejected, but in the course of a few days his melancholy gradually subsided, and he became at length as cheerful as any of his companions.

Departing from Kirwani on the morning of the 20th, we entered the Tenda wilderness of two days' journey. The woods were very thick, and the country shelved towards the south-west. About ten o'clock we met a coffle of twenty-six people and seven loaded asses returning from the Gambia. Most of the men were armed with muskets, and had broad belts of scarlet cloth over their shoulders, and European hats upon their heads. They informed us that there was very little demand for slaves on the coast, as no vessel had arrived for some months past. On hearing this, the Serawoollies, who had travelled with us from the Falemé River, separated themselves and their slaves from

the coffle. They had not, they said, the means of maintaining their slaves in Gambia until a vessel should arrive,
and were unwilling to sell them to disadvantage; they
therefore departed to the northward for Kajaaga. We
continued our route through the wilderness, and travelled
all day through a rugged country, covered with extensive
thickets of bamboo. At sunset, to our great joy, we
arrived at a pool of water near a large tabba tree, whence
the place is called Tabbagee, and here we rested a few
hours. The water at this season of the year is by no
means plentiful in these woods, and as the days were
insufferably hot, Karfa proposed to travel in the night.
Accordingly, about eleven o'clock the slaves were taken
out of their irons, and the people of the coffle received
orders to keep close together, as well to prevent the slaves
from attempting to escape, as on account of the wild
beasts. We travelled with great alacrity until daybreak,
when it was discovered that a free woman had parted from
the coffle in the night; her name was called until the woods
resounded, but no answer being given, we conjectured that
she had either mistaken the road, or that a lion had seized
her unperceived. At length it was agreed that four people
should go back a few miles to a small rivulet, where some
of the coffle had stopped to drink as we passed it in the
night, and that the coffle should wait for their return.
The sun was about an hour high before the people came
back with the woman, whom they found lying fast asleep
by the stream. We now resumed our journey, and about
eleven o'clock reached a walled town called Tambacunda,
where we were well received. Here we remained four days,
on account of a *palaver* which was held on the following
occasion:—Modi Lemina, one of the Slatees belonging to
the coffle, had formerly married a woman of this town,
who had borne him two children; he afterwards went to
Manding, and remained there eight years, without sending
any account of himself during all that time to his deserted
wife, who, seeing no prospect of his return, at the end of
three years had married another man, to whom she had
likewise borne two children. Lemina now claimed his

wife, but the second husband refused to deliver her up, insisting that, by the laws of Africa, when a man has been three years absent from his wife, without giving her notice of his being alive, the woman is at liberty to marry again. After all the circumstances had been fully investigated in an assembly of the chief men, it was determined that the wife should make her choice, and be at liberty either to return to the first husband, or continue with the second, as she alone should think proper. Favourable as this determination was to the lady, she found it a difficult matter to make up her mind, and requested time for consideration, but I think I could perceive that *first love* would carry the day. Lemina was indeed somewhat older than his rival, but he was also much richer. What weight this circumstance had in the scale of his wife's affections, I pretend not to say.

On the morning of the 26th, as we departed from Tambacunda, Karfa observed to me that there were no Shea trees farther to the westward than this town. I had collected and brought with me from Manding the leaves and flowers of this tree, but they were so greatly bruised on the road that I thought it best to gather another specimen at this place. The appearance of the fruit evidently places the Shea tree in the natural order of *Sapotæ*, and it has some resemblance to the *mudhuca* tree, described by Lieutenant Charles Hamilton, in the Asiatic Researches, vol. i. p. 300. About one o'clock we reached Sibikillin, a walled village; but the inhabitants having the character of inhospitality towards strangers, and of being much addicted to theft, we did not think proper to enter the gate. We rested a short time under a tree, and then continued our route until it was dark, when we halted for the night by a small stream running towards the Gambia. Next day the road led over a wild and rocky country, everywhere rising into hills, and abounding with monkeys and wild beasts. In the rivulets among the hills we found plenty of fish. This was a very hard day's journey, and it was not until sunset that we reached the village of Koomboo, near to which are the ruins of a large town, formerly destroyed by war. The inhabitants of Koomboo, like those of Sibikillin, have so bad a reputation that strangers seldom lodge in the village; we accordingly rested for the night in the fields, where we erected temporary huts for our protection, there being great appearance of rain.

May 28th.—We departed from Koomboo, and slept at a Foulah town, about seven miles to the westward; from which, on the day following, having crossed a considerable branch of the Gambia, called Neola Koba, we reached a well-inhabited part of the country. Here are several towns within sight of each other, collectively called Tenda, but each is distingui-hed also by its particular name. We lodged at one of them, called Koba Tenda, where we remained the day following, in order to procure provisions for our support in crossing the Simbani woods. On the 30th we reached Jallacotta, a considerable town, but much infested by Foulah banditti, who come through the woods from Bondou, and steal everything they can lay their hands on. A few days before our arrival they had stolen twenty head of cattle, and on the day following made a second attempt, but were beaten off, and one of them taken prisoner. Here one of the slaves belonging to the coffle, who had travelled with great difficulty for the last three days, was found unable to proceed any farther; his master (a singing man) proposed therefore to exchange him for a young girl belonging to one of the townspeople. The poor girl was ignorant of her fate until the bundles were all tied up in the morning, and the coffle ready to depart; when coming with some other young women to see the coffle set out, her master took her by the hand and delivered her to the singing man. Never was a face of serenity more suddenly changed into one of the deepest distress; the terror she manifested on having the load put upon her head, and the rope fastened round her neck, and the sorrow with which she bade adieu to her companions, were truly affecting. About nine o'clock we crossed a large plain covered with *ciboa* trees (a species of palm), and came to the river Nerico, a branch of the Gambia. This was but a small river at this time, but in the rainy season it is often dangerous to travellers. As soon as we had crossed this

Shea or the Buttertree

river, the singing men began to vociferate a particular song,
expressive of their joy at having got safe into the west
country, or, as they expressed it, *the land of the setting sun*.
The country was found to be very level, and the soil a
mixture of clay and sand. In the afternoon it rained hard,
and we had recourse to the common Negro umbrella, a
large ciboa leaf, which, being placed upon the head, completely defends the whole body from the rain. We lodged
for the night under the shade of a large tabba tree, near
the ruins of a village. On the morning following we
crossed a stream called Noulico, and about two o'clock, to
my infinite joy, I saw myself once more on the banks of
the Gambia, which at this place, being deep and smooth,
is navigable ; but the people told me that a little lower
down, the stream is so shallow that the coffles frequently
cross it on foot. On the south side of the river, opposite
to this place, is a large plain of clayey ground, called
Toombi Toorila. It is a sort of morass, in which people
are frequently lost, it being more than a day's journey
across it. In the afternoon we met a man and two women,
with bundles of cotton cloth upon their heads. They were
going, they said, for Dentila, to purchase iron, there being
a great scarcity of that article on the Gambia. A little
before it was dark, we arrived at a village in the kingdom
of Woolli, called Seesukunda. Near this village there are
great plenty of nitta trees, and the slaves in passing along
had collected large bunches of the fruit ; but such was the
superstition of the inhabitants that they would not permit
any of the fruit to be brought into the village. They had
been told, they said, that some catastrophe would happen
to the place when people lived upon nittas, and neglected
to cultivate corn.

June 2nd.—We departed from Seesukunda, and passed a
number of villages, at none of which was the coffle permitted to stop, although we were all very much fatigued ;
it was four o'clock in the afternoon before we reached
Baraconda, where we rested one day. Departing from
Baraconda on the morning of the 4th, we reached in a
few hours Medina, the capital of the king of Woolli's

dominions, from whom the reader may recollect I received a hospitable reception in the beginning of December 1795 in my journey eastward.[1]   I immediately inquired concerning the health of my good old benefactor, and learned with great concern that he was dangerously ill.   As Karfa would not allow the coffle to stop, I could not present my respects to the king in person ; but I sent him word by the officer to whom we paid customs, that his prayers for my safety had not been unavailing.   We continued our route until sunset, when we lodged at a small village a little to the westward of Kootakunda, and on the day following arrived at Jindey, where, eighteen months before, I had parted from my friend Dr. Laidley, an interval during which I had not beheld the face of a Christian, nor once heard the delightful sound of my native language.

Being now arrived within a short distance of Pisania, from whence my journey originally commenced, and learning that my friend Karfa was not likely to meet with an immediate opportunity of selling his slaves on the Gambia, it occurred to me to suggest to him that he would find it for his interest to leave them at Jindey until a market should offer.   Karfa agreed with me in this opinion, and hired, from the chief man of the town, huts for their accommodation, and a piece of land on which to employ them in raising corn and other provisions for their maintenance.   With regard to himself, he declared that he would not quit me until my departure from Africa.   We set out accordingly, Karfa, myself, and one of the Foulahs belonging to the coffle, early on the morning of the 9th ; but although I was now approaching the end of my tedious and toilsome journey, and expected in another day to meet with countrymen and friends, I could not part, for the last time, with my unfortunate fellow-travellers, doomed, as I knew most of them to be, to a life of captivity and slavery, in a foreign land, without great emotion.   During a wearisome peregrination of more than five hundred British miles, exposed to the burning rays of a tropical sun, these poor slaves, amidst their own infinitely greater sufferings,

[1] *Vide* page 27.

would commiserate mine; and frequently of their own accord, bring water to quench my thirst, and at night collect branches and leaves to prepare me a bed in the wilderness. We parted with reciprocal expressions of regret and benediction. My good wishes and prayers were all I could bestow upon them, and it afforded me some consolation to be told, that they were sensible I had no more to give.

My anxiety to get forward admitting of no delay on the road, we reached Tendacunda in the evening, and were hospitably received at the house of an aged black female called Seniora Camilla, a person who had resided many years at the English factory, and spoke our language. I was known to her before I had left the Gambia, at the outset of my journey; but my dress and figure were now so different from the usual appearance of a European, that she was very excusable in mistaking me for a Moor. When I told her my name and country, she surveyed me with great astonishment, and seemed unwilling to give credit to the testimony of her senses. She assured me that none of the traders on the Gambia ever expected to see me again; having been informed long ago, that the Moors of Ludamar had murdered me, as they had murdered Major Houghton. I inquired for my two attendants, Johnson and Demba, and learned with great sorrow that neither of them was returned. Karfa, who had never before heard people converse in English, listened to us with great attention. Everything he saw seemed wonderful. The furniture of the house, the chairs, etc., and particularly beds with curtains, were objects of his great admiration; and he asked me a thousand questions concerning the utility and necessity of different articles, to some of which I found it difficult to give satisfactory answers.

On the morning of the 10th, Mr. Robert Ainsley, having learnt that I was at Tendacunda, came to meet me, and politely offered me the use of his horse. He informed me that Dr. Laidley had removed all his property to a place called Kaye, a little farther down the river, and that he was then gone to Doomasansa with his vessel to purchase

rice, but would return in a day or two. He therefore
invited me to stay with him at Pisania until the Doctor's
return. I accepted the invitation, and being accompanied
by my friend Karfa, reached Pisania about ten o'clock.
Mr. Ainsley's schooner was lying at anchor before the
place. This was the most surprising object which Karfa
had yet seen. He could not easily comprehend the use of
the masts, sails, and rigging, nor did he conceive that it
was possible, by any sort of contrivance, to make so large
a body move forwards by the common force of the wind.
The manner of fastening together the different planks
which composed the vessel, and filling up the seams so
as to exclude the water, was perfectly new to him; and I
found that the schooner, with her cable and anchor, kept
Karfa in deep meditation the greater part of the day.

About noon, on the 12th, Dr. Laidley returned from
Doomasansa, and received me with great joy and satisfaction, as one risen from the dead. Finding that the
wearing apparel which I had left under his care was not
sold nor sent to England, I lost no time in resuming the
English dress, and disrobing my chin of its venerable in-
cumbrance. Karfa surveyed me in my British apparel
with great delight, but regretted exceedingly that I had
taken off my beard, the loss of which, he said, had converted me from a man into a boy. Dr. Laidley readily
undertook to discharge all the pecuniary engagements I
had entered into since my departure from the Gambia, and
took my draft upon the Association for the amount. My
agreement with Karfa (as I have already related) was to
pay him the value of one prime slave, for which I had
given him my bill upon Dr. Laidley before we departed
from Kamalia; for, in case of my death on the road, I was
unwilling that my benefactor should be a loser. But this
good creature had continued to manifest towards me so
much kindness, that I thought I made him but an inade-
quate recompense, when I told him that he was now to
receive double the sum I had originally promised, and Dr.
Laidley assured him that he was ready to deliver the goods
to that amount whenever he thought proper to send for

them. Karfa was overpowered by this unexpected token of my gratitude, and still more so when he heard that I intended to send a handsome present to the good old schoolmaster, Fankooma, at Malacotta. He promised to carry up the goods along with his own, and Dr. Laidley assured him that he would exert himself in assisting him to dispose of his slaves to the best advantage, the moment a slave vessel should arrive. These and other instances of attention and kindness shown him by Dr. Laidley, were not lost upon Karfa. He would often say to me, " My journey has indeed been prosperous ! " But, observing the improved state of our manufactures, and our manifest superiority in the arts of civilised life, he would sometimes appear pensive, and exclaim, with an involuntary sigh, *fato fing inta feng*, "black men are nothing." At other times he would ask me, with great seriousness, what could possibly have induced me, who was no trader, to think of exploring so miserable a country as Africa? He meant by this, to signify that, after what I must have witnessed in my own country, nothing in Africa could, in his opinion, deserve a moment's attention. I have preserved these little traits of character in this worthy Negro, not only from regard to the man, but also because they appear to me to demonstrate that he possessed a mind *above his condition;* and to such of my readers as love to contemplate human nature in all its varieties, and to trace its progress from rudeness to refinement, I hope the account I have given of this poor African will not be unacceptable.

No European vessel had arrived at Gambia for many months previous to my return from the interior ; and as the rainy season was now setting in, I persuaded Karfa to return to his people at Jindey. He parted with me on the 14th with great tenderness ; but as I had little hopes of being able to quit Africa for the remainder of the year, I told him, as the fact was, that I expected to see him again before my departure. In this, however, I was luckily disappointed, and my narrative now hastens to its conclusion, for, on the 15th, the ship Charlestown, an American vessel, commanded by Mr. Charles Harris, entered the river. She came for slaves, intending to touch at Goree to fill up, and to proceed from thence to South Carolina. As the European merchants on the Gambia had at this time a great many slaves on hand, they agreed with the captain to purchase the whole of his cargo, consisting chiefly of rum and tobacco, and deliver him slaves to the amount, in the course of two days. This afforded me such an opportunity of returning (though by a circuitous route) to my native country, as I thought was not to be neglected. I therefore immediately engaged my passage in this vessel for America; and having taken leave of Dr. Laidley, to whose kindness I was so largely indebted, and my other friends on the river, I embarked at Kaye on the 17th day of June.

Our passage down the river was tedious and fatiguing, and the weather was so hot, moist, and unhealthy, that before our arrival at Goree, four of the seamen, the surgeon, and three of the slaves had died of fevers. At Goree we were detained for want of provisions until the beginning of October.

The number of slaves received on board this vessel, both on the Gambia and at Goree, was one hundred and thirty, of whom about twenty-five had been, I suppose, of free condition in Africa, as most of them being Bushreens, could write a little Arabic. Nine of them had become captives in the religious war between Abdulkader and Damel, mentioned in the latter part of the preceding chapter; two of the others had seen me as I passed through Bondou, and many of them had heard of me in the interior countries. My conversation with them in their native language gave them great comfort; and as the surgeon was dead, I consented to act in a medical capacity in his room for the remainder of the voyage. They had, in truth, need of every consolation in my power to bestow, not that I observed any wanton acts of cruelty practised either by the master or the seamen towards them, but the mode of confining and securing Negroes in the American slave ships (owing chiefly to the weakness of their crews), being abundantly more rigid and severe than in British vessels employed in the same traffic, made these poor creatures to suffer greatly, and a general sickness prevailed amongst them. Besides the three who died on the Gambia, and six or eight while we remained at Goree, eleven perished at sea, and many of the survivors were reduced to a very weak and emaciated condition.

In the midst of these distresses, the vessel, after having been three weeks at sea, became so extremely leaky as to require constant exertion at the pumps. It was found necessary, therefore, to take some of the ablest of the Negro men out of irons, and employ them in this labour, in which they were often worked beyond their strength. This produced a complication of miseries not easily to be described. We were, however, relieved much sooner than I expected, for the leak continuing to gain upon us, notwithstanding our utmost exertions to clear the vessel, the seamen insisted on bearing away for the West Indies, as affording the only chance of saving our lives. Accordingly after some objections on the part of the master, we directed our course for Antigua, and fortunately made that island in about thirty-five days after our departure from Goree. Yet even at this juncture we narrowly escaped destruction, for on approaching the north-west side of the island we struck on the Diamond Rock, and got into St. John's harbour with great difficulty. The vessel was afterwards condemned as unfit for sea, and the slaves, as I have heard, were ordered to be sold for the benefit of the owners.

At this island I remained ten days, when the Chesterfield Packet, homeward bound from the Leeward Islands, touching at St. John's for the Antigua mail, I took my passage in that vessel. We sailed on the 24th of November, and after a short but tempestuous voyage, arrived at Falmouth on the 22nd of December, from whence I immediately set out for London, having been absent from England two years and seven months.

After his return from Africa, Park remained for a considerable time stationary in London, and was diligently employed in arranging the materials for the publication of his travels.

BOOK TWO

THE SECOND JOURNEY
THE JOURNAL
OF A
MISSION TO
THE INTERIOR OF
AFRICA
IN THE YEAR
1805

(Chapters XXVIII to XXXII are Park's journal almost verbatim, only astronomical observations, lists of stores, etc., being omitted. The style, as might be expected in a simple log written up en route, *is not so polished as in Book I ; indeed it is surprising, considering the difficulties which beset him, that Park was able to keep a journal at all.)*

CHAPTER XXVII

Introduction

PARK's return to Britain was a triumph. His family rejoiced as over one raised from the dead, the African Association were jubilant at the success of their envoy, and the public at large was greatly impressed not only by the importance of his discovery, but by the modesty of his bearing. The preparation of his journal for publication was a heavy burden to Park, but on its appearance in 1799 it was an immediate success, and several editions were called for. Success, however, did not turn Park's head. He refused to be lionised, and avoided talking about his exploits. Tall, well built, and handsome, he was nevertheless quite unspoilt and without vanity or affectation; indeed, strangers who looked to him for animation and lively conversation found instead considerable coldness and reserve. Among his friends, however, he was quite otherwise, and they all held him in great esteem and affection.

After the publication of his book, Park returned to Foulshiels and married his former master's daughter, Alison Anderson of Selkirk, in 1799. Two years of peace followed, in which Park lived on the proceeds of his book, and gradually regained the strength which his African journey had so severely taxed. At first he was haunted by a recurrence of stomach trouble—probably dysentery—and by terrifying dreams in which he thought himself again in Ali's power or in some other desperate situation in Africa. By the summer of 1800, however, he seems to have regained his strength and vigour, for he wrote to Sir Joseph Banks seeking further employment overseas. The possibility of a mission to New South Wales took him to London, and in a letter from there

281

on 12th March 1801 to his wife we may glimpse something of the man:

"My lovely Ailie, nothing gives me more pleasure than to write to you, and the reason why I delayed it a day last time was to get some money to send to you. You say you are wishing to spend a note upon yourself. My sweet Ailie, you may be sure I approve of it. What is mine is yours, and I receive much pleasure from your goodness in consulting me about such a trifle. I wish I had thousands to give you, but I know that my Ailie will be contented with what we have, and we shall live in the hope of seeing better days. I long very much to be with you, my love, and I was in great hopes of having things settled before now, but Sir Joseph (Banks) is ill, and I can do nothing till he recovers.

"I am happy to know you will go to New South Wales with me, my sweet wife. You are everything that I could desire; and wherever we go, you may be sure of one thing, that I shall always love you. Whenever I have fixed on this or any other situation I shall write to you. In the meantime, let nobody know till things are settled, as there is much between the cup and the lip.

"My lovely Ailie, you are constantly in my thoughts. I am tired of this place, but cannot lose the present opportunity of doing something for our advantage. When that is accomplished I shall not lose one moment. My darling, when we meet I shall be the happiest man on earth. Write soon, for I count the days till I hear from you, my lovely Ailie."

Nothing came of the Australian mission and Mungo returned to Foulshiels and examined other possibilities. Curiously, he seemed reluctant to engage in medical practice—he even considered taking a farm—and we must bear this in mind when considering his African travels. On neither expedition did Park show any attempt to facilitate his passage or earn his keep by the practice of his profession. Apart from a couple of pages on the ills and diseases of the Mandingoes (Book I, pp. 211 and 212), one could read Park's journals without guessing that he had had a medical training. The contrast with Livingstone is marked, and we cannot but think that had Park earned in Africa a reputation for healing as did Livingstone, his difficulties might have been much diminished. In fairness, however, we must remember that medicine was considerably more rudimentary in Park's time than in Livingstone's.

In October 1801, then, Park moved to Peebles and became a medical practitioner. There he soon acquired a high reputation for assiduity and kindliness, but the work was most uncongenial to him. Sir Walter Scott reports him as saying that he "would rather brave Africa and all its horrors than wear out his life in long and toilsome rides over cold and lonely heaths and gloomy hills, assailed by the wintry tempest, for which the remuneration was hardly enough to keep body and soul together."

Having kept in touch with Sir Joseph Banks, and no doubt having indicated to him his desire to make a further expedition to Africa, Park promptly obeyed a summons to London in 1803 to be offered by the Colonial Office another mission to the Niger.

Park accepted, and while he now had the resources and backing of the Government itself, he also had to endure its delays. Postponement followed postponement, and eventually Park returned to Scotland with a Moor from whom he was to receive instruction in Arabic until such time as an expedition could be sanctioned. In September 1804 he was again summoned to London, and in a memoir dated 4th October 1804 he set forth his proposals to Lord Camden. The expedition was to be for "the extension of British commerce and the enlargement of our geographical knowledge." He proposed to reconnoitre a route to the Niger by which trade could be carried on. He was to make a list of the articles which Africa would export and by barter ascertain their value in European goods. He was also to investigate the possibility of European settlement. He asked for 30 European soldiers, 6 carpenters, 15 to 20 negroes (preferably artificers), 50 asses, and 6 horses or mules. Equipment for the party was detailed, together with the necessaries for two boats of 40-foot length which were to be built on the Niger. In addition, he catalogued a stock of trade goods for barter *en route.* He proposed to buy the transport animals at the Canaries, and to collect the personnel at Goree. His policy while travelling was to attempt always to conciliate native potentates. Having reached the river and built his boats, he proposed to sail down stream for at least 1,400 miles. Then comes a typical Park understatement: "If the river should unfortunately end there, Mr. Park would feel his situation extremely critical . . . to return by the Niger to the westward he apprehends would be impossible; to proceed to the northward equally so; and to travel through Abyssinia extremely dangerous. The only remaining route that holds out any hopes of success is that towards the Bight of Guinea.' He realises, in fact, the great danger of his enterprise and pins his faith to a possible exit by the south, hoping that the Niger and Congo may prove to be the same river. He lists several reasons for feeling this to be the case.

His proposals were accepted. He was given a captain's commission, a credit of £5,000, and an assurance that in the event of his death a sum of £4,000 would be settled on his wife. He chose to accompany him two fellow countrymen, his brother-in-law Alexander Anderson to be his second-in-command, and George Scott, another Selkirkman, as artist to record the journey.

Further delays now ensued, not only mortifying but dangerous, for haste was needed if the expedition was to arrive before the rainy season, when travelling would be difficult. In the event, leaving England on 31st January 1805, they were in precisely the situation that Park had wished to avoid. He writes to his wife on arrival at Goree, however, without a hint of the worry that must have been in his mind.

"GOREE, *4th April* 1805.

"I have just now learnt that an American ship sails from this place for England in a few days; and I readily embrace the opportunity of sending a letter to my dearest wife. We have all of us kept our health very well ever since our departure from England. Alexander had a touch of the rheumatism at St. Jago, but is now quite recovered: he danced several country dances at the ball last night. George Scott is also in good health and spirits. I wrote to you from St. Jago, which letter I hope you received. We left that place on 21st March, and arrived here with the asses on the 28th. Almost every soldier in the garrison volunteered to go with me; and with the governor's assistance I have chosen a guard of the best men in the place. So lightly do the people here think of the danger attending the undertaking, that I have been under the necessity of refusing several military and naval officers who volunteered to accompany me. We shall sail for Gambia on Friday or Saturday. I am happy to learn that Karfa, my old friend, is at present at Jonkakonda; and I am in hopes we shall be able to hire him to go with us.

"We have as yet been extremely fortunate, and have got our business both at St. Jago and this place finished with great success; and I have hopes, almost to certainty, that Providence will so dispose the tempers and passions of the inhabitants of this quarter of the world, that we shall be enabled to *slide through* much more smoothly than you expect.

"I need not tell you how often I think about you; your own feelings will enable you to judge of that. The hopes of spending the remainder of my life with my wife and children will make everything seem easy; and you may be sure I will not rashly risk my life, when I know that your happiness, and the welfare of my young ones, depend so much upon it. I hope my mother does not torment herself with unnecessary fears about me. I sometimes fancy how you and she will be meeting misfortune half-way, and placing me in many distressing situations. I have as yet experienced nothing but success, and I hope that six months more will end the whole as I wish.

"PS. We have taken a ride this morning about twelve miles into the country. Alexander is much pleased with it; the heat is moderate, and the country healthy at present."

While he had no lack of European volunteers, it is ominous that no Africans would go with him. Park's personality and fame must have impressed the Europeans: doubtless also many of them were glad to snatch at any opportunity to be

quit of the boredom of garrison duties at Goree.   What
exactly he expected of them it is difficult to guess: in the
event they proved a total liability and their officer, Lieutenant
Martyn, quite failed to support Park, leaving the onus in
every way on the leader's shoulders.   Nowhere does Park
complain of Lieutenant Martyn, but nowhere is there any
evidence of his taking charge of the welfare of his men, much
less dealing with the military situation.

   In this company then, Park's journey began from Kayu,
near Pisania.   From the beginning difficulties arose, and the
convoy did not finally start inland until 4th May, at the height
of the hot season and with the rains imminent.   The long
column of animals and men at once proved difficult to manage,
and the military seemed quite unable to cope with the
situation.   As they penetrated inland and hostility appeared,
it was impossible to defend such a lengthy convoy effectively,
and much thieving went on.   News of the weakness of the
convoy spread like wildfire, and a swarm of predatory natives
followed it, darting in to steal in the most audacious manner
and, as the soldiers sickened and became listless, with ever
greater success.   It is difficult to see how Park could have
imagined any other fate for such a party.   He must have
realised also the folly of starting inland at such a season.
However, the alternative was a six to seven months' wait at
the coast, and this would doubtless have been even more
disastrous to health and morale.   In spite of the brave face
he put on, however, Park's heart must have been heavy
within him as the convoy blundered on.

                                                            (R. M.)

CHAPTER XXVIII

Departure from Kayee—Arrival at Pisania—Preparations there, and departure into the Interior—Samee—Payment to Mumbo Jumbo—Reach Jindey—Departure from Jindey —Cross the Wallia Creek—Kootakunda—Madina—Tabajang—Kingdom of Jamberoo—Visit from the king's son —Tatticonda—Visit from the son of the former king of Woolli—Reach Madina, the capital of Woolli—Audience of the king; his unfriendly conduct—Presents made to him and his courtiers—Barraconda—Bambakoo—Kanipe; inhospitable conduct of its inhabitants—Kussai—Nitta trees; restrictions relating to them—Enter the Simbani woods; precautions thereon, and sacrifice and prayers for success— Banks of the Gambia—Crocodiles and hippopotami—Reach Faraba—Loss of one of the soldiers—Rivers Neaulico and Nerico.

APRIL 27TH, 1805.—At ten o'clock in the morning took our departure from Kayee. The *Crescent,* the *Washington,* and Mr. Ainsley's vessel did us the honour to fire a salute at our departure. The day proved remarkably hot; and some of the asses, being unaccustomed to carry loads, made our march very fatiguing and troublesome. Three of them stuck fast in a muddy rice-field about two miles east of Kayee; and while we were employed in getting them out, our guide and the people in front had gone on so far that we lost sight of them. In a short time we overtook about a dozen soldiers and their asses, who had likewise fallen behind, and being afraid of losing their way, had halted till we came up. We in the rear took the road to Jonkakonda, which place we reached at one o'clock; but not finding Lieutenant Martyn nor any of the men who were in front, concluded they had gone by New Jermy, etc., therefore hired a guide and continued our march. Halted a few minutes under a large tree at the village of Lamain-Cotto, to allow the soldiers to cool themselves; and then proceeded towards Lamain, at which place we arrived at four o'clock. The people were extremely fatigued, having travelled all day under a vertical sun, and without a breath of wind. Lieutenant Martyn and the rest of our party arrived at half-past five, having taken the road by New Jermy.

.   .   .   .

April 28th.—Set out for Pisania. We passed two small Foulah towns and the village of Collin, and reached the banks of the Gambia at half-past eleven o'clock. Halted and gave our cattle water and grass; we likewise cooked our dinners, and rested till three o'clock, when we set forward and arrived at Pisania at sunset. Here we were accommodated at Mr. Ainsley's house; and as his schooner had not yet arrived with our baggage, I purchased some corn for our cattle, and spoke for a bullock for the soldiers.

April 29th.—Went and paid my respects to Seniora Camilla, who was much surprised to see me again attempting a journey into the interior of the country.

April 30th.—Mr. Ainsley's schooner arrived, and we immediately began to land the baggage and rice.

April 31st.—Gave out the ass saddles to be stuffed with grass, and set about weighing the bundles. Found that after all reductions, our asses could not possibly carry our baggage. Purchased five more with Mr. Ainsley's assistance.

May 1st.—Tying up the bundles and marking them.

May 2nd.—Purchased three asses, and a bullock for the people.

May 3rd.—Finished packing the loads, and got everything ready for our journey.

May 4th.—Left Pisania at half-past nine o'clock. The mode of marching was adjusted as follows. The asses and loads being all marked and numbered with red paint, a certain number of each was allotted to each of the six messes, into which the soldiers were divided; and the asses were further subdivided amongst the individuals of each mess, so that every man could tell at first sight the ass and load which belonged to him. The asses were also numbered with large figures, to prevent the natives from stealing them, as they could neither wash nor clip it off without being discovered.

Mr. George Scott and one of Isaaco's people generally went in front, Lieutenant Martyn in the centre, and Mr. Anderson and myself in the rear. We were forced to leave at Pisania about five cwt. of rice, not having a sufficient number of asses to carry it. We were escorted till we passed Tendicunda by Mr. Ainsley and the good old Seniora Camilla and most of the respectable natives in the vicinity. Our march was most fatiguing. Many of the asses being rather overloaded, lay down on the road; others kicked off their bundles, so that, after using every exertion to get forward, we with difficulty reached Samee, a distance of about eight miles. We unloaded our asses under a large Tabba tree at some distance from the town, and in the evening I went with Isaaco to pay my respects to the Slatee of Samee.

．　　．　　．　　．　　．

May 5th.—Paid six bars of amber to the Mumbo Jumbo boys, and set out for Jindey early in the morning. Found this day's travelling very difficult; many of the asses refused to go on; and we were forced to put their loads on the horses. We reached Jindey about noon. Purchased a bullock, and halted the 6th; fearing, if we attempted to proceed, we should be forced to leave some of our loads in the woods.

．　　．　　．　　．　　．

May 7th.—Left Jindey, but so much were our asses fatigued that I was obliged to hire three more, and four drivers to assist in getting forward the baggage. One of the St. Jago asses fell down convulsed when the load was put upon him; and a Mandingo ass, No. 11, refused to carry his load. I was under the necessity of sending him back to Jindey and hiring another in his place.

We travelled on the north side of the Wallia Creek till noon, when we crossed it near Kootakunda. Swam the asses over; and the soldiers, with the assistance of the Negroes, waded over with the bundles on their heads. Halted on the south side of the creek, and cooked our dinners.

At four o'clock set forwards, passed Kootakunda, and called at the village of Madina to pay my respects to Slatee

Bree.   Gave him a note on Mr. Ainsley for one jug of liquor. Halted at Tabajang, a village almost deserted; having been plundered in the course of the season by the king of Jamberoo, in conjunction with the king of Woolli.   Our guide's mother lives here; and as I found that we could not possibly proceed in our present state, I determined either to purchase more asses, or abandon some of the rice.

May 8th.—Purchased two asses for ten bars of amber and ten of coral each.   Covered the India bafts with skins, to prevent them from being damaged by the rain.   Two of the soldiers afflicted with the dysentery.

May 9th.—The king of Jamberoo's son came to pay his respects to me.   Jamberoo lies along the north side of the Wallia Creek, and extends a long way to the northward. The people are Jaloffs, but most of them speak Mandingo. Presented him with some amber.   Bought five asses and covered all the gunpowder with skins, except what was for our use on the road.

May 10th.—Having paid all the people who had assisted in driving the asses, I found that the expense was greater than any benefit we were likely to derive from them.   I therefore trusted the asses this day entirely to the soldiers. We left Tabajang at sunrise and made a short and easy march to Tatticonda, where the son of my friend, the former king of Woolli, came to meet me.   From him I could easily learn that our journey was viewed with great jealousy by the Slatees and Sierra-Woollis residing about Madina.

May 11th.—About noon arrived at Madina, the capital of the kingdom of Woolli.   We unloaded our asses under a tree without the gates of the town, and waited till five o'clock before we could have an audience from His Majesty. I took to the king a pair of silver-mounted pistols, ten dollars, ten bars of amber, ten of coral.   But, when he had looked at the present with great indifference for some time, he told me that he could not accept it; alleging, as an excuse for his avarice, that I had given a much handsomer present to the king of Kataba.   It was in vain that I assured him of the contrary; he positively refused to accept it, and I was under the necessity of adding fifteeen dollars, ten bars coral, ten amber, before His Majesty would accept it. After all, he begged me to give him a blanket to wrap himself in during the rains, which I readily sent him.

.   .   .   .   .

May 12th.—Had all the asses loaded by daybreak, and at sunrise, having obtained the king's permission, we departed from Woolli. Shortly after, we passed the town of Barraconda, where I stopped a few minutes to pay my respects to Jemaffoo Mamadoo, a very eminent Slatee. We reached the village of Bambakoo at half-past ten o'clock. Bought two asses, and likewise a bullock for the soldiers.

May 13th.—Departed from Bambakoo at sunrise, and reached Kanipe, an irregular built village, about ten o'clock. The people of the village had heard that we were under the necessity of purchasing water at Madina; and to make sure of a similar market, the women had drawn all the water from the wells, and were standing in crowds, drawing up the water as fast as it collected. It was in vain that the soldiers attempted to come in for their share: the camp kettles were by no means so well adapted for drawing water as the women's calabashes. The soldiers therefore returned without water, having the laugh very much against them.

I received information that there was a pool of water about two miles south of the town; and in order to make the women desist, I mounted a man on each of the horses and sent them away to the pool, to bring as much water as would boil our rice; and in the afternoon sent all the asses to be watered at the same place. In the evening some of the soldiers made another attempt to procure water from the large well near the town, and succeeded by the following stratagem. One of them having dropped his canteen into the well, as if by accident, his companions fastened a rope round him, and lowered him down to the bottom of the well; where he stood and filled all the camp kettles, to the great mortification of the women, who had been labouring and carrying water for the last twenty-four hours in hopes of having their necks and heads decked with small amber and beads by the sale of it. Bought two goats for the soldiers.

May 14*th*.—Halted at Kussai, about four miles east of Kanipe. This is the same village as Seesekunda, but the inhabitants have changed its name. Here one of the soldiers, having collected some of the fruit of the Nitta trees, was eating them, when the chief man of the village came out in a great rage, and attempted to take them from him; but finding that impracticable, he drew his knife, and told us to put on our loads and get away from the village. Finding that we only laughed at him, he became more quiet; and when I told him that we were unacquainted with so strange a restriction but should be careful not to eat any of them in future, he said that the thing itself was not of great importance if it had not been done in sight of the women. For, says he, this place has been frequently visited with famine from want of rain, and in these distressing times the fruit of the Nitta is all we have to trust to, and it may then be opened without harm; but in order to prevent the women and children from wasting this supply, a *toong* is put upon the Nittas until famine makes its appearance. The word *toong* is used to express anything sealed up by magic.

Bought two asses. As we entered the Simbani woods from this town, Isaaco was very apprehensive that we might be attacked by some of the Bondou people, there being at this time a hot war between two brothers about the succession: and as the report had spread that a coffle of white men were going to the interior, every person immediately concluded that we were loaded with the richest merchandise to purchase slaves; and that whichever of the parties should gain possession of our wealth, he would likewise gain the ascendancy over his opponent. On this account, gave orders to the men not to fire at any deer or game they might see in the woods; that every man must have his piece loaded and primed, and that the report of a musket, but more particularly of three or four, should be the signal to leave everything and run towards the place.

May 15*th*.—Departed from Kussai. At the entrance of the woods, Isaaco laid a black ram across the road and cut its throat, having first said a long prayer over it. This he considered as very essential towards our success. The flesh of the animal was given to the slaves at Kussai, that they might pray in their hearts for our success.

The first five miles of our route was through a woody country; we then reached a level plain nearly destitute of wood. On this plain we observed some hundreds of a species of antelope of a dark colour with a white mouth; they are called by the natives *Da qui*, and are nearly as large as a bullock. At half-past ten o'clock we arrived on the banks of the Gambia, and halted during the heat of the day under a large tree called *Teelee Corra*, the same under which I formerly stopped in my return from the interior.

The Gambia here is about a hundred yards across, and, contrary to what I expected, has a regular tide, rising four inches by the shore. It was low water this day at one o'clock. The river swarms with crocodiles. I counted at one time thirteen of them ranged along shore, and three hippopotami. The latter feed only during the night, and seldom leave the water during the day; they walk on the bottom of the river, and seldom show more of themselves above water than their heads.

At half-past three o'clock in the afternoon, we again set forward, and about a mile to the eastward ascended a hill, where we had a most enchanting prospect of the country to the westward; in point of distance it is the richest I ever saw. The course of the Gambia was easily distinguished by a range of dark green trees, which grew on its banks.

.   .   .   .   .

A mile and a half east of Prospect Hill is another on the north side of the road, from the top of which we had a charming view to the south. The course of the river is from the E.S.E.; no hills on the south side of it, the whole country being quite level. About ten miles E.S.E. the river passes near an elevated table land, which looks like an old fortification. At sunset reached a watering-place called Faraba, but found no water.

While we were unloading the asses, John Walters, one of the soldiers, fell down in an epileptic fit, and expired in about an hour after. The Negroes belonging to our guide set about digging a well, having first lighted a fire to keep off the bees which were swarming about the place in search of water. In a little time they found water in sufficient quantity to cook our suppers, and even supply the horses and asses in the course of the night.

Being apprehensive of an attack from the Bondou people, placed double sentries, and made every man sleep with his loaded musket under his head. Latitude by mer. alt. of the moon, 14° 38′ 46″ N.

About three o'clock buried John Walters, and in remembrance of him wish this place to be called Walters's Well.

May 16*th*.—Departed from the well as soon as day dawned, and reached the Neaulico at half-past eight o'clock. This stream is nearly dry at this season, and only affords water in certain hollow places which abound in fish. Saw Isaaco's Negroes take several with their hands, and with wisps of grass used as a net to frighten the fish into a narrow space. One of the fish was a new genus.

Saw in the bed of the river some Negroes roasting a great quantity of flesh on temporary wooden stages erected for the purpose.

This half roasting and smoking makes the meat keep much longer than it would do without it. The flesh was part of a *Da qui* which they found on the road; a lion had killed it during the night, and eat one leg of it.

At four o'clock p.m. departed from the Neaulico. At five, passed the ruins of Mangelli, where I formerly slept, and at six o'clock halted for the night at Manjalli Tabba Cotta, the ruins of a village so called. The wood during this day's march is in general small, and the road is much interrupted with dry bamboos. Plenty of water at the resting-place.

. . . . .

May 17*th*.—Left Manjalli Tabba Cotta, and after a fatiguing march of twelve miles, reached Bray, a watering-place. Endeavoured to take the meridional altitude of the sun, by the back observation with Troughton's pocket sextant; and after carefully examining his rise and fall, with the intervals betwixt each observation, I was convinced that it can be done with great accuracy, requiring only a steady hand and proper attention. This was a great relief to me; I had been plagued watching the passage of the fixed stars, and often fell asleep when they were in the meridian.

We left Bray at three o'clock p.m. and carried with us as much water as we possibly could, intending to rest at Nillin-dingcorro till the moon rose; but there being no water, our guide continued our march to the river Nerico, which we reached at eight o'clock, all the people and asses very much fatigued. Face of the country during this day an open and level plain with bushes and Cibi trees, making the prospect rich, though not grand. Saw plenty of lions' excrement in the wood: they deposit it only in certain places, and like the cats, claw up the ground in order to cover it

May 18th.—People employed all the morning in transporting the baggage and asses across the river; and as both men and asses were very much fatigued, I thought it best to halt on the east side of the river till the afternoon, as it would afford the soldiers an opportunity of washing their clothes.

. . . . . .

The breadth of the stream of the river Nerico is about sixty feet, the depth of water four feet, its velocity is two miles an hour. The heat of the stream at two o'clock 94° Fahrenheit.

CHAPTER XXIX

Arrival at Jallacotta — Maheena — Tambico — Bady; hostile conduct of the Faranba, or chief, and its consequences—Reach Jeningalla—Iron-furnaces. Mansafara—Attacked by wolves—Enter the Tenda wilderness—Ruins and Plain of Doofroo—Attacked by a swarm of bees—Arrival at Sibikillin—Shea trees—Badoo—Tambacunda—Ba deema river—Tabba Gee—Mambari—Julifunda; unfriendly conduct of its chief; and presents sent to him and the king—Visit from the latter—Reach Eercella—Baniserile—Celebrate His Majesty's birthday—Mode of fluxing iron—Madina—Falema river—Satadoo—Sickness and death of the carpenter—Arrival at Shrondo; commencement of the rainy season; and alarming sickness amongst the soldiers—Gold mines; process for procuring the gold—Dindikoo; gold pits—Cultivation—Arrival at Fankia.

MAY 18TH.—We left the Nerico about half-past three o'clock, and arrived at Jallacotta, the first town of Tenda, at sunset. From this place to Simbuni in Bondou is two days' travel.

May 19th.—Halted at Jallacotta in order to purchase corn and recruit the asses. Bought plenty of onions, which made our rice eat much better. Townspeople fishing in the woods, where the pools being nearly dry, the fish are easily taken.

May 20th.—Left Jallacotta, and about two miles to the east, passed the village of Maheena, close to which are the ruins of another village of the same name. It would appear from the number of ruins, that the population of Tenda is much diminished. We reached Tendico, or Tambico, about eight o'clock: we could not procure a bullock, the inhabitants having very few cattle. This village belongs to Jallacotta; and the Faranba of Jallacotta is subject to the king of Woolli. About half a mile from Tambico is a pretty large town called Bady, the chief of which takes the title of Faranba, and is in a manner independent. He exacts very high duties from the coffles, to the extent of ten bars of gunpowder for each ass-load.

We sent a messenger from Tambico to inform the Faranba of our arrival, and he sent his son in the evening with twenty-six men armed with muskets, and a great crowd of people, to receive what we had to give him. Sent him ten bars of amber by our guide; but as he refused to take it, went myself with five bars of coral, which he likewise refused. Indeed I could easily perceive from the number of armed men, and the haughty manner in which they conducted themselves, that there was little prospect of settling matters in an amicable manner. I therefore tore a leaf from my pocket-book, and had written a note to Lieutenant Martyn to have the soldiers in readiness; when Mr. Anderson, hearing such a hubbub in the village, came to see what was the matter. I explained my doubts to him, and desired that the soldiers might have on their pouches and bayonets, and be ready for action at a moment's notice. I desired Isaaco to inform him that we had as yet found no difficulty in our journey; we had readily obtained the permission of the kings of Kataba and Woolli to pass through their kingdoms, and that if he would not allow us to pass, we had then only to return to Jallacotta, and endeavour to find another road; and with this (after a good many angry words had passed between the Faranba's people and our guide) the palaver ended.

Matters were in this state, Faranba's son had gone over to Bady with the amber and coral, and we were preparing to return to Jallacotta early next morning, when about half-past six o'clock some of Faranba's people seized our guide's horse, as the boy was watering it at the well, and carried it away. Isaaco went over to Bady to inquire the reason of this conduct; but instead of satisfying him on this point, they seized him, took his double-barrelled gun and sword from him, tied him to a tree, and flogged him; and having put his boy in irons, sent some people back to Tambico for another horse belonging to an old man that was travelling with us to Dentila. I now told two of Isaaco's Negroes that if they would go with me into the village and point out the Faranba's people (it being quite dark) who had come to take the old man's horse, I would make the soldiers seize them, and retain them as hostages for Isaaco. They went and told this to the two chief men in the village, but they would not permit it. They were able, they said, to defend their own rights, and would not allow the horse to be taken; so after an immense hubbub and wrangling, the business at last came to blows, and the Faranba's people were fairly kicked out of the village.

I was now a little puzzled how to act; Isaaco's wife and child sat crying with us under the tree, his Negroes were very much dejected, and seemed to consider the matter as quite hopeless. We could have gone in the night and burnt the town. By this we should have killed a great many innocent people, and most probably should not have recovered our guide. I therefore thought it most advisable (having consulted with Mr. Anderson and Lieutenant Martyn) to wait till morning; and then, if they persisted in detaining our guide, to attack them in open day; a measure which would be more decisive, and more likely to be attended with success, than any night skirmishes. We accordingly placed double sentries during the night, and made every man sleep with his loaded musket at hand. We likewise sent two people back to Jallacotta, to inform the Dooty of the treatment we had received from Faranba, though at one of the towns belonging to the king of Woolli.

May 21st.—Early in the morning our guide was liberated, and sent back to us; and about ten o'clock a number of Faranba's people came and told me that Faranba did not wish to quarrel with me, but could not think of allowing a coffle to pass without paying the customary tribute; but as I had refused to do that the evening before, if I would now carry over to Bady such articles as I meant to give him, everything would be amicably settled. I told them that, after the treatment my guide had experienced, they could not expect that I would go to Bady alone; that if I went I would take twenty or thirty of my people with me. This seemed not so agreeable; and it was at last determined that the horse, etc., should be brought half way between the two villages, and delivered on receipt of the goods. I accordingly paid at different times goods to the amount of one hundred and six bars, being not quite one-third of what a coffle of Negroes would have paid. Faranba's people still kept our guide's gun and sword; alleging that they were sent away in the night to Bisra, a town in the neighbourhood, but would be sent after us as soon as the person returned who had gone in quest of them. We accordingly departed from Tambico about three o'clock, and halted for the night at Jeningalla near Bufra, or Kabatenda, where I formerly slept; my former landlord brought me a large calabash of milk.

.　　.　　.　　.　　.

May 22nd.—Halted at Jeningalla to purchase corn for our asses. Went and saw some iron-furnaces; they are smaller at the top than those of Manding.

.　　.　　.　　.　　.

The distance being very great between this place and the next water, we resolved to travel it by moonlight, and accordingly we left Jeningalla,

May 23rd.—At two o'clock in the morning, and at eight o'clock reached Nealo Koba. At the same place where I formerly crossed, the river is not flowing, but stands in pools, some of which are deep and swarming with fish. Oysters large, but of a greenish colour; did not eat any of them. About two o'clock resumed our journey, and at sunset reached a small Foula village; all very much fatigued, having travelled twenty-eight miles.

May 24th.—Halted at Mansafara, which is only four miles east of the Foula village. This consists of three towns, quite contiguous to each other; and near them is a large pool of water. From this town to the village of Nittakorra on the north bank of the Gambia is only eight miles due south. Bought corn for the asses in crossing the Samakara woods, and a bullock for the people. Much lightning to the south-east, and thunder. Got all the bundles covered with grass, etc. During the night the wolves killed one of our best asses within twenty yards of the place where Mr. Anderson and I slept.

May 25th.—Left Mansafara, and entered the Tenda or Samakara wilderness. About four miles to the east passed the ruins of Koba, where I formerly slept.[1]   The town was destroyed by the Bondou people about two years ago, and the Bentang tree burnt down.   At ten passed a stream like the Neaulico, running to the Gambia; and shortly after came in sight of the first range of hills, running from S.S.W. to N.N.E.; we came near them; and at half-past eleven halted at Sooteetabba, a watering-place within a mile of the hills.

.   .   .   .

Departing from Sooteetabba as soon as the heat of the day was over, we crossed the first range of hills.   Mr. Anderson and I ascended the top of one of the hills, which, from the amazing fine prospect all round, I have named Panorama Hill; it has a sugar-loaf looking top, with a number of wolf-holes in it.   The route across the hill, though very difficult for the asses, was extremely beautiful.   In the evening we descended into a romantic valley, where we found plenty of water, being one of the remote branches of Nealo Koba. There was plenty of fish in the pools; but they were too deep to catch them with the hands.   Close to the stream are the ruins of the village of Doofroo, destroyed by the Dentila people some time ago.   This is considered as an excellent place for shooting elephants; we saw the fresh dung and feet marks of many of them near the stream.   Watched for an eclipse of Jupiter's first satellite, but the planet became clouded.

May 26th.—At daybreak ascended from the plain of Doo-froo, and travelled over a rugged country, till ten o'clock, when we met a coffle (at a watering-place called Sootinimma) bound for Gambia to redeem a person who had been caught for a debt, and was to be sold for a slave if not ransomed in a few months.   There being no water here, we did not halt; but continued our march, two of the soldiers being unable to keep up.   The main body of the coffle still kept going on, and at half-past twelve reached Bee Creek; from whence we sent back an ass and two Negroes to bring up the two fatigued soldiers.

We had no sooner unloaded the asses at the creek than

[1] Called Koba Tenda on page 270.

some of Isaaco's people, being in search of honey, unfortunately disturbed a large swarm of bees near where the coffle had halted. The bees came out in immense numbers, and attacked men and beasts at the same time. Luckily most of the asses were loose, and galloped up the valley; but the horses and people were very much stung, and obliged to scamper in all directions. The fire which had been kindled for cooking being deserted, spread, and set fire to the bamboos; and our baggage had like to have been burnt. In fact, for half an hour the bees seemed to have completely put an end to our journey.

In the evening, when the bees became less troublesome, and we could venture to collect our cattle, we found that many of them were very much stung and swelled about the head. Three asses were missing; one died in the evening, and one next morning, and we were forced to leave one at Sibikillin: in all six; besides which, our guide lost his horse, and many of the people were very much stung about the face and hands.

*   *   *   *   *

May 27th.—Early in the morning we set forwards, and after travelling four miles arrived at Sibikillin. Here the water which supplies the town is collected in a deep rocky hollow. There are plenty of fish in the pool, but the natives will not eat any of them, nor allow them to be taken, imagining that the water would immediately dry up. Cautioned the soldiers against catching any of them. At night one of the townspeople found our guide's horse in the woods, and brought it to the town. Gave him fifteen bars of amber, and a barraloolo, etc.

May 28th.—At daybreak set forwards, and about three miles east of Sibikillin descended into a valley, where I saw the first *Shea* trees, some of them loaded with fruit, but not ripe. About eleven o'clock arrived at Badoo, a small town consisting of about three hundred huts. A little north of this is another town, called likewise Badoo; but they distinguish them by the names of Sansanding and Sansanba.

*   *   *   *   *

May 29th.—In the forenoon had an opportunity of sending two letters home to England, via Gambia.

[These two letters, to his wife and to Sir Joseph Banks, give a hasty note of his situation. They are very optimistic and state that he expects to be on the Niger on 27th June.]

In the evening left Badoo, and went to Tambacunda, about four miles east of Badoo. The river Gambia is only four miles distant, south of Badoo. Mr. Anderson and Mr. Scott went up a hill near the town, and had a fine view of it. The course is from the south-east, till it reaches the hills near Badoo; it then turns towards the south. It is called *Ba deema*, or the river which is *always a river*, i.e. it never dries. The distance between Badoo and Laby in Foota Jalla is five days' travel.

Purchased two asses.

May 30th.—Left Tambacunda, and entered the woods. Travelled very expeditiously till eleven o'clock, when we reached a watering-place called Fatifing, where we found some green dirty water, so bad that nothing but necessity would have made us drink it. Halted here till half-past two o'clock, when we again set forward and reached Tabba Gee just at dark: found no water. During the afternoon the country to the south hilly and beautiful. A little before we reached the halting-place some drops of rain fell.

May 31st.—Left Tabba Gee at daybreak, and a few miles to the east passed a round lump of quartz, called by the natives *Ta Kooro*, or the traveller's stone; all travellers lift up this stone and turn it round. The stone is worn quite smooth, and the iron rock on which it rests is worn hollow by this constant motion. Halted during the heat of the day at Mambari, where there is a small village built this season; the former one having been destroyed by war many years ago. Passed in the course of the forenoon two streams running towards Gambia.

.   .   .   .   .

Muianta, a hill resembling a castle, bearing by compass S. by E., is distant sixteen miles; Sambankalla bearing S..

the hills of Foota Jalla bearing by compass S.W. by W.S.W. and S.W. by S.—The town of Laby is immediately beyond those hills, which are three days' travel from this place. The river Gambia comes down the opening S.S.W. between Muianta and the hills of Foota Jalla. The latter have nearly the appearance of Madeira when seen from the sea, but the hills are not so sharp-pointed as those of Madeira.

In the afternoon again set forwards, and four miles to the east passed the dry bed of a torrent course towards Gambia; road rocky; plenty of white quartz in detached lumps and small pieces. Travelled till quite dark, when we were forced to halt for the night at a place where there was no water; and of course we all slept supperless.

June 1st.—At daybreak set forwards, and at ten o'clock arrived at Julifunda, a considerable town founded by people who formerly received goods in advance from the European traders on the Gambia, Rio Nunez, and Kajaaga; the road to Bambarra from these places frequently leading through this place when the other routes were stopped by war. These people, who trade on credit, are called *Juli* in distinction from the Slatee who trades with his own capital. Julifunda was formerly inhabited entirely by Soninkees; but the king of Foota Jalla made war on them, and obliged them, as a condition of peace, to embrace the Mahomedan religion. The town contains, I suppose, about two thousand people, including the suburbs.

In the evening sent our guide to the chief man, who is termed *Mansa Kussan*, and is reckoned one of the most avaricious chiefs in the whole of the road. Sent him some amber and scarlet as a present, and told him that I intended to remain one day at Julifunda in order to purchase rice.

June 2nd.—Bought some corn and two ass-loads of rice; presented Mansa Kussan with some amber, coral, and scarlet, with which he appeared to be perfectly satisfied, and sent a bullock in return; he even prayed for my safety, and told me that he would do his utmost to get us forwards. Bought an ass for twenty bars of amber. At four o'clock put on the loads and departed for Baniserile. The whole of the asses were gone, and only Mr. Anderson and myself remained, having sent our guide to inform Mansa Kussan of our departure. Our guide returned, and told us that Mansa Kussan had said that, unless I gave him ten bars of all the different sorts of merchandise, he would not allow us to pass farther up the country; and if we attempted to pass without his consent, he would do his utmost to plunder us in the woods.

Recalled the people and asses, and endeavoured to settle matters in a friendly manner. Suspecting that he would not have used such language unless he had received assurances from some other towns that they would join him in attacking us, sent him some more scarlet and amber by our guide; being unwilling to go singly into the town, having received information that it was the intention of the king to detain me, with a view to make me pay handsomely for my release.

Mansa Kussan seized the money which I paid for the ass in the seller's hands, and what evinced his hostile intentions still more, he seized the ass till such time as the palaver should be settled.

．　．　．　．　．　．

June 3rd.—Having sent him a number of presents, I concluded, and was assured by the king's brothers, that no further demands would be made; but was much surprised when our guide and the king's brothers told me on their return that I must send ten bars of gunpowder and ten of flints. Here I determined to put an end to the business; and told the king's brothers that I considered myself as having paid the king very well for passing through his territory; that I would neither give him a single charge of gunpowder nor a flint; and if he refused to allow me to pass, I would go without his permission; and if his people attempted to obstruct us we would do our utmost to defend ourselves. The king's brothers and some of the old Bushreens insisted on my sending the gunpowder or some other goods of equal value; but I assured them that Europeans would much rather run the risk of being plundered in a hostile manner than have their goods (which were brought to purchase provisions) extorted from them by such exorbitant demands. After going backwards and forwards to the king, His Majesty was pleased to say he was satisfied; and what surprised me, said that he was coming to pay us a friendly visit in the afternoon. He accordingly paid us a visit, attended by a parcel of parasites and singing women. Offered me a few Cola nuts, which I desired our guide to take and eat; he likewise told me that I should have a guide to Baniserile.

June 4th.—Early in the morning departed, and having passed the village Eercella, remarkable for a grove of large *Sitta* trees, about one o'clock arrived at Baniserile, and halted under a tree near the wells. This being His Majesty's birthday, pitched one of the tents, purchased a bullock and a calf for the soldiers; in the afternoon had them drawn up, and fired; and made it as much a day of festivity as our circumstances would permit; and though we were under the necessity of drinking His Majesty's health in *water* from our canteens, yet few of his subjects wished more earnestly for the continuance of his life and the prosperity of his reign.

Baniserile is a Mahomedan town; the chief man, *Fodi* Braheima, is one of the most friendly men I have met with. I gave him a copy of the New Testament in Arabic, with which he seemed very much pleased.

June 5th.—Employed in purchasing rice, having received information that there was a great scarcity of that article to the eastwards. Bought the rice both here and at Julifunda with small amber No. 5; and I found that though a scarcity existed almost to famine, I could purchase a pound of clean rice for one bead of amber, value *2d.* sterling.

Purchased three ass-loads, and on the 6th purchased two ass-loads more, making in all 750 lb. of rice. This day one of our guide's people went away to purchase slaves at Laby in Foota Jalla, distant three long days' travel. The people here assured me it was only three days' travel from Badoo to Laby. Had a squall with thunder and rain during the night. As the loads were put into the tent, they were not wetted, but one of our carpenters (old James), who had been sick of the dysentery ever since we crossed the Nerico, and was recovering, became greatly worse.

Dentila is famous for its iron; the flux used for smelting

the iron is the ashes of the bark of the Kino tree. These
ashes are as white as flour: they are not used in dyeing blue,
and must therefore have something peculiar in them. I
tasted them: they did not appear to me to have so much alkali
as the mimosa ashes, but had an austere taste. The people
told me, if I eat them, I would certainly die.

June 7th.—Departed early in the morning, and as the
carpenter before mentioned was very weak, appointed two
soldiers to stay by him, and assist him in mounting, and to
drive his ass. Four miles east of Baniserile came to the brow
of a hill, from which we had an extensive prospect eastwards.
A square-looking hill, supposed to be the hill near Dindikoo,
in Konkodoo, bore by compass due *east*.

Shortly after crossed the bed of a stream running towards
the Faleme river, called Samakoo on account of the vast
herds of elephants which wash themselves in it during the
rains. Saw their footmarks very frequently, and fresh dung.
Heard a lion roar not far from us. This day the asses
travelled very ill on account of their having eaten fresh grass,
as we supposed.

Obliged to load the horses, and at noon halted at a large
pool of water in the bed of the Samakoo, called Jananga.

From the time of our crossing the Samakoo to our halting-
place, we travelled without any road; our guide being apprehensive that as there existed a war a little to the south, and
the people were in arms, they might attempt to cut off some
of the fatigued asses in our rear.

In the afternoon resumed our march, and travelled without
any road over a wild and rocky country. Obliged to leave
two of the asses on the road, and load all the horses. We did
not reach the watering-place till quite dark, and were obliged
to fire muskets frequently to prevent us from straying from
each other.

June 8th.—Early in the morning resumed our march, and
about two miles to the east came to the brow of a hill, from
whence we could distinguish the course of the Faleme river
by the range of dark green trees which grew on its borders.
The carpenter unable to sit upright, and frequently threw
himself from the ass, wishing to be left to die. Made two of

the soldiers carry him by force and hold him on the ass. At noon reached Madina, and halted by the side of the Faleme river; which at this season is a little discoloured by the rain, but not sensibly swelled. The general course of this river as pointed out by the natives is from the south-east quarter; the distance to its source is six ordinary days' travel. The bed of the river here is rocky, except at the crossing-place, where it is a mixture of sand and gravel. The river abounds in fish, some of them very large: we saw several plunge and leap that appeared to be so large as to weigh 60 or 70 lb. The velocity of the stream is about four knots per hour.

In the afternoon got all the bundles carried over, and up the opposite bank, which very much fatigued the soldiers. When everything was carried over, I found the carpenter still more weakly and apparently dying. I therefore thought it best to leave him at Madina till the morning following. Went to the village, and hired a hut for him for six bars of amber, and gave the Dooty four bars, desiring him to make some of his people assist the soldier (whom I left to take care of the sick person) in burying him, if he died during the night. In the evening went to Satadoo, which is only one mile east of the river. As there was great appearance of rain, put all the baggage into one, and slept on the top of the bundles, leaving the other tent for the soldiers. We had a heavy tornado with much thunder and lightning.

June 9th.—In the morning the soldier, who had been left to take care of the sick man, returned, and informed us that he died at eight o'clock the preceding evening; and that with the assistance of the Negroes he had buried him in the place where the people of the village bury their dead. Purchased corn for the asses, and a large bullock for the people; likewise one ass.

Went into the town in the evening, and presented the Dooty with six bars, requesting a guide to Shrondo, which he readily granted. Satadoo is walled round, and contains about three hundred huts; it was formerly much larger.

Five of the soldiers, who did not go into the tent, but staid under the tree during the rain, complained much of headache and uneasiness at stomach.

June 10*th.*—The soldiers still sickly. Left Satadoo at sunrise: several of our canteens stolen during the night. This forenoon we travelled for more than two miles over white quartz, large lumps of which were lying all round; no other stone to be seen. Carried forwards a large skinful of water, being uncertain whether we should find any on the road. At eleven o'clock reached the bed of a stream flowing to the left, called Billalla, where we found some muddy water.

Resumed our journey at half-past three o'clock, and travelled over a hard rocky soil towards the mountains; many of the asses very much fatigued. The front of the coffle reached Shrondo at sunset; but being in the rear I had to mount one of the sick men on my horse, and assist in driving the fatigued asses; so that I did not reach the halting-place till eight o'clock, and was forced to leave four asses in the woods. Shrondo is but a small town. We halted as usual under a tree at a little distance; and before we could pitch one of the tents, we were overtaken by a very heavy tornado, which wet us all completely. In attempting to fasten up one of the tents to a branch of the tree, had my hat blown away, and lost. The ground all round was covered with water about three inches deep. We had another tornado about two o'clock in the morning.

The tornado which took place on our arrival had an instant effect on the health of the soldiers, and proved to us to be the *beginning of sorrow.* I had proudly flattered myself that we should reach the Niger with a very moderate loss; we had had two men sick of the dysentery: one of them recovered completely on the march, and the other would doubtless have recovered had he not been wet by the rain at Baniserile. But now the rain had set in, and I trembled to think that we were only half way through our journey. The rain had not commenced three minutes before many of the soldiers were affected with vomiting; others fell asleep, and seemed as if half intoxicated. I felt a strong inclination to sleep during the storm; and as soon as it was over I fell asleep on the wet ground, although I used every exertion to keep myself awake. The soldiers likewise fell asleep on the wet bundles.

June 11th.—Twelve of the soldiers sick. Went and waited on the Dooty, and presented him with five bars of amber, and two of beads, requesting his permission to go and look at the gold-mines, which I understood were in the vicinity. Having obtained his permission, I hired a woman to go with me, and agreed to pay her a bar of amber if she would show me a grain of gold. We travelled about half a mile west of the town, when we came to a small meadow spot of about four or five acres' extent, in which were several holes dug resembling wells. They were in general about ten or twelve feet deep; towards the middle of the meadow spot the holes were deepest, and shallower towards the sides. Their number was about thirty, besides many old ones which had sunk down. Near the mouths of these pits were several other shallow pits, lined with clay, and full of rain-water: between the mine pits and these wash pits laid several heaps of sandy gravel. On the top of each was a stone; some of the stones white, others red, others black, etc. These serve to distinguish each person's property. I could see nothing peculiar in this gravel; some silicious pebbles as large as a pigeon's egg, pieces of white and reddish quartz, iron stone, and killow, and a soft friable yellow stone, which crumbled to pieces by the fingers, were the chief minerals that I could distinguish. Besides the above there was a great portion of sand, and a yellow earth resembling *till*.

The woman took about half a pound of gravel with one hand from the heap, which I suppose belonged to her; and having put it into a large calabash, threw a little water on it with a small calabash; which two calabashes are all that are necessary for washing gold. The quantity of water was only sufficient to cover the sand about one inch. She then crumbled the sand to pieces, and mixt it with the water; this she did not in a rotatory manner, but by pulling her hands towards herself.

· · · · ·

She then threw out all the large pebbles, looking on the ground where she threw them, for fear of throwing out a piece of gold. Having done this, she gave the sand and water a rotatory motion, so as to make a part of the sand and water fly over the brim of the calabash. While she did this with her *right* hand, with her *left* she threw out of the centre of the vortex a portion of sand and water at every revolution. She then put in a little fresh water, and as the quantity of sand was now much diminished, she held the calabash in an oblique direction, and made the sand move slowly round, while she constantly agitated it with a quick motion.

I now observed a quantity of black matter, resembling gunpowder, which she told me was *gold rust*; and before she had moved the sand one quarter round the calabash, she pointed to a yellow speck, and said, *sanoo affilli*, see the gold. On looking attentively I saw a portion of pure gold, and took it out. It would have weighed about *one grain*. The whole of the washing, from the first putting in of the sand till she showed me the gold, did not exceed the space of *two minutes*. I now desired her to take a larger portion. She put in, as nearly as I could guess, about two pounds; and having washed it in the same manner, and nearly in the same time, found no fewer than *twenty-three* particles; some of them were very small. In both cases I observed that the quantity of *sanoo mira*, or *gold rust*, was at least forty times greater than the quantity of gold. She assured me that they sometimes found pieces of gold as large as her fist. I could not ascertain the quantity of gold washed here in one year; but I believe it must be considerable, though they wash only during the beginning and end of the rains.

．　　．　　．　　．　　．

Went in the afternoon to see a brother of Karfa Taura's; he had a very large collection of Arabic books, and I made him quite happy by adding an Arabic New Testament to the number.

June 12th.—Left Shrondo early in the morning; the sick being unable to walk, I gave them all the horses and spare asses. Travelled slowly along the bottom of the Konkodoo mountains, which are very steep precipices of rock, from eighty to two or three hundred feet high. We reached Dindikoo at noon; at which time it came on a tornado so rapidly, that we were forced to carry our bundles into the huts of the natives; this being the first time the coffle had entered a town since leaving Gambia. As soon as the rain was over, went with Mr. Anderson to see the gold pits which are near this town. The pits are dug exactly in the same manner as at Shrondo, with notches in the side of the pit to serve as a ladder to descend by. The gravel here is very coarse; some round stones larger than a man's head, and a vast number larger than one's fist were lying round the mouths of the pits, which were near twenty in number. Near the pits is a stream of water, and as the banks had been scraped away to wash for gold, I could distinguish a stratum of earth and large stones about ten feet thick, and under this a stratum of two feet of ferruginous pebbles about the size of a pigeon's egg, and a yellow and rusty-coloured sand and earth; under this a stratum of tough white clay. The rusty-coloured sand is that in which the gold is found. Saw plenty of the gold rust.

When I returned from the gold pits, I went with Mr. Scott to go to the top of the hill, which is close to the town. The hill was very steep and rocky. The rocks (like all the hills in Konkodoo) are a coarse reddish granite, composed of red feldspar, white quartz, and black shorl; but it differs from any granite I have seen, in having round smooth pebbles, many of them as large as a cannon shot. These pebbles, when broken, are granite, but of a paler colour and closer texture. The day was cool; but after fatiguing ourselves and resting six times, we found that we were only about half way to the top. We were surprised to find the hill cultivated to the very summits; and though the people of Dindikoo were but preparing their fields, the corn on the hill was six inches high. The villages on these mountains are romantic beyond anything I ever saw. They are built in the most delightful glens of the mountains; they have plenty of water and grass at all seasons; they have cattle enough for their own use, and their superfluous grain purchases all their luxuries; and while the thunder rolls in awful grandeur over their heads, they can look from their tremendous precipices over all that wild and woody plain which extends from the

Faleme to the Black river. This plain is in extent, from
north to south, about forty miles; the range of hills to the
south seem to run in the same direction as those of Konkodoo,
viz. from east to west.   There are no lions on the hills, though
they are very numerous in the plain.   In the evening Lieutenant Martyn fell sick of the fever.

June 13*th*.—Early in the morning departed from Dindikoo.
The sick occupied all the horses and spare asses; and as the
number of drivers was thus diminished, we had very hard
work to get on.   Ten of the loaded asses and drivers went a
different road.   Mr. Anderson and Mr. Scott being with
them, fired their muskets as soon as they observed that the
guide was leading them in a road where were no asses' footmarks.   Answered them; and sent the sergeant to their
assistance.   In half an hour they came up, having gone about
three miles too much to the right.   Reached a village almost
deserted about one o'clock, and found the coffle halted by a
stream to the east of it.   Very uneasy about our situation:
half of the people being either sick of the fever or unable to
use great exertion, and fatigued in driving the asses.   Found,
to my great mortification, that the ass which carried the
telescope and several other things was not come up.   Mr.
Anderson, the sergeant, and our guide rode back about five
miles in search of it; but returned at half-past three o'clock,
without being able to find it.   Presented the Dooty of the
village with five bars of amber; requesting him, if he heard
of it, to send it forward, and I would reward him for it.   Put
on the loads; and part of the coffle had departed, when one
of the Dooty's sons came and told us that he had seen the
ass, and brought it to the village.   Went to the village, and
paid the person who found it twenty bars, and the Dooty
ten bars.   Mounted the load on my horse, and drove it
before me.   I did not reach Fankia till seven o'clock; having
to walk slow, in order to coax on three sick soldiers who had
fallen behind, and were for lying down under every tree they
passed.   Fankia is a small village, four miles north-west from
Binlingalla.   Here we departed from my former route, and
did not touch on it again till we reached the Niger.

CHAPTER XXX

JUNE 14TH.—I halted at Fankia, in order to give the sick a little rest, knowing there was a steep hill to ascend near this place. Found myself very sick, having been feverish all night.

．　．　．　．　．　．

Bought corn for the asses, and plenty of fowls for the sick.

June 15th.—Left Fankia: men still very sickly, and some of them slightly delirious. About a mile north-east of this village is the passage in the Tambaura mountains, called Toombinjeena. The ascent is very steep and rocky: the perpendicular of the steepest place would not much exceed three hundred feet. The asses being heavily loaded, in order to spare as many as possible for the sick, we had much difficulty in getting our loads up this steep. The number of asses exceeding the drivers, presented a dreadful scene of confusion in this rocky staircase; loaded asses tumbling over the rocks, sick soldiers unable to walk, black fellows stealing; in fact it certainly was uphill work with us at this place.

Having got up all the loads and asses, set forwards; and about two miles from the steep came to the delightful village of Toombin. On collecting our loads, found that the natives had stolen from us seven pistols, two greatcoats, and one knapsack, besides other small articles. Sent back the horses for two sick soldiers, who were unable to ride on the horses, and were left at the steep. Pitched the tent, and secured the baggage from the rain.

June 16th.—Left Toombin. Just as the people and asses were gone, the good old schoolmaster whom I mentioned in my former travels came up.[1] He had heard the night before that I was with the party, and had travelled all night to come and see me. As the loads were gone on, I told him I wished him to go forward with me to the place where we should halt, that I might reward him in some degree for his former kindness. Recovered three of the pistols which had been stolen, and one greatcoat. Set forwards. About a mile to the east of the village found Hinton, one of the sick who rode Mr. Anderson's horse, lying under a tree, and the horse grazing at a little distance. Some of the natives had stolen the pistols from the holsters, and robbed my coat case, which was fastened behind the saddle, of a string of coral, all the amber and beads it contained, and one barraloolo. Luckily they did not fancy my pocket sextant, and artificial horizon, which were in the same place. Put the sick man on the horse and drove it before me; and after holding him on and using every exertion to keep him on the saddle, I found that I was unable to carry him on, and having fatigued myself very much with carrying him forwards about six miles, I was forced to leave him.

About a mile after I left Hinton, I came to two others lying in the shade of a tree. Mounted one on Mr. Anderson's horse, and the other on my own, and drove them before me. Reached the village of Serimanna about half-past twelve o'clock; sent back a horse in the cool of the evening for Hinton, and brought him to the village, being obliged to tie him on the horse.

Gave the schoolmaster five bars of scarlet, one barraloolo,

See pages 197 and 240.

ten bars of beads, fourteen of amber, and two dollars, which made him completely happy. I likewise gave him an Arabic New Testament, which he promised to read with attention.

June 17th.—Finding that Hinton was worse, and Sparks delirious, left them to the care of the Dooty of the village; having given him amber and beads sufficient to purchase victuals for them if they lived, and to bury them if they died. If they recovered, he engaged to join them to the first coffle travelling to Gambia. From Serimanna in two hours we reached Fajemmia: this is only a small village, but fortified with a high wall. The chief, from whom the village has its name, formerly resided at Faramba, to the east of this; but has lately retired here, leaving his people and slaves at Faramba. Fajemmia is the most powerful chief of Konkodoo, and holds under his subjection all the country from Toombin to the Ba fing.

The customs paid by travellers being always in proportion to the power and mischievous disposition of the chiefs, those paid at Fajemmia are of course very high.

.　　.　　.　　.　　.

June 18th.—Our palaver with Fajemmia was not finished till the morning of the 19th. During the 18th, 19th, and 20th I was very sick; and though in general I was able to sit up part of the day, yet I was very weak, and unable to attend to the marketing of corn, milk, and fowls. Mr. Anderson therefore bought these articles, and attended to the cattle, etc. Lieutenant Martyn, the sergeant, corporal, and half the soldiers sick of the fever. Boiled a camp kettle full of strong decoction of cinchona every day since leaving Dindikoo. Purchased three asses, and hired our guide's people to drive four of our asses in addition to the two they already drove, making altogether six asses, for one hundred and twenty bars.

On the 18th, Mr. Anderson and one of the soldiers went back to Serimanna to see the two men left there, and ascertain if they could possibly be carried forward. Returned on the 19th, and reported that they were both alive, but not in a state to be moved, and were themselves anxious to remain where they were, as it afforded them the only chance of recovery.

June 20th.—When we had loaded the asses, found one of the soldiers (old Rowe) unable to ride. Paid ten bars of amber, and measured eighteen days' rice for him to one of the best men in the village, who, I have no doubt, will take care of him. Shortly after leaving Fajemmia, it began to thunder, and by the time we had travelled four miles we experienced a smart tornado, which wetted many of the loads, and made the road very muddy and slippery. We reached a village nearly deserted, called Nealakalla, about noon. Here we found that the ass which carried the spare clothing was not come up; and as many of the men were very ill situated, particularly with respect to shoes, I thought it best to send back two of the men a few miles to see if they could find it. Felt rather uneasy about the men, as they did not return at sunset. Fired several muskets, but heard no answer. The village of Nealakalla is close to the Ba lee or "Honey river," which we found discoloured, but not sensibly swelled. Saw two crocodiles, and an incredible number of large fish.

June 21st.—As the two men had not yet arrived, sent forward the coffle to cross the river; desired Mr. Scott to fire a musket when they had all crossed. Mr. Anderson and myself agreed to stop at Nealakalla till noon, in hopes of hearing something concerning the two men. They arrived about eleven o'clock, having found the ass and load so near Fajemmia, that they had gone there and slept in the same hut with old Rowe, who, they told us was recovering and very well pleased with his situation. Set forwards; and about a mile to the north-east of the village crossed the river at a place where its course is interrupted by a bed of whinstone rock, which forms the stream into a number of small cataracts. The people had to carry over all the loads on their heads, and we found them cooking on the east bank of the river, and nearly ready to set forwards. Mr. Anderson and I stepped across the river from rock to rock without wetting our feet.

As soon as the men had finished their breakfast we set forwards, and about two miles east came to a narrow and deep creek, in which was a stream of muddy water. Crossed this with so much difficulty, that some were for calling it Vinegar Creek. About four o'clock passed the village of Boontoonkooran, delightfully situated at the bottom of a steep and rocky hill. Two miles east of this we halted for the night at the village of Dooggikotta; where the cultivation is very extensive, and we had much difficulty in keeping our cattle off the corn. A tornado during the night.

June 22nd.—Halted till near ten o'clock, as there was great appearance of rain. William Roberts, one of the carpenters who had been sick since leaving Fajemmia, declared that he was unable to proceed, and signed a note that he was left by his own consent. Passed a small village about four miles to the east, and travelled on the ascent near a river course almost the whole day. We had a fine view of Kullallie, a high detached and square rocky hill, which we had seen ever since we left Fajemmia. This hill is quite inaccessible on all sides, and level and green on the top. The natives affirm that there is a lake of water on its summit, and they frequently go round the bottom of the precipices, during the rainy season, and pick up large turtles, which have tumbled over the precipice and killed themselves. Saw many very picturesque and rocky hills during the march, and in the evening halted at the village of Falifing, which is situated on the summit of the ascent which separates the Ba lee from the Ba fing. Lost one ass, and 80 lb. of balls on the march.

June 23rd.—Early in the morning resumed our journey; and after travelling two hours on a level plain, bounded with high rocky precipices on our right and left, we descended slowly towards the east, and shortly came to the village of Gimbia, or Kimbia. I chanced to be in the rear, bringing on some asses which had thrown their loads; and when I came up I found all about the village wearing a hostile appearance, the men running from the corn grounds and putting on their quivers, etc. The cause of this tumult was, as usual, the *love of money*. The villagers had heard that the white men were to pass; that they were very sickly, and unable to make any resistance, or to defend the immense wealth in their possession. Accordingly when part of the coffle had passed the village, the people sallied out; and, under pretence that the coffle should not pass till the Dooty pleased, insisted on turning back the asses. One of them seized the sergeant's horse by the bridle to lead it into the village; but when the sergeant cocked his pistol and presented it, he dropped the bridle; others drove away the asses with their loads, and everything seemed going into confusion. The soldiers with great coolness loaded their pieces with ball, and fixed their bayonets: on seeing this the villagers hesitated, and the soldiers drove the asses across the bed of a torrent; and then returned, leaving a sufficient number to guard the asses.

The natives collected themselves under a tree by the gate of the village, where I found the Dooty and Isaaco at very high words. On inquiring the cause of the tumult, Isaaco informed me that the villagers had attempted to take the loads from the asses. I turned to the Dooty, and asked him who were the persons that had dared to make such an attempt. He pointed to about thirty people armed with bows; on which I fell a-laughing, and asked him if he really thought that such people could fight; adding, if he had a mind to make the experiment, they need only go up and attempt to take off one of the loads. They seemed by this time to be fully satisfied that they had made a vain attempt; and the Dooty desired me to tell the men to go forward with the asses. As I did not know but perhaps some of the sick might be under the necessity of returning this way, I thought it advisable to part on friendly terms; and therefore gave the Dooty four bars of amber, and told him that we did not come to make war; but if any person made war on us, we would defend ourselves to the last.

Set forwards, and half a mile to the east descended into a rocky valley: many of the asses fell in going down the steep. About noon reached Sullo, an unwalled village at the bottom of a rocky hill. Shortly after we halted Lieutenant Martyn's horse died. This was a godsend to the people of Sullo, who cut him up as if he had been a bullock, and had almost come to *blows* about the division of him; so much is horse-flesh esteemed at this place. Numbers of large monkies on the rocks over the town.

June 24th.—Left Sullo, and travelled through a country beautiful beyond imagination, with all the possible diversities of *rock*, sometimes towering up like ruined castles, spires, pyramids, etc.   We passed one place so like a ruined Gothic abbey, that we halted a little, before we could satisfy ourselves that the niches, windows, ruined staircase, etc., were all natural rock.   A faithful description of this place would certainly be deemed a fiction.

Passed a hill composed of one homogeneous mass of solid rock (red granite) without a detached stone or blade of grass; never saw such a hill in my life.   In the course of the march saw several villages romantically situated in the crescents formed by the rocky precipices; the medium height of these precipices is from one hundred to five or six hundred feet perpendicular.   The whole country between the Ba fing and Ba lee is rugged and grand beyond anything I have seen.

We reached Secoba at noon.   The Dooty of this town is Fajemmia's younger brother.   Presented him with goods to the amount of fifty bars; he was so much pleased that he said he would go with us till we had crossed the Ba fing, and see that the canoe people did not impose on us.

.   .   .   .   .

June 25th.—Halted at Secoba, in order to refresh the sick; bought plenty of fowls and milk for them.

June 26th.—Departed from Secoba, accompanied by the Dooty and several people.   Hired three of the Dooty's friends, as guides to Kandy, in that district of Fooladoo called Gangaran.   About seven miles east of Secoba came to the village of Konkromo, where we pitched our tents by the river side.   The day was too far spent before we had agreed with the canoe people, and, as we could not possibly carry all the loads over, thought it best to wait till next morning.

.   .   .   .   .

June 27th.—Early in the morning paid the canoe people fifty bars to carry over all our baggage and cattle, and likewise presented the Dooty of Secoba with some beads.   Four

canoes, sufficient to carry only an ass-load and an half at a
time, were provided for this purpose. Sent over Mr. Anderson and six men with their arms to receive the loads from the
canoes and carry them into the tents. The asses were made
to swim over, one on each side of the canoe, two boys sitting
in the canoe and holding them by the ears.

At this place I had an opportunity of seeing their mode of
smelting gold. Isaaco had purchased some gold in coming
through Konkodoo, and here he had it made into a large
ring. The smith made a crucible of common red clay and
dried it in the sun; into this he put the gold, without any flux
or mixture whatever; he then put charcoal under and over it,
and blowing the fire with the common double bellows of the
country, soon produced such a heat as to bring the gold into
a state of fusion. He then made a small furrow in the
ground, into which he poured the melted gold; when it was
cold he took it up, and heating it again, soon hammered it
into a square bar. Then heating it again, he twisted it by
means of two pairs of pincers into a sort of screw; and length-
ening out the ends, turned them up so as to form a massy
and precious ring.

When the baggage and cattle were all transported over, I
sent over the men, and embarked myself in the last canoe;
but as one of the soldiers in the other canoe had gone out to
purchase something, I made the canoe in which I was shove
off. telling the men to come off the moment the man returned.
I found it difficult to sit in the canoe so as to balance it,
though it contained only three people besides the rower.
We had just landed on the east bank, when we observed the
canoe, in which were the three soldiers, pushing off from
the opposite bank. It shortly after overset, and though
the natives from the shore swam in to their assistance, yet
J. Cartwright was unfortunately drowned. The natives dived
and recovered two of the muskets, and Cartwright's body;
they put the body in the canoe and brought it over. I used
the means recommended by the Humane Society, but in
vain. We buried him in the evening on the bank of the river.

The Ba fing is here a large river quite navigable; it is
swelled at this time about two feet, and flows at the rate of

three knots per hour. The people here are all thieves: they attempted to steal several of our loads, and we detected one carrying away the bundle in which was all our medicines. We could not sleep with the noise of the hippopotami, which came close to the bank and kept snorting and blowing all night.

.   .   .   .   .

June 28th.—Purchased an ass for four minkallis of gold, and a horse for forty-five bars. Set forwards about seven o'clock. After travelling four miles, the ass I had purchased lay down, and I found it impossible to raise him. Took off the load and left him. At ten o'clock came close to the bottom of a high rocky hill, which rises like an immense castle from the level plain: it is called Sankaree; and on inquiring about a large heap of stones near the foot of the precipice, I was told that the town of Madina, which was in the vicinity, was some years ago stormed by the Kaartans, and that the greater part of the inhabitants fled towards this hill. Some however were killed on the road, and these stones were collected over the grave of one of them. He said there were five more such near the hill, and that every person in passing, if he belongs to the same family or *contong*, thinks himself bound to throw a stone on the heap to perpetuate the memory of their friend. These heaps are precisely what in Scotland are called *cairns*. This hill is accessible only by one very narrow and difficult path. They assured me that there was abundance of water on the summit at all seasons, and that the huts built by the Madina people were still standing on the summit, though out of repair.

At eleven o'clock crossed a stream, like a mill stream, running north. We halted on the east side of it; found that one of the asses with a load of beads had not come up. The soldier who drove it (Bloore), without acquainting any person, returned to look for it. Shortly after the ass and load were found in the woods. Sent the sergeant after Bloore on one of the horses; he rode back as far as Sankaree without seeing him, and concluded he had lost the path. He found one of the sick (Walter) who had wandered from the track (for there was no road), and had laid himself down among

the bushes till some of the natives discovered him. Paid
the natives ten bars of amber, and desired them to look for
Bloore.

In the afternoon collected the asses for marching. Had
great difficulty in finding the horses, one of which (the
sergeant's) after all our search could not be found. As it was
in vain to wait for Bloore, put on the loads and departed. It
is to be observed that there is no pathway in these woods,
and we found much difficulty in keeping together: fired
muskets frequently to give intimation of our line of march.
After travelling about four miles, Shaddy Walter, the sick
man before mentioned, became so exhausted that he could
not sit on the ass. He was fastened on it, and held upright;
he became more and more faint, and shortly after died.
He was brought forwards to a place where the front of the
coffle had halted, to allow the rear to come up. Here when
the coffle had set forwards, two of the soldiers with their
bayonets, and myself with my sword, dug his grave in the wild
desert; and a few branches were the only laurels which
covered the tomb of the brave.

We did not come up to the coffle till they had halted for the
night near a pool of water shaded with ground palm trees.
Here I was informed that two of the soldiers were not come
up: one (Baron) was seen about a mile from the halting-place;
the other (Hill) was supposed to be three or four miles behind.
Fired two muskets every quarter of an hour: one to call
their attention, and the other about half a minute after to
give the direction. At half-past seven Hill came up, being
directed entirely by the sound of the muskets. At eleven
o'clock saw some lights in the woods, and heard people holla:
in a little time five people came, bringing with them Bloore,
the man who had gone in quest of the ass. He had gone
back as far as the Black river, crossed it, and made signs to
the people about the ass and the load. As they did not rightly
understand him, they thought that some party had fallen
on the coffle, and that this soldier had run away. They
therefore came with him to see if they could come in for their
share, or at least receive some reward for coming along with
the man. Paid them ten bars of amber, and desired them

to look for Baron, and I would give them ten bars more if they found him.

June. 29th.—At daybreak fired muskets for Baron; and as it was evident he must have wandered from the track made by the asses, and it was in vain to look for him in so extensive a wilderness, at half-past six o'clock loaded the asses and set out. Two more of the soldiers affected with the fever. Route in the morning rocky. Travelled twelve miles without halting, in order to reach a watering-place. About two miles before we came to the watering-place, Bloore, the soldier who had come up during the night, sat down under the shade of a tree; and when I desired him to proceed, he said he was rather fatigued, and when he had cooled himself, he would follow. I assured him that the halting-place was only a very little way off, and advised him by all means not to fall asleep. We halted on an elevated table land: the water was only rain collected in the hollow places of the rock. At half-past four o'clock, as Bloore had not come up, I sent the sergeant on one of the horses to bring him forward; he returned at sunset, having seen nothing of him, and having rode several miles past the place. I suspected that the sergeant might have rode past him asleep under the tree; I therefore got three volunteers to go with me, and look for him. It was now quite dark. We collected a large bundle of dry grass, and taking out a handful at a time, kept up a constant light, in order to frighten the lions which are very numerous in these woods. When we reached the tree under which he lay down, we made a fire. Saw the place where he had pressed down the grass, and the marks of his feet; went to the west along the pathway, and examined for the marks of his feet, thinking he might possibly have mistaken the direction. Found none; fired several muskets. Hollowed, and set fire to the grass. Returned to the tree and examined all round; saw no blood nor the footmarks of any wild beasts. Fired six muskets more. As any further search was likely to be fruitless (for we did not dare to walk far from the track for fear of losing ourselves), we returned to the tents. One of Isaaco's people shot an antelope in the evening, which more than supplied us all with meat. Much troubled in the night with wolves.

June 30th.—Early in the morning set forwards, and descended from the table land into a more fertile plain. Vast numbers of monkies on the rocks. Reached Kandy after a march of ten miles, all very much fatigued. This is but a small town; the large town having been taken and burnt by Daisy's son about two years ago, and all the people carried away. Mr. Anderson and Mr. Scott sick of the fever.

July 1st.—Covered a load of beads with the skin of the antelope. One of the bundles containing all our small *seed beads* stolen during the night; made all the search I could, but in vain: I could not recover it. As we were short of rice, and none could be purchased here, determined to push on as quick as possible; but the men were so very sickly, that I judged it imprudent to trust the baggage and asses without proper drivers. Employed in dividing the asses amongst the healthy men.

July 2nd.—Set forwards. Two more of the soldiers sick of the fever. When we had travelled about three miles, one of the soldiers (Roger M'Millan) became so delirious, that it was found impossible to carry him forwards. Left him at a village called Sanjeekotta. I regretted much being under the necessity of leaving in the hour of sickness and distress, a man who had grown old in the service of his country. He had been thirty-one years a soldier, twelve times a corporal, nine times a sergeant; but an unfortunate attachment to the *bottle* always returned him into the ranks.

We reached Koeena about three o'clock, all very much fatigued. I felt myself very sickly, having lifted up and reloaded a great many asses on the road. The village of Koeena is walled round, and it is surrounded on three sides with rocky precipices. Had a severe tornado at seven o'clock, which put out the watch-fire and made us all crowd into the tents. When the violence of the squall was over, we heard a particular sort of roaring or growling, not unlike the noise of a wild boar; there seemed to be more than one of them, and they went all round our cattle. Fired two muskets to make them keep at a distance; but as they still kept prowling round us, we collected a bunch of withered grass, and went with Lieutenant Martyn in search of the animals, suspecting them to be wild boars. We got near one of them, and fired several shots into the bush, and one at him as he went off among the long grass. When we returned to the tents, I learned by inquiring of the natives that the animals we had been in search of were not boars, but young lions; and they assured me that unless we kept a very good look out they would probably kill some of our cattle during the night. About midnight these young lions attempted to seize one of the asses, which so much alarmed the rest that they broke their ropes, and came at full gallop in amongst the tent ropes. Two of the lions followed them, and came so close to us that the sentry cut at one of them with his sword, but did not dare to fire for fear of killing the asses. Neglected to wind up the watch.

July 3rd.—Departed from Koeena, and halted during the heat of the day at Koombandi, distant six miles. Here the guides that I had hired from Kandy were to return; and I had agreed with them to carry back M'Millan's knapsack, and some amber and beads to purchase provisions for him; but three people came up to us with two asses for sale, and they informed me that they left Sanjeekotta early in the morning; that the soldier who was left there had died during the night, and the natives had buried him in a cornfield near the town. Purchased the asses in order to carry forwards the sick.

About three o'clock left Koombandi. Mr. Anderson and Mr. Scott were so sick, that they wished to remain here for the night; with much entreating, persuaded them to mount their horses and go on. Three miles east of the village, William Alston, one of the seamen whom I received from His Majesty's ship *Squirrel*, became so faint that he fell from his ass, and allowed the ass to run away. Set him on my horse, but found he could not sit without holding him. Replaced him on the ass, but he still tumbled off; put him again on the horse, and made one man keep him upright, while I led the horse. But as he made no exertion to keep himself erect, it was impossible to hold him on the horse, and after repeated tumbles he begged to be left in the woods till morning. I left a loaded pistol with him, and put some cartridges into the crown of his hat. At sunset reached

Fonilla, a small walled village on the banks of the Wonda, which is here called *Ba woolima* (Red river), and towards its source it has the name of *Ba qui* (White river), the middle part of its course being called *Wonda*. It had swelled two feet perpendicular by the rains which had fallen to the southward, and was very muddy; but cannot even in its present state be reckoned a large river.

July 4th.—Agreed with the canoe people to carry over our baggage and cattle for sixty bars. There being but one canoe, it was near noon before all the bundles were carried over. The transporting of the asses was very difficult. The river being shallow and rocky, whenever their feet touched the bottom they generally stood still. Our guide, Isaaco, was very active in pushing the asses into the water, and shoving along the canoe; but as he was afraid that we could not have them all carried over in the course of the day, he attempted to drive six of the asses across the river farther down where the water was shallower. When he had reached the middle of the river, a crocodile rose close to him, and instantly seizing him by the left thigh, pulled him under water. With wonderful presence of mind he felt the head of the animal, and thrust his finger into its eye; on which it quitted its hold, and Isaaco attempted to reach the farther shore, calling out for a knife. But the crocodile returned and seized him by the other thigh, and again pulled him under water; he had recourse to the same expedient, and thrust his fingers into its eyes with such violence that it again quitted him; and when it rose, flounced about on the surface of the water as if stupid, and then swam down the middle of the river. Isaaco proceeded to the other side, bleeding very much. As soon as the canoe returned I went over, and found him very much lacerated. The wound on the left thigh was four inches in length; that on the right not quite so large, but very deep; besides several single teeth wounds on his back. Drew the lips of the wounds together with slips of adhesive plaster secured with a roller; and as we were not far from a village, he thought it best for him to go forwards before his wounds had become very painful. He accordingly rode forwards to the village of Boolinkoomboo on one of our horses. Found myself very sick, and unable to stand erect without feeling a tendency to faint; the people so sickly that it was with some difficulty we got the loads put into the tents, though it threatened rain. To my great astonishment, Ashton,[1] the sailor whom I had left in the woods the evening before, came up quite naked, having been stripped of his clothes by three of the natives during the night. Found his fever much abated.

July 5th.—With great difficulty got the asses loaded, but had not a sufficient number of spare asses for the sick. Set one of them on my horse, and walked, feeling a remission of the fever, though still very giddy and unwell. We soon reached Boolinkoomboo, it being only two miles from the landing-place. This village is sometimes called Moiaharra: it does not contain above one hundred people. On collecting the asses, found that three were missing, besides a sickly one, which was too weak to cross the river, and was eaten by the people of Fonilla. All this diminished our means of carrying forward the sick.

I now found my situation very perplexing. To go forward without Isaaco to Keminoom, I knew, would involve us in difficulties; as Keminoom's sons are reckoned the greatest thieves and blackguards on the whole route. To stop till Isaaco recovered (an event which seemed very doubtful), would throw us into the violence of the rains. There was no other person that I could trust; and, what was worst of all, we had only *two days' rice,* and a great scarcity prevailed in the country. I determined to wait three days, to see how Isaaco's wounds looked, and in the meantime sent two of his people away to Serracorra with an ass and three strings of No. 5 amber to purchase rice.

July 6th.—All the people either sick, or in a state of great debility, except one. Bought all the milk I could find, and boiled a camp kettle full of strong decoction of barks every day.

July 7th.—Dressed Isaaco's wounds: they looked remarkably well.

---

[1] The name is thus written in Mr. Park's MS.; but it seems to be a mistake for *Alston, vide ante,* page 325.

July 8th.—Waiting very anxiously for the return of Isaaco's people with the rice, being now on very short allowance.

July 9th.—In the afternoon Isaaco's people returned, bringing with them 123 lb. of clean rice; Isaaco's wounds looking well, and beginning to discharge good pus.

July 10th.—Departed from Boolinkoomboo, and eight miles north-east passed the village of Serrababoo; close to which is a stream called Kinyaco, about knee deep, running to the north-west. It was very difficult to cross, on account of the fissures in the rocks which form its bed. Several of the asses fell, and their loads were of course wet. From this we travelled due north, over a ridge of rocks, which formed the only passage across a chain of hills. When we had crossed this, we travelled six miles on a rocky and almost impassable road, and a little before sunset, to our great joy, reached Sabooseera (Dooty Matta). This is a scattered unwalled village. Latitude by mer. alt. of moon 13° 50′.

CHAPTER XXXI

Arrival at Keminoom, or Manniakorro, on the Ba lee river—
Visit to the chief—Depredations upon the coffle by the
inhabitants—Continued attacks from banditti as far as the
Ba woolima river—Difficulties in passing it—Temporary
bridge made by the natives—Arrival at Mareena; inhospitable conduct of its inhabitants—Bangassi; interview with
the king—Continued sickness, and deaths among the soldiers
—Arrival at Nummasoolo—Obliged to leave five of the sick
behind—Reach Surtaboo—Sobee—Affray between Isaaco
and two soldiers—Balanding—Balandoo—More of the
soldiers fall behind—Koolihori—Greatly annoyed by wolves.

JULY 11TH.—From Sabooseera, or Mallaboo, we travelled
towards the west and north-west till noon, when we arrived
at Keminoom, or Maniakorro. This is a walled town fortified
in the strongest manner I have yet seen in Africa.

.   .   .   .   .

Pitched our tents under a tree near the Ba lee, which runs
here with great velocity, and breaks into small cataracts.
  July 12th.—Went in the morning with Isaaco and waited
on Keminoom, or Mansa Numma, as he is commonly called.

.   .   .   .   .

In the evening had such of the soldiers as were most healthy
dressed in their red coats; and at Numma's request went with
them to the town, where they went through some movements,
and fired.
  July 13th.—Very desirous to be gone, as we found the
people thieves to a man; in fact we have never yet been at a
place where so much theft and impudence prevails. This
can only be accounted for, by considering that Mansa Numma
is the reputed father of more than thirty children; and as
they all consider themselves as far above the common
people, they treat every person with contempt, and even steal

in the most open manner. By the side of the river are a great number of human bones (more than thirty skulls). On inquiring the reason, I was informed that Mansa Numma always inflicted capital punishments himself, and that the bones I saw were those of criminals. I had reason to regret, that capital punishments seldom or never extend to the real or reputed descendants of the king.

July 14th.—As soon as day dawned, struck the tents and loaded the asses. The townspeople gathered round us in crowds. They had stolen during our stay here four greatcoats, a large bundle of beads, a musket, a pair of pistols, and several other things. Before we had advanced a musket shot from the town (though we had one of the king's sons on horseback as a protector), one of the townspeople carried away a bag from one of the asses, containing some things belonging to one of the soldiers. The king's son, Lieutenant Martyn, and myself rode after him, and were lucky enough to come up with him, and recover the bag; but before we could rejoin the coffle, another had run off with a musket that was fastened on one of the loads.

We proceeded in this manner in a constant state of alarm; and I had great reason to fear that the impudence of the people would provoke some of the soldiers to run them through with their bayonets. About two miles from Mania-korro, as we were ascending a rocky part of the road, several of the asses fell with their loads. I rode a little from the path to see if a more easy ascent could not be found; and as I was holding my musket carelessly in my hand, and looking round, two of Numma's sons came up to me; one of them requested me to give him some snuff. Suspecting no ill treatment from two people, whom I had often seen with the king, and at our tents, I turned round to assure him that I never took snuff; at this instant the other (called Woosaba) coming up behind me, snatched the musket from my hand, and ran off with it. I instantly sprang from the saddle and followed him with my sword, calling to Mr. Anderson to ride back, and tell some of the people to look after my horse. Mr. Anderson got within musket shot of him, but seeing it was Numma's son, had some doubts about shooting him, and called to me if he should fire.

Luckily I did not hear him, or I might possibly have recovered my musket, at the risk of a long palaver, and perhaps the loss of half our baggage. The thief accordingly made his escape amongst the rocks, and when I returned to my horse, I found the other of the royal descendants had stolen my greatcoat.

I went and informed the king's son, whom we had hired as a guide, of what had happened; and requested to know how I should act if any of the people should steal from the baggage. He assured me that after what had happened, I should be justified in shooting the first that attempted to steal from the loads. Made such of the soldiers as were near me load their muskets and be ready. The sky became cloudy, and by the time that we had advanced about five miles from the town, we experienced a very heavy tornado. During the rain another of Numma's sons snatched up and ran off with one of the soldiers' muskets and a pair of pistols, which he had laid down while he was reloading his ass.

We halted amongst the rocks and put off the loads, all very wet. Turned the asses to feed, and cooked some rice, although it rained very heavily. One of the negro boys gave the alarm that three people were driving away our asses. I followed with some of our people: the thieves made their escape amongst the rocks, but without carrying away any of the asses, though they had untied the feet of three and fastened a fourth to a bush. Collected the asses and began to load. Whilst we were loading one of the asses strayed a little from the rest, about two hundred yards, and to my astonishment a man came from amongst the rocks, took off the load, and began to cut it open with his knife. Before any person could come at him, he left the load and ran up the rocks. Mr. Scott and one of the soldiers fired at him, but did not hit him. Went on. Road very rocky. Told the soldiers to shoot the first that took anything from the baggage. Found some of the asses and loads lying at the difficult places in the road, and often two loads with only one half-sick soldier to guard them. Kept in the rear, as I perceived they had a mind to take some of the loads and asses. I saw the thieves peeping over the rocks, and making signs to their comrades, who seemed very desirous of assisting us in putting on our loads.   Put one of the loads on my horse, and another on Mr. Anderson's, and luckily cleared the difficult passes of the rocks by sunset, without losing anything, though surrounded by at least a dozen experienced thieves.   When we reached the bottom of the rocky pass, we went on with more ease, and came up to the rest of the party about eight o'clock.   They had stopped for the night in the woods, and so were all our clothes;[1] and in fact we passed a very uncomfortable night amongst the wet grass, and exposed to a very heavy dew.

July 15*th*.—Early in the morning proceeded, and went on very slowly in the rear, by which means we were separated from the front.   Horses loaded as usual.   When we reached the cultivated land, which surrounds the village of Ganamboo, we came up to one of the soldiers, who informed us, that a man habited as a slave had come from amongst the bushes, and instantly seized on his musket and knapsack which were fastened on the top of his load.   The soldier struggled with him for his musket, and wrested it from him; on which the thief let go the knapsack, and attempted to make off; but when he heard the soldier cock his piece, expecting to be instantly shot, he threw himself down on the road and roared out in the most pitiable manner.   The soldier took a steady aim at him, but unfortunately his musket flashed in the pan, and the slave started up and ran in amongst the bushes.

Ganamboo is only a small walled village: it is situated about ten miles east half north from Maniakorro.

July 16*th*.—Left Ganamboo, but the soldiers and asses were so much fatigued that we were forced to stop at Ballandoo (Dooty Mari Umfa) during the night.   We had the most tremendous storm of thunder and lightning I ever saw. I was so confident that the tent would be struck by the lightning, that I went to some distance to avoid the explosion of our gunpowder.

July 17*th*.—Left Ballandoo at eight o'clock, and reached Seransang about noon.   All horses loaded; mine fell down

[1] It is thus in Mr. Park's MS.   There seems to be some omission.

under his load, and I was forced to sit by him till an ass was sent from the halting-place. Seransang is a scattered but populous town, and the land is cleared round it for a great distance. One of our best asses stolen during the night.

July 18th.—Departed from Seransang, having shifted the loads so as to have the horses free, in order to prevent theft. We had not travelled much above a mile, when two suspicious people came up. One of them walked slowly in the rear; and the other passed on, seemingly in great haste. I desired Mr. Anderson to watch the one in the rear, whilst I rode on at such a distance as just to keep sight of the other. The road making a turn, he was concealed from me by the bushes, and took advantage of this opportunity to carry away a greatcoat from a load which was driven by one of the sick men. I fortunately got a view of him as he was running off among the bushes, and galloping in a direction so as to get before him, quickly came so near him that he leaped into some very thick bushes. When I rode round, he went out at the side opposite to me; and in this manner I hunted him amongst the bushes for some time, but never losing sight of him. At last he ran past a spreading tree, and jumping back, stood close to the trunk of it. I thought I should certainly lose him if I did not avail myself of the present opportunity. I accordingly fired, and dropping my musket on the pummel of the saddle, drew out one of the pistols, and told him if he offered to move, I would instantly shoot him dead. "Do not kill me, white man," he exclaimed. "I cannot run from you, you have broke my leg." I now observed the blood streaming down his leg; and when he pulled up his cloth, I saw that the ball had passed through his leg about two inches below the knee joint. He climbed a little way up the tree, which was of easy ascent; always exclaiming in a pitiable tone of voice, "Do not kill me." Several of the people belonging to the coffle, on hearing the shot fired, came running; and amongst others the guide appointed us by Keminoom, who insisted that I should instantly shoot the thief dead; otherwise he said I did not fulfil the orders of his master, who had directed me to shoot every person that stole from me. I had great difficulty in preventing him from killing him, and was happy to recover the greatcoat, and leave the thief bleeding amongst the branches of the tree.

We proceeded without further molestation till about three o'clock in the afternoon, when it came on a tornado. During the rain one of the sick had fallen a little behind, and four people seizing him, stripped off his jacket. He followed them at a distance; and when they came up to Mr. Anderson and myself, he called out to us to shoot one of them, as they had taken his jacket. I had my pocket-handkerchief on the lock of my gun to keep the priming dry. When they observed me remove it, one of them pulled out the jacket from under his cloak, and laid it on one of the asses. Mr. Anderson followed them on horseback, and I kept as near him as I could on foot, my horse being loaded. After following them about three miles, they struck into the woods; and suspecting that they had a mind to return and steal some of the loads from the fatigued asses in the rear, I returned with Mr. Scott, and found that one of the soldiers had lost his knapsack, and another his jacket. But from their description, the robbers were not the same as had formerly passed.

Continued in the rear. When we came within a mile of the town of Nummaboo, the road passes near some high rocks. The asses being a little way before us, two of the robbers first seen came from amongst the rocks, and were going towards the asses; but when they observed us coming up, they attempted to slide off unobserved among the rocks. When I called to one of them to stop and tell me what they were looking after, they came near us; but as they had nothing of ours in their possession, we could not stop them, and they accordingly passed to the westward. Mr. Scott and I went and examined that part of the rocks where we observed them come out, and were lucky enough to find a soldier's coat, a camp kettle, and a number of other articles, which had probably been their share of the booty; for I learned on my arrival at the town, that the ass which carried the muskets belonging to the sick, had been stopped by four people near these rocks, and six muskets, a pair of pistols, and a knapsack taken away. To complete the business, J. Bowden, one of the sick, did not come up; and we had little doubt but that he had been stripped and murdered by these very people in the woods. We likewise had a very good ass stolen during the night.

July 19th.—Having purchased an ass in lieu of the one stolen, we left Nummaboo, which is a walled village, and proceeded onwards. Had two tornadoes; the last, about eleven o'clock, wetted us much, and made the road slippery. Two asses unable to go on. Put their loads on the horses, and left them. Mr. Scott's horse unable to walk: left it to our guide. At noon came to the ruins of a town. Found two more of the asses unable to carry their loads. Hired people to carry on the loads, and a boy to drive the asses. Past the ruins of another town at half-past twelve, where I found two of the sick, who had laid themselves down under a tree, and refused to rise (they were afterwards stripped by the Negroes, and came naked to our tents next morning). Shortly after this, came to an ass lying on the road unable to proceed with its load. Put part of the load on my horse, which was already heavily loaded. Took a knapsack on my back. The soldier carried the remainder and drove the ass before him.

We arrived on the banks of the Ba woolima at half-past one o'clock. This river is but narrow, not being more than fifty or sixty feet over; but was so swelled with the rains as to be twenty feet deep at the place where we proposed to cross it. Our first attempt was to fell a tree close to the river, that by its fall would reach across the stream and form a bridge: but after cutting down four, they all fell in such a manner as to be of no use; for though the tops of one reached the rocks on the farther shore when it fell, yet the violence of the current swept it away. In this manner we fatigued ourselves till sunset, when we gave up the attempt.

.   .   .   .   .

The passage of the river being the great desideratum, I proposed a raft to be hauled from side to side with ropes; whilst the Mandingoes were decidedly of opinion that nothing would answer our purpose but a bridge, which they said they would complete by two o'clock. I set to work with the carpenters to make a raft; but when the logs were cut into lengths, we could not muster healthy people enough to carry them to the water side. We were forced to give up the attempt and trust entirely to the Negro bridge.

.   .   .   .   .

Our people being all so sickly, I hired the Negroes to carry over all the baggage, and swim over the asses. Our baggage was laid on the rocks on the east side of the river; but such was our sickly state that we were unable to carry it up the bank. Francis Beedle, one of the soldiers, was evidently dying of the fever; and having in vain attempted, with the assistance of one of his messmates, to carry him over, I was forced to leave him on the west bank; thinking it very probable that he would die in the course of the night.

July 21st.—Hired Isaaco's people to carry the bundles up the bank, and assist in loading all the asses. One of the soldiers crossed the bridge, and found Beedle expiring. Did not stop to bury him, the sun being high; but set out immediately. Country woody, but level. About half-past ten o'clock came to Mr. Scott lying by the side of the path, so very sick that he could not walk. Shortly after Mr. Martyn laid down in the same state. My horse being loaded, and myself, as usual, walking on foot and driving an ass, I could give them no assistance. I came in sight of the town of Mareena a little before twelve; and at the same time was happy to see two of Isaaco's people coming back with two asses to take the loads off the horses in the rear. Sent them back for Mr. Scott and Mr. Martyn, and proceeded to the town. Some of the people who had crossed the river with us had informed the people of Mareena of the treatment we had experienced in passing from Maniakorro to the Ba woolima, which district is called Kissi; and withal had told the people that our coffle was a *Dummulafong,* a thing sent to be eaten, or in English *fair-game* for everybody. The inhabitants of Mareena were resolved to come in for their share; they accordingly stole five of our asses during the night; but felt themselves much disappointed next morning,

July 22nd.—when they understood, that instead of proceeding to Bangassi, we proposed to send forward a messenger to inform the king of the bad treatment we had experienced.

Three of them returned the asses they had stolen, but the other two would not. About noon we loaded all the horses and asses; and I hired two young men to carry forwards two trunks, the load of one of the asses which was stolen. Bangassi is only six miles distant from Mareena. It is a large town, fortified in the same manner as Maniakorro; but is four or five times as large. Pitched our tents under a tree to the east of the town.

July 23rd.—Received a present from Serenummo, the king, of a fine bullock and two very large calabashes of sweet milk; he likewise sent the two asses which the people of Mareena had stolen.

.   .   .   .   .

The town is large and populous, and is better fortified than even Maniakorro. We found Serenummo seated in a sort of shade, surrounded by only a few friends; orders having been given not to allow any person to enter it. He inquired if I was the white man who had formerly passed through the country, and what could induce me to come back again; with a number of such questions. To all which I gave the best answers I could; and then told him that I did not come to purchase slaves or gold; I did not come to take any man's trade from him or any man's money; I did not come to make money, but to spend it; and for the truth of these assertions I could appeal to every person who knew me or had travelled with me. I farther added, it was my intention at present to travel peaceably through his kingdom into Bambarra; and that as a mark of my regard for his name and character, I had brought a few articles which my guide would present to him. Here Isaaco spread out on the floor the various articles. The king looked at them with that sort of indifference which an African always affects towards things he has not before seen. However much he may admire them, he must never appear in the least surprised. He told me I should have permission to pass; and he would make his son take care of us till we arrived at Sego; but it would be some days before he was ready. I told him I was anxious to be in Bambarra, as I found my people very sickly; and if he would appoint me a guide, I would esteem it a favour. In fact I knew before, that this son proposed going to Sego with the annual tribute, which amounts to three hundred minkallis of gold or thereabouts; but I knew that the gold was not yet all collected, and that part of it would probably be bought with the merchandise I had given him.

July 25th.—Bought two asses for fifty-six bars of amber. During our stay at this town we were plentifully supplied with milk on moderate terms. I always purchased two camp kettles full every morning for the men, in hopes of recruiting them before we set forwards for the Niger; but they still continue sick and spiritless. Corporal Powal is dangerously ill of the fever, and M'Inelli is affected with the dysentery to such a degree, that I have no hopes of his recovery. He was removed yesterday to the shade of a tree at a small distance from the tents; and not being brought near in the evening, he was very near being torn to pieces by the wolves. They were smelling at his feet when he awakened, and then set up such a horrid howl, that poor M'Inelli, sick as he was, started up and came to the tents before the sentry could reach the place where he had slept.

July 26th.—Corporal Powal died during the night. Buried him this morning; two dollars and a half in his pocket, for which I am accountable. Overhauled the ass-saddles, and adjusted the loads, proposing to leave this to-morrow morning early.

·   ·   ·   ·   ·

July 27th.—The morning being rainy, we did not depart from Bangassi till about nine o'clock. Left here M'Inelli. Paid the Dooty ten bars of amber to purchase provision for him and give him lodging. Shortly after leaving the town, three of the soldiers laid down under a tree, and refused to proceed; their names Frair, Thomson, and Hercules. About a quarter of a mile farther, James Trott, one of the carpenters brought from Portsmouth, refused to go on, being sick of the fever. I drove on his ass, and desired him to return to Bangassi. Found myself very sick and faint, having to drive my horse loaded with rice, and an ass with the pit saws. Came to an eminence, from which I had a view of some very

distant mountains to the east half south. The certainty that
the Niger washes the southern base of these mountains made
me forget my fever; and I thought of nothing all the way but
how to climb over their blue summits.

Reached Nummasoolo at two o'clock. This has formerly
been a large town; but being destroyed by war some years
ago, nearly three-fourths of the town are in ruins. Before
we had time to pitch the tent properly, the rain came down
on us, and wetted us all completely, both men and bundles.
This was a very serious affair to us, many of our articles of
merchandise being perishable. Slept very uncomfortably
in wet clothes on the wet ground. Troubled in the night
with a lion; he came so near that the sentry fired at him, but
it was so dark that it was impossible to take a good aim. All
the asses pulled up the pins to which they were fastened, and
ran together as near the men as they could. As the sick
soldiers before mentioned did not come up before sunset, I
concluded they had all returned to Bangassi; and the Dooty's
son coming up on horseback, informed me that they had really
returned to his father's house, and wished to know what I
meant to do respecting them. I told him that I wished my
people to be taken proper care of, and gave him ten bars of
amber for his care in coming to inform me of them. I likewise put into his possession three strings of amber of forty
bars each, and told him how to dispose of them for the use of
the sick. I likewise told him that, if any of them should
recover, if he would send a proper person forward with them
to Bambakoo, I would give him an Indian baft, or ten bars
of scarlet, which he preferred. At the same time I wrote
the following note to the men.

"DEAR SOLDIERS,
"I am sorry to learn that you have returned to Bangassi.
I have sent in charge of the bearer of this three complete
strings of amber; one of which will procure rice for forty days;
the second will purchase milk or fowls for the same time;
and the third will buy provisions for you on the road till you
arrive at the Niger.
"Yours,
"M. PARK."

July 28th.—Rained all day. Remained in the tent at Nummasoolo.

July 29th.—Divided the men's clothes who were left behind amongst the other men; many of them being in great want of clothes, and the nights being now cold and damp. Found five dollars in J. Trott's knapsack, for which I am accountable. Spread out the rice to dry; found it hot and much damaged. Some people arrived from the east, who informed us that a stream on the road, which is usually dry, was so much swelled by the rain that no ass could cross it. Halted here during the day to dry the different articles.

July 30th.—Departed from Nummasoolo. Was under the necessity of leaving here William Allen sick. Paid the Dooty for him as usual. I regretted much leaving this man: he had naturally a cheerful disposition; and he used often to beguile the watches of the night with the songs of our dear native land.

About five miles east of Nummasoolo passed the stream before mentioned, flowing to the south-east. The water had subsided, and was only about eighteen inches deep, but flowed very rapidly. Many asses fell, and had their loads wetted. It likewise rained two hours on the march. Crossed a ridge of hills through an opening. Road tolerably good except in two places. We descended on the east side, and reached Surtaboo, a small ruined village, about two o'clock. Here I learnt that the front of the coffle had gone on to a village about four miles farther; but the asses in the rear being all very much fatigued, and lying down with their loads frequently, I judged it prudent to halt till some fresh asses should be sent to my assistance.

We had not halted here above an hour, when three of Isaaco's people and two asses came back; and with their help we arrived at Sobee at seven o'clock. On the road we passed the *last* of the St. Jago asses, the whole forty having either died or been abandoned on the road at different places. We were all very wet, for it rained almost the whole way; and all very hungry, having tasted nothing since the preceding evening. The town of Sobee has changed its situation *three* times. It was taken about ten years ago by Daisy, king of

Kaarta, with thirteen horsemen and some of his slaves on foot. They carried off five hundred slaves, two hundred of which were women. Such as escaped rebuilt the town about a mile to the east of its former situation; but when it had acquired some degree of prosperity, it was destroyed by Mansong, king of Bambarra. The present town is built nearer the foot of the hills; part of it is walled, which serves as a sort of citadel. There is plenty of corn and rice here on moderate terms; but they have not yet had time to recruit their herds of cattle.

July 31*st*.—Rained hard all the morning, and flying showers all day. Halted at Sobee. During the night one of the townspeople attempted to steal one of the soldiers' pieces, some of which were standing against a tree close to the tent. Lieutenant Martyn was sleeping under the tree; and hearing somebody moving the muskets, he no sooner observed that it was a Negro, than he snatched one of the muskets and fired at the thief as he was running off with one of the muskets. Whether the ball touched him or not we could not learn; but the thief dropped the musket, and we found it with the pouch and bayonet in the morning.

Aug. 1*st*.—Early this morning purchased an ass for a pistol, a baft, and a Mandingo cloth. We set out at seven o'clock. Immediately on the east of the town came to another stream flowing towards the S.S.W. It was so deep, that the whole of the bundles had to be carried over on men's heads. During this, being surrounded by thieves on all sides, Isaaco unfortunately struck two of the soldiers; which action had nearly cost him his life, one of the soldiers attempting to stab him with his bayonet, when Mr. Anderson prevented him; and as I reproved Isaaco for his conduct in the sharpest manner, he went off in a pet with his people, leaving us to find our way across the river in the best manner we could. I hired four people to carry over the loads; and stood myself as sentry over the thieves. In this manner the whole of the baggage was carried over with much less loss than we had sustained at any other river. The asses were swam over, and the whole only cost one string of No. 5; but I had to pay fifty stones to the Dooty's son for asses going on the corn. As soon as all was over we loaded the asses and set forwards. At sunset we reached Balanding. We had only time to pitch our tent, when the rain came on; indeed we had no time for cooking our victuals, for though all the soldiers cooked, yet the rain came on before our kettle was ready; and Messrs. Anderson, Scott, Martyn, and myself, all slept without having tasted anything during the day.

Aug. 2nd.—Rainy. Halted at Balanding.

Aug. 3rd.—Sun rose E. 3° S. Departed from Balanding, and halted at Balandoo, a walled village about four miles to the east by south. Bought two sheep for one barraloolo.

Aug. 4th.—Departed from Balandoo. About a mile to the east saw the hill of Sobee bearing north-west by compass. About this place Lawrence Cahill, one of the soldiers, who had complained of sickness for some days, fell behind; and I hired a person to drive his ass, telling him to come on at his leisure. At eleven o'clock crossed a stream running south-east which gave us great trouble, the banks being very steep and slippery. Crossed the same stream again at half-past twelve, running east by north. In the course of this day's march four of the soldiers were unable to attend to their asses. Mr. Scott, being very sick, rode my horse; and I drove one of the asses. So very much weakened were the men, that when their loads fell off they could not lift them on again. I assisted in loading thirteen asses in the course of the march. We reached Koolihori at three o'clock. This town is partly walled; but the greater part of the huts are without the walls. As soon as the tents were pitched, the rain commenced, and continued all night. We had not time to cook, and the rain prevented the watch-fire from burning; owing to which one of our asses was killed by the wolves. It was only sixteen feet distant from a bush under which one of the men was sleeping.

Aug. 5th.—Morning hazy. Halted, resolving to travel at two o'clock, and sleep in the woods, the Ba woolli being too far to reach in one march. Bought some ripe maize of this year's growth.

·   ·   ·   ·   ·

The whole route from Bangassi is marked with ruined towns and villages; some of them are rebuilt, but by far the greater number are still in ruins. We saw scarcely any cattle on the route, and the avidity of the people of Koolihori for animal food, or perhaps their own peculiar taste, made them eat what the wolves had left of our ass. The wolves had eat only the bowels and heart, etc., so that the people had the four quarters and head. The day having clouded up for rain, resolved to halt here for the night. In the course of the afternoon Lawrence Cahill came up; but William Hall, who had gone into a ruined hut near the road, and who did not appear to be very sick, did not arrive. Suspected that he might be killed by the wolves in the hut during the night. At sunset had all the asses properly tied near the tents; and watched myself with the sentries all night, as the wolves kept constantly howling round us.

CHAPTER XXXII

Departure from Koolihori—Ganifarra—Scarcity of provisions—
Distressing situation of the Author from deaths and sickness
of the party—Escapes from three lions—Intricate route to
Koomikoomi—Dombila—Visit from Karfa Taura—View
of the Niger—Reduced state of the party—Bambakoo—
Losses from wolves—Bosradoo; embark on the Niger;
incidents in the voyage to Marraboo—Isaaco sent to Sego
with presents for Mansong—Message from Mansong—Course
to Koolikorro — Deena — Yamina — Samee — Return of
Isaaco; account of his interview with Mansong—Messengers
sent by Mansong, and inquiries respecting the Author's
journey—Quit Samee—Excessive heat—Reach Sansanding
—Account of that city and its trade—Death of Mr Anderson
—Preparations for continuing the voyage eastward—
Information collected respecting various districts.

Aug. 6th.—Having hired two more ass-drivers at one bar
and their victuals per day, we left Koolihori early in the
morning, and travelled with considerable dispatch till three
o'clock; at which time we reached Ganifarra, a small beggarly
village. In the course of this march L. Cahill and J. Bird,
two of the soldiers, and William Cox, one of the seamen, fell
behind, and laid down. As soon as the front of the coffle
had reached Ganifarra, it came on a very heavy rain. Being
in the rear I was completely drenched; and two of the asses
carrying four trunks, in which were the gun stocks, pistols,
looking-glasses, etc., fell down in a stream of water near the
town, and all the contents were completely wet. I could
purchase nothing here, not so much as a fowl. Served out a
short allowance of rice, being very short of that article.

Aug. 7th.—During the night, some person had stolen one
of our best asses; and as the load must be left if we could not
recover it, Isaaco's people having traced the footmarks to a
considerable distance, agreed to go in search of it. Isaaco
gave them the strictest orders, if they came up to the thief

in the woods to shoot him; and, if not, to follow him to a town and demand the ass from the Dooty; if he refused to give it up, to return as soon as possible.

Spent the day in drying such things as were wet; cleaned and greased with Shea butter all the ornamented pistols, *ten pair*. Dried the looking-glasses, which were quite spoiled. In the afternoon sent two of the natives away with goods to a neighbouring town to purchase rice and corn. At sunset Bird came up, but had seen nothing of Cox nor Cahill.

Aug. 8th.—People not yet returned. Opened the trunk which contained the double-barrelled gun stocks; cleaned and greased them. About noon people returned with the rice and corn, but not quite sufficient for one day. Nearly at the same time Isaaco's people came up with the ass; they had traced his footmarks past Koolihori, and found him at Balandoo. Did not see the thief, but learned his name; which Isaaco promised to write to his friend at Bangassi, to inform Serinummo of him. In the afternoon agreed with the Dooty for thirty-five bars to carry everything over. Rained heavily all the evening.

Aug. 9th.—Michael May, a soldier, having died during the night, buried him at daybreak. Had all the loads taken to the crossing-place by eight o'clock. The Ba woolli is nearly of the same size as the one we formerly crossed of that name; it appeared to be exceedingly deep, and flowed at the rate of four or five miles per hour. There is a very good canoe here, which can carry over four ass-loads at once. As it threatened rain, sent over three men with one of the tents, and pitched it on the east side about half a mile from the river; the ground near the bank being marshy. Hired people to carry down the bundles, and put them into the canoe; and others to receive them on the other side, and carry them up the bank; so that the soldiers had nothing to move, being all weak and sickly.

By one o'clock all the baggage was over; but we found some difficulty in transporting the asses; the rapidity of the stream swept the canoe and the first six past the landing-place; and they went so far down the river, that I really thought the asses must be drowned; which would have been an irreparable loss in our situation. However, by the exertions of the Negroes, who swam in with ropes to the canoe, the asses were landed on the other side; where they stood by the water's edge until the Negroes with their corn hoes made a path for them up the steep bank. To prevent such an accident, we took the ropes from several of our loads, and fastened them together, so as to reach across the river; with this we hauled over the loaded canoe, and the Negroes paddled it back when empty. In this manner all the asses and horses were swam over without any loss.

When the bundles were all carried up to the tent, we found that we had not more rice than was barely sufficient for the present day; and as no more could be purchased, we had no alternative but to march early in the morning for Bambarra; the distance by all accounts would not exceed fourteen or fifteen miles.

Aug. 10*th.*—William Ashton declared that he was unable to travel; but as there was no place to leave him at, I advised him to make an exertion and come on, though slowly, till he should reach a place where he could have food. At eight o'clock set forwards; and travelled very expeditiously without halting till four in the afternoon, at which time the front of the coffle reached Dababoo, a village of Bambarra. Being in the rear, I found many of the men very much fatigued with the length of the journey and the heat of the day. At half-past four I arrived with the ass I drove at a stream flowing to the westwards.

Here I found many of the soldiers sitting, and Mr. Anderson lying under a bush, apparently dying. Took him on my back, and carried him across the stream, which came up to my middle. Carried over the load of the ass which I drove, got over the ass, Mr. Anderson's horse, etc. Found myself much fatigued, having crossed the stream sixteen times. Left here four soldiers with their asses, being unable to carry over their loads. Having loaded my ass and put Mr. Anderson on his horse, we went on to the village; but was sorry to find that no rice could be had, and I was only able to buy one solitary fowl.

Aug. 11*th.*—Bought a small bullock of the Moorish breed

for one barraloolo; and having purchased some corn, had it
cleaned and dressed for the people instead of rice. This
morning hired Isaaco's people to go back, and bring up the
loads of the soldiers who had halted by the side of the stream.
In the course of the day all the loads arrived; but was sorry
to find that in the course of the last two marches we had lost
four men, viz. Cox, Cahill, Bird, and Ashton. Mr. Anderson
still in a very dangerous way, being unable to walk or sit
upright. Mr. Scott much recovered. I found that I must
here leave one load, one of the horses being quite finished.
Left the seine nets in charge of the Dooty, till I should send
for them.

Aug. 12th.—Rained all the morning. About eleven o'clock,
the sky being clear, loaded the asses. None of the Europeans
being able to lift a load, Isaaco made the Negroes load the
whole. Saddled Mr. Anderson's horse; and having put a sick
soldier on mine, took Mr. Anderson's horse by the bridle,
that he might have no trouble but sitting upright on the
saddle. We had not gone far before I found one of the asses
with a load of gunpowder, the driver (Dickinson) being
unable to proceed (I never heard of him afterwards); and
shortly after the sick man dismounted from my horse, and
laid down by a small pool of water, refusing to rise. Drove
the ass and horse on before me. Passed a number of sick.
At half-past twelve o'clock Mr. Anderson declared he could
ride no farther. Took him down and laid him in the shade
of a bush, and sat down beside him. At half-past two o'clock
he made another attempt to proceed; but had not rode above
a hundred yards before I had to take him down from the
saddle, and lay him again in the shade. I now gave up all
thoughts of being able to carry him forwards till the cool of
the evening; and having turned the horses and ass to feed, I
sat down to watch the pulsations of my dying friend. At
four o'clock four of the sick came up; three of them agreed
to take charge of the ass with the gunpowder; and I put a
fourth, who had a sore leg, on my horse, telling him if he saw
Mr. Scott on the road to give him the horse.

At half-past five o'clock, there being a fine breeze from the
south-west, Mr. Anderson agreed to make another attempt,

and having again placed him on the saddle, I led the horse on pretty smartly in hopes of reaching Koomikoomi before dark. We had not proceeded above a mile, before we heard on our left a noise very much like the barking of a large mastiff, but ending in a hiss like the fuf [1] of a cat. I thought it must be some large monkey; and was observing to Mr. Anderson "what a bouncing fellow that must be," when we heard another bark nearer to us, and presently a third still nearer, accompanied with a growl. I now suspected that some wild animal meant to attack us, but could not conjecture of what species it was likely to be. We had not proceeded a hundred yards farther, when coming to an opening in the bushes, I was not a little surprised to see three lions coming towards us. They were not so red as the lion I formerly saw in Bambarra, but of a dusky colour, like the colour of an ass. They were very large, and came bounding over the long grass, not one after another, but all abreast of each other. I was afraid, if I allowed them to come too near us, and my piece should miss fire, that we should be all devoured by them. I therefore let go the bridle, and walked forwards to meet them. As soon as they were within a long shot of me, I fired at the centre one. I do not think I hit him; but they all stopt, looked at each other, and then bounded away a few paces, when one of them stopt, and looked back at me. I was too busy in loading my piece to observe their motions as they went away, and was very happy to see the last of them march slowly off amongst the bushes. We had not proceeded above half a mile farther, when we heard another bark and growl close to us amongst the bushes. This was doubtless one of the lions before seen, and I was afraid they would follow us till dark, when they would have too many opportunities of springing on us unawares. I therefore got Mr. Anderson's call, and made as loud a whistling and noise as possible. We heard no more of them.

Just at dark we descended into a valley where was a small stream of water; but the ascent on the opposite side was through a species of broken ground, which I have never seen anywhere but in Africa. It is of the following nature. A

[1] Thus in Mr. Park's MS.

stratum of stiff yellow clay fourteen or twenty feet thick (which, unless when it rains, is as hard as rock) is washed by the annual rains into fissures of a depth equal to the thickness of the stratum. There is no vegetation on these places, except on the summit or original level. Amongst these horrid gullies I unfortunately lost sight of the footmarks of the asses which had gone before; and finding no way to get out, led the horse up a very steep place in order to gain the original level, hoping there to find the footpath. But unluckily the ground was all broken as far as I could see; and after travelling some little way, we came to a gully which we could not cross; and finding no possibility of moving without the danger of being killed by falling into some of these ravines, or over some precipice, I thought it advisable to halt till the morning. On this rugged summit we fell in with Jonas Watkins, one of the sick; and with his assistance I lighted a fire. Wrapped Mr. Anderson in his cloak, and laid him down beside it. Watched all night to keep the fire burning, and prevent our being surprised by the lions, which we knew were at no great distance. About two o'clock in the morning two more of the sick joined us. Mr. Anderson slept well during the night, and as soon as day dawned,

Aug. 13*th.*—having found the footmarks of the asses, and having with difficulty even in daylight traced our way through this labyrinth, we found Mr. Scott and three more of the sick. They too had lost their way, and had slept about half a mile to the east of us. We reached Koomikoomi at ten o'clock. This is an unwalled village, but surrounded with extensive corn fields.

Aug. 13*th.*—Halted; rested at Koomikoomi.

Aug. 14*th.*—Jonas Watkins died this morning; buried him. Halted here to-day to see which way Mr. Anderson's fever was likely to terminate; and in the meantime sent two loaded asses forward to Doombila, the asses to return in the evening and carry loads to-morrow morning.

•   •   •   •   •

It is a common observation of the Negroes, that when the Indian corn is in blossom the rain stops for eleven days. The stopping of the rain evidently depends on the sun approaching the zenith of the place: the sun by this day's observation being only seventy-one miles north of us; and it is a wonderful institution of Providence, that at this time the maize here is all in full blossom; and on passing through the fields, one is like to be blinded with the pollen of the male flowers.

Aug. 15th.—Having slung a cloak like a hammock under a straight stick, had Mr. Anderson put into it, and carried on two men's heads; two more following to relieve them. Mr. Scott complained this morning of sickness and headache. Made one of the soldiers saddle Mr. Anderson's horse for him; and having seen him mount, and given him his canteen with water, I rode forwards to look after four Negroes whom I had hired to carry loads on their heads; but being strangers, I was apprehensive they might run away with them. Found everything going on well; and we travelled with such expedition, that we reached Doombila in four hours and a half, though the distance cannot be less than sixteen or eighteen miles, nearly south. It rained hard all the afternoon, and it was not till dark that all the sick soldiers came up. Only three of the soldiers were able to drive their asses to-day.

When I entered the town I was happy to meet Karfa Taura, the worthy Negro mentioned in my former travels; he heard a report at Boori (where he now resides) that a coffle of white people were passing through Fooladoo for Bambarra; and that they were conducted by a person of the name of Park, who spoke Mandingo. He heard this report in the evening; and in the morning he left his house, determined if possible to meet me at Bambakoo, a distance of six days' travel. He came to Bambakoo with three of his slaves to assist me in going forward to Sego, but when he found I had not come up, he came forwards to meet me. He instantly recognised me, and you may judge of the pleasure I felt on seeing my old benefactor.

At four o'clock, as Mr. Scott had not come up, and the people in the rear had not seen him lately, I sent one of Isaaco's people back on my horse as far as the next village, suspecting that he might have halted there when the rain came on. The man returned after dark, having been nearly at Koomikoomi without seeing or hearing anything of Mr. Scott. We all concluded that he had returned to Koomikoomi.

Aug. 17th.—Halted at Doombila in order to dry the baggage, and in hopes of Mr. Scott coming up. Told the four Negroes, who carried Mr. Anderson, and who returned to Koomikoomi this morning, to make every possible inquiry concerning Mr. Scott; and if he was able to ride, I would pay them handsomely for coming with him. If he had returned to Koomikoomi, I desired them to assure the Dooty that I would pay for every expense he might incur, and pay for a guide to conduct him to Marraboo. Received from the Dooty of Doombila a small bullock and a sheep. Paid him a barraloolo, five bars of amber, and fifty gun flints.

Aug. 18th.—Hearing no account of Mr. Scott, concluded he was still at Koomikoomi, but unable to travel. At seven o'clock left Doombila, and as the asses were now very weak, it was not long before I had to dismount and put a load on my horse. Only one of the soldiers able to drive an ass. Road very bad; did not reach Toniba till sunset, being a distance of eighteen or twenty miles south-east by south. Mr. Anderson's bearers halted with him at a village on the road, where there was some good beer. As soon as we had pitched the tent, it began to rain, and rained all night; the soldiers ran all into the village. I passed a very disagreeable night, having to keep our asses from eating the people's corn, which caused me to keep walking about almost the whole night.

In case it should escape my memory, I take this opportunity of observing that the standard law of Africa runs thus: If an ass should break a single stem of corn, the proprietor of the corn has a right to seize the ass; and if the owner of the ass will not satisfy him for the damage he thinks he has sustained, he can *retain* the ass. He cannot *sell* or *work* him, but he can *kill* him; and as the Bambarrans esteem ass-flesh as a great luxury, this part of the law is often put in force.

Aug. 19th.—Mr. Anderson's bearers having brought him forward early in the morning, we immediately loaded the asses, and departed from Toniba (Sergeant M'Keal appears to be slightly delirious). We kept ascending the mountains to the south of Toniba till three o'clock, at which time having gained the summit of the ridge which separates the Niger from the remote branches of the Senegal, I went on a little before; and coming to the brow of the hill, I *once more saw the Niger* rolling its immense stream along the plain!

After the fatiguing march which we had experienced, the sight of this river was no doubt pleasant, as it promised an end to, or to be at least an alleviation of, our toils. But when I reflected that three-fourths of the soldiers had died on their march, and that in addition to our weakly state we had no carpenters to build the boats in which we proposed to prosecute our discoveries; the prospect appeared somewhat gloomy. It however afforded me peculiar pleasure, when I reflected that in conducting a party of *Europeans,* with immense baggage, through an extent of more than five hundred miles, I had always been able to preserve the most friendly terms with the natives. In fact, this journey plainly demonstrates, first, that with common prudence any quantity of merchandise may be transported from the Gambia to the Niger, without danger of being robbed by the natives; secondly, that if this journey be performed in the dry season, one may calculate on losing not more than three or at most four men out of fifty.

But to return to the Niger. The river was much swelled by the rains, but did not appear to overflow its banks. It certainly is larger even here than either the Senegal or the Gambia. We descended with difficulty down the steep side of the hill towards Bambakoo, which place we reached at half-past six o'clock, and pitched our tents under a tree near the town. Of thirty-four soldiers and four carpenters, who left the Gambia, only six soldiers and one carpenter reached the Niger.

During the night the wolves carried away two large cloth bundles from the tent door to a considerable distance; where they eat off the skins with which they were covered, and left them.

Aug. 20*th.*—Received a bullock from the Dooty as a present. It was in the afternoon, and we fastened it to the tree close to the tent, where all the asses were tied. As soon as it was dark the wolves tore its bowels out, though within ten yards of the tent door where we were all sitting. The wolves here are the largest and most ferocious we have yet seen.

Aug. 21st.—Dried a bundle of beads, the strings of which were all rotten with the rain. Opened a leather bag which contained about thirty pounds of gunpowder for present use. Found it all wet and damaged. Spread it out in the sun; resolved to make something of it. Spoke for a canoe to carry down the baggage to Marraboo, the river being navigable over the rapids at this season. In the course of our march from Toniba to Bambakoo, we lost Sergeant M'Keil, Purvey, and Samuel Hill.

Aug. 22nd.—Early in the morning had all the bundles put on the asses, and carried to the place of embarkation, which is a village called Bossradoo, about a mile and a half east of Bambakoo. It rained hard all the forenoon. The canoes could not carry any of the soldiers, or any person except two to look after the goods. I resolved to go down with Mr. Anderson, leaving Mr. Martyn to come down with the men by land. They rode on the asses.

We embarked at ten minutes past three o'clock. The current, which is nearly five knots per hour, set us along without the trouble of rowing any more than was necessary to keep the canoe in the proper course. The river is full an English mile over, and at the rapids it is spread out to nearly twice that breadth. The rapids seem to be formed by the river passing through a ridge of hills in a south-easterly direction; they are very numerous, and correspond with the jetting angles of the hills. There are *three* principal ones, where the water breaks with considerable noise in the middle of the river; but the canoe men easily avoided them by paddling down one of the branches near the shore. Even in this manner the velocity was such as to make me sigh.

We passed two of the principal rapids, and three smaller ones, in the course of the afternoon. We saw on one of the islands, in the middle of the river, a large elephant; it was of a red clay colour with black legs. I was very unwell of the dysentery; otherwise I would have had a shot at him, for he was quite near us. We saw three hippopotami close to another of these islands. The canoe men were afraid they might follow us and overset the canoes. The report of a musket will in all cases frighten them away. They blow up the water exactly like a whale. As we were gliding along shore, one of the canoe men speared a fine turtle, of the same species as the one I formerly saw, and made a drawing of in Gambia. At sunset we rowed to the shore, landed on some flat rocks, and set about cooking the turtle and rice for our supper; but before this aldermanic repast was half dressed, the rain came on us, and continued with great violence all night.

Aug. 23rd.—At daybreak embarked again, very wet and sleepy. Passed the third rapid, and arrived at Marraboo at nine o'clock. Our guide soon found a large passage hut in which to deposit our baggage, for one stone of small amber per load. We carried the whole of it up in a few minutes. In the evening Mr. Martyn arrived, and all the people, except two, who came up next day.

Aug. 24th.—Received from the Dooty a small black bullock in a present, which our guide would not allow us to kill, it being of a jet-black colour. The Dooty's name is Sokee; and so superstitious was he, that all the time we remained at Marraboo he kept himself in his hut, conceiving that if he saw a white man, he would never prosper after.

Aug. 25th.—Paid Isaaco goods to the full value of two prime slaves, according to agreement. I likewise gave him several articles; and I told him, that when the palaver was adjusted at Sego, he should then have all the asses and horses for his trouble.

Aug. 26th.—Took out such things as I meant to give to Mansong.

．　　　．　　　．　　　．　　　．

I wished to put a stop to the malicious reports of the Moors and Mahomedans at Sego as soon as possible. I therefore resolved to send Isaaco forward to Sego with all the articles for Mansong, except certain which I desired him to say to

Modibinne would be given as soon as I heard accounts that Mansong would befriend us. This Modibinne is Mansong's prime minister; he is a Mahomedan, but not intolerant in his principles. Isaaco accordingly departed on the 28th with his wife and all his goods. Ever since my arrival at Marraboo I had been subject to attacks of the dysentery; and as I found that my strength was failing very fast, I resolved to charge myself with mercury. I accordingly took calomel till it affected my mouth to such a degree that I could not speak or sleep for six days. The salivation put an immediate stop to the dysentery, which had proved fatal to so many of the soldiers.

. . . . .

As soon as I recovered, I set about exchanging some amber and coral for cowries, which are the current money of Bambarra.

. . . . .

It is curious that in counting the cowries, they call eighty a hundred; whilst in all other things they calculate by the common hundred. Sixty is called a Manding hundred.

On the 6th Thomas Dyer (a private) died of the fever. I had to pay one thousand shells to Dooty Sokee, before he would allow me to bury him; alleging that if the ground was not bought where he was buried, it would never grow good corn after.

There is no wood proper for boat building in this neighbourhood; the best wood is near Kankaree, on a large navigable branch of the Niger; and almost all the Bambarra canoes come from thence; many of them are mahogany.

The travellers from Sego brought us every day some unfavourable news or other. At one time it was reported, and believed all over Marraboo, that Mansong had killed Isaaco with his own hand, and would do the same with all the whites who should come into Bambarra. Our fears were at length dispelled by the arrival of Bookari, Mansong's singing man, on the 8th, with six canoes. He told us he came by Mansong's orders to convey us and our baggage to Sego. That Mansong thought highly of the presents which Isaaco had brought, and wished us to be brought to Sego before he received them from Isaaco. We accordingly put our baggage in order; but it was not till the 12th that the singing man and his Somonies (canoe people) could be prevailed on to leave the Dooty Sokee's good beef and beer. We embarked, and left Marraboo at ten minutes past three o'clock.

.   .   .   .   .

Sept. 13th.—Bookari sent four of the Somonies over to a town on the opposite side of the river, to put in requisition a canoe for carrying part of our baggage. The people refused to give the canoe, and sent the Somonies back without it. Bookari immediately went with all the Somonies (38); and having cut the owner of the canoe across the forehead with his sword, and broken his brother's head with a canoe paddle, he seized one of his sons, and brought him away as a slave along with the canoe. He however set the boy at liberty, his father paying two thousand shells for his release.

We left Koolikorro at thirty-five minutes past eleven. I will not trouble your Lordship with transcribing the courses and compass bearings from this to Sansanding. I hope to give a tolerable correct chart of all its turnings and windings, when I return to Great Britain.

.   .   .   .   .

We travelled very pleasantly all day; in fact nothing can be more beautiful than the views of this immense river; sometimes as smooth as a mirror, at other times ruffled with a gentle breeze, but at all times sweeping us along at the rate of six or seven miles per hour. We halted for the night at Deena, a Somoni village on the south side. Had a tornado in the night, which wetted our baggage much. Most of us slept in the canoes to prevent theft.

Sept. 14th.—Departed from Deena early in the morning, and arrived at Yamina at forty-five minutes past four o'clock. Halted here the 15th, in order to purchase cowries.

.   .   .   .   .

On the 16th left Yamina, and in the evening reached Samee,

where we landed our baggage; and Bookari went forward to Segoto inform Mansong of our arrival.

.   .   .   .   .

Sept. 18*th.*—No accounts from Sego.

Sept. 19*th.*—About two o'clock in the morning, Isaaco arrived in a canoe from Sego, with all the articles I had sent to Mansong. Mansong had never yet seen any of them; and when he heard that I was arrived at Samee, he desired Modibinne to inform Isaaco that he had best take the articles up to Samee; and he would send a person to receive them from my own hand. Isaaco informed me that Mansong, at all the interviews he had with him, uniformly declared that he would allow us to pass; but whenever Isaaco mentioned us particularly, or related any incident that had happened on the journey, Mansong immediately began to make squares and triangles in the sand before him with his finger, and continued to do so, so long as Isaaco spoke about us. Isaaco said, that he thought Mansong was rather afraid of us; particularly as he never once expressed a wish to see us, but rather the contrary.

Sept. 22*nd.*—In the evening, Modibinne and four more of Mansong's friends arrived in a canoe. They sent for me, and Modibinne told me, that they were come by Mansong's orders to hear, from my own mouth, what had brought me into Bambarra. He said I might think on it during the night, and they would visit me in the morning; he said Mansong had sent me a bullock, which he showed me: it was very fat, and *milk white.*

Sept. 23*rd.*—As soon as we had breakfasted, Modibinne and the four grandees came to visit us. When they had seated themselves, and the usual compliments passed, Modibinne desired me to acquaint them with the motives which had induced me to come into their country. I spoke to them in the Bambarra language as follows: "I am the white man who nine years ago came into Bambarra. I then came to Sego, and requested Mansong's permission to pass to the eastwards; he not only permitted me to pass, but presented me with five thousand cowries to purchase provisions on the road;[1] for you all know that the Moors had robbed me of my goods.   This generous conduct of Mansong towards me has made his name much respected in the land of the white people. The king of that country has sent me again into Bambarra; and if Mansong is inclined to protect me, and you who are here sitting wish to befriend me, I will inform you of the real object of my coming into your country."

(Here Modibinne desired me to speak on, as they were all my friends.) "You all know that the white people are a trading people; and that all the articles of value, which the Moors and the people of Jinnie bring to Sego, are made by us.   If you speak of a *good gun*, who made it? the *white people*.   If you speak of a good pistol or sword, or piece of scarlet or baft, or beads or gunpowder, who made them? the *white people*.   We sell them to the Moors; the Moors bring them to Timbuctoo, where they sell them at a *higher rate*.   The people of Timbuctoo sell them to the people of Jinnie at a still higher price; and the people of Jinnie sell them to you.   Now the king of the white people wishes to find out a way by which we may bring our own merchandise to you, and sell everything at a much cheaper rate than you now have them.   For this purpose, if Mansong will permit me to pass, I propose sailing down the Joliba to the place where it mixes with the salt water; and if I find no rocks or danger in the way, the white men's small vessels will come up and trade at Sego, if Mansong wishes it.   What I have now spoken, I hope and trust you will not mention to any person, except Mansong and his son; for if the Moors should hear of it, I shall certainly be murdered before I reach the salt water."

Modibinne answered: "We have heard what you have spoken.   Your journey is a good one, and may God prosper you in it; Mansong will protect you.   We will carry your words to Mansong this afternoon; and to-morrow we will bring you his answer."   I made Isaaco show them the different things which I had allotted for Mansong and his son. They were delighted with the tureen, the double-barrelled guns, and in fact everything was far superior to anything of the kind they had ever before seen.

[1] Page 153.

When I had laid out everything for Mansong and his son, I then made each of the grandees, and Modibinne, a present of scarlet cloth. Modibinne now said that they had seen what I laid out for Mansong and his son, and that the present was great, and worthy of Mansong; but, added he, Mansong has heard so many reports concerning your baggage, that he wishes us to examine it. "Such of the bundles as are covered with skin, we will not open; you will tell us what is in them, and that will be sufficient." I told them that I had nothing but what was necessary for purchasing provisions; and that it would please me much if they could dispense with opening the bundles. They however persisted; and I ordered the bundles to be brought out, taking care, with the assistance of the soldiers, to secrete all the good amber and coral.

When all the loads were inspected, I asked Modibinne what he thought of my baggage? If he had seen any more silver tureens, or double-barrelled guns? He said he had seen nothing that was *bad*, and nothing but what was necessary for purchasing provisions; that he would report the same to Mansong. They accordingly went away to Sego; but without taking Mansong's present, till they had heard his answer.

Sept. 24th.—Seed and Barber (soldiers) died during the night; one of the fever, the other of the dysentery. Paid the Somonies twenty stones of amber for burying them.

Sept. 25th.—Modibinne and the same people returned with Mansong's answer, a literal translation of which I give as follows. "Mansong says he will protect you; that a road is open for you everywhere, as far as his hand (power) extends. If you wish to go to the east, no man shall harm you from Sego till you pass Timbuctoo. If you wish to go to the west, you may travel through Fooladoo and Manding, through Kasson and Bondou; the name of Mansong's stranger will be a sufficient protection for you. If you wish to build your boats at Samee or Sego, at Sansanding or Jinnie, name the town, and Mansong will convey you thither." He concluded by observing, that Mansong wished me to sell him four of the blunderbusses, three swords, a fiddle (violin) which belonged to Mr. Scott, and some Birmingham bead necklaces, which pleased above everything; that he had sent us a bullock, and his son another, with a fine sheep. I told Modibinne that Mansong's friendship was of more value to me than the articles he had mentioned, and that I would be happy if Mansong would accept them from me as a farther proof of my esteem.

I made choice of Sansanding for fitting out our canoe, because Mansong had never said he wished to see me, and because I could live quieter and freer from begging than at Sego. I therefore sent down the bullocks by land to Sansanding.

Sept. 26th.—We departed from Samee. The canoes were not covered with mats; and there being no wind, the sun became insufferably hot. I felt myself affected with a violent headache, which increased to such a degree as to make me almost delirious. I never felt so hot a day; there was *sensible heat* sufficient to have roasted a *sirloin*; but the thermometer was in a bundle in the other canoe, so that I could not ascertain the *actual* heat. We passed down a small stream to the north of Sego Korro, and halted opposite to Segosee Korro, near the sand hills, where I formerly waited for a passage. We waited here about an hour for Isaaco, who had gone to Segosee Korro to inform Mansong of our passing. When Isaaco returned, he made a sort of shade over our canoe with four sticks and a couple of cloaks; and in the evening I found myself more collected and less feverish. At sunset we rowed towards the north bank, where there are some flat rocks, on which passengers by water often sleep. We found the place occupied by a number of people. I counted between thirty and forty fires; we therefore passed on a little to the eastwards, and slept on a sand-bank covered with verdure.

Sept. 27th.—At daybreak we again proceeded, and in stretching over to gain the middle of the river, we passed a Somoni fishing village on an island; the huts occupied the whole of the dry ground, and it appeared, even when close to it, like a floating village. We reached Sansanding at ten o'clock. Such crowds of people came to the shore to see us, that we could not land our baggage till the people were beaten away with sticks, by Koontie Mamadie's orders, on whose premises we were accommodated with a large hut for sitting in, having another hut opening into it, in which we deposited our baggage.

Oct. 2nd.—Marshall and W. Garland (privates) died; one of the fever, the other of the dysentery. During the night the wolves carried away Garland, the door of the hut where he died being left open. Buried Marshall on the morning following, in a corn field near the church.

Oct. 4th.—Mansong sent down two broken gunlocks, and a large pewter plate with a hole in the bottom of it, for me to repair; and it was with much difficulty that I could persuade the messenger that none of us knew anything about such occupations.

Oct. 6th.—Da, Mansong's eldest son, sent one canoe as a present, and requested me to sell him a blunderbuss, and three swords, with some blue and yellow broad cloth. Sent him three swords, and ten spans of yellow cloth; received in return six thousand cowries.

Sansanding contains, according to Koontie Mamadie's account, eleven thousand inhabitants. It has no public buildings, except the mosques, two of which, though built of mud, are by no means inelegant. The market-place is a large square, and the different articles of merchandise are exposed for sale on stalls covered with mats, to shade them from the sun. The market is crowded with people from morning to night: some of the stalls contain nothing but beads; others indigo in balls; others wood-ashes in balls; others Houssa and Jinnie cloth. I observed one stall with nothing but antimony in small bits; another with sulphur, and a third with copper and silver rings and bracelets. In the houses fronting the square is sold scarlet, amber, silks from Morocco, and tobacco, which looks like Levant tobacco, and comes by way of Timbuctoo. Adjoining this is the salt market, part of which occupies one corner of the square. A slab of salt is sold commonly for eight thousand cowries; a large butcher's stall, or shade, is in the centre of the square, and as good and fat meat sold every day as any in England. The beer market is at a little distance, under two large trees;

and there are often exposed for sale from eighty to one hundred calabashes of beer, each containing about two gallons. Near the beer market is the place where red and yellow leather is sold.

Besides these market-places, there is a very large space, which is appropriated for the great market every Tuesday. On this day astonishing crowds of people come from the country to purchase articles in wholesale, and retail them in the different villages, etc. There are commonly from sixteen to twenty large fat Moorish bullocks killed on the market morning.

Oct. 8th.—As Mansong had delayed much longer in sending the canoes he promised than I expected, I thought it best to be provided with a sufficient quantity of shells to purchase two; particularly when I reflected that the river would subside in the course of a few days, having sunk this morning about four inches by the shore. I therefore opened shop in great style, and exhibited a choice assortment of European articles to be sold in wholesale or retail. I had of course a *great run,* which I suppose drew on me the envy of my brother merchants; for the Jinnie people, the Moors, and the merchants here joined with those of the same description at Sego, and (in presence of Modibinne, from whose mouth I had it) offered to give Mansong a quantity of merchandise of greater value than all the presents I had made him, if he would seize our baggage, and either kill us, or send us back again out of Bambarra. They alleged, that my object was to kill Mansong and his sons by means of charms, that the white people might come and seize on the country. Mansong, much to his honour, rejected the proposal, though it was seconded by two-thirds of the people of Sego, and almost all Sansanding.

From the 8th to the 16th nothing of consequence occurred. I found my shop every day more and more crowded with customers; and such was my run of business, that I was sometimes forced to employ *three tellers at once* to count my cash. I turned one market day twenty-five thousand seven hundred and fifty-six pieces of money (cowries).

The second day after my arrival at Marraboo, as no accounts

whatever had arrived concerning Mr. Scott, I sent a messenger to Koomikoomi, desiring him to bring Mr. Scott, or some account of him. He returned in four days, and told us that *Mr. Scott was dead*, and that the natives had stolen the pistols out of the holsters; but he had brought the horse to Bambakoo.

When Modibinne inquired of Isaaco what sort of a *return of presents* would be most agreeable to me, Isaaco (being instructed before) said he believed two large canoes, and Modibinne assured me, that the canoes would be sent down to Sansanding immediately on our arrival there.

. . . . . .

Oct 16th.—Modibinne and Jower arrived, and told me that they had brought a canoe from Mansong. I went to see it, and objected to one half of it, which was quite rotten. They sent up to Sego for another half; but when it arrived, it would not fit the one already sent. I was therefore forced to send Isaaco again to Sego; and as Mansong had requested me by Modibinne to sell him any spare arms I might have, I sent two blunderbusses, two fowling-pieces, two pair of pistols, and five unserviceable muskets; requesting in return that Mansong would either send a proper canoe, or permit me to purchase one that I might proceed on my journey. Isaaco returned on the 20th with a large canoe; but half of it was very much decayed and patched. I therefore set about joining the best half to the half formerly sent; and with the assistance of Abraham Bolton (private) took out all the rotten pieces; and repaired all the holes, and sewed places; and with eighteen days' hard labour, changed the Bambarra canoe into His Majesty's schooner *Joliba*; the length forty feet, breadth six feet; being flat bottomed, draws only one foot water when loaded.

Oct. 28th.—At a quarter-past five o'clock in the morning my dear friend Mr. Alexander Anderson died after a sickness of four months. I feel much inclined to speak of his merits; but as his worth was known only to a few friends, I will rather cherish his memory in silence, and imitate his cool and steady conduct, than weary my friends with a panegyric in which they cannot be supposed to join. I shall only observe that

364 Mungo Park's Travels in

no event which took place during the journey ever threw the smallest gloom over my mind, till I laid Mr. Anderson in the grave. I then felt myself as if left a second time lonely and friendless amidst the wilds of Africa.

Nov. 14th.—The schooner is now nearly ready for our departure; I only wait for Isaaco's return from Sego, that I may give him this paper in charge.

Nov. 15th.—Isaaco returned; and told us that Mansong was anxious that I should depart as soon as possible, before the Moors to the east had intimation of my coming. Bought bullock hides to form an awning to secure us from the spears and arrows of the Surka or Soorka and Mahinga who inhabit the north bank of the river betwixt Jinnie and Timbuctoo.

Nov. 16th.—All ready and we sail to-morrow morning, or evening.

CHAPTER XXXIII

The Last Letters and the Embarkation

So ends Mungo Park's journal as he hoists the sail of H.M.S. *Joliba*. Of the forty-four Europeans who left the Gambia in perfect health there remained only himself, three soldiers, one of whom was now crazy, and Lieutenant Martyn. The value to Park of the latter may be gauged by the letter he wrote to a friend in Goree while Park was building the *Joliba with his own hands*: "Whitbread's beer is nothing to what we get at this place, as I feel by my head this morning, having been drinking all night with a Moor."

Park obviously realised the extreme gravity of his situation but faced it with spirit and dignity. To Lord Camden he gives a brief report of casualties and continues: "I am afraid your lordship will be apt to consider matters as in a very hopeless state, but I assure you I am far from desponding. . . . I shall set sail to the east with the fixed resolution to discover the termination of the Niger or perish in the attempt. . . . My dear friend Mr. Anderson and likewise Mr. Scott are both dead, but though all the Europeans who are with me should die, and though I were myself half dead, I would still persevere; and if I could not succeed in the object of my journey, I would at least die on the Niger."

To Sir Joseph Banks he is full of plans and information, but to his wife he writes:

"Sansanding, 19*th November* 1805.

"It grieves me to the heart to write anything that may give you uneasiness; but such is the will of Him who *doeth all things well*! Your brother Alexander, my dear friend, is no more! He died of the fever at Sansanding, on the morning of 28th October; for particulars I must refer you to your father.

"I am afraid that, impressed with a woman's fears and the anxieties of a wife, you may be led to consider my situation as a great deal worse than it really is. It is true my dear friends Mr. Anderson and George Scott, have both bid adieu to the things of this world; and the greater part of the soldiers have died on the march during the rainy season; but you may believe me, I am in good health. The rains are completely over, and the healthy season has commenced, so that there is no danger of sickness; and I have still a sufficient force to protect me from any insult in sailing down the river to the sea.

"We have already embarked all our things, and shall sail the moment I have finished this letter. I do not intend to stop or land anywhere, till we reach the coast; which I suppose will be some time in the end of January. We shall then embark in the first vessel for England. If we have to go round by the West Indies, the voyage will occupy three months longer; so that we expect to be in England on the first of May. The reason of our delay since we left the coast was the rainy season, which came on us during the journey; and almost all the soldiers became affected with the fever.

"I think it not unlikely but I shall be in England before you receive this. You may be sure that I feel happy at turning my face towards home. We this morning have done with all intercourse with the natives; and the sails are now hoisting for our departure for the coast."

From Sansanding the choice was between success and death. Park clearly realised that his only hope was to follow the river to its end, hoping that this would be the sea. Accordingly he changed his tactics, meeting all opposition with force and shooting his way through. For a record of the end we must turn to the account given by the faithful Isaaco.

Isaaco had brought Park's letters and journals to the coast, from whence they had gone to England. Time passed, and no further messages arrived from Park; then rumours of disaster began to reach the coast, and eventually the Governor of Senegal sent Isaaco once more into the interior to seek for

news. He left Senegal early in 1810, and was back almost
two years later with an account not only of his own journey,
but with a statement which he had taken from the guide
Amadi Fatouma, whom he had the great good fortune to
encounter and who had been with Park almost to the end.
His statement, which as far as is known is a substantially
correct account, forms the following chapter.

(R. M.)

CHAPTER XXXIV

Amadi Fatouma's Journal

We departed from Sansanding in a canoe the 27th [1] day of the moon, and went in two days to Sellee,[2] where Mr. Park ended his first voyage. Mr. Park bought a slave to help him in the navigation of the canoe. There was Mr. Park, Martyn, three other white men, three slaves, and myself as guide and interpreter; nine in number, to navigate the canoe: without landing we bought the slave. We went in two days to Ginne. We gave the chief one piece of baft and went on. In passing Sibby, three canoes came after us, armed with pikes, lances, bows and arrows, etc., but no fire-arms. Being sure of their hostile intentions, we ordered them to go back, but to no effect; and were obliged to repulse them by force. Passed on; we passed Rakbara; three came up to stop our passage, which we repelled by force. On passing Timbuctoo we were again attacked by three canoes; which we beat off, always killing many of the natives. On passing Gouroumo seven canoes came after us, which we likewise beat off. We lost one white man by sickness: we were reduced to eight hands; having each of us fifteen muskets, always in order and ready for action. Passed by a village (of which I have forgotten the name), the residence of King Gotoijege; after passing which we counted sixty canoes coming after us, which we repulsed, and killed a great number of men. Seeing so many men killed, and our superiority over them, I took hold of Martyn's hand, saying, "Martyn, let us cease firing; for we have killed too many already"; on which Martyn wanted to kill me, had not Mr. Park interfered. After passing Gotoijege a long way, we met a very strong army on one side of the

---

[1] This Journal mentions no moon nor year.
[2] Called Silla in Mr Park's first voyage.

river, composed of the Poul nation; they had no beasts of any kind. We passed on the other side and went on without hostilities.

On going along we struck on the rocks. A hippopotamus rose near us, and had nearly overset the canoe; we fired on the animal and drove it away. After a great deal of trouble we got off the canoe without any material danger. We came to an anchor before Kaffo, and passed the day there. We had in the canoe before we departed from Sansanding, a very large stock of provisions, salted and fresh of all kinds; which enabled us to go along without stopping at any place, for fear of accident. The canoe was large enough to contain with ease one hundred and twenty people. In the evening we started and came to before an island; we saw on shore a great quantity of hippopotami; on our approach they went into the water in such confusion, that they almost upset our canoe. We passed the island and sailed. In the morning three canoes from Kaffo came after us, which we beat off. We came to near a small island, and saw some of the natives; I was sent on shore to buy some milk. When I got among them I saw two canoes go on board to sell fresh provisions, such as fowls, rice, etc. One of the natives wanted to kill me; at last he took hold of me, and said I was his prisoner. Mr. Park seeing what was passing on shore, suspected the truth. He stopped the two canoes and people, telling the people belonging to them, that if they should kill me, or keep me prisoner on shore, he would kill them all and carry their canoes away with him. Those on shore suspecting Mr. Park's intentions, sent me off in another canoe on board; they were then released. After which we bought some provisions from them, and made them some presents.

A short time after our departure, twenty canoes came after us from the same place; on coming near, they hailed and said, "Amadi fatouma, how can you pass through our country without giving us anything." I mentioned what they had said to Mr. Park; and he gave them a few grains of amber and some trinkets, and they went back peaceably. On coming to a shallow part of the river, we saw on the shore a great many men sitting down; coming nearer to them they stood up; we presented our muskets to them, which made them run off to the interior. A little farther on we came to a very difficult passage. The rocks had barred the river; but three passages were still open between them. On coming near one of them, we discovered the same people again, standing on the top of a large rock; which caused great uneasiness to us, especially to me, and I seriously promised never to pass there again without making considerable charitable donations to the poor. We returned and went to a pass of less danger, where we passed unmolested.

We came to before Carmasse, and gave the chief one piece of baft. We went on and anchored before Gourmon. Mr. Park sent me on shore with forty thousand cowries to buy provisions. I went and bought rice, onions, fowls, milk, etc., and departed late in the evening. The chief of the village sent a canoe after us, to let us know of a large army encamped on the top of a very high mountain, waiting for us; and that we had better return, or be on our guard. We immediately came to an anchor, and spent there the rest of the day, and all the night. We started in the morning; on passing the above-mentioned mountain, we saw the army, composed of Moors, with horses and camels; but without any fire-arms. As they said nothing to us, we passed on quietly, and entered the country of Haoussa, and came to an anchor. Mr. Park said to me, "Now, Amadi, you are at the end of your journey; I engaged you to conduct me here; you are going to leave me, but before you go, you must give me the names of the necessaries of life, etc., in the language of the countries through which I am going to pass"; to which I agreed, and we spent two days together about it, without landing. During our voyage I was the only one who had landed. We departed and arrived at Yaour.

I was sent on shore the next morning with a musket and a sabre, to carry to the chief of the village, also with three pieces of white baft for distribution. I went and gave the chief his present; I also gave one piece to Alhagi, one to Alhagi-biron, and the other to a person whose name I forget, all Marabous. The chief gave us a bullock, a sheep, three jars of honey, and four men's loads of rice. Mr. Park gave me seven thousand cowries, and ordered me to buy provisions, which I did; he told me to go to the chief and give him five silver rings, some powder and flints, and tell him that these presents were given to the king [1] by the white men, who were taking leave of him before they went away.   After the chief had received these things, he inquired if the white men intended to come back.   Mr. Park being informed of this inquiry, replied that he could not return any more.[2]   Mr. Park had paid me for my voyage before we left Sansanding; I said to him, "I agreed to carry you into the kingdom of Haoussa: we are now in Haoussa.   I have fulfilled my engagements with you; I am therefore going to leave you here and return."

Next day (Saturday) Mr. Park departed, and I slept in the village (Yaour).   Next morning, I went to the king to pay my respects to him; on entering the house I found two men who came on horseback; they were sent by the chief of Yaour.   They said to the king, "We are sent by the chief of Yaour to let you know that the white men went away, without giving you or him (the chief) anything; they have a great many things with them, and we have received nothing from them; and this Amadou fatouma now before you is a bad man, and has likewise made a fool of you both."   The king immediately ordered me to be put in irons; which was accordingly done, and everything I had taken from me, some were for killing me, and some for preserving my life.   The next morning early the king sent an army to a village called Boussa near the river side.   There is before this village a rock across the whole breadth of the river.   One part of the rocks is very high; there is a large opening in that rock in the form of a door, which is the only passage for the water to pass through; the tide current is here very strong.   This army went and took possession of the top of this opening.   Mr. Park came there after the army had posted itself; he nevertheless attempted to pass.   The people began to attack him,

[1] The king staid a few hundred yards from the river.
[2] These words occasioned his death; for the certainty of Mr. Park's not returning induced the chief to withhold the presents from the king.

throwing lances, pikes, arrows, and stones. Mr. Park defended himself for a long time; two of his slaves at the stern of the canoe were killed; they threw everything they had in the canoe into the river, and kept firing; but being overpowered by numbers and fatigue, and unable to keep up the canoe against the current, and no probability of escaping, Mr. Park took hold of one of the white men, and jumped into the water; Martyn did the same, and they were drowned in the stream in attempting to escape.   The only slave remaining in the boat, seeing the natives persist in throwing weapons at the canoe without ceasing, stood up and said to them, "Stop throwing now, you see nothing in the canoe, and nobody but myself, therefore cease.   Take me and the canoe, but don't kill me."   They took possession of the canoe and the man, and carried them to the king.

I was kept in irons three months; the king released me and gave me a slave (woman).   I immediately went to the slave taken in the canoe, who told me in what manner Mr. Park and all of them had died, and what I have related above.   I asked him if he was sure nothing had been found in the canoe after its capture; he said that nothing remained in the canoe but himself and a sword-belt.   I asked him where the sword-belt was; he said the king took it, and had made a girth for his horse with it.

CHAPTER XXXV

Epilogue

Amadi Fatouma gives an apparently accurate description of Mungo Park's journey down the Niger to Bussa. Having passed Timbuktu and Gao, the two main towns of the middle Niger, with no more than cursory attempts at contact with the inhabitants and more often a simple fusillade, Park's last and most serious miscalculation was to refuse the help and advice of the Emir of Yauri. According to information gathered several years later by Richard Lander, the Emir pointed out how dangerous the river was and advised the party to continue by land, for which he would give them a guide. But Park refused this generous offer and continued on down the river.

Although there seems no doubt that Park died at Bussa when he and the remaining three Europeans, their ammunition exhausted in a battle with people on the banks of the river, jumped overboard and were drowned, it is not clear who was attacking him or for what reason. He had had a relatively amicable interview with the local chief, representing the Emir of Yauri, and had given him presents; according to Amadi Fatouma, however, these presents were not passed on to the Emir himself. One version holds that it was the Emir, furious at Park's presumed discourtesy in passing by without leaving presents or calling in person, who sent his soldiers either to warn Park of the dangerous rapids ahead, or alternatively to capture Park and bring him back. Another version, gathered by Lander, was that Park and his companions were mistaken for Fulbe scouts from the holy war started two years previously by Uthman dan Fodio to purify the neighbouring Hawsa states. It is likely that the full story will never be known.

The final pieces in the jigsaw geography of the Niger were put in place by Clapperton who visited Bussa in 1826 from the south, and then by Richard and John Lander who finally in 1830 travelled down the river from Bussa to the coast. A quarter of a century later, quinine was used for the first time as a malaria prophylactic on a steamship expedition upstream from the mouth of the Niger, and as a result no lives were lost from fever. With these two events a new era opened in the history of the Niger and of inland west Africa.

(J.J.S.)

APPENDIX

Some information on prices and exchange rates in the Bambara Kingdom of Segu on the Niger

Mungo Park records in the journal of his second trip the prices of articles in October 1805 at Sansanding, an important market on the Niger. The following details are taken from the first edition of his book: *The Journal of a Mission to the Interior of Africa in the year 1805, together with other documents, official and private, relating the same mission.* London: John Murray, 1815.

Prices of European and African goods:

EUROPEAN ARTICLES.

	Value in Cowries
A musket – – – – – –	6 to 7000
A cutlass – – – – –	1500 to 2000
A flint – – – – – – – –	40
Gunpowder, one bottle – – – – –	3000

Amber No. 1. – – – – – –	1000
Ditto No. 2. – – – – – –	800
Ditto No. 3. – – – – – –	400
Ditto No. 4. – – – – – –	160
Ditto No. 5. – – – – – –	80
Ditto No. 6. – – – – – –	60
Coral No. 4. each stone – – – – –	60
Black points, per bead – – – – –	20
Red garnets, per string – – – – –	40
White ditto, per string – – – – –	40
Blue agates, per string – – – – –	100
Round rock coral, per bead – – – –	5
Long ditto, per bead – – – –	5
Short arrangoes, per bead – – – –	40
Gold beads, per bead – – – – –	10
An Indian baft – – – – –	20,000
A barraloolo, or five-bar piece – – – –	8000
Scarlet cloth 10 spans – – – –	20,000
If sold to the Karankeas *in retail* – –	30,000

Light yellow cloth nearly the same as scarlet;
    blue not so high

Paper per sheet – – – – – –	40
A dollar – – – – – from 6 to	12,000

Or from 1*l*. 5*s*. to 2*l*. 10*s*.

AFRICAN PRODUCE.

Value in Cowries

A minkalli of gold (12*s*. 6*d*. sterling) – – –	3000

Four minkallies are equal to £3. 3*s*.

Ivory, the very largest teeth, each　–　　–　　10,000
The medium size　–　　–　　–　　–　　–　　–　7000
The smaller　–　　–　　–　　–　　–　　–　3 or 4000
Indigo leaves beat and dried in lumps larger than
　ones fist, each　–　　–　　–　　–　　–　　–　40
A prime slave, (male)　–　　–　　–　　–　40,000
A ditto, (female)　–　　–　　–　from 80 to 100,000
A girl　–　　–　　–　　–　　–　　–　　–　40,000
A horse from two to ten prime male slaves
A cow (fat)　–　　–　　–　　–　　–　　–　15,000
An ass　–　　–　　–　　–　　–　　–　　–　17,000
A sheep　–　　–　　–　　–　　–　　–　3 to 5,000
A fowl　–　　–　　–　　–　　–　　–　–　250 to 300
As much *excellent fat beef* as will be sufficient for
　seven men one day　–　　–　　–　　–　　–　620
As much *good beer* as the same number can drink
　in one day　–　　–　　–　　–　　–　　–　　–　300

Elsewhere (pp. 57–8) Park records that in the gold producing area of the Faleme river the exchange rate between gold and amber is as follows: one bead of amber no. 4 will purchase one sixth of a minkalli of gold, which is about one third of the price recorded in Sansanding, and that gold can be bought at a better rate with beads or scarlet, and especially with gunpowder.

INDEX

377

Previously published by
ELAND BOOKS

MEMOIRS OF A
BENGAL CIVILIAN

JOHN BEAMES
**The lively narrative of a Victorian
district-officer**

With an introduction by Philip Mason

They are as entertaining as Hickey . . . accounts like
these illuminate the dark corners of history.
Times Literary Supplement

John Beames writes a splendidly virile English and
he is incapable of being dull; also he never hesitates
to speak his mind. It is extraordinary that these
memoirs should have remained so long unpublished
. . . the discovery is a real find.
John Morris, The Listener

A gem of the first water. Beames, in addition to being
a first-class descriptive writer in the plain Defoesque
manner, was that thing most necessary of all in an
autobiographer – an original. His book is of the
highest value.
The Times

*If you wish to receive details of forthcoming publications,
please send your address to
Eland Books, 53 Eland Road, London SW11 5JX*

VIVA MEXICO!

CHARLES MACOMB FLANDRAU
A traveller's account of life in Mexico

With a new preface by Nicholas Shakespeare

His lightness of touch is deceiving, for one reads *Viva Mexico!* under the impression that one is only being amused, but comes to realise in the end that Mr Flandrau has presented a truer, more graphic and comprehensive picture of the Mexican character than could be obtained from a shelful of more serious and scientific tomes.
New York Times

The best book I have come upon which attempts the alluring but difficult task of introducing the tricks and manners of one country to the people of another.
Alexander Woollcott

Probably the best travel book I have ever read.
Miles Kington, Times

His impressions are deep, sympathetic and judicious. In addition, he is a marvellous writer, with something of Mark Twain's high spirits and Henry James's suavity ... as witty as he is observant.
Geoffrey Smith, Country Life

TRAVELS WITH MYSELF AND ANOTHER

MARTHA GELLHORN

Must surely be ranked as one of the funniest travel books of our time — second only to *A Short Walk in the Hindu Kush* . . . It doesn't matter whether this author is experiencing marrow-freezing misadventures in war-ravaged China, or driving a Landrover through East African game-parks, or conversing with hippies in Israel, or spending a week in a Moscow Intourist Hotel. Martha Gellhorn's reactions are what count and one enjoys equally her blistering scorn of humbug, her hilarious eccentricities, her unsentimental compassion.
Dervla Murphy, Irish Times

Spun with a fine blend of irony and epigram. She is incapable of writing a dull sentence.
The Times

Miss Gellhorn has a novelist's eye, a flair for black comedy and a short fuse . . . there is not a boring word in her humane and often funny book.
The New York Times

Among the funniest and best written books I have ever read.
Byron Rogers, Evening Standard

If you wish to receive details of forthcoming publications,
please send your address to
Eland Books, 53 Eland Road, London SW11 5JX

Previously published by
ELAND BOOKS

THE WEATHER IN AFRICA

MARTHA GELLHORN

This is a stunningly good book.
Victoria Glendinning, New York Times

She's a marvellous story-teller, and I think
anyone who picks up this book is certainly not
going to put it down again. One just wants to go
on reading.
Francis King, Kaleidoscope, BBC Radio 4

An authentic sense of the divorce between Africa
and what Europeans carry in their heads is
powerfully conveyed by a prose that selects its
details with care, yet remains cool in their
expression.
Robert Nye, The Guardian

This is a pungent and witty book.
Jeremy Brooks, Sunday Times

*If you wish to receive details of forthcoming publications,
please send your address to
Eland Books, 53 Eland Road, London SW11 5JX*

MOROCCO
THAT WAS

WALTER HARRIS

With a new preface by Patrick Thursfield

Both moving and hilariously satirical.
Gavin Maxwell, Lords of the Atlas

Many interesting sidelights on the customs and
characters of the Moors. . .intimate knowledge of
the courts, its language and customs. . .thorough
understanding of the Moorish character.
New York Times

No Englishman knows Morocco better than Mr W.
B. Harris and his new book. . .is most entertaining.
Spectator (1921)

The author's great love of Morocco and of the Moors
is only matched by his infectious zest for life. . .
thanks to his observant eye and a gift for felicitously
turned phrases, the books of Walter Harris can claim
to rank as literature.
Rom Landau, Moroccan Journal (1957)

His pages bring back the vanished days of the
unfettered Sultanate in all their dark splendour; a
mingling of magnificence with squalor, culture with
barbarism, refined cruelty with naive humour that
reads like a dream of the Arabian Nights.
The Times

*If you wish to receive details of forthcoming publications,
please send your address to
Eland Books, 53 Eland Road, London SW11 5JX*

Previously published by
ELAND BOOKS

HOLDING ON

A Novel by
MERVYN JONES

This is the story of a street in London's dockland
and of a family who lived in it. The street was built in
the 1880s, and the Wheelwright family (originally
dockers) lived there until its tragic demolition in
the 1960s, when it was replaced by tower blocks.
  As a social document, the book rings with truth,
but it is much more than that: its compelling
narrative brings the reader right into the life of the
Wheelright family and their neighbours.

Moving, intelligent, thoroughly readable…
it deserves a lot of readers.
Julian Symons, Sunday Times

A remarkable evocation of life in the East End of
London… Mr Jones fakes nothing and blurs little…
It is truthful and moving.
Guardian

Has a classic quality, for the reader feels
himself not an observer but a sharer in the life of
the Wheelwrights and their neighbours.
Daily Telegraph

*If you wish to receive details of forthcoming publications,
please send your address to
Eland Books, 53 Eland Road, London SW11 5JX*

Previously published by
ELAND BOOKS

A DRAGON APPARENT

NORMAN LEWIS
Travels in Cambodia, Laos and Vietnam

A book which should take its place in the permanent
literature of the Far East.
Economist

One of the most absorbing travel books I have read
for a very long time. . .the great charm of the work is
its literary vividness. Nothing he describes is dull.
Peter Quennell, Daily Mail

One of the best post-war travel books and, in
retrospect, the most heartrending.·
The Observer

Apart from *The Quiet American*, which is of course a
novel, the best book on Vietnam remains *A Dragon
Apparent*.
Richard West, Spectator (1978)

One of the most elegant, witty, immensely readable,
touching and tragic books I've ever read.
Edward Blishen, Radio 4

*If you wish to receive details of forthcoming publications,
please send your address to
Eland Books, 53 Eland Road, London SW11 5JX*

THE
HONOURED
SOCIETY

NORMAN LEWIS
The Sicilian Mafia Observed

New epilogue by Marcello Cimino

One of the great travel writers of our time.
Eric Newby, Observer

Mr Norman Lewis is one of the finest journalists
of his time. . .he excels both in finding material
and in evaluating it.
The Listener

It is deftly written, and every page is horribly
absorbing.
The Times

The Honoured Society is the most penetrating book
ever written on the Mafia.
Time Out

If you wish to receive details of forthcoming publications,
please send your address to
Eland Books, 53 Eland Road, London SW11 5JX

Previously published by
ELAND BOOKS

NAPLES '44

NORMAN LEWIS

As unique an experience for the reader as it must
have been a unique experience for the writer.
Graham Greene

Uncommonly well written, entertaining despite its
depressing content, and quite remarkably evocative.
Philip Toynbee, Observer

His ten novels and five non-fiction works place him
in the front rank of contemporary English writers . . .
here is a book of gripping fascination in its flow of
bizarre anecdote and character sketch; and it is
much more than that.
J. W. Lambert, Sunday Times

A wonderful book.
Richard West, Spectator

Sensitive, ironic and intelligent.
Paul Fussell, The New Republic

One goes on reading page after page as if eating
cherries.
Luigi Barzini, New York Review of Books

*If you wish to receive details of forthcoming publications,
please send your address to
Eland Books, 53 Eland Road, London SW11 5JX*

Previously published by
ELAND BOOKS

A VIEW
OF THE WORLD

NORMAN LEWIS
Selected Journalism

Here is the selected journalism of Norman Lewis, collected from a period of over thirty years. The selection includes ten of the best articles from *The Changing Sky*, eight more which have never been collected within a book, and two which have never previously been published.

From reviews of *The Changing Sky*:

He really goes in deep like a sharp polished knife. I have never travelled in my armchair so fast, variously and well.
V. S. Pritchett, New Statesman

He has compressed into these always entertaining and sophisticated sketches material that a duller man would have hoarded for half a dozen books.
The Times

Outstandingly the best travel writer of our age, if not the best since Marco Polo.
Auberon Waugh, Business Traveller

If you wish to receive details of forthcoming publications, please send your address to Eland Books, 53 Eland Road, London SW11 5JX

Previously published by
ELAND BOOKS

KENYA DIARY (1902–1906)

RICHARD MEINERTZHAGEN

With a new preface by Elspeth Huxley

Those who have only read the tranquil descriptions of Kenya between the two Wars may be surprised by Meinertzhagen's often bloodthirsty diaries. They do not always make pleasant reading, but they offer an unrivalled and startlingly vivid account of life during the early days of the colony.

One of the best and most colourful intelligence officers the army ever had.
Times, Obituary

This book is of great interest and should not be missed
New Statesman

One of the ablest and most successful brains I had met in the army.
Lloyd George, Memoirs

Anybody at all interested in the evolution of Kenya or the workings of 'colonialism' would do well to read this diary.
William Plomer, Listener

*If you wish to receive details of forthcoming publications,
please send your address to
Eland Books, 53 Eland Road, London SW11 5JX*

Previously published by
ELAND BOOKS

LIGHTHOUSE

TONY PARKER

What is it that leads a man to make lighthouse-keeping his life's occupation? Why does he select a monotonous, lonely job which takes him away from his family for months at a stretch, leaving him in a cramped, narrow tower with two other men not of his own choosing?

Lighthouse-keepers and their families have opened their souls to Tony Parker, and his portrait of their lives is as compelling as any novel, and gives us an exceptional insight into the British character.

A very human book; and a pleasure to read.
John Fowles

Immediate, vivid, and absorbing... one of the most fascinating social documents I have ever read.
William Golding

A splendid book which has enriched my understanding of human nature.
Anthony Storr, The Sunday Times

*If you wish to receive details of forthcoming publications,
please send your address to
Eland Books, 53 Eland Road, London SW11 5JX*

Previously published by
ELAND BOOKS

A CURE FOR SERPENTS

THE DUKE OF PIRAJNO
An Italian doctor in North Africa

The Duke of Pirajno arrived in North Africa in 1924. For the next eighteen years, his experiences as a doctor in Libya, Eritrea, Ethiopia, and Somaliland provided him with opportunities and insights rarely given to a European. He brings us stories of noble chieftains and celebrated prostitutes, of Berber princes and Tuareg entertainers, of giant elephants and a lioness who fell in love with the author.

He tells us story after story with all the charm and resource of Scheherazade herself.
Harold Nicolson, Observer

A delightful personality, warm, observant, cynical and astringent. . .Doctors who are good raconteurs make wonderful reading.
Cyril Connolly, Sunday Times

A very good book indeed. . .He writes a rapid darting natural prose, like the jaunty scutter of a lizard on a rock.
Maurice Richardson, New Statesman

Pirajno's book is a cure for a great deal more than serpents.
The Guardian

In the class of book one wants to keep on a special shelf.
Doris Lessing, Good Book Guide

*If you wish to receive details of forthcoming publications,
please send your address to
Eland Books, 53 Eland Road, London SW11 5JX*

Previously published by
ELAND BOOKS

A FUNNY OLD QUIST

The Memoirs of a Gamekeeper
EVAN ROGERS
EDITED BY CLIVE MURPHY

An octogenerian gamekeeper tells us his story.
He has worked for sixty-eight years on the same
Herefordshire estate, and can remember the time
when wooden clogs were worn and young women
gave birth in the fields while gathering stones for a
shilling a ton.

Although he is a downright traditionalist who
dislikes new-fangled ways, he doesn't pretend that
life was always easy, and he is sometimes sharply
critical of his former masters. From this truthful
and vivid account, we get an unsentimental picture
of life on a semi-feudal estate – a way of life that
has almost completely disappeared.

A refreshing and informative book, a social
document of permanent value, as well as a
good read.
Times Literary Supplement

Extraordinary is the proper word for it.
Country Life

*If you wish to receive details of forthcoming publications,
please send your address to
Eland Books, 53 Eland Road, London SW11 5JX*